Stir Ups

...a round-up of recipes
from the
Junior Welfare League
of Enid, Oklahoma

...featuring over 700 tested recipes,
'stirred-up' with a heap o' flavor from the
heartland of America.

The purpose of the Junior Welfare League is: "...to give aid to less fortunate citizens of our community and to work in harmony with the established civic, professional and welfare organizations. The object of the organization shall be to foster interest among the members in the social, economic, educational, health, cultural and civic conditions of this community, and to make efficient their volunteer service."

To order copies of **STIR-UPS,**
Send check for $17.00* total.
($14.95 plus $2.05 postage, handling, and applicable tax)
to
Junior Welfare League of Enid
P.O. Box 5877
Enid, Oklahoma 73702
*Price subject to change.

ISBN: 0-9609340-0-6

First Printing	October, 1982	10,000 copies
Second Printing	January, 1983	10,000 copies
Third Printing	March, 1984	10,000 copies
Fourth Printing	September, 1985	10,000 copies
Fifth Printing	December, 1987	10,000 copies

Printed by S. C. Toof and Company
Memphis, Tennessee

At Home on the "Range"

STIR-UPS, from America's heartland, salutes the unique flavor of today's Home on the Range. How times have changed since our Grandmothers spent many an hour at the range...stirring up those tempting flavors we all remember. The Great Plains Region with its vast blue skies and golden fields of grain offers its own unique flavor to America's cooking heritage. We have come a long way since Grandmother's day, when stirring up something for supper meant an entire day by the stove including the extra chores of putting food by for the long months of winter...to the pre-packaged cooking helpers and quick tricks in the microwave of today. We won't be content with cardboard quickies or microwave magic. STIR-UPS is for the cook who wishes to please with the best possible flavor through "tried and true" techniques.

STIR-UPS doesn't claim to be a purely regional cookbook...we like to think the selections included are treasures and favorites from this cross-roads of America in which we live. Thus, we include selections from near and far to tempt even the most discriminating cook. Each section in STIR-UPS is named to enhance the spirit of the Great Plains. Some of the recipes in the "Territory Treats" section were tried-and-true secrets of our Grandmothers before Oklahoma became a state. Shortcuts on time but not on flavor will be found in "Pony Express-ohs"! The "Salad Stampede" and "Slim Pickins" sections include a health-conscious variety of ideas and suggestions. "Kids Korral" is a round-up of creativity for wranglers of all ages. Recipes in "Dough-Si-Dough" bring the unequaled aroma of homebaked breads to your kitchen. It is entirely appropriate that we consider these recipes for golden goodness to be our most unique contribution to Regional American Cooking.

Just as we harvest wheat to send around the world, STIR-UPS represents a harvest of kitchen ingenuity and flavor. As you browse through the next 400 pages, you will find over 700 tested recipes, some of which are marked with the JWL seal of approval. These recipes received the highest ratings by all who tested and tasted them and are guaranteed to stir-up blue-ribbon compliments. Helpful hints, time and money-saving ideas, as well as tempting variations are expressed through the Stir-Ups symbol.

Whether stirring up a gourmet treat for a fancy shindig or simply making play dough on a rainy afternoon...STIR-UPS will bring a unique flavor to your HOME ON THE "RANGE."

S.J.
July, 1982

*This cookbook is dedicated to
the city of Enid
in grateful appreciation for
its financial and moral support
over the last fifty-three years.
AND
to the State of OKLAHOMA in honor of its
DIAMOND JUBILEE.
We proudly designate our first edition of
STIR-UPS as the
DIAMOND JUBILEE EDITION.*

You're doin' fine, Oklahoma! · 1907 Diamond Jubilee 1982 · '75

Acknowledgements

To the general membership of our organization for their hours of tasting and testing hundreds of recipes.

To those friends and relatives who tasted, tested, and waited patiently on cookbook committee members who put their own dinner on the back burner while busily meeting deadlines.

To the Provisional Class of 1982 for their efforts in compiling and organizing the index.

To all who submitted over 1100 recipes for "Stir-Ups"...our sincere appreciation. We regret that we were unable to publish each of them...due to lack of space, similarity, test results, and duplication.

To the Honorary and Sustaining members of the Junior Welfare League for their service to this project...without whose efforts "Stir-Ups" would not have been possible.

EDITOR-CHAIRMAN

Sherrel Jones

CO-CHAIRMEN

MARKETING & PROMOTION
Gail Wynne

TESTING & TYPING
Ann Frazee Riley

COMMITTEE CHAIRMEN

SHINDIG STARTERS
Nancy Fry
Judy Puerta

CAIN'T SAY NO
Mona Payne
Sharon Blythe

CIMARRON—SIMMER-ON'
Pat Anderson
Kay Nicholas

FANCY FIXINS
Gail Wynne
Jean Mitchell

SALAD STAMPEDE
Ila Nicholas
Cecelia Beck

CELLAR DWELLERS
Carolyn Bules

DOUGH-SI-DOUGH
Sue Taylor

KIDS KORRAL
Pat Reeves
Susie Devoll

HARVEST HEAPIN'S
Florelee Day

ARE YOU "GAME"?
Jackie Batchelder

HOE'N AND GROW'N
Beverly Evans
Mary Helen Iselin

TERRITORY TREATS
Ruth Dobbs
Donita Mitchell

ART & COVER DESIGN
Ruth Ann Sailors

THEME & LAY-OUT
Judy Halstead

PRINTING & THEME DEVELOPMENT
Pat Anderson

EDITORIAL ASSISTANT
Lynda Nelson

TREASURER
Eleanor Taylor

LIBRARIAN
Carolyn Bules

Thanks to our Special Consultants:
A. J. Petree
Jean Mitchell
Donita Mitchell
Barbara Lewis, Jo Barnes
Cyndy Butler
Pat H. Fredeman, Ph.D.

Appetizers
Gourmet
Frozen Desserts
Indexing
Proof Reading
Editorial Consultant

Symbols Used in Stir-Ups

 The Junior Welfare League seal of approval. These recipes received the highest ratings by all who tested and tasted them.

 Stir-Up a tempting variation, or enjoy a time-saving tip. This symbol gives helpful hints to the cook.

TABLE OF CONTENTS

Appetizers and Beverages. . . . "Shindig Starters". 11

Soups and Stews. . . . "Cimarron—(Simmer-On)". 51

Salads. . . . "Salad Stampede". 65

Breads. . . . "Dough-Si-Dough". 95

Main Dishes. . . . "Harvest Heapins". 125

Vegetables. . . . "Hoe'n and Grow'n". 177

Desserts. . . . "Territory Treats". 207

Cookies and Candy. . . . "Cain't Say No". 249

Gourmet. . . . "Fancy Fixins". 273

Low-Cal. . . . "Slim Pickins". 307

Pickles and Preserves. . . . "Cellar Dwellers". 317

Kid's Specialties. . . . "Kids Korral". 325

Easy-to-dos. . . . "Pony Express-ohs!". 351

Sportsman's Pleasure. . . . "Are You "Game"?". 373

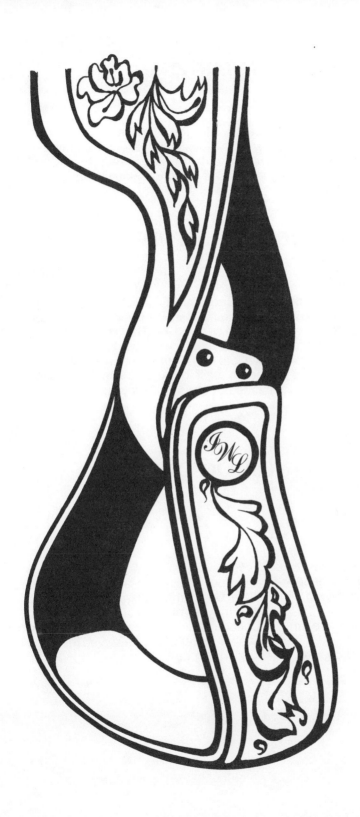

SHINDIG STARTERS

APPETIZERS AND BEVERAGES

SHINDIG STARTERS

Your next "shindig," whether a barbeque after the wheat is "in" or a spring tea party, is sure to have some star attractions with teasers from this section. Everything from Prairie Firewaters to dainty little Green Onion Sandwiches, your guests are sure to be "pleased as punch" you included them in your shindig.

A. J.'s SUGGESTIONS ON SERVING CAVIAR

Caviar is one of the finest delicacies. Good quality caviar has light, large grains. Caviar should be served in its original state on *ice*. It can be served in a small bowl and set in a larger bowl of crushed ice. Garnishes should be served on a separate tray. Melba toast, lemon wedges, finely chopped onions and hot Blintzes (small buckwheat cakes) and sour cream are good accompaniments. If caviar is served on toast, great care should be taken in spreading the eggs so that they are not bruised. Always use parsley or fresh mint leaves for color effect.

A. J. Petree

BRAVO AVOCADO

Serves: 8-10

3 to 5 ripe avocados, mashed
1 bunch green onions, chopped
1 (2-1/4-oz.) can chopped
ripe olives
1 (16-oz.) carton sour cream
16 oz. Picante sauce
8 to 10 oz. Cheddar cheese,
shredded

Layer avocados, green onions, olives and sour cream on large round chop plate. Cover and seal with Picante sauce (you may not need all of it). Cover all with Cheddar cheese. Cover with Saran Wrap and refrigerate. May be served the same day or next day.

Ila Nichols

BAKED CHICKEN STRIPS

Serves: 8

7 or 8 deboned chicken breasts
2 cups fine bread crumbs
1 cup Parmesan cheese
   (canned)
1-1/2 tsp. salt
1 Tbsp. thyme
1 Tbsp. basil
1 cup butter, melted

Cut chicken into 1-1/2" strips. Combine dry ingredients. Dip chicken strips into butter and then coat in crumbs. Place on lightly greased cookie sheet. Bake for 20 minutes at 400°. Turn strips after 10 minutes. This is a super recipe for appetizers or perfect for a Tailgate Picnic. The thyme and basil can be adjusted to your family liking. Can be reheated in the microwave.
For some creative variations: Try other spices such as lemon pepper or barbecue spice.

Lou Ann Smith

BEER-CHEESE PINECONES

Serves: 30

2 (8-oz.) cream cheese,
   softened
1/3 cup beer
2 Tbsp. fresh parsley,
   finely snipped
1 tsp. paprika
3 cups smoked sharp Cheddar
   cheese, shredded (12-oz.)

Sliced almonds
* Apple slices
* Pear slices
Assorted crackers
 * Dip apple and pear slices
in a mixture of water and lemon
juice or ascorbic acid color
keeper to prevent the fruit from
darkening.

In a large bowl, beat together the softened cream cheese, beer, parsley and paprika until well blended. Stir in the Cheddar cheese. Cover and chill 1 hour. Divide mixture in half. With hands, mold each portion into a pinecone shape; place on a baking sheet. Insert sliced almonds in rows over molded cheese to resemble pinecones. Cover and chill several hours. To serve, transfer pinecones to platter with wide metal spatula. Serve with apple slices, pear slices and assorted crackers. Makes 4 cups spread.

Stefani Schram

BRONCO BUSTERS

Serves: 36

1 cup *Swiss cheese, grated*
4 *green onions, chopped fine*
1/4 *cup mayonnaise*
1-4.2 *oz. can chopped ripe olive*
1/4 *cup crumbled bacon*
    (use 100% Wilson's real
    bacon in a can)
1 *tsp. Worcestershire sauce*
Pepperidge Farm Party Rye
    bread

Mix all ingredients together. Spread on rye bread, bake at 375° for 10 to 15 minutes. Serve hot.

Diana Allen

BITE-SIZE PEPPERONI PIZZAS
Great for Teenage Parties

Serves: 96 bite-size pizzas

2 *(8-oz.) cans flaky biscuits*
1 *(8-10-oz.) pkg. pepperoni*
    slices
1 *(16-oz.) jar bottled spaghetti*
    sauce
1/2 *cup Parmesan cheese*
8-10 *oz. pkg. Mozzarella*
    cheese, shredded

Remove biscuits from can and separate each into 4 flat layers. (Each can of 12 biscuits will make 48 layers.) Place on cookie sheet. Add 1 tsp. sauce to top of each layer. Top with 1 or 2 pieces pepperoni and then top with Parmesan and Mozzarella cheeses. Bake at 400° for 6-8 minutes.
Note: If freezing, freeze on cookie sheet before adding cheese. Remove when frozen and store in plastic bag in freezer. When ready to serve, remove from freezer and top with cheese. Bake at 400° for 10 minutes.

JoAnn Nicholas

BACON AND SAUSAGE QUICHELETS

Serves: 8 pie servings or 24 quichelets

CRUST:
1 cup Bisquick mix
Milk

FILLING:
1/2 lb. bacon
1/2 lb. sausage
1/2 large onion, chopped
1/2 green pepper, chopped
3 eggs, beaten
1 can (5.33-oz.) evaporated milk
Dash of salt
Dash of pepper
Sliced mushrooms (optional)
1/2 lb. Cheddar cheese, grated
    (or cheese of your choice)

Moisten Bisquick with enough milk to form a ball-like pie crust. Press dough into bottom and sides of a 9" pie pan and set aside.

Fry bacon until crispy and drain on paper towel. Set aside. Fry sausage, onion and green pepper until sausage is done. Drain on paper towel and set aside. Combine eggs, milk, salt and pepper. Stir in fried bacon and sausage mixture. Sprinkle grated cheese on uncooked pie. Save some cheese for later. Place crust in oven at 400° until cheese melts. Remove and pour egg mixture on top of melted cheese. Top with more grated cheese. Bake at 400° for 25-30 minutes —until knife comes out clean. Quiche can be reheated later. Cool 10 minutes before cutting.
Note: For individual Quichelets, roll dough thin and cut with biscuit cutter. Press into muffin pan or tartlet tins and fill. Decorate each with mushroom slice or thin slice of pimento or green pepper.

Mona Payne

CANDIE'S GOODY

Serves: 6-8

1 (8-10-oz.) pkg. cream cheese, softened
1 medium onion, chopped
1 large green pepper, chopped
1 (8-1/2-oz.) can small shrimp, drained (or 1 cup chopped fresh)
6 oz. cocktail sauce
Fritos (large size for dipping)

Spread cream cheese in center of tray. Scatter onions, pepper and shrimp over cream cheese. Pour cocktail sauce over entire mixture and dip with Fritos.

Jeanne Dillingham

CALICO PECAN BALL

Serves: 20

2 (8-oz.) cream cheese,
  softened
1 cup crushed pineapple,
  drained
1/2 cup sweet pepper, chopped
1 cup pecans, chopped
1 tsp. onion salt
1 tsp. seasoned salt
3/4 cup additional pecans,
  chopped

Combine 1 cup crushed pineapple and remaining ingredients. Mix well on low speed of mixer or with fork. Form into ball and roll in additional chopped pecans. Wrap to chill until ready to serve. Keeps well—may be stored for several days in advance for party. Serve with celery sticks and/or Ritz crackers.

Ruth Dobbs

CHEESE FONDUE

4-5 slices bacon, crumbled
1/4 cup onion, chopped
2 Tbsp. flour
1 lb. brick Velveeta, cut in cubes
2 cups sour cream
French bread, chips or raw
  vegetables

In large skillet, fry bacon until crisp. Remove bacon to drain. Brown onions in same skillet then add flour. Adjust heat to low and melt cheese cubes. Stir in sour cream. Serve in fondue pot, crock pot, or chafing dish. You may crumble bacon on top or stir crumbled bacon into hot cheese mixture just before serving. Dippers: Cut French bread into cubes and toast at low temperature for 20 or 30 minutes to use as dippers. Raw vegetables and chips are also good.
Variation: Add chopped jalapeño peppers.

Meme Wheeler

 Garnish a cheese fondue with a flower or other design such as a Christmas tree with green pepper slices.

CATTLEMEN'S SPREAD

A Hot 'n Hearty "He-Man's" Delight!

Makes: 2 pounds of spread

1 cup pecans, chopped
2 Tbsp. butter
16 oz. cream cheese, softened
5 oz. dried beef, minced
1/2 tsp. garlic powder
1 cup sour cream
4 tsp. onion, minced

Sauté pecans in butter, reserve all. Soften cream cheese in mixer or processor. (If you choose to use food processor, mince beef and onion and remove before softening cream cheese.) Then blend in sour cream and garlic salt. Add onion and beef last, being careful not to over-process. (If using mixer, this is not necessary.) Spread evenly in 1-1/2 qt. lightly greased baking dish. Top with pecan mixture and bake for 20 minutes at 350.° Spread on crackers. Additional beef may be added for a group of hungry poker players!

Committee Variation: For a hearty ham spread, you may wish to use shaved ham and chopped green onions.

Margaret Wright

CHEESIES

Yield: about 4 dozen

1 egg white
1 tsp. water
1-1/2 cups Swiss cheese,
    finely grated
1/4 cup Parmesan cheese,
    grated
1/2 cup margarine, softened
3/4 cup all-purpose flour
3/4 tsp. salt
1/8 tsp. nutmeg
Paprika

Combine egg white with water, beating slightly with a fork—set aside. Combine cheese and margarine, room temperature, mixing well. Add flour, salt and nutmeg. Stir with a fork until a stiff dough is formed. Wrap in aluminum foil and chill for 15 minutes. Shape dough into 3/4 inch balls. Place on greased cookie sheet. Flatten each with a fork—brush with egg white mixture. Bake at 425° for 10 minutes or just until edges begin to brown. Cool and sprinkle lightly with paprika. Especially nice with salads.

Isabel Biggs

CHEESE CASSEROLE DIP

Serves: 12

1-1/4 lbs. Monterey Jack
    cheese
1 lb. Cheddar cheese
5 (4-oz.) cans green chilies,
    chopped and drained
5 eggs, beaten

Shred the cheese, if you have time, or use a food processor; if not, small cubes work fine. Layer the cheese and chilies in a 7"x 12" pyrex pan. Pour eggs over cheese. Bake in 350° oven approximately 20 minutes. Serve with crackers, heavy chips, zucchini strips or cauliflowerettes. Serve hot.

Judy Anderson

CHEESE ONION ROUNDS

Very quick and a good spur of the moment trick.
(Must microwave)

Serves: 6

1/2 cup mayonnaise
1/4 cup Parmesan cheese,
    grated
2 green onions, finely chopped
1 box Old London Sesame
    Rounds

Mix mayonnaise, cheese and onions and chill until serving time. Spread a small amount on each sesame round. Put about 18 on a plate and microwave on full power for 15 seconds or just until they begin to bubble. Serve hot.

Florelee Day

CLAM DIP

Yield: 2-1/2 cups

1 (8-oz.) pkg. cream cheese
    softened
1 (7-1/2-oz.) can minced
    clams, drained
1/2 cup mayonnaise
1/2 tsp. Worcestershire sauce
1/2 tsp. garlic salt (optional)
1/2 cup celery, diced
1/4 cup onion, diced finely

Combine all ingredients. Allow to stand in refrigerator half a day. Serve with potato chips or cauliflower.

Edith Davis

COCKTAIL MEATBALLS

Yield: 8 dozen

2 lbs. lean ground beef,
    finely ground
2 eggs, slightly beaten
1 cup fine bread crumbs
2/3 cup milk or half and half
1/2 tsp. sage or poultry
    seasoning

Combine these ingredients and blend very thoroughly. Make into 70-75 small balls and brown in skillet which has had 1 Tbsp. butter added and melted. Pour off all fat.

SAUCE:
3 (4-1/2-oz.) jars apricot
    baby food
1 cup brown sugar
1 cup catsup
1 cup vinegar
1 cup barbeque sauce
1 tsp. salt
4 tsp. soy sauce
2 tsp. ground ginger
Garlic salt to taste

Mix ingredients and simmer for 30 minutes, stirring often. Pour over meatballs. Simmer 15 minutes. Keep hot to serve. Chafing dish works well.

Margaret Lillibridge

CHEESEY CHUTNEY SPREAD

Serves: 6

8 oz. cream cheese
Several tsp. cream
1 Tbsp. curry powder
1 tsp. Worcestershire sauce
1/2 tsp. salt
Dash paprika

Mix cream cheese in blender or processor with cream. Add remaining ingredients. Form into a round and top with chutney. Garnish with green onions on top of chutney. _Chill 24 hours_. Serve with favorite crackers.

GARNISH:
Major Grey's Chutney (unless
    you are fortunate to have
    your own homemade)
Few green onions, tops
    and all, chopped

Jeannine Bowers

CUCUMBER TEA SANDWICHES

An elegant delight shared by a professional.

Yield: 66 servings

1 loaf thin-sliced white
sandwich bread (22 slices)
3 cucumbers (not over 2" in
diameter and medium
length)
3 (3-oz.) pkgs. cream cheese
with chive
1 cup Hellmann's mayonnaise
1 cup fresh celery, chopped
1/4 tsp. salt

Freeze loaf of bread. Wash, score and slice cucumbers 1/16" thick and pat dry. Set aside. Mix cream cheese, salt and 1/2 cup of mayonnaise until smooth. Should be the consistency of cake icing. Set aside. Cut frozen bread with 2" round cutter. 3 rounds from each slice with no crust. Use immediately or re-freeze until needed. Frozen bread is easy to handle and will not dry out. Fill *small* decorating bag and *small* star tip with 1/2 cup mayonnaise. Pressure one star in center of each bread round. All rounds should be placed on cookie sheets. This dab of mayonnaise will keep the cucumber slices from sliding off the bread. Place one slice of cucumber on each bread round, and press down in center. Fill *large* decorating bag and *large* star tip with cream cheese mixture. Pressure a large star leaving a very small edge of cucumber showing. Garnish with parsley. These dainty sandwiches will hold several hours in refrigerator. Do not freeze. Note: 1/2 cup Creamy Cucumber salad dressing can be used instead of mayonnaise when blending the cream cheese.

A. J. Petree

CHILI CHEESE ROLLS

Serves: 30

1 lb. Velveeta cheese,
softened
6 oz. cream cheese, softened
1/4 tsp. garlic powder
1 cup pecans, finely chopped
Chili powder

Combine Velveeta cheese, cream cheese and garlic powder. Add pecans. Divide into three equal parts. Sprinkle chili powder on wax paper and roll each cheese ball until completely covered with powder. Shape and chill several hours. Slice and serve with Triscuits.

A. J. Petree

CREAMY ARTICHOKE BOTTOMS

(Microwave)

Yield: 4-5 servings

8-10 artichoke bottoms (canned)
1 (3-oz.) pkg. cream cheese
3 Tbsp. chives, chopped
2 Tbsp. butter, softened
2 Tbsp. sour cream
1/4 cup Parmesan cheese,
    freshly grated
Schilling Salad Supreme

Arrange artichoke bottoms on plate bottom side up. Sprinkle with salt and pepper. Soften cream cheese and mix with chives, butter and sour cream. Add a large teaspoonful of mixture to each artichoke and sprinkle liberally with Parmesan cheese. Microwave full power for 3 minutes, turning plate twice. Garnish with Schilling Salad Supreme. Serve 1 or 2 per person on a plate with a fork.

Nancy Fry

CURRIED CHICKEN APPETIZERS

Yield: 6 dozen

2 lbs. raw chicken meat
    (about 4 cups)
1 medium onion
2 egg yolks
2 tsp. salt
2 tsp. curry powder

In a food chopper, grind chicken and onion. Mix with egg yolks, salt and curry powder. Form into marble-sized balls, flatten slightly, and fry in deep fat at 370° until lightly browned. Serve promptly on toothpicks. May be prepared ahead of time and warmed in microwave oven. Note: Partially frozen boned chicken breasts work best for chopping in a food processor or in grinder. Onion may be cubed and ground with chicken or minced and combined after chicken is ground.

Joy Marler

To slice or grind chicken or other meat in a food processor, freeze slightly before processing.

CRAB PILLOWS

Yield: 24

Crab meat from 1 leg
1 pkg. Won Ton Wrappers
1 (8-oz.) pkg. cream cheese
2 Tbsp. mayonnaise (or enough
to soften cream cheese)
1 green scallion, chopped
Dash of salt
3-4 drops Tabasco sauce

Mix crab, cheese and seasonings. Drop 1-2 tsp. of mixture on Won Ton wrapper. Pinch four corners together into a point. Deep fry in hot oil until lightly browned, 1-2 minutes.
Note: A small amount of egg white or water may be brushed on corners to help seal won tons. Pillow resembles a small apple dumpling.

Judith A. Jackson

CRAB QUICHE

Yield: 16 servings

3 eggs, slightly beaten
1 cup commercial sour cream
1/2 tsp. Worcestershire sauce
3/4 tsp. salt
1 cup Swiss cheese, shredded
1 (7-1/2-oz.) can crab, drained
and flaked
1 (3-oz.) can French fried onions
2-9" baked pastry shells

Heat oven to 300°. Combine eggs, sour cream, Worcestershire and salt. Stir in cheese, crab meat and fried onions. Pour into 2 baked pastry shells. Bake 1 hour or until set. Serve hot in small wedges.

Pat Anderson

 Make small individual quichelets, using tart pans or bottoms of muffin tins as forms. Flakey canned refrigerator biscuits may be divided and quickly pressed into use as crust.

DIANA'S CLAM DIP

Serves: 8

1 (7-1/2 oz.) can minced or
     whole clams, drained
8 oz. cream cheese
1/2 cup sour cream
1 Tbsp. lemon juice
1/4 tsp. garlic salt
1/4 tsp. pepper
1/4 tsp. Lowry's seasoned salt
1/4 cup green onions, chopped
1/4 cup green pimento olives,
     chopped
1 tsp. Worcestershire sauce

Mix all ingredients and chill. Serve with Doritos or potato chips.

Diana Allen

CHIPPED BEEF BALL

Serves: 6

8 oz. cream cheese, softened
2 tsp. horseradish
1 tsp. prepared mustard
1 (5-oz.) pkg. smoked chipped
     beef, cut up

Blend cream cheese, horseradish and mustard and roll into ball. Frizzle chipped beef in butter. Roll creamed mixture in frizzled chipped beef. Serve with crackers.
Note: To frizzle chipped beef, separate and tear beef slices apart. Drop into skillet with 1-2 Tbsp. hot melted butter. Stir lightly just until it is heated enough to begin to sizzle. This makes it easy to combine with cheese.

Jean Mitchell

 Always garnish cheese spreads and dips with a touch of green whether a sprig of parsley or a garden-fresh choice...pleases the eye and tempts the palate.

CURRY DIP

Makes: 2-1/2 cups

2 cups Hellmann's mayonnaise
2 Tbsp. onion juice
6 Tbsp. catsup
2 Tbsp. curry powder
2 Tbsp. Worcestershire sauce
2 pinches ground cloves
Garlic, to taste, 1-2 cloves
    pressed

Combine all ingredients and chill. Good with zucchini squash, raw and sliced. Also cauliflower, carrots, green pepper, etc.
Note: If just a pinch of garlic is desired, mix all ingredients the day before and place peeled garlic clove on toothpick and insert in center dip. Cover and refrigerate overnight and remove toothpick with garlic and stir well before serving.
Meme Wheeler

DANDY DILLY DIP

Makes: 2 cups

2/3 cup sour cream
2/3 cup Hellmann's mayonnaise
1 Tbsp. dry onion flakes
1 Tbsp. parsley
1 tsp. Beau Monde seasoning
1 tsp. dill weed or seed

Mix all ingredients together. Refrigerate overnight. Serve with raw vegetables— green pepper and zucchini strips, cauliflower and broccoli flowerettes, celery and carrot sticks or fresh mushrooms.
Barbara Caddell

Janie Word's Variation: Add 1 tsp. Worcestershire, 2 drops Tabasco and 1/2 tsp. Accent and use one 1/2-oz. pkg. green onion dip mix (Frito Lay) instead of onion flakes.

Patty Ricketson's Variation: Hollow out a large round of rye bread. Double recipe and fill hollowed bread. Serve with cubes of rye bread for dipping.

GREEN ONION SANDWICHES

Any kind of bread
Small green onions
Butter or margarine

Remove the crusts from bread. Wash, drain and peel onion tops down to the delicate green part and chop. Mix butter and onions and spread on bread. Refrigerate. Yummy with fried chicken.
Note: To keep sandwiches fresh, cover with dampened carefully wrung dish towels or paper towels both while working with and storing sandwiches prior to serving.

Suzy Traynor

GAZPACHO
A Good Outdoor Party Starter Sunday Picnic Treat!

Serves: 6-8

4 tomatoes, peeled
1 large cucumber, chopped
1 small to medium onion,
    chopped
1 green pepper, chopped
1 qt. tomato juice
3 Tbsp. wine vinegar
2 Tbsp. olive oil
1 garlic clove, pressed
Salt and pepper to taste
1 tsp. Worcestershire sauce
Dash of Tabasco
1/4 cup lemon juice
Pinch of sugar

Combine finely chopped vegetables with other ingredients. Chill overnight or several hours. Serve cold. Garnish with a lemon slice or small celery stick with leaves left on.
Note: For winter zip when those best of summer flavored tomatoes are not to be found, you can use a can of Del Monte tomato wedges chopped in blender.

Ruth Ann Sailors

Tomatoes are peeled easily if dipped for a few seconds in scalding water.

HOT WALNUT 'N BEEF DIP

Serves: 10

1 (8-oz.) pkg. cream cheese
1/2 cup sour cream
2 Tbsp. milk (or half and half)
Dash Worcestershire sauce
1 (2-1/2-oz.) pkg. dried beef,
    chopped
2 Tbsp. green pepper, chopped
2 Tbsp. green onion, chopped
2 oz. English walnuts, chopped

Mix together and serve *warm* in small chafing dish. Serve with crackers or chips.

Janie Roney

HOT BROCCOLI DIP

Serves: 30-40

GROUP #1:
1 lb. fresh mushrooms, sliced
1 large onion, chopped
3-4 sticks celery, diced

GROUP # 2:
1 can cream of mushroom soup
2 (10-oz.) pkgs. frozen broccoli,
    chopped, and cooked
    according to pkg.
    directions, drained
2-6 oz. tubes of garlic cheese
1 tsp. lemon
Salt and pepper

Saute Group #1 in butter.
Mix Group #2 in a sauce pan and add #1. Heat. Add a generous squeeze of lemon. Salt and pepper to taste. Serve warm in a chafing dish or a fondue pot with Doritos or raw vegetables.

Judy Chambers

 Put a favorite dip in a bowl and slip the bowl into a sombrero or a ten-gallon hat. Add other Western or South of the Border touches to the table and enhance the mood of your shindig.

HUMMAS BI TAHINI

A middle eastern dish....This one will make a visiting Sheik
feel right at home.

Yield: 5 servings

*1/3 cup tahini (available in
 specialty and gourmet
 food stores)*
1/2 cup (scant) lemon juice
1/2 tsp. salt
2 cloves garlic (more if desired)
2 Tbsp. parsley, chopped
*1 cup garbanzo beans (drained
 and heated)*
Fresh parsley
Olive oil
*Arabic Bread (may substitute
 Pita bread)*

Place all ingredients in blender except
garbanzo beans. Blend. Then add beans
and blend until beans are all mixed and
chopped (almost blended). Place in a
low round serving dish. Put fresh parsley
in center and around the parsley make
a trench with a spoon. In trench place
olive oil. To eat, take a small piece of
pita bread and use it as a scoop. Scoop
the Hummas and end up in the olive oil.
It's delicious!

Jane Ford

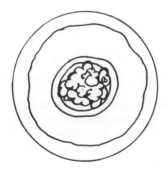

...OR WITH THE BACK OF A LARGE SPOON
SWIRL A PINWHEEL DESIGN IN THE
TAHINI MIXTURE.

HOT CRAB DIP

1 (8-oz.) pkg. cream cheese
1/2 cup crab meat
1 Tbsp. milk
2 Tbsp. onion, chopped
1/2 tsp. horseradish
1/4 tsp. salt & pepper
1/3 cup slivered almonds

Mix all ingredients except almonds.
Bake in 375° oven for 15 minutes. Top
with almonds. Serve with crackers. Use
small round soufflé dish for baking
and surround with crackers for serving.

Robin Sigler

HOT CRAB COCKTAIL

16 oz. cream cheese, softened
    to room temperature
1/2 cup mayonnaise
1/2 cup sherry
1/4 tsp. garlic salt
2 tsp. prepared mustard
1 tsp. onion juice
1 lb. fresh crab meat, cooked
    and flaked
Crackers

Soften cream cheese and mix other ingredients except for crab. Place the blended ingredients in a double boiler and heat over simmering water, stirring occasionally. When heated, gently fold in the crab meat. Place in a chafing dish and serve with crackers.

Note: Crab should be boiled just until meat turns white. Remove from shell and carefully flake, removing bits of bone and shells. If making ahead, do not add crab meat until ready to heat and serve.

Nikki Baker

HOT CLAM CHEESE DIP

Yield: 3 cups

1/4 large green pepper,
    chopped
1/2 bunch green onions,
    chopped
2 (5-oz.) jars Kraft sharp
    cheddar cheese
1 (7-oz.) can minced clams,
    drained
2 dashes Tabasco sauce
Garlic to taste

Sauté green pepper and green onions in butter. Drain off butter. Mix ingredients into 1-1/2 qt. casserole dish. Heat uncovered in microwave for 3 minutes or until cheese is melted. Stir ingredients every minute. Serve in chafing dish with chips.

Janie Roney

 Be creative with dippers: use a variety of vegetables and in the fall add crisp apples and pears.

JEANNINE BOWER'S HOT ARTICHOKE SPREAD

Serves: 8

1 (14-oz.) can artichoke hearts,
   drained, rinsed and
   chopped
1 cup Hellmann's mayonnaise
1 cup Parmesan cheese, grated
   (canned)
1/2 tsp. garlic powder
Lemon juice to taste
Dash of Tabasco

Combine all ingredients, mixing well. Spoon into a lightly-greased casserole. Sprinkle with paprika and bake at 350° for 20 minutes. Serve hot with assorted crackers. This is not only easy, but it is a super hit at any cocktail party.

Patricia Loomis

LA PUERTA TACO DIP

8 oz. cream cheese
1 cup sour cream
Garlic salt
Lots of green onions (tops
   included), chopped
Cheddar cheese, shredded
Tomatoes, chopped
2 or 3 avocados, thinly sliced
Lettuce, shredded
Lawry's Taco Sauce (powdered)
Doritos

Cream together: cream cheese, sour cream and garlic salt. Layer on a flat plate: Cream cheese mixture, green onions, Cheddar cheese, tomatoes, avocados, lettuce, Lawry's powdered taco sauce as garnish. Serve with large pkg. plain Doritos.

Judy Puerta

HAM ROUNDUPS
(A Champagne Party Favorite)

1-6 oz. package thin-sliced
   ham
1-8 oz. package softened cream
   cheese
1/2 cup finely chopped green
   onions
1/3 cup stuffed green olives,
   chopped
Garlic powder to taste
White pepper to taste

Combine cheese, onions, olives, garlic powder and pepper. Separate ham slices and pat excess moisture from each. Spread cheese mixture on each ham slice and roll up pinwheel style. Chill until firm. When ready to serve, slice 1/2 inch slices for colorful pinwheels. Variation: Fry and crumble 4 slices of bacon and add to filling.

Cookbook Committee

PARTY PIZZAS

1 loaf party rye bread
1 lb. hot sausage
1 lb. regular sausage
1 lb. Velveeta cheese
1 tsp. oregano
1 tsp. A-1 sauce
1 tsp. catsup
Picante sauce
Parmesan cheese

Mix sausages together and cook until done, but not browned. Drain well. Melt cheese and mix with seasonings and sausages. Spread mixture on party rye and top with picante sauce and Parmesan cheese. Bake in 425° oven for 10 minutes or until bubbly.

Jeanne Dillingham

PICKLED MUSHROOMS

Yield: 25-30 mushrooms

1/2 lb. mushrooms, cleaned and
     stemmed (3-1/2 cups)
2/3 cup tarragon vinegar
1 Tbsp. sugar
1/2 cup olive oil
Dash pepper
1 garlic clove, minced
1-1/2 tsp. salt
2 Tbsp. water
1 medium onion, sliced
     in rings
2 tsp. parsley, fresh, chopped
1 Tbsp. prepared mustard

Mix all ingredients and refrigerate at least 3 days to fully marinate. Serve at room temperature with party picks.

VARIATION:
Add 1 bay leaf
Use brown sugar instead of
     granulated

Sally Shipley
Ila Nicholas

MUCHO GRANDE LAYERS

Seves: 30-40

1 (16-oz.) can refried beans
3 oz. Jalapeño cheese roll
3 medium ripe avocados,
    mashed
1 Tbsp. lemon juice
1/2 tsp. salt
1/4 tsp. pepper
Picante Sauce
1 cup sour cream
1/2 cup mayonnaise
1 (1-1/2-oz.) pkg. Taco
    seasoning mix
1 cup green onions, with tops,
    chopped
2 cups tomatoes, cored, seeded
    and chopped
2 (3-1/2-oz.) cans pitted ripe
    olives, drained and
    chopped
1 (8-oz.) pkg. sharp Cheddar
    cheese, shredded

Heat beans and cheese and spread in bottom of 9" x 13" dish. Cool. In separate bowl, mix avocados, lemon juice, salt and pepper. Spread over bean and cheese mixture. Cover with thin layer of picante sauce. Next, layer the mixture of sour cream, mayonnaise and taco mix. Top with onions, tomatoes and olives. Last, add cheese. Serve with Doritos.

Ann Long

MUSHROOMS SUPREME

Serves: 8-10

4 slices bacon, cooked
1/2 lb. fresh chopped
    mushrooms
1 medium onion, chopped
1 clove garlic, minced
2 Tbsp. flour
1/4 tsp. salt
1/8 tsp. pepper
8 oz. cream cheese, cubed
2 tsp. Worcestershire sauce
1 tsp. soy sauce
1/2 cup sour cream

Cook bacon, drain and reserve 2 Tbsp. grease—crumble bacon. Cook mushrooms, onion and garlic in bacon grease. Stir in flour, salt and pepper. Add cream cheese, Worcestershire sauce and soy sauce. Heat and stir until cheese is melted. Stir in sour cream and bacon. Heat but do not boil. Serve warm with party rye bread or assorted rye crackers.

Lou Ann Smith

PLUM PLEASURES (Plum Soup)

Serves: *8

1 (13-oz.) can prune plums with
    liquid
3/4 cup apple juice
2 Tbsp. light rum
1 Tbsp. sugar
1/8 tsp. cinnamon
Pinch of cloves

Remove pits from plums. Pureé plums and plum syrup in blender or food processor. Stir in remaining ingredients; strain. Refrigerate until cold. Additional rum can be added to taste.

Serving suggestions: Pour in champagne glasses to serve. A special tip: I have served this as a soup before a main course of beef stroganoff.

*If you wish to use fresh sand plums, simmer 1 qt. of fresh plums with 1 cup water and 1 cup apple juice. Let cool. Drain plums from liquid and squeeze to remove pits. Return plums to liquid. Blend well. Add rum and 1/2 cup sugar. Heat until sugar dissolves. Add 1 Tbsp. lemon juice and spices. Blend thoroughly. Cover and chill 24 hours before serving.

Jane Ford

POTACHOS

2 medium size potatoes, baked
Oil
1 cup sour cream
4 whole green onions, sliced
1 cup Cheddar cheese,
    shredded
4 slices bacon, fried and
    crumbled

Cut potatoes into eighths. Scoop out leaving 1/2" meat with skins. Deep fry skins at 400° for 1-2 minutes. Arrange on platter in sunburst design. In middle of platter put sour cream. Top with cheese, bacon and green onion.

Optional toppings: sliced black olives, sliced mushrooms.

Cookbook Committee

RUTH BONDURANT'S SALSA

Yield: 1-1/2 cups

4 tomatoes
2 bunches green onions
1 (4.2-oz.) can ripe olives,
    chopped
1 (4-oz.) can green chilies,
    chopped
1 Tbsp. olive oil
1 Tbsp. vinegar
1 Tbsp. garlic salt (or regular
    salt to taste)
Doritos

Chop tomatoes, including skin, and green onions. Mix these and all remaining ingredients and chill. Serve with Doritos.

Florelee Day

SAUSAGE STUFFED MUSHROOMS

Serves: 20

1-1/2 lbs. mushrooms
1/2 lb. sausage
1/4 cup dry bread crumbs,
    seasoned
1/4 cup green onions,
    chopped
1/4 cup green pepper,
    chopped
1/2 cup Mozzarella cheese,
    shredded

Wash and dry mushrooms, Remove stems from mushrooms and chop stems. Cook sausage until well browned. Drain on paper towel. In 2 Tbsp. sausage drippings, cook mushroom stems, onion and green pepper until tender. Combine with sausage, cheese and dry bread crumbs. Fill mushrooms with mixture. Bake at 375° for 15 minutes.

Jana Harvey

RASPBERRY SOUP

You can rustle this up in a hurry for a real treat.

Serves: 5

1 (10-oz.) pkg. frozen red
    raspberries (sweetened)
8 oz. sour cream
1/3 cup rosé wine
1/2 cup half and half
1/2 cup whole milk

Place all ingredients in blender. Pureé mixture. Serve chilled.

Margaret Buvinger

RANCHO DE CHIMAYO

A Great Beginning for Your Next Fiesta!

Serves: 8

4 ripe avocados
1 Tbsp. onion, chopped
1 fresh tomato, chopped
1/8 tsp. lemon juice
1 tsp. salt
1/4 tsp. monosodium glutamate
1/4 tsp. white or black pepper
1/2 tsp. Worcestershire sauce
1 tsp. garlic salt
1/2 tsp. green chilies, chopped
1/2 Tbsp. mayonnaise

Peel avocados. Add all remaining ingredients together—mash. Put in a covered container, seal tightly and keep refrigerated. Excellent served on lettuce leaves as salad or with chips as dip.

Betty Shuttee

RONEY EGG ROLLS

1 whole chicken, stewed
1 lb. pork cubed steaks
1/2 cup celery, thinly sliced
3 Tbsp. green onions
1 small can (8-oz.) water
    chestnuts
1 can (16-oz.) bamboo shoots
3 Tbsp. soy sauce
1 Tbsp. ginger
1 Tbsp. salt
1 Tbsp. pepper
1 cup rice (cooked)
1/2 cup carrots, shredded
4 egg whites
1 pkg. egg roll wrappers

Cook meats and cut up into small pieces and set aside. Sauté celery, onion, water chestnuts, bean sprouts, bamboo shoots, soy sauce, ginger, salt and pepper. Add carrots, meats and rice. Place 2 Tbsp. of mixture into each egg roll. Seal well with egg whites and roll up. Deep fat fry until golden brown. Serve with sweet and sour sauce. These can be frozen up to 3 months after cooking. When reheating, reheat in a conventional oven to make crisp again. Do not use a microwave.

Mrs. Steve Roney (Janie)

SWEET-SOUR SMOKIES

Serves: 8

1 (6-oz.) jar plum jam
1 (8-oz.) jar mustard
2 (5-oz.) pkgs. smokie link
    sausages ("little smokies")

Combine all ingredients. Cover and simmer slowly for 1 hour. Serve warm with party picks.
Variation: You may use red currant jelly in place of plum jam.

Carolyn Bules

SUNNY'S FABULOUS CHEESE DIP

Serves: 30

2-1/2 (6-oz.) tubes Kraft
    pasteurized processed
    cheese spread, sharp
1/2 medium onion, chopped
2 (8-oz.) pkgs. cream cheese
1 (12-oz.) jar Marie's Blue
    Cheese Salad Dressing
    (no substitute)
1/2 cup pecans
Parsley flakes

Mix dressing and cheeses well. Add remaining ingredients. Sprinkle with Parsley flakes. *Set overnight.* Serve with raw vegetables or crackers.

Janie Roney

SHOW STOPPER SANDWICHES

8 oz. cream cheese, softened
1/3 cup chopped stuffed olives
2 Tbsp. olive juice
1/4 cup pecans, chopped
8 slices bacon, cooked
    and crumbled

Combine all ingredients and spread on sandwich bread (crust removed) and serve in quarters or mini-triangles. Garnish with olive slice.

Janie Word

STUFFED MUSHROOMS WITH BACON

Serves: 20

1-1/2 lbs. fresh mushrooms
6-8 slices bacon, diced
1/4 cup green onion, chopped
1/4 cup green pepper, chopped
1/2 tsp. salt
1 pkg. (3-oz.) cream cheese
1/2 tsp. Worcestershire sauce
1 Tbsp. butter
1/2 cup dry bread crumbs

Wash and dry mushrooms. Remove stems and dice. Sauté bacon and drain on paper towel. Sauté onion, green pepper and stems in small amount of bacon drippings. Combine bacon, onion, green pepper, mushroom stems, salt, cream cheese, and Worcestershire sauce. Mix bread crumbs with butter. Brown and mix with other ingredients. Stuff mushroom caps and bake at 375° for 15 minutes. Note: If large caps are used they make a nice vegetable garnish for steak dinner.

Jana Harvey

SAUSAGE SWIRLS

Yield: 40

4 cups flour, sifted
1/4 cup corn meal
2 Tbsp. baking powder
1 tsp. salt
2/3 cup vegetable oil
1 cup milk
2 lbs. sausage

Combine flour, cornmeal, baking powder, salt, vegetable oil and milk in food processor. Divide into 2 sections. Roll out mixture then spread on 1/2 of the sausage. Roll into log and slice off pieces 1/2" thick. Do the same with other mixture. Bake at 350° for 15-20 minutes. Can freeze.

Pat Diehl

SEASONED PECANS

4 cups whole pecans
1/2 cup butter
2 Tbsp. seasoned salt

Melt butter. Add to pecans and salt. Mix well. Spread out on a cookie sheet. Bake at 350° for 20 minutes, stirring twice.

Pam Boyle

SESAME CHICKEN WITH HONEY DIP

A Unique Crowd Pleaser.

Serves: 6

1/2 cup Hellmann's mayonnaise
1 tsp. dry mustard
1 tsp. instant minced onion
1/2 cup fine dry bread crumbs
1/4 cup sesame seeds
2 cups cooked chicken or
    turkey, cubed

HONEY DIP:
1 cup Hellmann's mayonnaise
2 Tbsp. honey

Mix first 3 ingredients, set aside. Mix crumbs and sesame seeds. Coat chicken with mayonnaise mixture, then crumb mixture. Place on baking sheet. Bake in 425° oven for 12 minutes or until lightly browned. Serve hot with honey dip. Serve with cocktail forks or toothpicks.

Linda Downs

SOY CHESTNUTS

Serves: 6

1 (7-1/2-oz.) can water
    chestnuts, drained
Soy sauce
4 slices bacon
Sugar

Soak water chestnuts in soy sauce from 30 minutes to 2 hours. Roll in sugar. Cut bacon slices in quarters. Wrap each chestnut in uncooked bacon and secure with toothpick. Bake at 350° for 20 minutes. Best when made ahead and warmed at same temperature for 5 minutes.

Judy Puerta

SHRIMP SPREAD

Serves:4

1 (4-1/2-oz.) can shrimp,
    chopped or 1/2 cup fresh,
    cooked, chopped,
    deveined
1/3 to 1/2 cup mayonnaise
2 Tbsp. celery, chopped
2 Tbsp. onion, chopped
2 Tbsp. parsley, chopped

Mix all ingredients and let stand several hours or overnight. Serve as dip or spread on crackers.

Ila Nicholas

SHRIMPLY "DEVINE"

A man's shrimp dip—A divine dip from a divine cook.

Makes: 3 cups

8 oz. cream cheese
1 cup (8-oz. carton) sour cream
2 pkgs. Good Season's Italian
    Dressing Mix
1 cup minced shrimp (fresh
    is a must!)

Let cream cheese soften. Prepare shrimp (peel, devein and cook). Drain well and chop. Combine cream cheese, sour cream and salad dressing powder. Beat until well mixed. Stir in minced shrimp. Best to refrigerate 2 hours before serving. Excellent with carrots, broccoli and celery, in addition to Escort crackers.

Mrs. Libbus Devine
Houston, Texas

SWEDISH NUTS

4 cups nuts, halves
2 egg whites, room temperature
1 cup sugar
Dash of salt
1/4 to 1/2 cup butter

Toast nuts in 325° oven until lightly browned. Beat egg whites until frothy. Fold sugar and salt into egg whites and beat until stiff. Melt butter in jelly roll pan. Combine nuts and egg whites and spread over butter. Bake for 30 minutes, stirring every 10 minutes or until light brown. Great for a tea party or as a festive finish with fruits and cheeses.

Ann Frazee Riley

TOO EASY TAMALE DIP

Serves: 20 with other hors d'oeuvres

2 (15-oz.) cans tamales
1 (16-oz.) can chili without
    beans
1 (8-oz.) jar picante sauce
2 (5-oz.) jars Old English
    cheese
1 onion, chopped

Chop the tamales and add rest of ingredients and blend. Put in fondue or crock and keep warm. Serve with anything "dippable". Easy and very good.

Nancy Rooks

SUPER SPINACH DIP

Serves: 20

1 pkg. (10-oz.) frozen chopped
    spinach, thawed and
    drained well
1 cup sour cream
1 cup mayonnaise (Hellmann's)
1/2 cup green onions,
    chopped
1/2 cup chopped parsley
1 tsp. salt
1 tsp. Beau Monde Seasoning
1 tsp. dill weed
2 to 3 Tbsp. lemon juice
    (or more)

Combine all ingredients and mix well. Chill 24 hours. Serve with crackers, party rye or raw vegetables. This is one of the best vegetable dips.

Eadie Lowenhaupt
Ann Maxwell

"SQUARE DANCERS"
A Quick-Step Chili Quiche-like Appetizer

Yield: 3 dozen squares

1 (4-oz.) can whole green
    chilies, drained, peeled
    and chopped (or use diced
    green chilies)
2 cups Cheddar cheese,
    shredded
1 cup Bisquick
1 cup light cream
4 eggs

Heat oven to 375°. Grease square pan, 9" x 9" x 2". Sprinkle chilies and cheese in pan. Beat remaining ingredients until smooth—15 seconds in blender on high speed. Pour into pan. Bake until golden brown, about 30 minutes. Let stand 10 minutes before cutting. Cut into 1-1/4" squares. Black olive slices or stuffed olive slices make a nice garnish.

Judy Anderson

SUPREME SALMON SPREAD

Serves: 10-12

1 can (16-oz.) Alaskan Red
    Sockeye Salmon, drained
    and flaked
1 pkg. (8-oz.) cream cheese,
    softened
1/4 cup green onion, finely
    chopped
1 Tbsp. lemon juice
2 tsp. prepared horseradish
1/4 tsp. salt
1/2 cup parsley, chopped
1/2 cup walnuts, chopped
Assorted crackers

In a medium bowl, blend salmon, cream cheese, onions, lemon juice, horseradish, salt. Wrap in wax paper to form ball. Chill 1 hour or until firm. Roll in parsley and nuts. Chill until ready to use. Serve with crackers or party rye.

Ruth Dobbs

SMOKED HAM BALLS

Yield: 60 small appetizers

1 lb. ground smoked ham
1/2 lb. ground fresh pork
3/4 cup soft bread crumbs
2 eggs, beaten
1/2 cup milk
2 Tbsp. onion, chopped

GLAZE:
1 cup canned crushed pine-
    apple, drained slightly
1/3 cup brown sugar
1 Tbsp. vinegar
3 Tbsp. mustard

Mix together ham, pork, crumbs, eggs, milk and onion. Form balls. Combine glaze and spoon over meat mixture. Bake in 350° oven for 1 hour, basting occasionally with glaze mixture.

Meme Wheeler

SMOKED OYSTER DIP

Serves: 12-14

1 (8-oz.) pkg. cream cheese, softened
1-1/2 cups Hellmann's mayonnaise
4 dashes hot sauce
1 Tbsp. lemon juice
1 (4-1/4-oz.) can chopped black olives, drained
1 (3.66-oz.) can smoked oysters, drained and chopped

Combine first 4 ingredients, mixing well. Stir in olives and oysters.
Serving suggestions: Serve with raw vegetables and 1 pkg. crackers.
Note: One recipe is enough for a party of 20 when other hors d'oeuvres are served.

Linda Downs

WALNUT CHEESE SPREAD

Serves: 16

1 lb. sharp cheddar cheese, grated
2 green onions, chopped
1/2 cup walnuts, roasted and chopped fine
1/4-1/2 cup mayonnaise
Pepper and liquid smoke to taste

Combine all ingredients. Best if made and let stand in refrigerator overnight. To roast walnuts: place in shallow pan in a slow oven (250°) until roasted. Watch carefully—they burn easily. Serve with crackers.

Gail Wynne

WILD WEST HOT DIP

Serves: 20 with other foods

1 lb. sausage or 1/2 lb. sausage and 1/2 lb. hamburger
1 lb. Velveeta cheese
1 (10-oz.) can Ro-Tel Green Chilies and tomatoes, drain and reserve

Brown meat and drain well. Melt cheese and combine with Ro-Tel sauce. Add meat, and simmer 30 minutes. Thicker dip, drain Ro-Tel; for thinner dip, add all the liquid in can. Serve in chafing dish with large corn chips.
Note: This also makes a good cheese sauce for your favorite enchiladas!

Donna Messall

ZUCCHINI APPETIZERS

These are great served warm with your favorite green salad.

Yield: 4 dozen, serves 12

3 cups zucchini, thinly sliced,
    unpared (about 4 small
    ones)
1 cup Bisquick
1/2 cup onion, chopped
3/4 cup Parmesan cheese,
    grated
2 Tbsp. parsley, snipped
1/2 tsp. salt
1/2 tsp. seasoned salt
1/2 tsp. dried marjoram or
    oregano
Dash pepper
1/2 tsp. garlic powder
1/2 cup vegetable oil
4 eggs, beaten

Mix all ingredients in large mixing bowl. Spread in oiled 13"x 9"x2" baking pan. Bake 25 minutes at 350°. Should be golden brown. Cut in 2"x1" pieces. Freezes well.

Kathy Risley

BEVERAGES

BANANA FRUIT PUNCH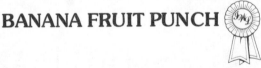

Makes 2 gallons

4 cups sugar
6 cups water
48 oz. pineapple juice
2 (12-oz.) cans frozen orange
    concentrate, thawed
1 (12-oz.) can frozen lemonade
    concentrate, thawed
5 bananas
3 qts. ginger ale

Mix sugar and water. Heat to boiling. Remove from heat and cool. When mixture is cool, add pineapple juice, orange concentrate and lemonade concentrate. Mash bananas by hand or in blender, then add to above mixture. Mix all by hand and put into three 1/2-gallon milk cartons. Freeze. Take out 2 hours before serving. When ready to serve, add 3 qts. ginger ale.

Janet Jones Hinson

BOURBON SLUSH

Makes 24 cups

1 (12-oz.) can frozen orange
    juice
2 (12-oz.) cans frozen lemonade
7 cups water
1-1/2 cups sugar
2 cups strong tea
2 cups bourbon
1 large bottle 7-Up

Set frozen juice out for 10 minutes. Mix all ingredients together except 7-Up. Put in freezer. Stir occasionally. When ready to serve, use 2/3 parts slush to 1/3 part 7-Up.
Note: Keep this in freezer for use as desired.

Jane Ford

BUNDLE TEA SPICED TEA

Serves: 50

6 qts. boiling water
1-1/2 lb. sugar
2 lemons, juice and rind
4 oranges, juice and rind
4 tsp. of whole cloves
8 sticks of cinnamon
3 Tbsp. of tea

Let first 6 ingredients stand 20 minutes, keeping hot but not boiling. Add tea. Let stand 5 minutes and strain.
Note: A regular event in early spring was a tradition of Junior Welfare League in years past. Station wagons were lined up in front and bundles were brought to stock the thrift shop. With the increase in public awareness of the Thrift Shop and its purpose, bundle teas have become a thing of the past, but the recipe remains a favorite.

CRÈME DE MENTHE

Makes 1 quart

2 cups vodka
2 cups light corn syrup
1/2 tsp. peppermint extract
2 tsp. vanilla
Green food coloring

Combine vodka, corn syrup, peppermint, and vanilla in a 4-cup screw top jar; stir in just enough food coloring to tint. Close jar. Store in cool, dry place for one month.

Mary Hendley

CHAMPAGNE PUNCH

Makes 2 gallons

4 fifths iced Brut champagne
5 oz. iced kirsch liqueur
   (not kirschwasser)
5 oz. iced Olorose (cream
   Sherry)
4 oz. iced lemon juice
16 oz. iced orange juice

Pour all ingredients into punch bowl. Stir lightly. For less tart punch, omit lemon juice.

Judy Chambers

COFFEE FRAPPE
(a winter evening delight)

Makes 24 cups

4 qts. strong hot coffee
1 qt. milk
1 cup sugar
2 tsp. vanilla
1/2 gal. vanilla ice cream

Mix coffee, milk, sugar, and vanilla. Pour over ice cream, stirring to blend and serve in punch bowl.
Variation: Add 1 cup Kahlúa or your favorite brandy.
Committee Suggestion: Garnish with cinnamon stick.

Florelee Day

CRANBERRY TEA

Makes 1 gallon

1/2 cup tea leaves
1/2 tsp. each: nutmeg,
   cinnamon and allspice
5 cups boiled water
3 cups hot water
1-1/2 cups sugar
1 cup orange juice
1/2 cup lemon juice, fresh
   squeezed
2 qts. cranberry juice

Put tea leaves, nutmeg, cinnamon, and allspice in cheese cloth and place in 5 cups of boiled water. Set aside. In larger pan combine hot water, sugar, orange juice, lemon juice, and cranberry juice. Add tea mixture and serve hot.

Bonnie Alexander
Stillwater, OK

GOLDEN WASSAIL

(Combine 4 golden fruit juices, add spices,
and heat! Result: a perfect holiday drink.)

Makes 2 quarts

4 cups unsweetened pineapple
   juice
1-1/2 cups (1 12-oz. can)
   apricot nectar
4 cups apple cider or apple
   juice
1 cup orange juice
6 inches stick cinnamon
1 tsp. whole cloves
1/4 tsp. whole cardamom seeds,
   crushed

Combine all ingredients in a large pan. Heat to boiling point; reduce heat and simmer 15 to 20 minutes. Remove from heat and strain. Pour hot wassail into mugs; garnish with floaters of thin orange slices studded with cloves.

Ruth Dobbs

 Use a bundt pan for a uniquely-shaped ice ring. Freeze a layer at a time, adding fruit arrangements with each. Different flavors of fruit juice will not dilute punch as melting occurs and will also add a rainbow of color.

HOT BUTTERED RUM

Serves: 16

Base:
1/4 lb. butter
1 lb. dark brown sugar
1/4 tsp. cinnamon
1/4 tsp. ground nutmeg
1/4 tsp. ground cloves
Dark rum

Mix all ingredients except rum. May be stored in refrigerator until ready to use. Drink: Into each cup or mug, place one heaping Tbsp. of base. Add 1-1/2 oz. dark rum. Fill with boiling water, stir, and serve. Great for ski trips!

Nancy Fry

HOT BUTTERED RUM 'N CREAM

"A good treat to keep on hand for winter hibernation."

Makes 30-40 cups

1 lb. brown sugar
1 lb. butter
1 lb. powdered sugar
1 qt. vanilla ice cream
2 tsp. nutmeg
2 tsp. ground cloves
Rum

Mix ingredients and keep in a covered container in freezer. Use 2 Tbsp. of mix per cup. Add hot water and 1 jigger rum. Sprinkle with nutmeg and serve.

Mary Hendley

HOT CINNAMON CIDER

Makes 2 quarts

2 qts. cider
1 tsp. whole cloves
1 tsp. whole allspice
1-3" stick cinnamon
1/2 unpeeled lemon, sliced
1/4-1/2 cup sugar

Bundle spices in cheesecloth. Heat and stir all ingredients well. Pour into cups or mugs to serve.

Ruth Dobbs

INDIAN TEA

Serves: 16

4 lemons
1 tsp. almond extract
1 qt. ginger ale
1 cup strong tea

Squeeze lemons. Reserve juice. Heat lemon rinds with 2 cups water. Dissolve 2 cups sugar in 2 cups of water (remove rinds). Add 1 cup strong tea. Cool. Add almond extract. Add ginger ale immediately before serving. Serve over crushed ice.

Colleen Jantzen

KAHLÚA

Makes 2 quarts

4 cups water
7 cups sugar
4 oz. instant coffee,
   (Maxwell House)
1 vanilla bean
1 qt. vodka

Boil water; add sugar and instant coffee to boiling water. Stir until all is dissolved well, then let cool. While boiling water, put vanilla bean in vodka. When first mixture is cool, pour into vodka and vanilla bean mixture. Stir well; then pour into tinted bottle and store in dark place for 2 weeks. Then ready to use. Excellent alone or with coffee.

Debbie Hardesty

OKLAHOMA JOY JUICE

Makes 3 quarts

1/2 gal. sauterne
1 qt. ginger ale
1 cup vodka

Mix all ingredients and chill. Easy, quick, and cheap.

Ruth Dobbs

LEGACY WINE PUNCH

Makes 2 gallons

1-1/2 cups water
2 cups sugar
2 sticks cinnamon
2 tsp. cloves
1/8 tsp. salt
2 fifths Burgundy
1 pt. chilled cranberry juice
    (2 cups)
1 qt. chilled apple cider
Thinly sliced lemons

Bring sugar, water, and spices to boil. Lower heat; simmer 10 minutes. Strain spices. Cool to serve. Combine half of syrup with wine, juice, and cider. Add ice and lemon. Syrup may be prepared ahead and refrigerated.

Mary Suzan Chambers

MINT JULEP

Makes 1/2 gallon concentrate

7 cups water
7 cups sugar
1 (6-oz.) can frozen orange juice
2 (16-oz.) bottles of lemon juice
3 double handsful mint leaves
Ginger ale or 7-Up

Bring water and sugar to boil. Add orange juice and lemon juice. Let mixture reheat and pour over mint leaves. Cover and let steep for at least 4 hours but best if left overnight. Strain. Use 1/3 cup of concentrate to a tall glass of ice. Finish filling with Ginger ale, 7-Up, or water.

Carole Smith

OPEN HOUSE PUNCH

Makes 3 quarts

2-1/2 cups Southern Comfort
6 oz. lemon juice
1 (6-oz.) can frozen orange juice
2 (6-oz.) cans frozen lemonade
2-1/4 qt. 7-Up

Combine all ingredients, adding 7-Up just before serving. Add lemon and orange slices as garnish.

Colleen Jantzen

SPICED APPLE CIDER

Makes 3 quarts

1/2 cup packed brown sugar
1 cinnamon stick
1 Tbsp. whole cloves
2 cups water
1-1/2 qt. apple cider or juice
1/2 cup lemon juice (best if
  fresh)
4 cups orange juice

Combine sugar, spices, and water in sauce pan. Heat to boiling, stirring until sugar dissolves. Reduce heat and simmer 10 minutes. Strain and discard spices. Pour spiced syrup into large kettle or dutch oven. Add cider, lemon juice, and orange juice. Heat to a simmer to serve or may be served chilled. Garnish with thinly sliced lemon and orange.

Sandra Davis

PUNCHY SANGRIA

(Delicious and refreshing on a hot summer night!)

Makes 2 quarts

2 (6-oz.) cans frozen pink
  lemonade concentrate
  (thawed and undiluted)
4-1/2 cups rosé wine,
  chilled
Juice of one lime
2 cups club soda, chilled
1 lemon, thinly sliced
1 orange, thinly sliced

Combine lemonade, rosé, and lime juice. Stir until blended. Slowly stir in club soda. Garnish with lemon and orange slices. Serve over ice.

Diana Allen

VODKA ORANGE SLUSH

Prairie Firewater

Makes 1 gallon

9 cups water
2 cups sugar
1 (12-oz.) can orange juice
1 (12-oz.) can lemonade
2 cups vodka
7-Up

Put sugar and water in large pan. Bring to boil and simmer 20 minutes. Add orange juice, lemonade, and vodka. Pour into 2 large cake pans and freeze. Stir occasionally. Fill glass 1/2-3/4 full of this mixture and fill with 7-Up. Garnish with mint.

Janet Stehr

WEDDIN' PARTY PUNCH (with sherbet)

Makes 1 gallon

1/2 gal. pineapple sherbet
1 qt. ginger ale (or 7-Up),
    chilled
1 qt. unsweetened pineapple
    juice, chilled

One hour before party, thaw pineapple sherbet in punch bowl to soften. When guests first arrive, add ginger ale and pineapple juice. Let set in punch bowl until ready to serve. Mix thoroughly. Add more pineapple juice and ginger ale if needed.

Diana Allen

WEDDING PUNCH
(For 100 people)

1 (16-oz.) can frozen orange
    juice concentrate
1 (12-oz.) can frozen lemonade
    concentrate
1 (6-oz.) can frozen limeade
    concentrate
2 (46-oz.) cans unsweetened
    pineapple juice
2-1/2 qts. water
2 qts. ginger ale

Combine all juices. Ginger ale should be added just before serving. An ice ring may be made with the juices (all except ginger ale) several days before serving. Slices of fruit and mint leaves may be frozen in ring. Use a ring mold or a bundt pan.

Mrs. Earl Mitchell (Jean)

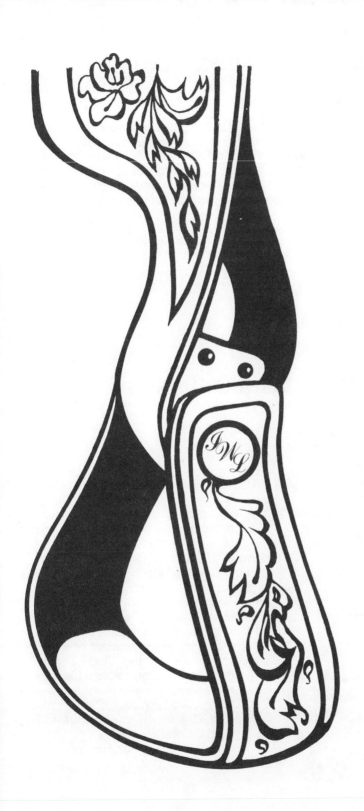

CIMARRON
SOUPS AND STEWS

"CIMARRON (SIMMER-ON)"

"Cimarron you soups!" Just as you won't find many cowboys who haven't heard of the Cimarron River, you won't find many cooks out west or anywhere who don't have a favorite and ever-reliable soup or stew. In the Mid-West we are supposed to be famous for our hearty robust flavors. You may wish to alter seasonings a bit, but that slow, low, simmerin' will bring that best in the West flavor to your Home on the Range. Cimmarron!

CREAM OF ASPARAGUS SOUP

Serves: 4

1 lb. fresh asparagus
4 cups chicken stock
1 small onion, finely chopped
2 Tbsp. butter
1-1/2 Tbsp. flour
Salt and pepper

FOR LIAISON:
2 egg yolks
6 Tbsp. heavy cream

Trim asparagus stalks, rinse in cold water and remove lower, tough ends. Cut in one-inch pieces and put in pan with stock and onion. Cover, bring to boil and simmer until tender (approximately 8 minutes). Reserve a few tips for garnish and purée remainder in food processor or blender. Melt butter in a large pan, stir in flour and cook, stirring until straw-colored. Add asparagus purée, season and bring soup to a boil, stirring constantly. Simmer 2-3 minutes. Mix egg yolks and cream together. Add a little of hot soup before adding liaison to remaining soup. Reheat carefully without boiling. Add reserved asparagus tips. Serve. Note: May be made ahead, but add liaison just before serving.

JoAnn Nicholas

AVOCADO CREAM SOUP

Serves: 8

4 large ripe avocado, peeled and diced
1-1/2 cups whipping cream
6 cups chicken broth
1 tsp. salt
1/4 cup dry sherry
Dried parsley
Paprika
Lemon slices

Blend 2 avocados with 1/2 cup of whipping cream in electric blender. Remove mixture from blender, repeat procedure with remainder of avocado and cream. Bring broth to a boil, reduce heat to low and stir in avocado purée. Add salt, mixing well. Add sherry. Chill thoroughly. Top with sprinkle of dried parsley and paprika and lemon garnishes.

Linda Downs

BLACK BEAN SOUP

Serves: 6

1 lb. black beans
1-1/2-lbs. smoked ham hock
1 Tbsp. dried minced onion
1 tsp. salt
1/4 tsp. dillweed
1/4 tsp. dry mustard
1/4 tsp. rosemary
2 tsp. cumin
2 bay leaves

Soak beans overnight. Drain soaking water, cover with fresh water in large covered kettle and bring to boil, then simmer for 2 hours. Drain this water and replace with fresh. (This eliminates most of the "problem" with eating beans and may also be used for navy beans.) Again, simmer over low heat for 3 more hours with remaining ingredients added. When beans are tender, remove ham, separate meat from bones and return meat to soup. It helps to remove lid the last hour of cooking to thicken soup.

Florelee Day

 Soup garnishes add a touch of enthusiasm and appetite and appeal; use celery sticks, a mushroom slice, parsley, a slice of zucchini, a small tomato slice, a green onion, or a carrot curl.

BEER CHEESE SOUP

Serves: 6

1/4 cup butter
1/2 cup onion, chopped
1/2 cup carrot, shredded
1/4 cup all-purpose flour
Dash of salt and pepper
2-1/2 cups milk
16 oz. jar Cheese Whiz
1/2 cup beer

Melt butter in saucepan. Add shredded carrot and chopped onion. Cook until tender. Blend in flour, salt and pepper. Add milk, stirring constantly until thickened. Add Cheese Whiz. Stir to melt. Blend in beer and heat.

Ann Frazee Riley

CHILI QUEEN'S CHILI

2 lbs. lean chili meat
1/2 lb. lean ground chuck
1 onion, chopped
1/4 cup green pepper, chopped
2 cloves garlic, minced
1 Tbsp. chili powder
1 Tbsp. cumin
3/4 tsp. oregano
1/2 tsp. sage
2 Tbsp. cornmeal
1 1-oz. Williams chili seasoning
1 tsp. salt
1/4 tsp. black pepper
1 Tbsp. Worcestershire sauce
1/4 to 1/2 cup chili sauce
1 6-oz. can tomato paste
1 1-lb. can whole tomatoes

Sauté ground meats, onion, green pepper, and garlic in 6 qt. roasting pan. Add remaining ingredients, blending well. Bring to a boiling point. Reduce heat and simmer covered two hours. Beans may be added, if desired.

Mrs. Glenn Devoll (Susie D'z Chili)

 Instant mashed potatoes can be added as a thickener for no-lump gravies and white sauces, added to stews and casseroles for a richer taste, or to create creamy, smooth soups.

CORN AND CHEESE CHOWDER

Serves: 8-10

2 cups water
2 cups diced potatoes
1/2 cup chopped onion
1/2 cup diced celery
2 Tbsp. margarine
1/2 tsp. dried whole basil
1 large bay leaf
1 17-oz. can cream style corn
2 cups milk
1 cup canned tomatoes,
    chopped
2 tsp. salt
1/8 tsp. pepper
1 Tbsp. minced fresh parsley
1/2 cup shredded Chedder
    cheese

Combine first seven ingredients in a large Dutch oven; bring to a boil. Reduce heat and simmer about 10 minutes or until potatoes are tender. Discard bay leaf. Stir in corn, milk, tomatoes, salt and pepper; heat thoroughly. Add cheese; cook over low heat, stirring constantly, until cheese is melted. Sprinkle fresh parsley over chowder.

Gayle Hackett

CHEESE SOUP

Serves: 10

1/2 cup onions, minced
1/2 cup butter
2/3 cup flour
1 tsp. dry mustard
1 tsp. paprika
1/4 tsp. Cayenne pepper
1 tsp. salt
1 can (10-1/2 oz.) chicken broth,
    or about 1-1/3 cup
5 cups milk
3 cups (12 oz.) sharp Cheddar
    cheese, shredded

Sauté onions in butter until soft; blend in flour and dry seasonings. Gradually stir in broth and milk. Cook over low heat, stirring constantly until soup thickens. Stir in cheese until smooth. Continue stirring until heated thoroughly. Garnish and serve.

Diana Allen

CHINESE STEW

Serves: 6

2 lbs. stew meat
2 Tbsp. cooking oil
1-1/2 tsp. salt

1 small head cabbage, shredded
1 lb. carrots, cut into strips
1 can water chestnuts, sliced
1 can bamboo shoots or
    bean sprouts
3 large onions, sliced
1 cup celery, chopped

Soy sauce

Dredge stew meat in flour and brown in oil. Cover with water and cook until tender. Add salt. In another cooking vessel, use 2 Tbsp. cooking oil and add vegetables, cooking until tender.
Mix vegetables with meat, serve over chow mein noodles or hot rice. Sprinkle soy sauce over meat and noodles or rice to suit individual taste.

Mrs. Robert H. Gengler

CHILI CON CARNE

Serves: 10

2 Tbsp. corn oil
1 cup onions, coarsely chopped
3 cloves garlic, finely crushed
1/2 cup green peppers, diced
2 lbs. lean ground beef, coarsely
    ground
4 Tbsp. chili powder
4 cups canned stewed tomatoes
4 cups canned chili beans
1 tsp. salt
1 cup boiling water

Heat oil in extra large skillet or Dutch oven, sauté onions, garlic and pepper; add ground beef and brown. Add remaining ingredients, except water, and simmer at least 1 hour. Add water. Cook slowly 4-6 hours. Yields approximately 4-1/2 lbs.

Ralph Evans

 Use crispy Chinese noodles, canned onion rings, or potato sticks for an unusual crunch to the top of soup or stew.

CURRIED BROCCOLI SOUP

Serves: 4-5

1 10-oz. pkg. frozen broccoli
1/2 cup water
2 rounded Tbsp. flour
2 Tbsp. butter
1 Tbsp. curry powder (or less,
    to taste)
Dash Tabasco sauce
1/2 tsp. salt
1 14-oz. can chicken broth
1 cup half and half

Cook broccoli in boiling water until barely tender. Place flour, butter and seasonings in blender. Add half the broth and the broccoli (including water). Purée the mixture. Return to pan and add remainder of broth and half and half. Bring to boiling point, stirring frequently, and serve.

Margaret Buvinger

CHICKEN-MUSHROOM SOUP

Serves: 4-6

4 cups chicken stock (skimmed)
1 clove garlic, minced
1 tsp. parsley flakes
1 small jar pimiento
2 cups fresh mushrooms, sliced
1 tsp. lemon juice
Salt to taste
Flour paste (equal parts flour
    and water), if desired

Bring broth to boil—reduce heat to low. Add all ingredients except flour paste. Simmer over low heat 30 minutes in a covered pot. Thicken to desired consistency with flour paste. Can be served with croutons, a dollop of sour cream, or plain.
Note: Thicken to gravy consistency and serve over chicken kiev, rice and other chicken entrées.

Charla Hicks

Slow low simmering for flavor: to get the full benefit of flavor in a soup or stew, start the final cooking process on the lowest heat possible. Let soup come to its hot serving temperature slowly while covered. This allows flavors to blend to the best possible advantage ...and the cook a chance to relax before dinner time.

CABBAGE SOUP

Serves: 6-8

3 or 4 lb. roast, cubed
5 beef bouillon cubes
1 clove garlic
1 tsp. parsley flakes
1 2-lb. bag carrots
1 onion, diced
1 head cabbage

Cover cubed roast with water and simmer 3 hours with bouillon, garlic, parsley, carrots & onion. Cut up cabbage. Add to beef and broth and cook slowly one hour.

Mrs. Ken Boyle (Pam)

GRANDMOTHER THOLE'S GREEN BEAN SOUP

Serves: 10-12

1 large hambone with some
    meat
1 large onion, chopped
1 Tbsp. salt
4 cans #202 whole green beans
    or fresh green beans
    in season
2 lbs. lean, chopped ham
6 chopped potatoes, large

1 pt. heavy cream
1/2 stick butter
1 qt. milk

First Day: Bring to boil in a large pot: large ham bone, onion, salt and water to cover by an inch or two. Turn down heat and simmer two or three hours; turn off heat, cover and let set out all night. Second Day: Remove bone and skim off fat. Add green beans and chopped ham. Bring to a boil, reduce to simmer and cook slowly. Add potatoes.

Add cream, butter and milk. Heat on low heat. Variation: Add 1 tsp. vinegar to each bowl just before serving. Note: Does not freeze well but will keep well in refrigerator.

Anne Cromwell

 Always save ham and other bones for hardy stocks. Wrap and freeze until needed, or prepare stocks and freeze in a milk carton for a flavor-filled addition to your favorite soup.

JOHN'S ONION SOUP

Serves: 6

3 medium onions, finely sliced
4 Tbsp. butter
1 Tbsp. flour
2-1/2 pts. beef stock, canned
    broth or consommé
    will do
Salt and pepper to taste
French bread or croutons
Swiss cheese, shredded
Additional butter

Cook onions in butter in heavy pot. When browned, sprinkle with flour. Allow to brown a little longer; then add beef stock, salt and pepper. Cook for 15 minutes. Slice bread 1/4 inch thick, butter lightly, and brown in oven. Put onion soup in casserole, put bread on top, then layer of Swiss cheese and a dab of butter. Put under broiler until golden brown.

John Wynne

FRENCH ONION SOUP

Serves: 6

1 qt. beef bouillon or brown
    stock or 2 cans commercial
    and 1 can water
3 cups yellow onions, sliced
1/4 cup butter
1-1/2 tsp. salt
1/4 cup sugar
2 Tbsp. flour
1/2 tsp. dry mustard
1/4 cup dry vermouth or cognac
1 cup Parmesan cheese, grated
Croutons, melba toast, etc.,
    if desired

Cook sliced onions in butter, covered, for 15 minutes. Uncover and add salt, sugar, flour, dry mustard and vermouth. Add to bouillon. Cook 6-8 hours in crock pot. Add cheese before serving. If desired, add croutons before serving.
Note: May be baked in microwave to melt cheese or broiled in oven. In restaurants the toast is placed on top of soup, then layered with cheese, then broiled.

Sally Shipley
Ruthie Dillingham

MAMA SESSIONS VEGETABLE STEW

Serves: 4

Note: My grandmother made this stew forever and my mother, too. My grandmother, Callie Sessions, came to Oklahoma in a covered wagon when she was 5 years old, back in 1890. She lived to be 92. The key to this vegetable stew is the garlic salt—really makes the difference.

6 cups water
2 short ribs
1/2 lb. hamburger meat
4 large stalks celery, chopped
6 carrots, chopped
3 potatoes, chopped
1 medium onion, chopped
1/2 cup elbow macaroni
1 can (16-oz.) stewed tomatoes
1 can (15-oz.) tomato sauce
1 tsp. salt
1 tsp. pepper
2 tsp. garlic salt

Put water on to boil in Dutch oven kettle on top of stove. Add short ribs and hamburger meat and let boil at a rolling boil while preparing vegetables. Add rest of ingredients and turn down to medium temperature or slow boil. Cover and cook for 2 hours on stove, stirring occasionally. You may add other vegetables according to your taste.

Diana Allen

MOTHER'S BEAN SOUP

Serves: 12

2 lbs. small Michigan Navy beans
4 qts. hot water
1-1/2 lbs. smoked ham or ham hocks
1 onion, chopped
Butter
Salt and pepper to taste
1 tsp. garlic salt

Wash navy beans and run through hot water until beans are white or let soak overnight. Put beans into a large pot with the 4 qts. hot water and bring to a boil. Add smoked ham hocks and boil slowly for about 3 hours, covered. Braise onion in a little butter and when light brown, add to bean soup. Season to taste.
Note: Can cook in a crock pot overnight. Can add a carrot while beans are cooking to absorb gas from beans. Then throw carrot away. Do not eat the carrot.

Diana Allen

POTATO BACON CHOWDER

Serves: 6

8 slices bacon, cut up
1 cup onion, chopped
4 cups potatoes, cooked
    and cubed
1 cup water
1 can cream of chicken soup
1 cup sour cream
1-3/4 cup milk
1/2 tsp. salt
Dash pepper

Fry bacon until crisp. Remove bacon and sauté onion in drippings. Remove onion and drain on paper towel. Cube potatoes and cook in the 1 cup water, add soup, onion and bacon, sour cream and milk, plus seasonings, saving some bacon to crumble on top. Simmer, but do not boil.

Peggy Harmon

POTATO SOUP

Serves: 4-6

3 or 4 medium potatoes, peeled,
    sliced or cubed
2 medium onions, chopped
1 cup celery
1-1/2 Tbsp. butter
Boiling water to cover
1/2 tsp. salt
1 bay leaf
2 Tbsp. butter
Chicken stock
Salt to taste

Sauté potatoes, onions and celery in 1-1/2 Tbsp. butter. Add boiling water, salt and bay leaf.
Boil vegetables until potatoes are tender (about 20 minutes). Put vegetables through blender until there are no lumps. Beat 2 Tbsp. butter into the blended vegetables. Thin soup to desired consistency with chicken stock. Add salt to taste.
Serving suggestions: For lunch or light supper. Serve with hot French bread and a fresh fruit salad.

Claudell Thomas

 Small amounts of leftover vegetables may be added to a large container in the freezer for use in family stew. It's time to make stew when the container is full of a variety of frozen vegetable layers.

OVEN STEW

Serves: 4-6

2 lbs. stew meat, trimmed
3 Tbsp. tapioca
Carrots
Onions
Potatoes
Celery
1 lb. can tomatoes

Cut all ingredients into chunks (except tomatoes and tapioca). Put all into Dutch oven or similar pot, cook for 5 hours in 225° oven.
Note: Good for busy day (prepare early), since this cooks so slowly and long, can put in and leave house easily.

Suzy Traynor

SPINACH CHEESE SOUP

Serves: 8-10

2 Tbsp. salad oil
3/4 cup onion, chopped
1 large clove garlic, pressed
6 cups water
6 chicken bouillon cubes
8 oz. fine egg noodles (about
    4 cups)
1 tsp. salt
6 cups milk
2 pkgs. (10 oz.) frozen chopped
    spinach, thawed and
    drained
1/2 lb. Cheddar cheese,
    shredded (about 2 cups)
1/2 lb. Swiss cheese, shredded
    (about 2 cups)
Paprika
Packaged croutons

In large saucepan, heat oil. Add onion and garlic; sauté over medium heat, stirring occasionally, until onion is tender (about 5 minutes). Add water and bouillon cubes. Heat to a rapid boil, stirring occasionally to dissolve cubes. *Gradually* add noodles and salt so water continues to boil. Cook uncovered, stirring occasionally until tender (about 6 minutes). Stir in milk, spinach, both cheeses.Cook until heated through and cheeses are melted. Stir constantly, do not boil (or it will burn on bottom of pan!). Sprinkle with paprika and croutons. Serve immediately. Note: Leftover soup can be covered, chilled and reheated (covered) by adding milk as necessary for desired consistency.

Chris Smith
Ann Frazee Riley

 A leaf of lettuce dropped into a pot absorbs grease from the top of soup. Remove the lettuce and throw it away as soon as it has served its purpose.

STEAK SOUP

Serves: 8-10

2 lbs. ground chuck
2 sticks (1 cup) butter
1 cup flour
2 qts. water
4 potatoes, diced
2 carrots, diced
1 or 2 onions, chopped
2 cans mixed vegetables
1/2 to 1 bottle of B.V., or
    Schilling beef base

Brown meat and drain. In Dutch oven melt butter and add flour. Mix. Add 2 qts. of water. Add vegetables, meat and B.V. Simmer as long as you like.
Note: gets better every day.

Dee Everitt

TIFFANY'S BEAN POT SOUP

Serves: 8-10

2 cups dried pinto beans
1 lb. ham (cubed)
1 qt. water
1 large can tomato juice (22-oz.)
4 cups chicken stock
3 onions chopped
3 cloves garlic
3 Tbsp. chopped parsley
1/4 cup chopped green peppers
4 Tbsp. brown sugar
1 tsp. chili powder
1 tsp. m.s.g.
1 tsp. salt
1 tsp. crushed bay leaf
1 tsp. oregano
1/2 tsp. each rosemary, celery
    seed, thyme, marjoram,
    basil, curry powder
4 whole cloves
1 cup Sherry

Soak cleaned beans overnight, drain. Add all other ingredients except Sherry. Bring to boil and cook slowly until beans are tender. Add Sherry. Serve in generous bowls topped with onion flakes. May be frozen for future use.

Julie Barnard

NOTES:

Your own favorite Soup or Stew.

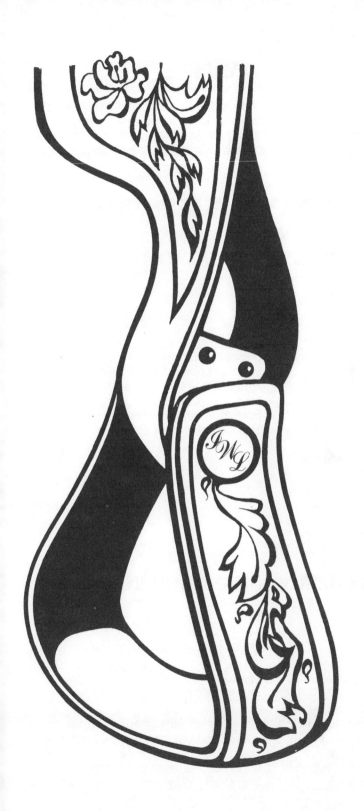

SALAD STAMPEDE

SALADS

"SALAD STAMPEDE"

Never before have so many of us stampeded to salad bars! With so much enthusiasm and awareness of health and fitness—we are always on the lookout for some exciting varieties of salads. Whether you're racing against the scale or looking for a crisp contrast in your menu, the Salad Stampede is sure to provide some ideas.

FRUIT SALADS

BLUEBERRY SALAD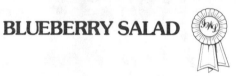

Serves: 12

2 pkgs. raspberry, blackberry or blueberry Jello
2 cups hot water
1 (15-oz.) can blueberries (undrained)
1 small can drained crushed pineapple
1 (8-oz.) pkg. cream cheese, softened
1 cup sour cream
1/2 cup Cool Whip
1/4 cup sugar
1/2 tsp. vanilla
Chopped pecans

Dissolve Jello in hot water in 9" x 13" pan. Let cool. Add blueberries and pineapple. Let jell. Combine cream cheese, sour cream, Cool Whip, sugar and vanilla. Spread this mixture on top of Jello mixture. Sprinkle chopped nuts on top.

Colleen Jantzen
Marcia Seals

BLUEBERRY BANANA BONANZA

CRUST:
3/4 cup butter
1-1/2 cups flour
3/4 cup chopped pecans

Mix and press into 9 x 13-inch oblong pyrex pan. Bake at 350° for 15-20 minutes.

FILLING:
8 oz. cream cheese, softened
1/2 cup butter
2 eggs, slightly beaten
1 tsp. vanilla
2 cups powdered sugar

Combine cream cheese, butter, eggs, vanilla and powdered sugar and spread over cooled crust. Top with 3 to 4 sliced bananas, 1 (21-oz.) can blueberry pie filling, Cool Whip and 1/2 cup chopped pecans.

Eleanor Taylor

CHRISTMAS SALAD

Serves: 6

1 3-oz. pkg. lime Jello
1-1/2 cups boiling water
1 cup crushed pineapple,
   drained
1 3-oz. pkg. cream cheese
1 jar (7-oz.) marshmallow creme
3/4 cup nuts, chopped
1/4 cup maraschino cherries,
   chopped
1 cup whipped cream or
   1 small Cool Whip

Dissolve Jello in boiling water. Let cool until somewhat thick. Mix pineapple and cream cheese. Add marshmallow creme, nuts and cherries. Add whipped cream and jello. Pour into mold and chill.

Mrs. J. D. Boyer (Jane)

CRANBERRY FREEZE

Serves: 6

1 16-oz. can whole cranberry
   sauce
1 8-3/4-oz. can crushed pineapple, drained
1 cup dairy sour cream
1/4 cup confectioners sugar,
   sifted
3 pineapple rings, well drained

Combine cranberry sauce and crushed drained pineapple. Stir together the sour cream and the sifted powdered sugar. Add to the fruit and mix well. Line a 3 cup refrigerator tray with foil and pour in fruit mixture. Freeze until firm. Remove frozen salad and foil from the pan. Let set a few minutes at room temperature. Remove foil and cut into pie wedges. Place one-half a pineapple ring on top of each wedge. This may be served on lettuce.

Mrs. Robert Harper (Sue)

 It is easy to remove the white membrane from oranges for fancy desserts or salads—by soaking them in boiling water for five minutes before you peel them.

CRANBERRY SALAD

Serves: 4-6

1 (8-oz.) can crushed pineapple
1 (3-oz.) pkg. cherry Jello
1/2 cup sugar
1 cup hot water
1 Tbsp. lemon juice
1 cup ground fresh cranberries
1 cup diced celery
1 small orange, remove seeds
    and membrane,
    grind whole
1/2 cup chopped pecans

Drain pineapple. Add water to syrup to make 1/2 cup. Dissolve Jello and sugar in hot water. Add 1/2 cup syrup mixture and lemon juice. Chill till partially set in 9 x 13 inch pan. Add remaining ingredients.

Mary Susan Chambers

PEACHES 'N CREAM SALAD

Serves: 9-12

1 pkg. (3 oz.) lemon gelatin
1 cup boiling water
1 cup orange juice
1 pkg. whipped topping mix
1 pkg. (3 oz.) cream cheese,
    softened
1/4 cup chopped pecans

PEACH LAYER:
1 pkg. (3 oz.) lemon gelatin
1 cup boiling water
1-1 lb. 6 oz. can peach pie
    filling

Dissolve gelatin in boiling water; add orange juice. Refrigerate until slightly thickened. Prepare topping mix according to package directions; blend in cheese; stir in pecans. Fold into gelatin mixture and pour into a 9 x 9 x 2 inch pan. Chill until almost firm. Prepare Peach Layer: Dissolve gelatin in boiling water; stir in pie filling. Pour over top of first layer. Chill until firm. Cut in 9 squares or 12 pieces. Serve on crisp salad greens, if desired.

Marjorie Collier

FRUIT SALAD

Serves: 6-8

1 can mandarin oranges
1 lb. can apricot halves
1 lb. can pineapple chunks
1 lb. can peach slices
1 small pkg. vanilla instant
   pudding
1 small carton strawberries,
   frozen
3 bananas, sliced

Drain cans of fruit, except pineapple juice and save. Put fruit together in large bowl. Sprinkle pudding over it. Then put partially thawed strawberries on top. Let set overnight. When ready to serve, pour pineapple juice over bananas. Drain and put in salad. Mix and serve. Will keep for 2 or 3 days.

Danette Tucker

PINEAPPLE A LA CHANTILLY

Serves: 4-8

2 pineapples
1 pt. strawberries
2 cups green grapes
2 large bananas, sliced
1/4 cup sugar, or to taste

CHANTILLY SAUCE:
2 cups whipped cream
1/2 cup chocolate, grated
2 Tbsp. sugar
2 Tbsp. light rum

Cut pineapples in half lengthwise. Scoop out pineapple, leaving 3/4 inch rim. Dice fruit and mix with strawberries, green grapes and bananas (banana slices should be stirred gently in lemon juice to keep them from turning). Add sugar and chill thoroughly. Pile fruit back in shell and top with chantilly sauce. Fruit may be assembled early if bananas are treated with lemon juice.
Note: For single servings used as a main course (as for a ladies luncheon) half pineapples should be used. For a pre-meal appetizer the pineapple could be cut in fourths, canoe fashion, leaving stem and leaf section.

Sauce: Whip cream. While still beating, add sugar and rum. Gently fold in chocolate. Top fruit with sauce just before serving. Allow 1/4 to 1/2 cup per serving.

Mrs. Jere Sturgis (Vicki)

FROZEN FRUIT SALAD

Serves: 25

6 bananas, mashed
2 (16-oz.) cans apricots, drained
2 (15-oz.) cans crushed
    pineapple with half the
    juice drained
1 (12-oz.) can frozen orange juice
2 cups sugar
1 orange juice can of water
2-1/2 Tbsp. lemon juice

Combine all the ingredients and freeze in muffin tins lined with cupcake liners.

Mrs. David Bules (Carolyn)

MELLOW CRANBERRY SALAD

Serves: 6-8

12 oz. fresh cranberries
1-1/4 cups sugar
1 lb. tokay grapes
8 oz. small marshmallows
8 oz. whipping cream
1 cup pecans

Grind cranberries and add sugar. Let stand while you seed the grapes. Drain the juice from the cranberries. Add grapes, marshmallows, pecans and whipping cream. Mix well. Refrigerate over night.

Mrs. Gary Dickenson (Rosanne)

PINEAPPLE YUM YUM

Serves: 8

2 cups crushed pineapple
Juice of one lemon
1 cup sugar
2 Tbsp. gelatin
1/2 cup cold water
1 cup Colby cheese, grated
1/2 pint whipping cream,
    whipped

Heat pineapple. Add lemon and sugar. Stir until sugar is dissolved. Soak gelatin in cold water for 5—10 minutes. Add to pineapple mixture. Cool. Then add cheese and whipped cream. Chill and serve.

Mrs. Fred Blythe (Sharon)

SALAD DELIGHT

Serves: 8

1 3-oz. cream cheese, diced
1 10-oz. jar maraschino cherries
1 15-oz. can pineapple chunks
1 large green pepper, diced
1 cup miniature marshmallows
1 11-oz. can mandarin oranges
1 8-oz. carton whipping cream,
    whipped
1 cup pecans, chopped

Drain juice from all ingredients. Mix and chill. (For desired color add small amount of cherry juice.)

Mrs. Bruce Simon (Cindy)

7-UP SALAD

1 large or 2 small pkgs. lemon
    Jello
2 cups hot water
2 cups 7-Up
2 8-oz. cans crushed pineapple,
    well drained
1 cup marshmallows
2 bananas, sliced

TOPPING:
2 Tbsp. flour
1/2 cup sugar
1 egg, well beaten
1 cup pineapple juice
2 Tbsp. butter
2 cups (1 pkg.) prepared
    Dream Whip

Mix Jello and water. Let cool slightly. Add 7-Up and let set until ropey. Stir sliced bananas into pineapple and let set 10 minutes so that bananas will not darken. Add marshmallows and combine all with 7-Up-Jello mixture. Pour into pan and chill.

Mix flour, sugar, egg and juice. Cook until thick, stirring constantly. Add butter and cool. Fold in Dream Whip. When salad is set, spread on topping. Sprinkle with grated cheese, nuts, cherries, etc.

Ann Frazee Riley

VEGETABLE SALADS

AVOCADO JELLO SALAD

Serves: 4-6

1 small pkg. lime Jello
2 cup hot water
1 large Philadelphia cream
   cheese
1/4 cup green pepper, diced
1/2 cup celery, diced
2 Tbsp. onion, diced
1/8 tsp. salt
1/2 cup mayonnaise
1 tsp. vinegar
1 avocado, well mashed

Dissolve Jello in hot water, add Philadelphia cream cheese and stir with a whisk until cheese is mostly dissolved. Add green pepper, celery, onion, salt, mayonnaise and vinegar and avocado. Stir. Refrigerate until set.

Sharon Blythe

AVOCADO-SPINACH SALAD

Serves: 6

1 lb. spinach
Salt
1 clove garlic, peeled
2 Tbsp. lemon juice
6 Tbsp. olive oil
Freshly ground black pepper
2 hard-cooked eggs
1/2 red or yellow onion, sliced
1 or 2 large avocados, sliced

Wash spinach well. Cut off tough stems with scissors. Drain spinach leaves and chill in damp paper towel. Tear into bite-sized pieces. Sprinkle bottom of wooden bowl with salt and rub with garlic. Add lemon juice and oil and chill in bowl. When ready to serve, add spinach, pepper, eggs, onion and avocado. Toss lightly and serve.

Mrs. Jim Nicholas (Ila)

MARINATED BROCCOLI

Serves: 8-10

3 bunches fresh broccoli
1 cup cider vinegar
1 Tbsp. dillweed
1 Tbsp. sugar
1 Tbsp. monosodium glutamate
1 tsp. salt
1 tsp. pepper
1 tsp. garlic salt
1-1/2 cups olive oil or
    vegetable oil

Trim off large leaves of broccoli. Remove tough ends of lower stalks, and wash broccoli thoroughly; cut flowerettes from stems, reserving stems for use in other recipes. Combine remaining ingredients; mix well and pour over broccoli flowerettes. Cover and chill 8 hours or overnight. Drain, marinade before serving.

Mrs. Ray Downs (Linda)

MAKE AHEAD COLE SLAW

Serves: 12-15

1 medium head of cabbage,
    chopped or shredded
1 green pepper, thinly sliced
1 onion, thinly sliced
10 stuffed olives, thinly sliced
1/2 cup sugar
1 cup vinegar
1/2 cup salad oil
1 tsp. dry mustard
1 tsp. celery salt
1 tsp. salt
1/2 tsp. black pepper

Layer cabbage, pepper, onion and olives in a large bowl. Combine sugar, vinegar, salad oil, dry mustard, celery salt, salt and pepper in small covered sauce pan and boil for three minutes. Pour the hot mixture over vegetables. Mix and refrigerate *at least 24 hours*.

Mrs. Richard Risley (Kathy)
Mrs. Tom Sailors (Ruth Ann)

CALICO SALAD

Serves: 10-12

1 can diced carrots, drained
1 can whole kernel corn, drained
1 can yellow wax or green beans,
    drained
1 medium bell pepper, chopped
1 red bell pepper, chopped
1 medium onion, chopped
1 tsp. salt
3/4 cup sugar
2/3 cup wine vinegar
1/3 cup salad oil

Combine all vegetables. Mix together salt, sugar, vinegar, oil. Add to vegetables, mixing well. Refrigerate overnight. Keeps a week.

Mrs. Dennis Iselin (Mary Helen)

CAULIFLOWER-BACON

Serves: 10-12

1 medium head cauliflower,
    broken into flowerets
1 small head Iceberg lettuce,
    shredded
1 small red onion, thinly sliced
    and separated into rings
1 lb. bacon, cooked and
    crumbled
2 to 4 Tbsp. sugar
1/4 cup grated Parmesan,
    canned
1 cup salad dressing or
    mayonnaise

In large bowl, layer all ingredients in order given. Cover and refrigerate 3 to 4 hours. Toss gently *just* before serving as it does not hold well if tossed too early.

Linda Downs

CUCUMBERS IN SOUR CREAM

Serves: 4

1 cucumber, thinly sliced, (peel
    if desired)
1 tsp. salt
1/2 cup dairy sour cream
1 Tbsp. vinegar
1 or 2 drops bottled hot
    pepper sauce
2 Tbsp. chopped chives
1 tsp. dill seed
Dash of pepper

Sprinkle cucumber slices with salt, let stand 30 minutes, drain. Combine remaining ingredients; pour over cucumbers. Chill about 30 minutes. Makes 4 or 5 servings. Serve on lettuce leaf.

Meme Wheeler

MARINATED GREEN BEANS

Serves: 12

2 lbs. whole, cooked green
    beans, drained

MARINADE:
2 Tbsp. vegetable oil
1 Tbsp. cider vinegar
1 small onion, minced
1/2 tsp. salt
1/4 tsp. freshly ground pepper

DRESSING:
1/2 cup dairy sour cream
1/2 cup mayonnaise
1 Tbsp. lemon juice
1 Tbsp. horseradish
2 tsp. onion, minced
1 tsp. dry mustard

Place drained beans in a bowl. Blend marinade ingredients and pour over the beans. Let marinate overnight in refrigerator. Next day, drain beans. Blend dressing ingredients in food processor or blender until smooth. Add dressing to beans and toss. Garnish with cherry tomatoes, whole mushrooms, and slivered blanched almonds. Dressing can be made the night before.

Mrs. Richard Risley (Kathy)

BACON FLAVORED GREEN BEANS

Serves 4

9 oz. pkg. frozen green beans
   (French cut)
2 Tbsp. lemon juice
1/4 cup mayonnaise
1 Tbsp. grated onion
1 tsp. Dijon mustard
1/4 cup crisp bacon, crumbled
Salt and pepper

Partially thaw and chop beans. Blanch 1 minute in boiling water with 1 Tbsp. lemon juice. Drain, mix mayonnaise, onion and mustard. Fold cooled beans into sauce with 1 Tbsp. lemon juice and bacon. Season and chill. Serve on green lettuce.

Mrs. Bill Word (Janie)

CREAMY MUSHROOM SALAD

Serves: 4

4 cups fresh mushrooms, sliced
8 oz. cream cheese
1/3 cup mayonnaise
1/2 tsp. salt
1/4 tsp. white pepper
2-1/2 Tbsp. grated onion

Whip together all the ingredients except the mushrooms. Gently mix with the mushrooms. Serve on lettuce leaf.

Mrs. Bill Word (Janie)

SWISS MUSHROOMS

Serves: 8-10

1 lb. mushrooms, sliced
3/4 lb. Swiss Cheese, shredded
1 bunch green onion with 1'' of
   stem, chopped
1/2 cup oil
1/4 cup red wine vinegar
3 Tbsp. Cavender Seasonings

Combine mushrooms, cheese, green onions. Combine oil, vinegar, seasonings, then pour over mushroom mixture, when ready to serve.

Judy Halstead
Mrs. James Cox (Janet)

MARINATED GARDEN SALAD

Serves: 6-8

*1 6-oz. jar marinated artichoke
    hearts, drained
2 medium carrots, thinly sliced
1 green pepper, cut into strips
2 large green onions, sliced
2 cups cauliflower flowerettes
2 cups fresh mushrooms, sliced
2 cups celery, chopped
1 8-oz. can water chestnuts*

*MARINADE:
1/4 cup vegetable oil
1/2 cup sugar
1/2 cup vinegar
1 Tbsp. water
1/8 tsp. salt*

Pour marinade over the vegetables and let stand over night.

Mrs. Bruce Harvey (Jana)

MARINATED SALAD

Serves: 4-6

*1 pkg. broccoli spears
    (use tops only)
2 tomatoes, cut in wedges
1 medium avocado, cubed
1 cup artichoke hearts
1 cucumber, sliced*

*DRESSING:
1/2 cup Italian dressing
Dash of wine vinegar
1/2 tsp. chervil*

Cook and drain broccoli just until crisp. Cut off tops. Mix marinade dressing. Prepare vegetables. Combine all ingredients and let set in refrigerator for at least one hour. Toss lightly and serve on lettuce leaves.

Mrs. Dick Allen (Diana)

LEMON-MARINATED VEGETABLES

Serves: 12

1-1/2 cups pure vegetable oil
1 cup lemon juice
2 Tbsp. parsley
4 tsp. salt
1 tsp. sugar
1/4 tsp. hot pepper sauce
1 clove garlic, crushed
1 lb. Zucchini, sliced
1 head cauliflower, separated
2 cans artichoke hearts, halved

Combine oil, lemon juice, parsley, salt, sugar, hot sauce, and garlic in large screw-top jar. Place vegetable in separate bowl. Shake oil (mix well) mixture and pour over vegetables. Cover and marinate overnight. Drain vegetables and serve.

Mrs. Tim Crowley (Melanie)

PRAIRIE PEA SALAD

Serves: 6

6 Tbsp. mayonnaise
Juice of 1 lemon
4 or 5 green onions, minced
2 cups frozen peas, (not thawed)
1 cup Cheddar cheese, strips
Salt & pepper to taste
2 cups lettuce, torn in bite-size
    pieces
8 slices crisp bacon, crumbled

One day before serving, combine all ingredients except bacon and lettuce. Stir well; cover and refrigerate. Just before serving add lettuce and bacon.

Mrs. John Wynne (Gail)

 Tossed salad for a crowd: use an extra large plastic bag. This makes for easy tossing and storage in the pre-party crowded refrigerator as well as ease in the last minute no-spill arrangement in your favorite salad bowl.

SLICED POTATO SALAD

Serves: 6

8 medium potatoes
2 tsp. salt
1 cup sour cream
1 tsp. celery seed
1/4 cup parsley flakes
1-1/2 cups mayonnaise
1-1/2 tsp. horseradish
1/2 tsp. salt
2 medium onions, minced

Boil potatoes with jackets in the 2 tsp. salt. Cool. Peel and slice. Combine the remaining ingredients. Arrange a layer of potatoes in serving dish. Top with mixture and repeat. Chill 6-8 hours.

Mrs. Bruce Harvey (Jana)

GERMAN POTATO SALAD

Serves: 6-8

5 slices bacon
1 small Bermuda onion,
    chopped
2 Tbsp. flour
2/3 cup white vinegar
1-1/3 cups water
1/4 cup sugar
1 tsp. salt
Dash pepper
6 cups potatoes, sliced and
    cooked

Fry the bacon until crisp and drain. Save 2-3 Tbsp. drippings. Crumble the bacon. Sauté onion in drippings. Blend in flour slowly. Stir in vinegar and water. Cook until mixture boils and thickens slightly. Add sugar, salt and pepper. Simmer 10 minutes. Layer potatoes, bacon and sauce in top of a double boiler. Keep warm over hot water for 6 to 8 hours to allow flavors to blend. Serve warm.

Mrs. Richard Davis (Dr. Elaine)

 A few drops of lemon juice in water will whiten boiled potatoes.

LAYERED POTATO SALAD

Serves: 12

6-8 medium boiled potatoes
1/2 onion, cut large in rings
Seasoned salt
6 eggs, boiled and sliced
1 large carton (16 oz.)
   cottage cheese
2 cups mayonnaise
3 Tbsp. Wesson oil

Slice potatoes and layer in bottom of 9" x 13" dish. Then layer onions which have been sprinkled with seasoned salt, eggs, cottage cheese, and mayonnaise which has been combined with the Wesson oil. Garnish with dried parsley. Wishbone Italian is good added to the mayonnaise mixture.

Ruth Bennett

JANE LEE'S VEGETABLE MARINADE

Serves: 12

2 lbs. carrots
1 stalk celery
1 head cauliflower, separated
1 pint cherry tomatoes
2 green peppers
2 cans black olives, pitted
1 15-oz. jar green olives, stuffed
1 sweet red onion

DRESSING:
1-1/2 cups salad oil
2/3 cup vinegar
2-1/2 tsp. salt
1 tsp. pepper
1-1/2 tsp. sugar
3 garlic cloves

Cut carrots and celery into bite sizes. Do not cut cherry tomatoes. Cut green peppers into strips. Drain olives. Separate red onion into rings. Place in bowl. Mix dressing ingredients and pour over vegetables. Marinate in refrigerator 24 hours. Remove garlic cloves. May be served with toothpicks if used as an hors d'oeuvre.

Mrs. John Scott (Marsha)

 When slicing hard-cooked eggs, wet the knife before each cut to keep yolks from crumbling.

"CITY SLICKER" CARROTS

Serves 8

2 lbs. carrots
2 green peppers
2 medium onions
1 can tomato soup
1/2 cup salad oil
3/4 cup vinegar
1 cup sugar
1 tsp. salt
1/2 tsp. pepper
1 Tbsp. prepared mustard
1 Tbsp. Worcestershire sauce

Peel, slice and cook carrots until *just* tender. Drain and cool. Slice pepper and onions into rings. Combine other ingredients and pour over vegetables. Refrigerate overnight. Keeps well one week.

Ruth Ann Sailors

WHEATHEART TABOULI SALAD

6 servings

1 cup bulgar (cracked wheat)
Warm water
6 tomatoes, chopped
6 green onions, chopped whole
2 cups chopped fresh parsley
2 cloves garlic crushed
1/3 cup olive oil
1/2 cup lemon juice
Salt and pepper to taste
Possible additional ingredients:
1/2 cup chopped cucumber,
    seeded
1/3 cup chopped green pepper
1/4 cup chopped black olives
1 cup finely chopped mint
    leaves

Prepare wheat. In a medium bowl, soak wheat in warm water to cover. Let set one hour. Drain if needed. Chop and prepare remaining ingredients. Toss with wheat. Chill. Tabouli may be served on lettuce leaves for individual appetizers, or as a dip with Doritos. This salad originated in the middle east and is a favorite on the Great Plains. It keeps well in the refrigerator, and provides a chewey contrast to the traditional steak and baked potato crowd.

The Enid News and Eagle and
The Cookbook Committee

*Please note: this recipe is not the last word in tabouli salad, and ingredients can vary to please your preference. The salad is so popular in our region, that every kitchen has a special way to prepare it. We selected this one as it included our favorite ingredients. Any way you enjoy it, tabouli is packed with nutrition!

SPAGHETTI SALAD

Serves: 24

1 pkg. (12 oz.) thin spaghetti
1 large cucumber
2 bunches green onions
2 bunches radishes
4 hard-boiled eggs
1 tsp. sugar
1/2 tsp. celery salt
1-1/2 tsp. salt
3/4 tsp. white pepper

DRESSING:
2 cups mayonnaise
3/4 cup sour cream
3/4 cup half & half
4 Tbsp. Durkee's dressing
1 Tbsp. yellow mustard

Break spaghetti in quarters and boil. When done, drain and cool. Thinly slice cucumber, onions, radishes, and eggs. Mix in large bowl. Add spaghetti to vegetables. Add the seasonings, then dressing and toss until well blended.
This can be made the day before. You may want to reserve a little bit of the dressing and add more before ready to serve. The spaghetti really soaks up dressing.

Mrs. Stanley Stoner (Bobbie)

SPINACH GELATIN

Serves: 8-10

1 3-oz. pkg. lemon Jello
1 cup hot water
1/2 cup cold water
1-1/2 tsp. vinegar
Salt and pepper
1 tsp. minced onion
1/2 cup mayonnaise
1 cup spinach, cut fine
1/2 cup cottage cheese
1/2 cup celery, chopped fine

Dissolve Jello in hot water, add cold water, vinegar, salt and pepper to taste, and onion. Chill until partially set then beat until real fluffy. Blend in mayonnaise and spinach. Add cottage cheese and celery. Refrigerate.

Hidy Eby

LAYERED SPINACH SALAD

Serves: 15

1 bunch spinach, chopped
1/2 head lettuce
2 bunches green onions,
    finely chopped
8 hard-boiled eggs, sliced
1/2 head cauliflower, finely
    chopped
1 lb. crisply fried bacon,
    drained and crumbled
1 pkg. frozen green peas,
    uncooked

Layer ingredients in large bowl as they are listed.

TOPPING:
1 cup sour cream
2 cups Hellmann's mayonnaise
1 to 2 cups Cheddar cheese,
    grated
Croutons

Mix sour cream with mayonnaise. Cover above ingredients. Top with cheese. Refrigerate overnight. Toss gently before serving, adding croutons.
Will serve 30 if lettuce & cauliflower are doubled. Use very large bowl for mixing.
Mrs. Jim Henderson (Bonnie)

SERENDIPITY SALAD

1 small package lime Jello
1 small package lemon Jello
2 cups hot water
1 cup mayonnaise
2 cups cottage cheese
1 cup sour cream (optional)
2 Tbsp. onion, finely chopped
4 Tbsp. green pepper,
    finely chopped
6 Tbsp. carrots, grated

Dissolve Jello in hot water. Add mayonnaise, cottage cheese, sour cream, onion, green pepper and carrots. Stir briskly and refrigerate until set.

Mrs. Fred Blythe (Sharon)

MARINATED VEGETABLE SALAD

Serves: 8-10

3/4 cup vinegar or red
wine vinegar
1/2 cup vegetable oil
1 tsp. salt
1 cup sugar
1 Tbsp. water
1 can French-style green beans,
drained
1 can English peas, drained
1 can shoe peg corn, drained
1 jar chopped pimientos,
drained
1 cup celery, chopped
1 green pepper, chopped
1 small onion, chopped
1 cup purple onion, chopped

Combine the first five ingredients in a saucepan and bring to a boil to dissolve the sugar. Cool. Combine vegetables and stir in the vinegar mixture. Cover and place in the refrigerator over night.

Linda Dunlap
Linda Lovell

24 HOUR LAYERED SALAD

Serves: 6

1 head lettuce, medium
1 cup onion, thinly sliced
1 cup celery, sliced
1 can (6 oz.) water chestnuts,
drained
1 10-oz. pkg. frozen peas
2 cups mayonnaise
1 tsp. sugar
1/2 tsp. salt
1/4 tsp. pepper
1 cup mozzarella cheese, grated
Parmesan cheese to taste
Bacon Bits & chopped parsley

Shred lettuce and place it in bottom of 9" x 13" glass dish. Top with layers of onion, celery, and sliced water chestnuts. Sprinkle with layers of frozen peas, spread with layer of mayonnaise. Sprinkle with mixture of sugar, salt & pepper. Top with mozzarella cheese and Parmesan cheese. Do not toss. Cover tightly with foil or plastic wrap and refrigerate 24 hours or 48 hours, if desired. When ready to serve, garnish with bacon bits and parsley. Refrigerate leftover. Covered, will stay fresh 3-4 days.

Mrs. Gary Hansen (Patti)
Variation: For a touch of Italian, the Cookbook Committee recommends omitting the water chestnuts and adding 1 cup freshly sliced mushrooms and black olives to taste.

MAIN DISH SALADS

CHICKEN SALAD

Serves: 8

8 chicken breasts (3 lbs. 12 oz.)
3 peppercorns
1/2 medium onion, chopped
1 small bay leaf
1 medium stalk celery including
    leaves, finely chopped
1 cup frozen peas, cooked as
    directed

DRESSING:
1 cup mayonnaise
1/2 tsp. salt
1-1/2 Tbsp. pimiento, chopped
1/3 cup green onions, chopped
1/2 cup sour cream
1/4 tsp. pepper
1/4 tsp. curry powder
1-1/2 Tbsp. lemon juice

Add bay leaf, peppercorns, celery, onion and enough water to cover chicken. Add 1 tsp. salt per quart of water. Bring to a boil. Add chicken. Return to a boil, then reduce to simmer for 30 minutes. Remove from heat and let chicken stand in the broth until lukewarm. Drain chicken and remove skin. Bone and cube the meat. (Should have 1-1/2 to 1-3/4 lb.) Mix dressing ingredients and combine with chicken. Refrigerate overnight. Store peas in a separate container. Before serving, gently add peas and 1-1/2 cup celery, finely chopped. Serve in individual dishes lined with butter lettuce. Garnish with two thin avocado slices.

Mrs. Everett Crews (Helen)

CHICKEN SALAD MOLD

Serves: 8

3 cups chicken, cooked
    and cubed
2 hard boiled eggs, chopped
1/2 cup stuffed olives, chopped
2 Tbsp. capers
1 Tbsp. onion or chives, minced
1/2 cup celery, chopped
1 envelope plain gelatin
1/4 cup cold water
2 cups Kraft mayonnaise

Combine first six ingredients. Soak gelatin in cold water and then dissolve over hot water. Add gelatin to mayonnaise, stirring well. Fold mayonnaise mixture into first mixture. Pour into molds and chill. Garnish with tomato, avocado, cucumber, etc.

Mrs. Joe Champlin (Jane)

CRAB LOUIE

Serves: 6

1 head lettuce
3 lbs. fresh crab meat (frozen
    can be used)

DRESSING:
2 cups mayonnaise
1/2 cup cocktail sauce
2 Tbsp. Worcestershire sauce
1/2 cup milk
2 Tbsp. vinegar
1 cup sweet pickle relish
2 chopped hard-boiled eggs
1 thick slice onion, grated

Before serving, place crisp, whole lettuce leaves to form cups in chilled bowls. Shred lettuce to form beds of salad and place on top of leaves. Combine dressing ingredients and mix thoroughly. Add enough dressing to crab to moisten and place on top of lettuce. Spoon dressing over salads and garnish. Serve with garlic bread.
Optional garnishes: crab legs, tomato wedges, olives, carrot curls, green pepper rings, lemon wedges or parsley.

Mrs. Jim Riley (Robin)

CRABACADO

Serves: 8

1 cup Hellmann's mayonnaise
    (more may be used if
    desired)
4 tsp. horseradish
    (more to taste)
3 tsp. lemon juice
1 tsp. Worcestershire sauce
2 Tbsp. onion, minced
1/2 tsp. garlic, minced
1/2 tsp. Cayenne
1 Tbsp. dill pickle relish
3 large boiled eggs, chopped
8 oz. snow crab meat
4 avocado halves, peeled
1 can Roland white asparagus
    spears
Tomato wedges

Combine all ingredients except avocados, asparagus and tomato wedges. Chill mixture and fill avocado shells. Garnish with white asparagus and tomato wedges.

Mrs. Wally Hite (Karol)

CRÊPE TWISTS

Serves 12

1-1/4 cup flour
Pinch of salt
3 eggs beaten
1-1/2 cups milk
2 Tbsp. butter, melted

Place all ingredients in blender or mixer and beat well. Let batter stand one hour for more perfect crêpes. Note: If pan is either too hot or too cold, the crepe will not adhere. If crêpes are too thin or have a lacy appearance, add more flour to the batter. After crêpes are cooked, cut in one to 1/2 inch strips about three inches long. Place about 10 or so in hot oil. Stir so they will twist. Deep fat fry about one minute. Place on paper towels to dry. Sprinkle Parmesan cheese and salt over them. Serve warm, soon after frying.

Jane Ford

HAM 'N POTATO SALAD

Serves: 8-10

1 Tbsp. or 1 envelope
    unflavored gelatin
1/2 cup water
1-1/2 cups cooked ham, diced
1/4 cup chili sauce
1 Tbsp. onion, finely chopped
2 tsp. prepared mustard
1 tsp. horseradish
1 cup mayonnaise or salad
    dressing
2 cups diced potatoes (about
    4 or 5, boiled)
1/2 cup celery, diced
2 Tbsp. green pepper, finely
    chopped
1 Tbsp. onion, finely chopped
2 Tbsp. vinegar
1 tsp. salt
1/2 tsp. pepper

Stir gelatin in water until dissolved. First layer—combine ham, chili sauce, chopped onion, mustard, horseradish and mixture of 1/4 cup gelatin and 1/2 cup mayonnaise. Leave remaining 1/4 cup gelatin at room temperature. Mix ingredients and place in 10"x 6"x 1" baking dish and chill until almost set. Second layer—combine potatoes, celery, green pepper, onion, vinegar, salt and pepper and mixture of 1/4 cup gelatin and 1/2 cup mayonnaise. Spread over first layer. Refrigerate and let set. Cut into squares. Garnish with parsley.

Mrs. Harold Henson (Marietta)

HAM SALAD MOLD

Serves: 8

1 Tbsp. unflavored gelatin
1/2 cup cold water
2 Tbsp. lemon juice
2 Tbsp. horseradish
2 tsp. mustard (prepared)
1 cup mayonnaise
1 cup diced celery
1 Tbsp. chopped chives
2 Tbsp. minced onion
2 cups diced ham (tuna, chicken
    or corned beef is good)

Soften the gelatin in cold water. Dissolve over hot water. Add next 4 ingredients to gelatin. Stir well. Add remaining ingredients. Pour into oiled mold (8 inch) and chill until firm. Unmold on lettuce and garnish if serving on buffet.

Tina Swanson

PARADISE CHICKEN SALAD

Serves: 8+

2-1/2 cups cooked chicken,
    cubed
3/4 cup celery, diced
3/4 cup Hellmann's Mayonnaise
2 Tbsp. chutney, chopped
    (Col. Gray's)
1 tsp. curry powder
1 medium banana, sliced
1/3 cup salted peanuts
1 can pineapple tidbits
    (not chunks)
1/2 cup flaked coconut
1 11-oz. can mandarin oranges
    (chilled & drained)

Combine chicken, celery, and pineapple. In separate bowl, mix mayonnaise, chutney and curry. Cover each bowl and refrigerate.
Day of party—Drain chicken mixture; add bananas and peanuts. Toss with mayonnaise mixture and oranges and sprinkle with coconut.

Mrs. Don Gooch (Corinne)

MACARONI-SALMON SALAD

Serves: 6-8

3 cups macaroni, chilled,
    cooked (1-1/2 cups
    uncooked)
8 oz. can red salmon
1 cup cucumber, seeds
    removed and diced
1 10-oz. box frozen peas,
    steamed and chilled
1/2 lb. cheddar cheese, cubed
1 cup celery, chopped
2 Tbsp. onions, minced
2 Tbsp. parsley, chopped
1/4 cup green pepper, minced
Salt and pepper to taste
1/2 to 3/4 cup Miracle Whip

Toss all ingredients together with salad dressing. Serve chilled on crisp lettuce leaf. You may want to garnish with chopped hard cooked eggs.

Colleen Harris

SHRIMP POTATO SALAD

Serves: 8-10

4 cups boiled potatoes, cubed
1/4 cup stuffed olives, sliced
3 hard-cooked eggs, chopped
1 cup celery, chopped
1/4 cup onion, chopped
1/2 cup green pepper, chopped
1/2 lb. boiled shrimp, peeled
    deveined & halved
1/2 cup mayonnaise
1/2 tsp. salt

Combine all ingredients, mixing well. Chill thoroughly before serving.

Mrs. Ray Downs (Linda)

 For easy peeling of hard boiled eggs, add a few drops of oil to some water. Crack the eggs and let stand in oil and water solution for a few minutes.

SHERREL'S FAVORITE TUNA SALAD

Serves: 6

2 pkgs. cream cheese (3 oz.)
1 envelope gelatin
1/4 cup cold water
3/4 cup boiling water
1/2 cup mayonnaise
1 tsp. grated onion
5 large stuffed olives, chopped
1/2 cup celery, chopped
Salt and white pepper
Pinch of Lawry's seasoned salt
1 can (7 oz.) white albacore tuna,
    drained

Let cream cheese soften at room temperature. Mix gelatin with cold water then hot water until thoroughly dissolved. Combine with softened cream cheese. (You may want to use mixer to get a smooth texture.) When mixture is smooth add mayonnaise and beat until mixture is well blended. Stir in remaining ingredients and pour into loaf pan or ring mold. Six individual salad molds could be used. Serve loaf slices or individual molds on lettuce leaves. Garnish with parsley and an olive or a thin slice of cucumber with a sliver of pimento on top.

Mrs. L. W. Jones (Gladys)

SHRIMP WITH AVOCADOS

Serves: 8

2 lbs. shrimp, shelled and
    deveined (cooked)
1 cup salad oil
1 cup thinly sliced onion
3/4 cup white wine vinegar
1/2 cup minced celery
1/4 cup undrained capers
7 bay leaves
1 tsp. salt
1 tsp. celery seed
1 tsp. pepper
Few drops of tabasco
Lettuce leaves
2 avocados

In large bowl toss shrimp, oil, onion, vinegar, celery, capers, bay leaves, salt, celery seed, pepper and tabasco. Chill for 24 hours. Just before serving, arrange lettuce leaves on plates, add peeled and diced avocados to shrimp mixture. Toss lightly, then spoon on plates.

Carole Smith

SHRIMP REMOULADE (New Orleans Style)

Serves: 8

1/2 cup Tarragon vinegar
4 Tbsp. horseradish mustard
1/2 tsp. Cayenne pepper
1 Tbsp. paprika
2 Tbsp. tomato ketchup
1 tsp. salt
1 whole clove garlic, pressed
1 cup salad oil
1/2 cup green onions with tops,
    finely minced
1/2 cup celery finely minced
Shrimp, cooked, deveined,
    peeled and chilled
    (allow 5 or 6 per person,
    depending on size
    of shrimp)

Mix vinegar, mustard, pepper, paprika, tomato ketchup, salt and garlic. Add oil, beat thoroughly and add green onion and celery. Pour over cooked shrimp. To really be delicious, the shrimp should marinate for at least 4 or 5 hours. Serve cold on lettuce.

Mrs. Tim Ferguson (Norma)

SHRIMP MOUSSE

Serves: 12

1 can (10-3/4 oz.) tomato soup
1 envelope Knox gelatin
1/2 cup cold water
4 oz. cream cheese, softened
1/2 small bottle green olives,
    chopped
1 Tbsp. green onion, minced
1/2 cup mayonnaise
1 green pepper, chopped
1 rounded cup whole, small,
    boiled shrimp

Bring tomato soup to a boil. Dissolve gelatin in cold water and add to soup. Dissolve cream cheese in soup while hot. Cool. Add other ingredients, except shrimp. Place paper muffin cups into 12 muffin tins. Put 1 small shrimp in bottom of paper liner and cover with cooled mixture. Refrigerate to congeal. Remove from cups, place bottom side up on lettuce leaves.
Note: You may wish to add an additional 1/2 to 1 cup minced shrimp to gelatin mixture.

Mrs. Dennis Iselin (Mary Helen)

LINDA WILSON'S BANANA DRESSING

2 ripe bananas
2 Tbsp. lemon juice
1/4 cup brown sugar
1/4 cup honey
1 cup cream, whipped

Combine first four ingredients in blender and blend until smooth. Fold in whipped cream. Great over fruit.

Mrs. John Wynne (Gail)

THE CURRY CONNECTION

Makes: 1 cup

1 Tbsp. Curry powder
   (or more to taste)
1 cup mayonnaise
(If you feel guilty that this is so
easy, add a squirt of lemon juice.)

Mix together. Good sauce for vegetables. Makes fancy sandwiches (over sliced roast beef or turkey on French bread). Great as a vegetable dip. Chop up hard boiled eggs in it and put on toast for brunch.

Sharon Iorio

POPPY SEED DRESSING

Serves: 3-1/2 cups

1-1/2 cups sugar
2 tsp. dry mustard
2 tsp. salt
2/3 cup vinegar
3 Tbsp. onion juice
   (1 large onion)
2 cups salad oil
3 Tbsp. poppy seeds

Mix together sugar, mustard, salt and vinegar. Add onion juice and mix well. Slowly add oil, beating constantly. Beat until thick, then beat five minutes longer. Add poppy seeds and beat again. Store in cool place.

Pat Hackett
Donna Neal Messall

MARTY'S SPECIAL DRESSING

1-3/4 cup white sugar
1/2 cup salad oil
3/4 tsp. salt
1-1/4 cup vinegar
3/4 cup water
1/2 tsp. celery seed

Mix all ingredients in a shaker, mixing bowl or blender. Serve on coleslaw or lettuce type salads or even vegetable or bean type salads.

Mrs. Larry Keeler (Sally)

KITTY'S MAYONNAISE

Makes: 2 cups

2 egg yolks
1 tsp. salt
1/2 tsp. sugar
1/4 tsp. paprika
1/2 tsp. dry mustard
2 Tbsp. vinegar
2 cups corn oil
2 Tbsp. lemon juice
1 Tbsp. hot water

Mix dry ingredients. Put egg yolks (room temperature), vinegar and lemon juice in blender or mixing bowl. Mix well on medium speed. Add dry ingredients with blender or mixer running. Blend for 1 to 2 minutes. Add salad oil, 1/2 cup at a time, with blender running. High speed will be required as more oil is added. Add hot water last—this helps take away the oily taste. Store covered in refrigerator.

Note: The more whipping, the fluffier the mayonnaise.

Mrs. Robert Jantzen (Colleen)

HOT BACON DRESSING

8 slices bacon
1-1/2 cups sugar
3 tsp. cornstarch
1/2 tsp. salt
1/4 cup water
1/2 cup vinegar

Fry bacon until crisp, crumble and set aside. Mix dry ingredients, adding vinegar and water gradually; pour mixture over bacon and cook, stirring constantly until mixture thickens. Serve on endive, iceberg lettuce, dandelion greens, cucumbers, or on cabbage for hot slaw.

Mrs. Stephen Jones (Sherrel)

ROYAL FRENCH DRESSING

Serves: 8

1/2 cup sugar
1/4 cup vinegar
1 Tbsp. lemon juice
1 small onion
4 Tbsp. ketchup (1/4 cup)
1/2 cup oil
1 tsp. salt
1 tsp. paprika

Place all ingredients in blender and blend until desired consistency.

Mrs. Jon Ford (Jane)

My Favorite Salad

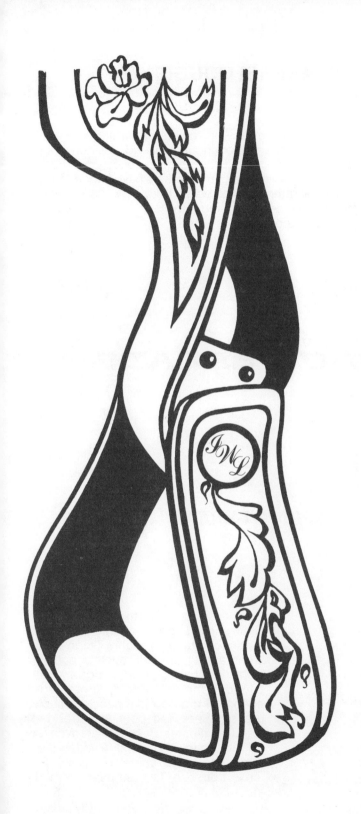

DOUGH-SI-DOUGH

BREADS

"DOUGH-SI DOUGH"

It is with pride that we live in the midst of golden grain and share the goodness of our harvest with others throughout the world. It is no wonder that this Heartland of America presents an outstanding collection of home-baked breads. Many of our mothers and grandmothers have handed these recipes and techniques down through the years. With pleasure we share these traditions and treasures—perhaps some of these recipes may become traditions in your household, too!

QUICK BREADS

APRICOT BREAD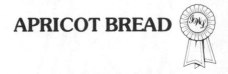

Yield: 1 loaf

1 cup dried apricots
1 cup sugar
2 Tbsp. butter, softened
1/4 cup water
1/2 cup orange juice
2 cups flour, sifted
2 tsp. baking powder
1/4 tsp. soda
1 tsp. salt
1/2 cup nuts, chopped

Soak apricots in warm water to cover. Drain and cut up apricots. Mix sugar and butter together thoroughly. Stir in water and orange juice. Sift together and stir in the flour, baking powder, soda and salt. Blend in the nuts and apricots. Line bottom of greased loaf pan with paper, grease paper, and pour in batter. Let stand 20 minutes. Bake in 350° oven for 55 to 60 minutes or until wooden pick thrust into center comes out clean. Remove from pan. Take off paper immediately. Let cool on rack.

Mrs. Earl Mitchell (Jean)

CZECH CARAWAY SEED LOAF

Yield: 1 loaf

3 Tbsp. caraway seeds
3/4 cup milk
1 cup margarine
1-1/2 cups powdered sugar
5 egg yolks
3 cups flour
2-1/2 tsp. baking powder
1/4 tsp. salt
1/2 tsp. mace
1/2 tsp. cinnamon
5 egg whites

Soak caraway seeds in milk for 30 minutes. Cream margarine, sugar, and egg yolks. Add flour, baking powder, salt, mace, cinnamon, seeds and milk. Beat egg whites until stiff and fold into cake batter. Bake in greased loaf pan for 1 hour at 350°.

Colleen Jantzen

KONA INN BANANA BREAD

Yield: 2 loaves

2 cups granulated sugar
1 cup softened butter
6 bananas, ripe and mashed
    (3 cups)
4 eggs, well-beaten
2-1/2 cups cake flour
2 tsp. baking soda
1 tsp. salt

With electric beater, cream together sugar and butter until light and fluffy. Add bananas and eggs, beating until well-mixed. Sift together dry ingredients three times. Blend with banana mixture but *do not* overmix. Pour into 2 lightly-greased loaf pans. Bake 45 minutes to one hour, at 350°, until firm in the centers and the edges begin to separate from pans. Cool on a rack for 10 minutes before removing from pan. These freeze beautifully.
Committee Variation: You may want to add slivered almonds or pecans to taste.

Mrs. Cecil Stuart (Helen)

 Over ripe bananas may be frozen and saved for use as needed.

MEXICALI CORN BREAD

Yield: 12-15 servings

1/2 large green pepper
1 large onion
2 (4-oz.) cans green chilies
chopped (about 1/4 cup)
1 cup grated cheese, Cheddar
3 eggs
1/2 cup vegetable oil
1/2 cup flour
1 cup cornmeal, yellow
1 tsp. salt
1/2 tsp. soda
3 tsp. baking powder
1 cup buttermilk
1/4 tsp. garlic powder
1 cup Mexican-style corn

Chop green pepper, onion, and hot peppers and set aside. Combine eggs and and oil. Add dry ingredients and buttermilk. Fold in garlic powder, canned corn (well drained), cheese and chopped onion mixture. Pour into well-greased 13" x 9" glass pan. Bake at 450° for 25-30 minutes.

Mrs. Elbert Wheeler (Meme)

POPOVERS

Serves: 6-8

2 eggs
1 cup milk
Pinch of salt
1 tsp. melted butter
1 cup flour

Beat eggs until light and foamy. Add milk, salt, and melted butter and beat together. Dump in flour and beat until light and bubbly—do not overbeat, should be somewhat lumpy. Pour into smoking hot greased muffin, custard or popover cups, filling 2/3 full. Bake in preheated 450° oven for 10 minutes. Turn down heat to 350° and bake for 20 minutes more.

Mrs. Joe Champlin (Jane)

LEMON NUT BREAD

Yield: 3 loaves

2 cups flour
1 lb. chopped nuts
1 lb. white raisins
1 lb. butter (not oleo)
2 cups sugar
6 eggs
2 oz. lemon extract

Combine flour with 1/2 cup nuts and 1/2 cup raisins. Set aside. Cream butter and sugar. Add eggs, flour mixture and remainder of nuts, raisins and extract. Bake in 3 greased loaf pans (8"x 3-1/2" x 2-3/4") at 250° for 2-1/2 hours. Place shallow pan of water underneath loaves in oven while cooking. Let cool in pans after baking.

Mrs. George Holmes (Jerri)
Mrs. Curtis Horral (Thelma)

PUMPKIN BREAD

Yield: 1 bundt pan plus 1 small loaf pan

3-1/3 cups all purpose flour
3 cups sugar
1-1/2 tsp. salt
2 tsp. soda
1 tsp. nutmeg
2 tsp. cinnamon
2 cups canned pumpkin
1 cup vegetable oil
4 eggs, beaten
2/3 cup water

Sift dry ingredients together. In another bowl mix pumpkin, water, oil, and eggs. Pour dry mixture into liquid mixture and mix well. Fill greased and floured bundt pan and 1 small loaf pan (greased and floured). Bake 350° for 1 hour-15 minutes. Remove the small loaf pan after approximately 45 minutes.

Cookbook Committee Suggestion: Small round loaves may be made by using well greased 10-oz. soup cans. To remove loaf, invert can, open bottom with can opener and push loaf out. Makes great little round tea sandwiches with cream cheese filling. Chilled loaves slice better for this purpose.

Lana Heath
Stillwell, Kansas

PUMPKIN DATE BREAD

Yield: 3 loaves

3-1/3 cups flour
3 cups sugar
1 tsp. salt
2 tsp. soda
1 tsp. nutmeg
2 cups pumpkin
1 cup cooking oil
4 eggs, beaten
2/3 cup water
1 cup nuts, chopped
1 cup dates, chopped

Mix the flour, sugar, salt, soda and nutmeg. Add the pumpkin, cooking oil, eggs and water. Mix until smooth and add nuts and dates. Bake at 350° for 1 hour in loaf pans. Makes 3 loaves.

Mrs. Eldred Harmon (Jeannine)

STRAWBERRY BREAD

Yield: 2 loaves

3 cups flour
1 tsp. soda
1 tsp. salt
3 tsp. cinnamon
2 cups sugar
2 (10-oz.) pkg. frozen
     strawberries
4 eggs
1-1/4 cups cooking oil
1-1/4 cups pecans, chopped

Mix dry ingredients together. Mix with an electric mixer, strawberries, eggs, oil and pecans. Add to dry ingredients and stir carefully. Pour into 2 greased loaf pans and bake 1 hour at 350° Cool in pans 10 minutes. To make 3 loaves, use smaller size loaf pans, and bake 40 minutes.

Mrs. Steve Harmon (Peggy)

 Always chill fruit breads for ease in slicing.

WHOLE WHEAT BREAD

Yield: 2 loaves

3 cups whole wheat flour
1 cup white flour
2 cups brown sugar
1 tsp. salt
4 tsp. baking powder
2 cups milk
1 egg, beaten
2 cups nuts, chopped

Mix dry ingredients in large mixing bowl. Add egg and milk. Mix well. Add chopped nuts. Pour into 2 well greased loaf pans. Bake 1 hour at 325°-350°. Turn out on rack to cool. Especially good sliced, buttered and warmed.

Mrs. John Day (Florelee)

ZUCCHINI BREAD

Yield: 2 loaves

3 eggs, beaten
1 cup vegetable oil
2 cups sugar
2 tsp. vanilla
3 cups flour
1 tsp. soda
3 tsp. cinnamon
1/4 tsp. salt
1/2 tsp. baking powder
1/2 cup nuts, chopped
3 cups zucchini, shredded

Combine first four ingredients and mix well. Add remaining ingredients and mix well. Pour into well greased and floured loaf pans. Bake at 325° for 1 hour.
Rosanne Dickinson Variation: Add 1/2 cup raisins.

Mrs. Bruce Harvey (Jana)

Softened creme cheese with crushed pineapple or pecans stirred in makes a nice filling for tea sandwiches with a favorite fruit bread. These sandwiches may be made ahead, and keep well in the refrigerator.

SOUR CREAM BISCUITS

Serves: 1 dozen biscuits

2 cups sifted flour
3 tsp. baking powder
1/2 tsp. soda
1 tsp. salt
1/2 cup shortening
1 cup sour cream

Sift dry ingredients together and cut in shortening. Gradually add sour cream. Mix lightly. Turn on lightly floured board and knead a few turns. Pat or roll about 1/2 or 3/4 inch thick. Cut with biscuit cutter. Place on ungreased baking sheet. Bake 450° 12-15 minutes.

Pat Diehl

GRANDMOTHER'S ANGEL BISCUITS

Yield: 5-6 dozen

1 pkg. dry yeast
5 Tbsp. warm water (115°-120°)
5 cups flour
5 tsp. baking powder
1/2 tsp. soda
1 tsp. salt
3 Tbsp. sugar
1 cup shortening
2 cups buttermilk

Sprinkle yeast over warm water. stir with fork to dissolve. Set aside. Sift dry ingredients together. cut in shortening with pastry blender or knives. Mix yeast and buttermilk together. Add to dry ingredients. Mix well. Pour on floured board, knead lightly, roll and cut with biscuit cutter. Bake on cookie sheets in 450° oven for 8-10 minutes or until lightly browned. Dough will keep in refrigerator and can be used as needed.

Jana Harvey

 Turn cinnamon rolls or biscuits into orange rolls with the addition of concentrated orange juice or sugar to make a paste to spread on dough. Make cinnamon roll style and top with melted butter, grated orange rind, and slivered almonds.

THE "BERRY-BEST" MUFFINS

Yield: 16-18 muffins

1 cup butter
2 cups sugar
4 eggs
2 tsp. vanilla
4 cups flour
1 cup milk
4 tsp. baking powder
1 tsp. salt
4-5-1/2 cups fresh or frozen
    blueberries, blackberries,
    raspberries or cranberries*
* If using frozen fruit, partially
thaw and combine with 1/4
cup flour. Fresh berries should
be rinsed, drained and well-
dusted with flour, before
folding into batter.

Cream butter and sugar in large mixing bowl. Add eggs (one at a time) and vanilla. Blend thoroughly. Combine flour, baking powder and salt. Alternately add flour mixture and milk to first mixture. (The batter will be very thick.) Blend well. Fold in berries. Grease muffin tins. (Because batter will need to expand over the rim, it is best to grease or oil muffin tin beyond rims of cups. You may use paper liners, but top of tin should still be oiled to allow for overage.) So that muffins will take on a mushroom shape, heap batter above rim of muffin tins. This will produce a beautiful shape. Sprinkle generously with sugar and bake in preheated 425° oven for 10 minutes. After 10 minutes of baking, turn oven temperature down to 375° and bake an additional 15 minutes until muffins are done in center and a rich golden brown on top.

Mrs. James Sears Bryant (Ann)

CHOCOLATE MUFFINS (Brownie Texture)

Yield: 12-18 muffins

4 squares semi-sweet chocolate
2 sticks margarine
1-1/2 cups chopped nuts
1 cup flour
1-1/2 cups sugar
4 eggs
1 tsp. vanilla

Melt chocolate and margarine, add nuts, set aside. Mix together flour, sugar and eggs. Add to chocolate mixture and add vanilla. Fill greased muffin tins 1/2 full. Bake 350° for 20-25 minutes. Paper muffin cups can be used.

Pamela Buller

CHOCOLATE CHIP ORANGE MUFFINS

Serves: 12 muffins

1-1/2 cups all purpose flour
1/2 cup white sugar
2 tsp. baking powder
1/2 tsp. salt
1 egg
1/2 cup milk
1/4 cup vegetable oil
3/4 cup Hershey's milk
    chocolate chips
2 tsp. grated orange peel

Sift flour, sugar, baking powder, and salt. Beat egg and add to the flour mixture. Add milk and vegetable oil—stir to moisten. Mix in the chips and the orange peel. Fill greased muffin tins about 2/3 full. Bake 400° for 20-25 minutes. Usually served on Thanksgiving or Christmas, but good anytime.

Mrs. Paul Baker (Nikki)

MUFFINS BY THE PAIL FULL

Serves: Approximately 4 dozen

4 cups All-Bran
2 cups 100% Bran
1 tsp. salt
2 cups boiling water
2-1/2 cups sugar
1 cup shortening
4 eggs
1 quart buttermilk
5 cups sifted flour
4-1/2 tsp. soda

Combine brans, salt, boiling water. Let mixture cool. Cream together sugar and shortening. Add eggs one at a time to sugar mixture. Add buttermilk to bran mixture. Combine bran and sugar/shortening mixtures. Add flour, soda. Bake at 375° for 20-25 minutes in greased muffin pans. Keep batter refrigerated. Will keep 4-6 weeks. This is an excellent after school snack.

Mrs. Franklin Forney (Judy)
Mrs. Howard Best

 Non-buttermilk drinkers can save buttermilk easily by freezing small measured quantities to be thawed as needed.

PURE BRAN MUFFINS

Yield: 10-12

*1 cup Pure Bran (Bran flakes
   from health store)*
3/4 cup flour
1/2 tsp. soda
1/4 cup brown sugar
1/4 cup oil
1 egg
3/4 cup buttermilk

Mix ingredients in order given. Bake in greased muffin tin at 375° for 15-20 minutes. May be served at breakfast or dinner. Easily frozen in aluminum and reheated when needed. Great way to get your fiber for the day!

Mrs. Mark Cromwell (Amy)

REFRIGERATOR GINGERBREAD MUFFINS

Yield: 6 dozen

1 cup shortening
1 cup sugar
1 cup dark molasses
4 eggs
2 tsp. soda
1 cup buttermilk
4 cups all purpose flour
2 tsp. ginger
1/2 tsp. cloves (ground)
1/2 tsp. allspice
1/2 tsp. cinnamon
1 cup chopped pecans
1 cup raisins (optional)

Combine shortening and sugar, creaming until light and fluffy. Stir in molasses; add eggs, one at a time, beating well after each addition. Dissolve the soda in the buttermilk. Combine flour and spices; add to creamed mixture alternately with buttermilk; beating well after each addition. Stir in pecans and raisins. Store in air tight container in refrigerator. When ready to bake, fill greased 1-1/2" muffin cups 2/3 full. Bake at 350° about 20 minutes or until muffins test done. Batter may be stored for several weeks in refrigerator. Do not stir.
Note: To bake without chilling batter, reduce baking time to 15 minutes.
Loretta Jantzen's Variation: Omit cloves and reduce allspice to 1/4 tsp. and increase cinnamon to 1 tsp.

Mrs. C. A. Howard

BANANA OATMEAL MUFFINS

Serves: 12 muffins

1 cup oatmeal
1/2 cup sour milk*
1 egg
1/2 cup brown sugar
1/2 cup mashed banana
    (about 1)
1 cup flour
1/2 tsp. soda
1 tsp. baking powder
1/2 tsp. salt
1/3 cup vegetable oil
1/2 cup pecans, chopped
* To make sour milk, add 1-2/3
tsp. vinegar to 1/2 cup lukewarm milk, stir well and set
aside for a few minutes.

Mix in the order given. Do not over mix. Fill greased muffin tins 2/3 full. Bake in 400° oven for 15-20 minutes. These freeze beautifully. Use muffin papers and when they are cool, put in a plastic bag to store in the freezer. To thaw quickly, can be placed in the microwave for a few seconds. These are great for breakfast.

Mrs. Terry Lewis (Barbara)

PANCAKES

GERMAN PANCAKES

Serves: 6-8

1 stick butter-melted
1 cup flour
1/2 tsp. salt
6 eggs
1 cup milk

Mix well and pour into pan. Bake at 450° for 20 minutes. Sprinkle with powdered sugar on top before serving.

Mrs. Jim Lovell (Linda)
Danette Tucker

BLINTZES

Serves: 8

Crepes: page 367

Prepare crepes:

FILLING:
2 lb. (1 carton) cream style
cottage cheese (drained)
2 eggs
1/3 cup sugar
1-1/2 tsp. vanilla
1/3 cup butter
1 can cherry pie filling
1 carton (16-oz.) sour cream

Mix cheese, eggs, sugar, vanilla, and butter together. Place 3 Tbsp. cheese filling in center of crêpe. Overlap 2 opposite sides over filling. Then fold up ends toward middle seam. Melt butter. Brown crêpes seam side down, turning to brown on the other side. Keep warm until all are browned. Serve warm with topping. The topping is prettier if you just pour the cherries over them and dob a spoon of sour cream on top.
Note: The trick in turning the crêpes to brown on the opposite side is SPEED (no one will know if you don't turn them). If serving 12, then double the recipe and put two crêpes on each plate.

Jane Ford

FILL   FOLD   TUCK

JANIE'S BUTTERMILK PANCAKES

Number of cakes	20	15	10	5
Eggs	4	3	2	1
Buttermilk	1-1/2 cups	1-1/8	3/4	3/8
Flour	1 cup	3/4	1/2	1/4
Salt	1/2 tsp.	3/8	1/4	1/8
Soda	3/4 tsp.	1/2	1/3	1/4
Melted bacon grease	4 Tbsp.	3	2	1

In bowl, beat eggs, add buttermilk. Mix together dry ingredients, add to liquid. Add bacon grease. Mix together well. Cook on hot griddle.

Mrs. Bill Word (Janie)

DUTCH BABY

Serves: 6

1/2 cup sifted flour
1/2 tsp. salt
1/2 cup milk
2 eggs (or 3 for an
    "eggy" pancake)
2 Tbsp. melted butter
1 Tbsp. lemon juice
1-1/2 pint strawberries
1 pkg. sliced peaches, drained
Powdered sugar
Dairy sour cream or whipped
    cream (may add brown
    sugar and cinnamon)

Heat oven to 450°. Put a little butter in a 9 inch skillet with a heat proof handle and place in the oven to heat while mixing the batter. Sift flour and salt together. Add with the milk to the beaten eggs; beat until smooth. Stir in 2 Tbsp. melted butter. Pour into pan. Bake on bottom shelf 20 minutes. Reduce heat to 350°. Prick shell; bake 10 more minutes. At the table have ready the plates of fruit, lemon wedges, sugar and cream. Other fruits can be substituted according to the season or to the tastes of the cook. Drizzle the shell with lemon juice; sprinkle with sugar. Fill with fruit. Cut in wedges and top with cream. Serve at once.

Mrs. Stuart Meulpolder (Barbara)

BEST IN THE WEST WAFFLES OR PANCAKES

(Truly easy—your family will want these every morning.)
The batter is ready before the griddle is hot!

6 Tbsp. oil
1 large egg
1-1/4 cups milk
1-1/4 cups flour
2 Tbsp. wheat germ
2 tsp. baking powder
1/4 tsp. salt
3 Tbsp. sugar

Place liquid ingredients in blender and blend well. Stir dry ingredients together and slowly add to liquid mixture. Blend for about 30 seconds after stopping blender a few times to scrape down sides. Pour on griddle, turn and serve.
Variations: *You may use 1/4 cup honey in place of the sugar and add one additional Tbsp. oil.
*You may choose to omit wheat germ and use 2 Tbsp. grated orange rind and 1/3 cup chopped pecans. Use finely chopped for waffles.
Serving Suggestions: Use orange honey butter—so good you may not want syrup. We like to simply fold pancake in half and eat with the orange honey butter in between.

Mrs. Stephen Jones (Sherrel)

FRENCH ORANGE SAUCE

1 small can frozen orange juice
1 small can Milnot
1-1/2 cups sugar
1/2 stick butter

Warm all ingredients slowly over low flame. Delicious over pancakes, waffles, French toast or pound cake.

Carolyn Wells

GRANDMOTHER'S BROWN SUGAR SYRUP

1 cup brown sugar
1 cup white sugar
1 cup hot water
1 tsp. maple flavoring

Mix together first three ingredients and boil 4 minutes. Add 2 Tbsp. cold water immediately, then add maple flavoring. This is wonderful served warm. The aroma makes breakfast a special memory and treat as well.

Colleen Harris

ORANGE HONEY BUTTER

1/2 cup honey
1/2 cup butter
2-4 Tbsp. finely grated
    orange rind

Combine all ingredients and whip until light and fluffy. Keeps well in refrigerator. Serve with "Best in the West Waffles."

Sherrel Jones

PECAN BUTTER

1/2 cup honey
1/2 cup butter
1/4 cup pecans, finely chopped

Mix ingredients, add pecans. Cream until light and fluffy. This makes an excellent topping for toast, pancakes or gingerbread.

Linda Downs

YEAST BREADS

ANGEL WINGS

Yield: 4-5 dozen

1 pkg. dry yeast
4 Tbsp. warm water
5 cups flour
1/2 cup sugar
1 Tbsp. baking powder
1 tsp. soda
1 tsp. salt
1 cup shortening
2 cups buttermilk
1/2 cup butter

Dissolve yeast in warm water. Set aside. Combine dry ingredients. Cut in shortening. Add yeast to buttermilk. Stir liquids into dry ingredients. Roll onto floured surface about 1/2" thick. Cut with a roll cutter of 2-1/2" circle. Dip one side into melted butter and fold over with buttered side in. Place in baking pan, bake at 425° for 15 minutes. Angel Biscuits may be prepared and frozen. Freeze on cookie sheets. When frozen, place in plastic sheets for easy storage. It is not necessary to thaw before baking.

Mrs. Bob Wooldridge (Martha)

BLUE RIBBON BREAD

Yield: 4 loaves

3 cups milk, scalded and
    cooled until lukewarm
1/2 cup honey
2 pkgs. dry yeast
7-1/2 cups sifted flour
3 egg yolks, slightly beaten
6 Tbsp. melted butter
1/2 cup sour cream
1 Tbsp. salt

In large bowl, mix 2 cups lukewarm milk, honey and yeast and let stand 15 minutes. Add 3 cups flour and beat until smooth. Add egg yolks and beat 1 minute. Mix 6 Tbsp. melted butter with sour cream. Add this to the mixture and again beat 1 minute. Add 4-1/2 cups flour and 1 Tbsp. salt and mix with a wooden spoon. Add 1 cup milk to make a medium-soft dough. Beat with spoon until batter is smooth and shiny. Cover bowl and let rise in a warm place until doubled. Punch down and knead for 10 minutes. Shape into four loaves and place in greased 9" x 5" loaf pans. Let rise until doubled and bake 30 minutes at 350° Brush top of loaves with melted butter.

Janice Semrad

CREAM CHEESE SWEET ROLLS

Yield: 2-2-1/2 dozen

1 cup sour cream
1/2 cup sugar
1/2 cup melted butter
1 tsp. salt
2 pkgs. dry yeast
1/2 cup warm water
4 cups flour
2 eggs, beaten

FILLING:
1 (8-oz.) pkg. cream cheese
*   softened*
3/4 cup sugar
1 egg
2 tsp. vanilla
1/2 tsp. salt

GLAZE:
2 cups powdered sugar
1/4 cup milk
2 tsp. vanilla

Combine sour cream, butter, sugar and salt. Mix well. Dissolve yeast in warm water in large bowl. Stir in sour cream mixture, then eggs. Add flour, one cup at a time. Dough will be soft. Cover bowl and chill overnight. Divide dough into 2 equal portions. Turn each out on a lightly floured surface and knead 4-5 times. Roll each into a 10"x 16" rectangle and spread with half of the filling (1 cup per half). Roll up in jellyroll fashion and pinch ends to seal. Cut each roll in 1-1/2" slices and place 2" apart on greased baking sheets. Cover and let rise in a warm place 1-1/2 hours or till doubled in bulk. Bake at 375° for 12 minutes or till rolls are golden brown. Drizzle glaze over each.

Linda Dunlap

HOBO BREAD

Yield: 3 loaves

2 cups raisins
2 cups boiling water
4 tsp. soda

2 cups sugar
1/8 tsp. salt
4 cups flour
1/4 cup vegetable oil

Pour boiling water over raisins and let stand till cool. Add soda and stir well. Let stand overnight.

Stir sugar, salt, flour and vegetable oil until well mixed (will be thick). Add to raisin mixture. Bake in greased, floured 1 lb. coffee cans filled 1/2 full at 350° for 1 hour 15 minutes. Makes three loaves.
Mrs. Dean McCullough (Jean)

COUNTY FAIR EGG BREAD

Yield: 2 loaves

2 pkgs. active dry yeast
1/2 cup warm water
1/2 cup sugar
1/2 cup shortening
4 tsp. salt
2 cups milk, scalded (heated to
   steaming—not boiling)
1/2 cup cold water
4 eggs, beaten
9-10 cups all purpose flour

Soften yeast in warm water. In large mixing bowl combine scalded milk with salt shortening and sugar. Mix until shortening melts, then add cold water. Cool this mixture to lukewarm. Stir in yeast and beaten eggs. Gradually add flour to form a stiff dough. Knead on lightly floured board until smooth and satiny (about 5-7 minutes). Place in greased bowl, turning to grease all sides. Cover. Let rise in warm place 1-1/2 to 2 hours or until doubled. Punch down dough. Cover and let rise again 30 minutes. Divide dough into 6 portions and braid into two loaves. These will fit best at an angle on greased cookie sheets which have been lightly sprinkled with corn meal. Tuck ends of braids under and using fingers underneath, spread braids apart in center of loaves as they are placed on cookie sheets. This makes a nice oval appearance. Bake at 375° until golden. Brush with melted margarine.

Sherrel Jones

HONEYED WHOLE WHEAT BREAD

Yield: 2 loaves

2-1/2 cups warm water
   (100°-115°)
2 pkgs. yeast
2 cups unsifted whole
   wheat flour
4 cups sifted all purpose flour
1/4 cup honey or brown sugar
3 tsp. salt
1/2 cup shortening

Dissolve yeast in water and let stand a few minutes. Add whole wheat flour, shortening, and honey. Mix until smooth. Add salt and white flour slowly. Cover and let stand 30 minutes or until doubled in size. Punch down and work. Divide in half and put in 2 greased 9" x 5" x 3" loaf pans. Grease tops and let rise. Bake at 400° for 20-30 minutes.

Ann Frazee Riley

BRAN REFRIGERATOR ROLLS

Yield: 4 dozen

1 cup Crisco
3 tsp. salt
1/3 cup sugar
1 cup Nabisco 100% Bran
2 well beaten eggs
1 cup hot water
2 pkgs. dry yeast
1/2 cup warm water
(100-115°)
5-1/2 cups flour

Cream Crisco, salt, sugar, and bran. Add eggs and hot water. Dissolve yeast in warm water. Add 2 cups flour. Beat well. Add yeast mixture, mix well. Add remaining flour, 1 cup at a time, mixing well after each addition until dough is smooth. Put in greased bowl in refrigerator overnight (covered). Next day make into rolls and put into well buttered pans. Let rise 3-1/2 hours. You can freeze the rolls in the pans and take out about 4 hours before serving. Let rise about 4 hours. Bake 375° 15-20 minutes. Makes 48 rolls.

Mrs. Boyd Freeman, Jr. (Ruth)

CREOLE DOUGHNUTS

Serves: 40

3/4 cup milk
1/4 cup sugar
1/2 tsp. salt
2 Tbsp. butter
1 pkg. dry yeast
1/3 cup warm water
(105°-115°F)
1 egg
3-1/2 cups flour

Heat milk until bubbles form around edge of pan. Remove from heat. Add sugar, salt, and butter, Stir until butter melts. Cool. In large bowl, sprinkle yeast over warm water. Stir and add egg and milk mixture. Add 2 cups flour and mix with mixer until smooth. Add rest of flour and beat with spoon till smooth. Dough will be soft. Place in greased bowl and cover with waxed paper. Refrigerate 4 hours. Heat oil to 360°F for frying. Take half of dough out (leave rest cold) and roll out on lightly floured surface to a square about 9" x 9". Cut into 20 squares. Drop 4 at a time into hot oil. Fry till golden brown—about 3 minutes. Drain on paper towel and sprinkle with powdered sugar. Makes about 40.

Mrs. Bill Word (Janie)

GRANDMOTHER'S WHITE BREAD

(Makes wonderful toast)

Makes: 2 large or 3 small loaves

1 cup warm water
1 cup warm milk
1/2 cup melted butter
1 Tbsp. salt
1/4 cup sugar
1 egg
2 pkgs. dry yeast
1 cup warm water
7 to 7-1/2 cups flour, sifted

Mix 1 cup water, milk, butter, salt and sugar. Add 2 to 3 cups flour, beating well with mixer. Soften yeast in 1 cup warm water, then add along with egg, to flour mixture. Beat with mixer as long as possible, gradually adding flour. Knead in remaining flour, kneading approximately 10 minutes. Place in greased bowl, cover with plastic wrap, and let rise in warm place until doubled in size. Punch down. Place on floured board and divide into loaves. Grease tops, cover and again let rise until double. Bake at 350° for 35 to 40 minutes. (I turn my bread out into a mitted hand to see if the sides are brown, and I thump the sides or bottom to see if it is done.)

Mrs. Earl Mitchell (Jean)

MOTHER WILES' ROLLS

Makes: 3 dozen rolls

2/3 cup shortening
1/2 cup sugar
2 eggs
1 cup milk
1 cup water
1 cup cooked and very wetly
    mashed potato
2 pkgs. dry yeast
1/2 cup warm water
    (110°-115°)
7-8 cups flour
1 tsp. baking powder
1/2 tsp. soda
3 tsp. salt

Cream together shortening, sugar and eggs. Add milk, water and potato. Beat well. Dissolve yeast in warm water. Add to first mixture. Blend in and cover. Let rise for 1 hour. Sift 3 cups flour with baking powder, soda and salt. Add to yeast mixture. Add remaining flour, cup at a time, to make a sticky dough. Place in well-greased bowl, cover and let rise for about 40 minutes or until doubled. Make into rolls. Place in well-greased pans. Cover. Let rise until double. Bake at 400° for 15-20 minutes.

Mrs. Boyd Freeman, Jr. (Ruth)

PITA BREAD

1 pkg. dry or compressed yeast
1/4 cup warm water
1 Tbsp. sugar
2 cups warm water
1-3/4 tsp. salt
2 Tbsp. sugar
2 Tbsp. melted shortening or oil
2 cups cake flour
5-6 cups all purpose
    unbleached or Better for
    Bread flour

Dissolve yeast in warm water (110°-118°) with 1 Tbsp. sugar. Stir with fork. In large bowl, measure 2 cups warm water with salt, sugar, shortening and 2 cups all purpose flour. Beat with spatula until smooth. Add cake flour and sufficient amount of remaining flour until soft, workable dough. Turn onto floured surface or in mixer with dough hook and knead for 10 minutes. Place in warm, greased bowl, turning to coat the top. (Use butter to coat the bowl. Oil will be absorbed by the dough.) Cover loosely. Set aside to rise for 1-1/2-2 hours or until doubled. Punch down, knead lightly and allow to rest 10 minutes. (This is important in order to roll out your pita bread.) Cut portions of dough a little smaller than a tennis ball and round each ball and allow to rise for 45 minutes. Roll each ball in 1/4" thick circle. Spread these circles of dough in an area, cover and let rest 30 minutes. Preheat oven to 550° (500°, if your oven will not go to 550°). Place pizza stone, quarry tile or baking sheet in oven to preheat (stone or tiles are best). With spatula, slide Pita bread onto baking sheet. Bake 3-5 minutes. Watch for pita to puff up like a balloon and brown lightly. Do not bake too long or you will have a nice big cracker instead of a soft bread. They bake very fast and it is helpful if you have two ovens going. These breads puff in baking and then fall after taking out of the oven. Wrap each pita in foil as it comes out of the oven and they will fall beautifully. You are now ready to fill with your favorite sandwich stuffing or serve with butter and a hot bowl of soup. After the breads have cooled, they may be stacked in plastic bags and frozen.

Donita Mitchell

 When bread is baking, a small dish of water in the oven will help to keep the crust from getting hard.

NO-FAIL FRENCH BREAD

Serves: 2 loaves

1/2 cup warm water
2 pkgs. active dry yeast
2 cups hot water
3 Tbsp. sugar
1 Tbsp. salt
1/3 cup melted shortening
6 cups flour
1 egg white, beaten
Sesame seeds (optional)

Dissolve yeast in warm water. In large glass mixing bowl combine hot water, sugar, salt, shortening and allow to stand until lukewarm. Add dissolved yeast and 3 cups flour. Beat with wire whisk until smooth and well blended. Add remaining flour to make a soft dough that can still be mixed with a wooden spoon. Leave spoon in batter and allow dough to rest 10 minutes. Stir batter down, let rest 10 minutes again. Repeat this process of stirring dough followed by 10 minute rest until it has been done a total of 5 times. Turn dough out onto floured board and knead only enough to coat dough with flour so it can be handled. Divide dough in half. Roll each half into a rectangle 9"x 12". Roll up jellyroll style. Arrange each length-wise on greased cookie sheet, allowing room for both loaves. Brush tops with a beaten egg white, then sprinkle generously with sesame seeds. With a sharp knife, slash top diagonally about 3 times across each loaf and cover and let rise until double in bulk, about 30-60 minutes. Bake at 400° for 35 minutes or until done. This can be made with an electric mixer (heavy duty) following same directions.

Dana Chambers

CREATIVE BREAD BAKING IDEAS
Great little Stir-ins for added flavor and nutrition—
Stir in extra nutrition with the substitution of special flours such as whole wheat, barley, or rye to part of regular flour.

Add oatmeal, candied fruit, granola, cracked wheat, wheat germ, crushed shredded wheat cereal or even chopped green onion to a favorite bread roll to create unique flavors and your own personal touch. Begin with small amounts and increase to your taste.

NO-KNEAD OATMEAL BREAD

Yield: 2 loaves

1/2 cup warm water
2 pkgs. active dry yeast
1-1/2 cups boiling water
1 cup quick-cooking oats
1/2 cup light molasses
1/3 cup shortening
1 Tbsp. salt
6-1/4 cups sifted all purpose
    flour
2 slightly beaten eggs

Soften yeast in 1/2 cup warm water. In large bowl, combine the boiling water, the rolled oats, molasses, shortening and salt. Cool to lukewarm. Stir in 2 cups of the flour; add eggs; beat well; stir in softened yeast; beat well. Add remaining flour, 2 cups at a time, mixing well after each addition to make a moderately stiff dough. Beat vigorously till smooth about 10 minutes. Grease top lightly. Cover tightly. Place in refrigerator at least 2 hours or overnight. Turn out on well floured surface; shape in 2 loaves. Place in greased 8-1/2"x 4-1/2"x 2-1/2" loaf pans. Cover, let rise in warm place till double—about 2 hours. Bake at 375° about 40 minutes. If crust browns too quickly, cover with foil last half of baking. Makes 2 loaves.

Virginia Gregory

ENGLISH MUFFIN BREAD

Yield: 2 loaves

2 pkgs. dry yeast
6 cups flour (unsifted)
1 Tbsp. sugar
2 tsp. salt
1/4 tsp. baking soda
2 cups milk
1/2 cup water
Cornmeal

Combine 3 cups flour, yeast, sugar, salt and soda in processor. Heat liquids until very warm (120-130°). Add to dry mixture. Beat well. Stir in rest of flour to make a stiff batter. Spoon into 2 loaf pans that have been greased and sprinkled with cornmeal. Sprinkle with cornmeal. Cover, let rise 45 minutes in warm place. Bake at 400° for 25 minutes. Remove from pans immediately. Makes 2 loaves! (8-1/2"x 4-1/2"x 2-1/2")

Mrs. Mark Cromwell (Amy)

THE JUDGE'S FAVORITE COFFEE CAKE

Yield: 2 coffee cakes or
3 loaves or
2 dozen rolls or any combination of above

Basic Refrigerator Dough:
2 pkg. dry yeast
2-1/2 cups warm water
3/4 cup sugar
7-1/2-8 cups flour
3/4 cup oil
2 eggs
2-1/2 tsp. salt

In large mixing bowl add yeast to warm water. Let soften. Using electric mixer, blend in sugar, oil, eggs, salt and flour (4 cups only). Blend until smooth. Using dough hooks on mixer or large wooden spoon, add remaining flour (this is a soft dough). Using 1/2 tsp. oil, coat top with oil. Place in refrigerator to rise overnight or let rise at room temperature. After letting rise until double in bulk, shape. Let rise until double again. Bake. Dough can be used for the following:

THE COFFEE CAKE

One-half of recipe makes 1 bundt cake pan. Pinch off 1" balls. Drop into melted butter, then into cinnamon-sugar mixture (1 cup sugar—1 Tbsp. cinnamon). Place in bundt pan until you have 1 layer. Sprinkle with nuts. Add 2nd layer. Pour another 2 Tbsp. butter and extra sugar-cinnamon. Let rise overnight in refrigerator or until double. Just before baking pour the following mixture over coffee cake (1/2 cup heavy cream, whipped; 1/2 cup light brown sugar, 1 tsp. cinnamon). Bake 30-40 minutes at 350.° Do not preheat oven. Turn up-side down, drizzle with glaze.

HOT ROLLS

Shape, let rise, bake 20 minutes at 350.°

BREAD

Divide into thirds—shape, let rise, bake 20-30 minutes, depending on size of loaves, in oven that has been preheated to 400° Reduce heat to 375° during baking.

Lavonn Meier

 Here is a good mixture to keep in your refrigerator to grease and flour pans all in one step. Nancy Parker's Pan Preparation:
1 cup flour
2/3 cup shortening
1/4 cup oil
Mix well. This keeps indefinitely in your refrigerator.

HANNAH'S ROLLS

Yield: 3 dozen rolls

2 eggs
2 Tbsp. sugar
2 tsp. salt
2/3 cup shortening
1/4 cup water
1 cup water, cold
1 Tbsp. sugar
1/4 cup warm water
2 pkgs. dry yeast
4 cups flour

Put eggs in large bowl, mix slightly. In pan mix sugar, salt, shortening and 1/4 cup water, heat until shortening melts. Remove from heat. Add 1 cup cold water to cool mixture. Mix sugar, yeast and warm water (110°-115°) in small bowl. Combine shortening with eggs, add 2 cups flour and beat until smooth. Add yeast mixture. Blend together. Then add 2 more cups flour. Beat until smooth. Turn out on lightly floured board. Knead until smooth. Place dough in warm greased bowl. Cover. Allow to rise double in size, 1 to 1-1/2 hours. Shape into rolls. Put in buttered baking sheets. Cover. Let rise about 1 hour. Bake in preheated oven 375° 15-20 minutes.

Hannah Weber

MOTHER TEMPLEMAN'S BUTTER HORN ROLLS

Yield: 3 dozen

1 cake yeast
1 cup sweetmilk (lukewarm)
1/2 cup sugar
1/2 cup butter, melted
2 eggs, well beaten
1/2 tsp. salt
4-1/2 cups sifted flour

Crumble yeast with 1 Tbsp. sugar until it becomes liquid. Add milk, sugar, butter. Blend well with mixer. Add eggs, salt, and gradually add flour to make a soft dough, stiff enough to knead. Cover and place in refrigerator overnight. The next day, place dough on bread board, knead briefly, and cut into thirds. Work with 1/3 at a time. Roll out round, about 1/4" thick. Spread thinly with butter and cut into 12 pie shaped pieces. Roll toward small end and place in buttered pans. Set aside to rise about 3 hours. Repeat with remaining dough. Bake 15 minutes at 350°. If using dry yeast, dissolve in 1/4 cup warm water and 3/4 cup milk at 110° in place of 1 cup milk.

Jo Ann Nicholas

HERB PARMESAN BREAD

Serves: 1 large loaf

2 cups warm water
  (110°-115°)
2 pkgs. dry yeast
2 Tbsp. sugar
2 tsp. salt
2 Tbsp. soft margarine or butter
1/2 cup plus 1 Tbsp. grated
  Parmesan cheese
1-1/2 Tbsp. dried oregano
4 cups sifted all purpose flour

Sprinkle yeast over warm water in large bowl of electric mixer. Let stand for a few minutes. Stir to dissolve. Add sugar, salt, butter, 1/2 cup cheese, oregano and 3 cups flour. Beat at low speed until blended. At medium speed, beat until smooth —about 2 minutes. With a wooden spoon, gradually beat in remainder of flour, cover bowl, with wax paper and a towel. Let rise for about 45 minutes in a warm place. Stir down batter with wooden spoon. Beat vigorously 1/2 minute. Turn into lightly greased 1-1/2 or 2-qt. casserole. Sprinkle evenly with 1 Tbsp. cheese. Bake 45-50 minutes at 375° or until nicely browned. Turn out onto wire rack. Let cool or serve slightly warm, cut into wedges.

Mrs. Bruce Harvey (Jana)

BEER BREAD
A Quick and Easy Favorite

Yield: 1 loaf

3 cups self-rising flour
3 Tbsp. sugar
1 (12-oz.) can of beer
1/4 cup (1/2 stick) butter or
  margarine, melted

Additional butter or margarine
  for brushing on top

Mix first four ingredients. Pour into well greased 9" x 5" pan. Bake at 350° for 45 minutes. Pour additional butter over bread and bake for 15 more minutes to brown. Serve warm or cool. Makes great green onion sandwiches. Leftovers are good bread crumbs for topping casseroles and vegetables. Sue Taylor's Suggestion: A great way for a bachelor to have homemade bread.

Pat Howard Preble

RUTH'S RAISED CINNAMON ROLLS

Serves: 16 rolls

1 pkg. active dry yeast
1/4 cup water
1 cup milk, scalded
2 Tbsp. shortening
2 Tbsp. sugar
1 tsp. salt
1 egg, beaten
3-1/2 cups enriched flour

1/4 cup melted butter
1/4 cup brown sugar
1 tsp. cinnamon

1 cup brown sugar
2 Tbsp. white syrup
1 Tbsp. butter

Soften dry yeast in warm water. Combine milk, shortening, sugar, salt; cool to lukewarm. Add softened yeast and egg. Gradually stir in flour to form soft dough. Beat vigorously. Cover and let rise in warm place (82°F) till double in bulk. About 2 hours. Roll 1/2 of the dough at a time on a lightly-floured surface to a rectangular shape 1/4 inch thick. Brush on melted butter or margarine and sprinkle on 1/4 cup brown sugar and cinnamon. Roll up in long roll. Seal edges and cut into 1" slices. Combine 1 cup brown sugar, 2 Tbsp. white syrup, 1 Tbsp. butter. Heat slowly in greased shallow casserole pan. Place rolls over mixture. Cover. Let rise till double in bulk. Bake in moderate oven 375° for 25 minutes. Remove from pan to cool bottom side up.

Ruth Earl

EASY BUTTERSCOTCH PULL-APARTS

1 pkg. frozen hot rolls
(unraised dough)
1 cup brown sugar
1/4 cup granulated sugar
1 (3-5/8-oz.) pkg. regular
butterscotch pudding mix
1 tsp. cinnamon
1 stick margarine, melted

The night before baking, place individual rolls in well-greased tube or bundt pan. Mix sugars, pudding mix and cinnamon and sprinkle over rolls. Pour melted margarine over top of dry mixture. Leave on cabinet, uncovered, all night. The next morning, bake in 350° oven for 30 minutes. Remove from oven and let stand in pan for 5 minutes before inverting.

Mrs. Bruce Harvey (Jana)

MANNA BREAD

Serves: 16

2 pkgs. dry yeast
3-1/2 to 4 cups flour,
    sifted all-purpose
1/4 cup dry onion soup mix
8 slices bacon
1 (12-oz.) can beer
1/4 cup milk
,1 Tbsp. sugar
2 Tbsp. yellow cornmeal

Combine yeast, 1-1/4 cup flour and onion soup mix. Cook bacon till crisp, drain, reserving 2 Tbsp. drippings. Heat together beer, milk, sugar and reserved drippings just till warm (mixture will appear curdled). Add to dry ingredients in mixing bowl. Beat at low speed with electric mixer for 1/2 minute. Beat 3 minutes at high speed. Stir in crumbled bacon and enough of the remaining flour to make a moderately stiff dough. Knead until smooth. Place dough in greased bowl, turn to grease both surfaces. Cover, let rise until almost double, 40-45 minutes. Punch down. Shape into rolls. Place in two 9 x 1/2 inch round pans. Cover top of rolls with a little melted margarine and sprinkle with cornmeal. Let rise until almost double, about 25 minutes. Bake 375° for 25 minutes or until golden. Can be made in ring form and tear off your own piece. Will freeze and reheat.

Betty Behring

SIMPLE CINNAMON PECAN BREAD

2 cans biscuits, 10 in can
1/3 cup sugar
1-1/4 tsp. cinnamon
1 cup pecans, chopped
3/4 stick margarine
1/2 cup brown sugar

Cut biscuits into fourths and dust with 1/4 tsp. cinnamon and 1/3 cup sugar. Grease bundt pan and pour 1/2 cup nuts in bottom of pan. Distribute 1 can biscuits on bottom of pan. Sprinkle 1/2 cup pecans next. Add remaining biscuit pieces. Heat in saucepan margarine, 1 tsp. cinnamon and brown sugar. Pour over biscuits and nuts. Bake at 350° for 20 minutes. Pulls apart for easy eating.

Mrs. E. M. Wheeler (Meme)

RANDALL'S ROLL-UPS

(The committee specially requested this recipe from Beth)

Yield: 48

2 cups lukewarm water
1/2 cup sugar
1-1/2 tsp. salt
2 pkgs. dry yeast
1 egg
1/4 cup vegetable oil
6-1/2 cups + flour
Melted margarine

Mix water, sugar, salt and yeast together until dissolved. Add egg, and shortening. Mix in flour with spoon or dough hook on mixer. *Do not knead.* Let rise until double, 1 to 1-1/2 hours. Divide dough into 4 balls. Roll out in circle, brush with melted margarine, cut into 12 pie shaped pieces, roll up. Bake in 375° oven for approximately 12 minutes. The dough can be mixed and placed in refrigerator up to 4 days. You may also shape the dough and refrigerate. Take out for 2 hours and bake. The same dough can be used for sweet rolls.
Cookbook Committee Suggestion: Spread pie shape with orange marmalade, raspberry jam or cinnamon-sugar and butter mixture before rolling up crescent style. A super brunch attraction!

Beth Randall

"ANN'S AN ANGEL" ROLLS

(You can be an angel too with this quick, simple method of preparing home-made yeast rolls.)

Yield: 24

2 cups lukewarm water
1 pkg. yeast
3/4 stick oleo, melted (not hot)
1/4 cup sugar
1 egg, beaten
4 cups self-rising flour

Sprinkle yeast over 1/2 cup water and stir until dissolved. Add remaining water. Mix all ingredients together, adding the flour last. Fill greased muffin tins half full and bake at 375° for 15-20 minutes. (Dough may be stored in refrigerator.)

Ann Frazee Riley

 In the final addition of flour to dough, add only a small amount at a time, then mix well. It is better to have dough a little sticky as you can always knead in more flour.

WHOLE WHEAT EGG BREAD

Makes: 2 large or 3 small loaves

2 cups boiling water
1/2 cup powdered milk
1/2 cup butter
2 tsp. salt
1/2 cup honey
2 pkgs. dry yeast
2 eggs, beaten
4 cups whole wheat flour
4-1/2 cups white flour

Pour boiling water over dry milk, butter, salt and honey. Allow to cool. Add yeast and eggs. Add flour, 1 cup at a time, starting with whole wheat. Mix with electric mixer about 7 minutes at medium speed. Stir in additional flour until stiff enough to knead. Turn dough on floured board and knead until smooth and elastic. Place in greased bowl, cover and let rise until double, about 1-1/2 hours. Punch down and turn on lightly floured board. Shape into loaves and place in greased pans. Cover and let rise again to double. Bake 350° for 30-35 minutes.

Connie grinds her own whole wheat flour from wheat grown on her farm.

Note: Warm draft free area makes nice place for bread to rise.

Mrs. Loscoe Hunter (Connie)
Waukomis

CREATIVE BREAD CRUSTS
Brush tops of warm bread with milk or butter for a soft crust.

Egg white and water mix brushed on several times during baking makes a crisp flaky crust.
Sesame seeds or poppy seeds may be sprinkled on top of this.

Whole egg beaten with 2 Tbsp. water makes a golden glistening crust to a favorite bread.

Add 2 Tbsp. sugar to a sweet bread topper.

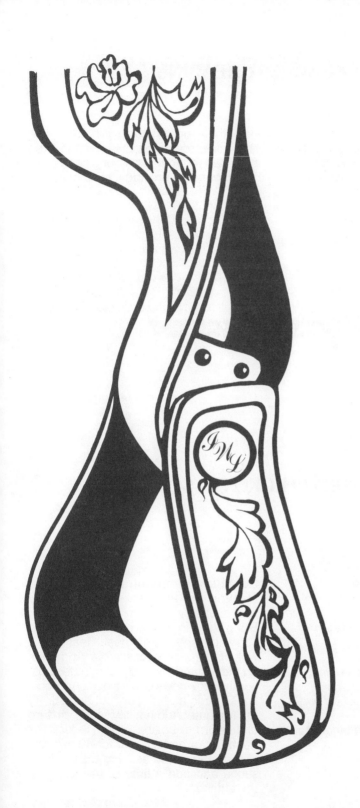

HARVEST HEAPIN'S

MAIN DISHES

"HARVEST HEAPINS' "

He-man delights, hearty, and heaped with flavor. You, too, will be delighted with these flavor-lickin' selections. These are crowd pleasers—tried and true. Whether you're looking for a new main dish for your family, or a company's-a-comin' treat, our main dishes are guaranteed to provide a heap of compliments to the cook.

CHICKEN

BRAISED CHICKEN IN SOY SAUCE

Serves: 6-8

1 3 to 4 lb. chicken
3/4 cup soy sauce
3 Tbsp. sherry
1-1/2 cup chicken broth
1/2 Tbsp. sugar
3 Tbsp. oil
3 whole scallions, cut in
    1 inch pieces
1 clove garlic, crushed and
    minced
2 thin slices fresh ginger root,
    minced

Cut chicken through the bone with a cleaver into 2" pieces. Combine soy sauce, sherry, chicken broth and sugar. Bring liquid to boiling point. Cover saucepan and remove from heat. Heat oil in a wok or flame-proof casserole. Add chicken pieces and stir fry for 3 minutes until lightly browned on all sides. Add scallions, garlic and ginger root and stir fry for 1 minute. Add hot soy sauce mixture and return to boiling point. Reduce the heat. Cover and simmer for 40 minutes. Place chicken in serving dish. Strain sauce and add a little of the sauce to the chicken.

Mrs. Brent Chapel (Jan)

126

CASHEW CHICKEN

Serves: 4

1 whole chicken breast,
    boned and cubed
1 Tbsp. cornstarch
1 Tbsp. soy sauce
1 Tbsp. sherry
1 clove garlic, minced
Salt
4 Tbsp. oil
1 slice of ginger root, minced
1/2 cup onion, chopped
1/2 cup celery, chopped
4 water chestnuts, sliced
1/4 lb. mushrooms, sliced
1/4 lb. sugar peas
1/2 cup cashew pieces, raw

GRAVY MIX:
1 Tbsp. cornstarch
1 Tbsp. soy sauce
1/2 cup chicken broth

Combine cornstarch, soy sauce, sherry, garlic, salt, 1 Tbsp. oil and ginger root. Marinate meat for 20 minutes. Sauté onions and celery with 2 Tbsp. oil over high heat for 1 to 2 minutes. Remove to platter. Sauté chicken in 1 Tbsp. oil over high heat until browned. Add mushrooms, sugar peas and cashew pieces. Mix well. Add vegetables and gravy mix till thick. Serve over rice.

Mrs. Paul Baker (Nikki)

CHICKEN ALBERGHETTI

Serves: 6

3 chicken breasts, boned,
    skinned and cut in half
Salt and pepper to taste
2 eggs, slightly beaten
3/4 cup dry bread crumbs
1/2 cup butter
8 oz. prepared Italian Cooking
    Sauce
1/2 cup light cream
6 slices Mozzarella cheese
6 slices Swiss cheese
Parmesan cheese, canned
Butter

Season chicken with salt and pepper. Dip in egg and roll in crumbs. Sauté in butter until browned. Dilute spaghetti sauce with light cream (reserve 2 Tbsp.). Pour sauce in bottom of covered casserole. Add chicken. Top each piece with 1 slice Swiss and Mozzarella cheese. Add reserved sauce. Sprinkle with butter and Parmesan. Cover and bake at 350° for 45-60 minutes.

Mrs. Ron Barnes (Jo)

CHICKEN BREASTS IN LEMON CREAM

Serves: 4-8

1 cup heavy cream
3 Tbsp. lemon juice
5 Tbsp. butter
1/2 lb. mushrooms, stemmed
    and sliced
8 halves of chicken breasts,
    skinned and boned
Small can Le Sueur peas, drained
Onion salt
Flour
1 Tbsp. vegetable oil
1 pkg. Lipton Cup-a-Soup broth
    or 1 chicken bouillon cube
    dissolved in 1/3 cup water

Mix cream and lemon juice; reserve. Heat 3 Tbsp. butter in large skillet (electric fry pan is excellent) over medium high heat. Sauté mushrooms in butter until nicely browned; remove with slotted spoon; reserve. Sprinkle chicken breasts with onion salt; dredge lightly with flour, shaking off excess. Add remaining 2 Tbsp. butter and the 1 Tbsp. oil to skillet. Brown chicken in this mixture over medium heat about 5 minutes per side. Remove chicken from skillet. Add broth to skillet keeping heat at medium; add lemon cream mixture. Put chicken breasts in this mixture, add mushrooms and peas and simmer gently for about 20 minutes or until cream mixture is fairly thick.

Mrs. John Day (Florelee)

CHICKEN ELIZABETH

Chicken breasts, number
    desired
Ham slices, cut in strips
Swiss cheese slices, cut in
    strips
Corn flake crumbs
Oregano

Remove bones from chicken breast and salt and pepper to taste. In middle of breast lay strips of ham and strips of Swiss cheese. Roll breast together and tie with string. Roll in corn flake crumbs which have had a dash of oregano added to them. Put in flat baking pan and bake 45 minutes at 350°. Take out of oven, remove string, add sauce and bake 45 minutes more at same temperature.

SAUCE
2 Tbsp. oleo
2 Tbsp. flour
2 cups chicken broth
1/2 cup white wine
1/2 pint sour cream

Melt oleo, add flour and stir till bubbly. Add chicken broth and stir till the mixture is smooth. Then add white wine and sour cream.

Mrs. Gary Hansen (Patti)

CHICKEN CACCIATORE

Serves: 6

2-1/2 lbs. chicken breasts,
    boned
1/4 cup olive oil
2 medium onions, slightly
    chopped
2 cloves garlic minced
1 (16-oz.) can whole tomatoes
1 (15-oz.) can tomato herb
    sauce
1 tsp. salt
1 tsp. dried oregano or basil
    leaves, crushed
1/2 tsp. celery seed
1/4 tsp. pepper
1 to 2 bay leaves
1/4 cup Sauterne cooking wine
Hot cooked spaghetti
Grated Parmesan cheese

Brown chicken in olive oil in a large skillet. Remove chicken and set aside. Add onion and garlic to pan drippings. Sauté until tender. Combine next 7 ingredients, stirring well. Return chicken to skillet and add sauce. Cover and simmer 30 to 45 minutes. Stir in cooking wine. Cook, uncovered 15 to 20 minutes over very low heat until chicken is tender, turn chicken occasionally. Skim off excess fat. Serve chicken and sauce over spaghetti; sprinkle with Parmesan cheese.

Mrs. Larry Dobbs (Ruth)

CHINESE CHICKEN

1 chicken, cooked and boned
1 can cream of mushroom soup
1/2 cup milk
1 (16-oz.) can Chinese
    vegetables, drained
1 (16-oz.) can French green
    beans, drained
1 (14-oz.) can bean sprouts,
    drained
1 (8-oz.) can sliced water
    chestnuts, drained
1 (2.8-oz.) can French fried
    onion rings
1 cup cheddar cheese, grated
(More of any of the above
    vegetables may be added,
    if desired)

Mix all ingredients together, except onion rings and cheese. Bake at 325° for 45 minutes. Top with French fried onion rings and 1 cup grated cheese. Bake 15 minutes more.

Mrs. John Taylor (Sue)

CHICKEN PARMESAN

Serves: 6

3 whole chicken breasts, split,
    boned and skinned
2 eggs, slightly beaten
1 tsp. salt
1/8 tsp. pepper
3/4 cup fine bread crumbs
1/2 cup salad oil
1 (15-oz.) can tomato sauce
1/4 tsp. dried basil
1/8 tsp. garlic powder
1 Tbsp. butter
1/2 cup Parmesan cheese,
    grated
8 oz. thinly sliced Mozzarella
    cheese cut into triangles

Place chicken on wax paper and flatten to 1/4" thick, using meat mallet. Combine eggs, salt and pepper. Dip breasts into egg mixture, then roll each in bread crumbs. Brown in hot oil in a large skillet; drain on paper towels. Place chicken in lightly greased 13"x9"x2" pan. Drain oil from skillet. Combine tomato sauce, basil, garlic in skillet. Bring to a boil and simmer 10 minutes, or until thickened. Stir in butter. Pour mixture over chicken and sprinkle with Parmesan cheese. Cover and bake at 350° for 30 minutes. Uncover and arrange Mozzarella slices on top. Bake an additional 10 minutes.

Vivi Johnson

CHICKEN KAPAMA (Greek)

Serves: 6

1 chicken, cut into serving
    pieces
Salt and pepper to taste
1 dash cinnamon
6 Tbsp. butter
2 cups canned tomatoes
1 (6-oz.) can tomato paste
1 tsp. sugar
3/4 cup water
3 sticks cinnamon
3 onions, minced
3 cloves garlic, minced
1 lb. macaroni
1/2 cup cheddar cheese,
    grated

Sprinkle chicken with salt, pepper and cinnamon. In a heavy kettle melt 2 Tbsp. butter and brown chicken until golden on all sides. Combine tomatoes, tomato paste, sugar and water and pour sauce over chicken. Add cinnamon sticks. Sauté minced onion and garlic in another 2 Tbsp. butter and add to chicken. Bring the sauce to a boil, cover, and simmer until the chicken is tender.

Cook macaroni according to directions on the package. Drain and empty into serving dish. Brown remaining 2 Tbsp. of butter and pour over macaroni. Pour over sauce from chicken and sprinkle grated cheese on top. Serve chicken separately.

Mrs. Joe Farrant (Susie)

CHICKEN TETRAZZINI

Serves: 8

*3-4 cups cooked chicken
(best to use breasts, cut
in chunks)*
7 oz. broken spaghetti
1 green pepper, chopped
1 large can mushrooms, sliced
1 can water chestnuts, sliced

SAUCE
3 Tbsp. margarine
3 Tbsp. flour
2 cups milk
1 cup chicken broth
*1/2 lb. Old English cheese,
grated (or Sharp Cheese)*
*1/2 lb. American cheese,
grated (or Monterey
cheese)*

Bake chicken and debone. Cook spaghetti, drain. To make sauce, melt margarine, stir in flour, heat with milk to make a white sauce. Add chicken broth. When cool stir in grated cheese. Combine chicken, vegetables and spaghetti. Pour into greased 11-1/2" x 7-1/2" pyrex dish. You may wish to refrigerate 24 hours ahead. Bake at 350° for 40 minutes to 1 hour.

Linda Dunlap's variation: Add 1/2 cup chopped celery.

May be garnished with any of the following: black olive slices, pimiento slices, or paprika.

Committee Suggestion: This recipe can accommodate left-over turkey from Thanksgiving and be frozen ahead for the hectic days preceding Christmas.

Mrs. Don Diehl (Pat)

CURRIED CHICKEN WITH SAFFRON RICE

Serves: 6

1 pkg. (6-oz.) saffron rice
3 chicken breasts, halved
1-1/2 tsp. curry powder
1/4 tsp. ginger
1 Tbsp. instant minced onion
*1 can condensed cream of
chicken soup*
1 can (6-oz.) mushroom caps
3 Tbsp. parsley, chopped
1/2 cup sour cream

Cook rice as directed on package. Arrange chicken breasts in large shallow baking dish. Combine curry powder, ginger and instant minced onion. Stir in undiluted soup. Blend in mushrooms and their liquid. Pour over chicken. Place in preheated 375° oven and bake uncovered about 45 minutes, until chicken is tender. Place hot rice on warm serving platter. Arrange chicken breasts on rice. Sprinkle with chopped parsley. Stir sour cream into drippings left in pan. Pour into warm sauce boat and serve with chicken and rice.

Mrs. Richard Puerta (Judy)

CRANBERRY-STUFFED CORNISH HENS

Serves: 4

2/3 cups chopped fresh
   cranberries
2 Tbsp. sugar
1 tsp. finely shredded
   orange peel
1/8 tsp. ground cinnamon
3 cups toasted raisin bread
   cubes
2 Tbsp. butter, melted
4 tsp. orange juice
4 (1 to 1-1/2 lb.) Cornish
   game hens
Cooking oil
1/4 cup orange juice
2 Tbsp. butter, melted

In bowl, combine chopped cranberries, sugar, orange peel, cinnamon and 1/2 tsp. salt. Add raisin bread cubes; sprinkle with 2 Tbsp. melted butter and 4 tsp. orange juice. Toss lightly to mix. Season cavities of hens with salt. Lightly stuff birds with cranberry mixture. Pull neck skin to back of each bird and fasten securely with a small skewer. Tie legs to tail; twist wing tips under back. Place hens, breastsides up, on a rack in a shallow roasting pan. Brush with cooking oil; cover loosely with foil. Roast in 375° oven for 30 minutes. Combine 1/4 cup orange juice and 2 Tbsp. melted butter. Uncover birds; baste with orange juice-butter mixture. Roast, uncovered, about 1 hour longer or till done, basting once or twice with orange juice-butter mixture.

Mrs. Kirk Fry (Nancy)

KEELER'S FAVORITE BEER BATTER FOR FISH OR CHICKEN

1 (12-oz.) can of beer—room
   temperature
1 cup flour
Salt and pepper to taste

Fold flour into beer, salt and pepper to taste. Dip fish or chicken into batter and deep fry. This makes a crispy batter and tastes fantastic. It can be used on any food to be deep fried. Excellent on catfish.

Mrs. Larry Keeler (Sally)

 When pan frying or sautéing, always heat pan a little before adding the butter or oil. Not even eggs will stick.

"MISS BONNIE'S FRIED CHICKEN
with her original Chicken Fried Biscuits"

Mama has made these biscuits for years and for years I have tried to duplicate them — finally for this Cookbook she shared her secret...They are wonderful when accompanied with your favorite fried Chicken.

1 whole fryer, cut into pieces
Buttermilk
Flour
Salt
Pepper
Crisco Oil

Wash and dry chicken parts. Marinate in buttermilk 1 hour. Preheat oil in electric skillet, 375° while preparing chicken. (Tip — heat skillet slightly before pouring in oil). Put 2 cups flour into large brown bag. Place chicken parts which have been coated in buttermilk into bag and shake well. Place in heated oil and sprinkle with salt and pepper. Cover and cook 20 minutes per side. For crispy chicken do not cover. Larger pieces can finish cooking in a 325° oven. Cover with foil if you don't wish to have a crisp crust. Note: Removing skin from chicken does get rid of extra fatty layers and some extra calories as well. This buttermilk method allows for a good crisp crust. If you desire a few extra crunchies, add 1/4 cup grits or cracker crumbs to the flour. Salt and pepper the chicken as you begin frying. The salt will help the chicken to bleed and give up some of its own juices — thus making more flavorful biscuits as well as gravy.

BISCUITS
2 cups flour
1 Tbsp. baking powder
1 Tbsp. sugar
1/2 tsp. salt
1-1/4 cups milk

Remove chicken from frying pan (hold in oven to keep warm). Sift dry ingredients together. Stir in milk. Mixture will be gooey. Drop by teaspoonsful into 375° or 400° oil in skillet in which you have just prepared chicken. All the little crunchies will adhere to these biscuits. Turn once. Each side should be a golden brown. Make sure oil is correct temperature. These biscuits are light and crisp and they do not absorb oil. Drain on paper towels.

*This is a favorite summer meal with fresh corn on the cob and a good salad. With fresh strawberries and your favorite homemade ice cream — big city guests will be in for a fantastic country dinner!

Sherrel Jones

GOURMET CHICKEN IN MUSHROOMS

Serves: 4

1 frying chicken, cut in serving pieces (or 2-1/2 lbs. thighs or breasts)
1/2 cup milk
1/4 cup flour
Salt and pepper
1/2 cup butter
1/2 lb. fresh cleaned mushrooms, sliced
2 cups sour cream

Dip chicken pieces in milk and roll in flour seasoned with salt and pepper. Melt butter in heavy skillet. Brown chicken in hot butter, and remove to greased casserole. Sauté mushrooms in the hot butter and spoon over chicken. Cover the chicken and mushrooms with sour cream. Bake at 325° for 45 minutes or until chicken is tender. Can also be baked in a microwave oven on high for 20 minutes. Whole quail or dove breasts can also be used.

A.J.'s tip: Clean a large amount of mushrooms by spinning in water in a salad spinner. Change water, spin again. Do not let mushrooms stand in water. Drain well.

Mrs. John Day (Florelee)

IMPERIAL CHICKEN

Serves: 4

2 chicken breasts, boned and cut in half
1/2 cup fine dry bread crumbs (1 slice)
1/3 cup Parmesan cheese, grated
2 Tbsp. parsley, minced
1 tsp. salt
1/8 tsp. pepper
1 stick butter or margarine
1/4 tsp. dried minced garlic flakes
2 Tbsp. lemon juice

Blend bread crumbs, cheese, parsley, salt and pepper. Combine melted butter and garlic. Dip chicken into butter, then into crumb mixture, coating thoroughly. Roll each piece into firm roll, skewer with toothpick and arrange in glass baking dish. Drizzle lemon juice over chicken with any remaining butter. Sprinkle with paprika. Place in 350° preheated oven and bake 1 hour. Can be prepared ahead of time and baked later. Just as good heated the next day.

Mrs. Ruhal Wells (Carolyn)

PARISIAN CHICKEN DINNER

Serves: 4

1 fryer cut in pieces
1/3 cup flour
1 tsp. salt
1 tsp. paprika
Dash pepper
2 cups new potatoes with
    jackets sliced 1/2" thick
3/4 cup sliced whole green
    onions
2 chicken bouillon cubes
1 cup hot water
1 cup dairy sour cream
1 stick butter
Fresh parsley for garnish

Combine flour, salt, paprika and pepper in sack. Add chicken pieces a few at a time and shake to coat. In large skillet, brown chicken in butter. Push chicken pieces to center of pan to arrange sliced potatoes around chicken. Season potatoes with salt and pepper. Sprinkle sliced green onions over all. Dissolve bouillon cubes in the water, pour over chicken. Cover and simmer about 35 minutes or until chicken is tender. Remove chicken and potatoes to platter. Stir sour cream into pan drippings. Cook and stir until heated through. Electric skillet works best.

Mrs. Jerry McCune (Sharon)

CHICKEN DIVAN

Serves: 8

2 (10-oz.) pkg. broccoli
2 cups cooked chicken, sliced
2 cans cream of chicken soup
1 cup mayonnaise
1 tsp. lemon juice
1/2 tsp. curry powder
1/2 cup cheddar cheese,
    shredded
1/2 cup soft bread crumbs
1 Tbsp. butter

Cook broccoli, drain and place in greased shallow baking pan. Arrange chicken slices over broccoli. Combine soup, mayonnaise, lemon juice, and curry powder and pour over chicken and broccoli. Cover with cheese, then with bread crumbs. Bake at 350° for 25-30 minutes. Note: Can use Pepperidge Farm Herbed Stuffing Mix.

Delores McCoy

RANCH HOUSE "CHICKENCHILADA"

Serves: 6

1 can cream of chicken soup
1 can cream of mushroom soup
1 medium onion, grated
1/2 cup white wine
1 doz. soft corn tortillas,
    shredded
1 cup (7-oz.) jalapeño
    peppers, chopped
1 lb. Telenook sharp cheese or
    Colby sharp, grated
1 lb. Monterey Jack cheese,
    grated
6 whole chicken breasts,
    cooked, boned and
    chopped

Combine soups, onion and wine together. In an 11-1/2"x7-1/2" greased pyrex baking dish, layer the tortillas,cream mixture, peppers, cheese and chicken. Bake at 350° for 30 minutes.
Variation: In place of jalapeño peppers, a can of Ro-Tel sauce may be used. Sliced black olives or jalapeño peppers may be used as a garnish.

(For meeker tastes, substitute chopped green chilies for jalapeños.)

Mrs. Bill Word (Janie)

SWEET 'N SOUR BAKED CHICKEN

Serves: 6

1/4 cup butter
1/2 cup onion, chopped
1/2 cup green pepper, chopped
1/2 cup carrots, chopped
1/2 cup celery, chopped
3/4 cup ketchup
1/2 cup pineapple juice
2 Tbsp. vinegar
1/4 cup brown sugar, packed
2 Tbsp. soy sauce
1/2 tsp. garlic salt
1/8 tsp. pepper
1/8 tsp. ground ginger
1/2 cup pineapple juice
3 Tbsp. cornstarch
1 cup chunk pineapple drained
3 lbs. chicken, cut-up

Melt butter on low heat. Add onion, green pepper, carrots and celery. Cook 5 minutes. Add ketchup, 1/2 cup pineapple juice, vinegar, brown sugar, soy sauce, garlic salt, pepper and ginger. Blend 1/2 cup pineapple juice with cornstarch, add to vegetable mixture, stirring constantly until mixture boils. Cook until thick. Add pineapple chunks. Arrange chicken, skin side up in oblong pan. Pour sauce over chicken. Bake covered at 350° for 1-1/2 hours. Uncover and bake 30 minutes longer.
Variation: Pork cutlets may be used in place of chicken. The entire sauce may be made ahead of time and added when ready to serve.

Mrs. Glenn Devoll (Susie)

PARMESAN CHICKEN WITH PASTA

Serves: 4

3 whole chicken breasts
Salt and pepper
Flour
6 Tbsp. butter
1 cup mushrooms, sliced
1/2 cup Parmesan, freshly
grated
1/2 cup cream

Bone, skin and slice thin and flatten chicken breasts with mallet. Season and coat with flour. Melt butter over low heat and sauté chicken on each side until it stiffens (only takes a couple of minutes on each side). Place chicken in casserole. Sauté mushrooms in remaining butter and place over chicken. Add cream and sprinkle with Parmesan. Bake at 350° for 12 minutes.
Serving suggestions: Delicious served with pasta.

PASTA
1/2 cup onion, chopped
3 Tbsp. butter
1-1/2 cups pasta
1/4 cup vermouth
2 cups chicken broth

Sauté 1/2 cup chopped onion in 3 Tbsp. butter. Add pasta (use a good brand) and stir for a minute. Add vermouth and stir until it is absorbed. Add chicken broth and simmer for about 20 minutes, stirring frequently. The secret to success is the slow cooking. If you double this recipe remember that you *never* double the alcohol.

Mrs. Dan Mitchell (Donita)

GINGERED PEACH NUGGETS

Serves: 4

1 (#2-1/2) can cling peach
halves
1 (1/2") piece dried ginger root
1 tsp. lemon rind
2 Tbsp. lemon juice
Whole cloves

Night before: drain syrup from peaches and add ginger root, lemon juice and rind. Simmer 5 minutes. Stick 3 cloves into each peach half and place in hot syrup and simmer for 5 minutes. Discard ginger root and let peaches stand over-night at room temperature. Drain at serving time. Good with ham or chicken.

Mrs. Jerry Shipley (Sally)

CORNBREAD DRESSING

Serves: 8-10

CORNBREAD

1-1/2 cups cornmeal
1/2 cup flour
4 tsp. baking powder
1/2 tsp. salt
1 cup milk
1 egg, beaten
1/4 cup shortening, melted

Mix together cornmeal, flour, baking powder, salt. Add shortening, milk, and egg. Stir only enough to mix. Fill greased 9"x9" pan 1/2 full and bake for 25 minutes at 425°.

BROTH

4 cups cold water
Gizzard, liver and neck
    portions of turkey
1 celery stalk
Bay leaf
Peppercorns
Onion slice

Combine ingredients and simmer until tender, removing liver after first 10 minutes. Stock not used in stuffing can be used in gravy.

STUFFING

3 cups cornbread
3 cups soft white bread crumbs
3 stalks celery, diced
1 medium onion, diced
2 eggs, beaten
1 tsp. sage
1 tsp. poultry seasoning

Add just enough broth to hold mixture together, but not wet or pasty. Stuffing will look the same when it is done as it looked when put in oven. Rub turkey lightly inside with salt. Stuff with the dressing. Bake turkey according to directions. Can also be baked separately in 9"x13" greased pan at 350° for 30 minutes.
Note: You may prefer all cornbread, or a smaller portion of white crumbs. Keep total crumb mixture to 6 cups.

Sharon Iorio

 To prevent chance of food poisoning, do not store stuffing inside cavity of turkey or chicken. Refrigerate or freeze all stuffings separately. Temperature plays a big role in the development of bacteria. As soon as meat has cooled to room temperature, wrap and chill at once.

BEEF

OUTDOOR SMOKED BRISKET

Serves: 6-8

4 lb. packaged corned beef brisket
Powdered Bar-B-Q spice

Remove brisket from package and coat well with Bar-B-Q powder. Place on rack with fat side up. Smoke in smoker for 4 hours. Slice diagonally across grain of meat. Great for picnics!

Mona Payne

BAR B Q BRISKET

(Good to fix ahead for company)

Serves: 8-10

5-6 lb. brisket
Seasoning salt
Garlic salt
Worcestershire sauce
Pepper

SAUCE
1 cup ketchup
1/3 cup Worcestershire sauce
3/4 cup brown sugar
1 Tbsp. lemon juice

Sprinkle brisket generously with seasoning salt, garlic salt, Worcestershire sauce and pepper. Bake 30 minutes at 450°. Wrap brisket in foil and bake 7-8 hours at 225°. It's a good idea to place in a pan with sides in case some juices escape during baking. Remove juice, add water to make 2 cups for use in making sauce. Sauce: Combine all sauce ingredients with the 2 cups water-juice mixture from the cooked brisket. Chill brisket, slice thin, pour sauce over and return to oven till hot.

Mrs. Jesse Beck (Cecelia)

 Spray grill with cooking spray for a non-stick surface during a cookout. If spray is not at hand, use cooking oil saturated on paper towel. Rub toweling over rods of grill before use.

MARINATED BRISKET

Serves: 6-8

3-5 lb. brisket
1/3 cup lemon juice
1 cup beef consommé
1/4-1/2 (6-oz.) bottle liquid
    smoke
1 small bottle soy sauce
1/4 tsp. garlic salt or powder
1/4 tsp. black pepper

Put brisket in plastic cooking bag. Mix all remaining ingredients and pour over meat in bag. Close bag tightly and marinate 24 hours, turning several times. Leave in bag, make 5 or 6 small slits in bag and cook in 275° oven for 5-6 hours. To serve, remove meat from bag and slice, trimming away excess fat. Skim marinade to remove fat, and serve with meat.

Note: The marinade can be made thicker by adding about 2 Tbsp. flour.

Variation: You may use 1/3 cup vinegar instead of lemon juice.

Brisket Serving Suggestions: Slice thin for a good buffet meat to serve with an assortment of mustards and small buns.

Judy Halstead
Mrs. Richard Davis (Elaine)

RUTH'S BRISKET

Brisket
Garlic salt
Onion salt
Celery salt
1 onion, minced
1/2 bottle liquid smoke
2-1/2 oz. Worcestershire
    sauce

Line a baking pan with foil to seal brisket. Place brisket, fat side down in lined pan and sprinkle generously with garlic, onion and celery salt. Add onion, smoke. Seal foil and refrigerate overnight. Next day—add Worcestershire and salt and pepper all over the brisket. Bake 275° for 5-6 hours.

Shred or slice meat and pour Bar-B-Q Sauce all over then serve warm or refrigerate for later use.

Note: Plastic cook-in bag simplifies marinating.

Ruth Earl

CABBAGE ROLLS

About 25 cabbage rolls

1/2 cup raw rice, cooked
1 lb. ground beef
1/2 tsp. cinnamon
1 tsp. salt
1/4 tsp. pepper
1 egg
1 tsp. thyme
1/4-1/2 cup chopped onion
1 head of cabbage (you may
    need to buy 2, if smaller
    heads are used)

Put cooked rice and next seven ingredients in a large bowl. Mix well to be sure all spices are evenly mixed. Set aside. Put head of cabbage in large pan and cover with water. Boil about 5 minutes and then leaves should separate easily. Put about 1/2 cup of the meat mixture on one leaf of cabbage and roll tightly and tuck ends in. Repeat with remaining meat mxture and cabbage leaves. Place rolls in large greased baking dish. Spoon sauce over rolls and cover dish tightly with lid or foil. Bake in 325° oven for 1 to 1-1/2 hours. Check about every 20-30 minutes to see if extra liquid is needed. They may use about 1 cup of water during the baking time.

SAUCE
1 (8-oz.) can tomato sauce
2 Tbsp. brown sugar
1/2 tsp. cinnamon
2 Tbsp. lemon juice

Combine all sauce ingredients.

Mrs. Gary Dickinson (Rosanne)

 Use greased muffin tins as molds when baking stuffed green peppers.

ITALIAN CHEESE-IT CASSEROLE

Serves: 8

FIRST LAYER

2 lbs. ground beef
1 tsp. salt
1/4 tsp. pepper
1/8 tsp. garlic, minced

Cook meat and seasoning in skillet until pink color disappears. Drain well. Spoon into greased 9 x 13 inch baking dish.

SECOND LAYER

2-1/2 to 3 lbs. summer or
   zucchini squash or 2
   packages (20-oz.) frozen
   cut zucchini
1 (4-oz.) can green chili pepper,
   chopped (Old El Paso
   Brand, if using Del Monte
   Brand only use 1/2 can)
1 medium onion, chopped
2 Tbsp. butter
1 cup mild cheddar cheese,
   shredded

Cook squash in salted water until tender. Drain well. Stir in chili pepper, onion and butter. Spread over meat mixture and sprinkle with cheese.

THIRD LAYER

2 eggs
2 cups cottage cheese
2 tsp. Parmesan cheese, grated
2 tsp. parsley, chopped

Beat eggs until light; fold in cottage cheese and parsley, spoon over squash layer. Sprinkle with Parmesan cheese. Bake in 350° oven for 35-45 minutes or until set.

Mrs. Ray Downs (Linda)

 Make a great spaghetti casserole from left over spaghetti makings. Grease casserole dish and layer sauce, pasta, and grated mozzarella or provolone cheese. Cover and freeze for a busy day supper.

ITALIAN SPAGHETTI SAUCE

Makes 1 — 1-1/2 quarts

*1-1/2 cups onion, chopped
  (1 large)
1/2 cup celery, chopped
1/2 cup green pepper, minced
1/2 cup carrots, chopped
1/4 cup fresh parsley, snipped
1 clove garlic, minced
1/2 lb. ground beef
3 Tbsp. olive or vegetable oil
4 medium tomatoes, peeled,
  seeded, chopped
  (approximately 2 cups)
1 can (8-oz.) tomato sauce
2 Tbsp. tomato paste (can use
  as much as 2 small cans)
1 cup water
1-1/2 tsp. dried oregano leaves
3 fresh basil leaves or 1/2 tsp.
  dried leaves
1/4 tsp. dried thyme leaves
1 bay leaf
1 can (3 oz.) mushrooms,
  chopped
2 tsp. salt
1 tsp. sugar
1/2 tsp. pepper
1/2 cup burgundy*

Sauté onions, celery, green pepper, carrots, parsley, garlic and ground beef in hot oil in dutch oven over medium heat, stirring frequently, until vegetables are tender and meat is browned (approximately 10 minutes). Stir in tomatoes, tomato sauce, tomato paste and 1 cup water. Simmer uncovered, stirring frequently (approximately 5 minutes). Stir in remaining ingredients, except wine, simmer uncovered until thick (approximately 2 to 2-1/2 hours). Remove bay leaf; add wine. Taste and adjust seasonings; if sauce is too thick, may wish to use whole (1) can of tomato paste and 1 to 2 cups water and 1/3 cup wine. Can be frozen.

Mrs. Robert Stormont (Betsy)

To keep spaghetti or noodles from boiling over, add 1 tsp. oleo or salad oil to boiling water before cooking. Add 2 tsp. and it will keep the noodles from sticking together.

POP OVER PIZZA

Serves: 8

1 lb. ground beef
1 large onion, chopped
1 envelope or 1-1/2 oz.
    spaghetti sauce mix
1 (15-oz.) can tomato sauce
1/2 cup water
1 (8-oz.) pkg. Mozzarella
    cheese
2 eggs
2 cups milk
1 Tbsp. vegetable oil
1 cup flour, sifted
1 tsp. salt
1/2 cup Parmesan cheese,
    grated

Preheat oven to 400°.Grease a 13"x9"x 2" pan. Brown meat and onion in a large skillet. Break it into chunks with a spoon. Rinse off excess fat. Stir in sauce mix, tomato sauce and water; simmer 10 minutes. Spoon into pan and top with slices of cheese. Place in oven to keep hot. Then beat eggs, milk and oil in a bowl with an electric mixer until foamy. Beat in flour and salt. Pour batter over hot meat filling, spreading to cover completely. Sprinkle with Parmesan cheese. Bake in hot oven at 400° for 30 minutes until puffed and deep golden brown. Cut in squares and serve while hot and puffy.

Mrs. Dick Allen (Diana)

BEEF AND SNOW PEAS

Serves: 4

2 Tbsp. dry sherry
4 Tbsp. soy sauce
4 tsp. cornstarch
1 clove of garlic, crushed
1 lb. top sirloin of beef,
    cut in small thin slices
4 Tbsp. pure vegetable oil
1/4 lb. fresh mushrooms,
    thinly sliced
1 pkg. (8-oz.) frozen snow peas,
    thawed
1 tsp. sugar
1/2 tsp. monosodium glutamate
1 cup canned consommé
1-1/2 tsp. cornstarch
1 Tbsp. water

Combine sherry, 2 Tbsp. soy sauce, 4 tsp. cornstarch and garlic. Add beef; mix well; let stand 15 minutes. Sauté beef quickly in 3 Tbsp. hot oil in skillet until color disappears, stirring constantly. Add mushrooms; cook 2 minutes. Remove meat and mushrooms from skillet; reserve. Add remaining oil and snow peas to skillet. Sauté 1 minute. Return beef and mushrooms to skillet. Add remaining 2 Tbsp. soy sauce, sugar, monosodium glutamate, and consommé. Dissolve 1-1/2 tsp. cornstarch in water; stir into sauce in skillet. Simmer until sauce thickens.

KATHRYN MASTERYANNI'S SPAGHETTI SAUCE

Serves: 6

1 lb. lean ground beef
1 medium onion, minced
1-1/2 Tbsp. olive oil
1 clove garlic, sliced
1 (1-lb.) can whole tomatoes
1 large (15-oz.) can tomato
sauce
1/2 cup water
3/4 tsp. oregano
1/2 tsp. ground thyme
1/2 tsp. salt
Pepper, to taste
1 tsp. parsley
2 Tbsp. sugar
1 bay leaf
Mushroom lovers may like
to add mushrooms

Brown beef, onion and garlic in olive oil in large skillet. Pour off excess grease. Add all other ingredients to browned mixture and cook until mixture begins to thicken. Stir occasionally to prevent sticking.

Note: The longer and slower this cooks the better. Remove bay leaf before serving. When preparing spaghetti, add 1 Tbsp. olive oil to the salted cooking water to keep from sticking. Rinse with cold water to remove starch, then hot water to warm.

Ruth Earl

RICE DRESSING (HASHWAH)

Serves: 8

1 cup Uncle Ben's Long Grain
white rice
3 lb. chili ground beef or lamb
1/2 cup rendered butter
1/2 tsp. salt
1/2 tsp. cinnamon
1/2 tsp. pepper
1/4 tsp. allspice
2 cups chicken broth
1/2 cup pine nuts
2 Tbsp. butter

Soak rice in warm salted water for at least 1 hour. Sauté meat in butter in heavy saucepan. Add salt and spices and cook covered over low heat until meat is tender and liquid is gone. Drain water off rice and rinse and add to meat. Cook together for 5 minutes. Add chicken broth and bring to boil. Reduce heat, add pine nuts that have been sautéed in butter and continue cooking until liquid is gone and rice is done. Great with turkey, chicken and quail as a side dish.

Mrs. Jim Nicholas (Ila)

STUFFED SQUASH (KOUSA)

Serves: 15-20

1-1/2 cup rice
1/2 cup oleo or butter
2 tsp. salt
1/4 tsp. pepper
1/2 tsp. cinnamon
1/4 tsp. allspice
3 lb. chili ground lean beef
    or lamb
1/2 cup water
15-20 medium yellow squash
1 (6-oz.) can tomato paste or
    tomato juice to cover
    squash
1 Tbsp. lemon juice
1 tsp. salt
3 cups water

Place rice in mixing bowl and rinse, drain well. Add butter and spices and mix. Combine rice with meat adding water to mix. Scrape squash well, slice off necks. Core by hollowing out squash and remove all seeds. Wash squash and drain. Be careful not to break it. Stuff squash with filling. Do not pack too tightly. Place in flat pyrex dishes. Cover with tomato juice and lemon or with tomato paste which has been added to the 3 cups water. Bake covered in 350° oven until squash are tender and sauce is thick. Great with salad and bread. This filling can be used for cabbage rolls, grape leaf rolls and small eggplant.

Mrs. Jim Nicholas (Ila)

LASAGNA

Serves: 8-10

1/2 cup onion, chopped
1-1/2 lbs. ground beef
1 clove garlic
Salt and pepper to taste
2 Tbsp. parsley
1 tsp. fennel seed
2 tsp. sweet basil
1 Tbsp. oregano
2 cans (28-oz.) whole tomatoes
1 (8-oz.) can tomato paste
1 lb. lasagna noodles
1/2 lb. Mozzarella cheese
1-1/2 cups cottage cheese
1-1/2 cups grated Parmesan
    cheese

Saute onion, add ground beef, garlic and spices. Simmer 15 minutes. Add tomatoes that have been mashed lightly and tomato paste. Simmer another 20 minutes. Cook noodles according to directions. Spoon sauce in bottom of 9"x13" pan. Layer with noodles, Mozzarella cheese, cottage cheese, Parmesan cheese. Repeat layers, ending with sauce. Sprinkle with Parmesan cheese. This can be frozen for a short period of time. Bake at 350° for 30 to 40 minutes.

Mrs. John J. Allen (Jeannette)

JERRY'S VEAL PARMESAN

Serves: 6

SAUCE
1/2 cup onion, chopped
1 clove garlic, minced
2 Tbsp. olive oil
1 (16-oz.) can Italian tomatoes
2 tsp. sugar
1 tsp. salt
1/2 tsp. oregano
1/4 tsp. basil
1/4 tsp. pepper

Sauté onion and garlic in hot oil until soft, but not brown. Add remaining ingredients. Simmer while preparing meat.

1-1/2 lbs. veal
2 eggs, beaten
Seasoned bread crumbs
Olive oil
1 (8-oz.) pkg. Mozzarella
cheese, sliced
1/4 cup Parmesan cheese

Dip veal in eggs, then crumbs and brown in oil. Place in large baking dish, cover with Mozzarella cheese and Parmesan cheese. Cover with foil and bake at 350° for 30-45 minutes. Serve with sauce. May be frozen.

Mrs. Wally Hite (Karol)

MEATBALLS ROSÉ

Serves: 4

1 lb. ground beef
1/4 cup milk
1/2 cup bread crumbs
1 tsp. "Spice Islands"
Beaumonde Seasoning
Salt and pepper, to taste
1 can beef bouillon
1/2 cup rosé wine
2 Tbsp. flour

Combine beef, milk, bread crumbs, seasoning, salt and pepper and form into small balls. Brown in butter. Remove to casserole. In fat left in pan, blend flour, undiluted can beef bouillon and wine. Pour over meatballs and bake 30 minutes in 350° oven. Serve with noodles or rice.

Mrs. Bob Anderson (Pat)

CHEESE PLEASE MEAT LOAF

Serves: 8

2 lbs. ground round steak
1 cup sharp cheese (Old
    English), grated
2 cups fresh bread crumbs
1 egg
1 tsp. salt
Pepper to taste
1/2 cup onion, chopped
1/2 cup celery, chopped
1 (8-oz.) can tomato sauce

Mix all ingredients except 1/2 cup of the cheese and all of the tomato sauce. Mound in a round or oblong pan. Bake at 350° for 1 hour. Remove and spread the tomato sauce over the top and sprinkle the remaining 1/2 cup cheese over this. Cook 15 minutes longer. With spatulas lift out onto serving platter.

Jean Mitchell

MEAT LOAF SUPREME

Serves: 8-10

1 lb. ground pork
1 lb. ground beef
1 cup carrots, shredded
1 cup crushed Ritz Crackers
1 cup dairy sour cream
1/4 cup onion, chopped

Combine pork, beef, carrots, crackers, sour cream and onion. Mix and press into 9"x5"x3" loaf pan. Bake at 350° for about 1-1/2 hours. Let stand 10 minutes; remove from pan. Serve with Mushroom Sauce.

MUSHROOM SAUCE
1 beef bouillon cube
Meat loaf drippings
1/2 cup sour cream
1 Tbsp. flour
3 oz. can broiled, sliced
    mushrooms, undrained

Dissolve bouillon cube, crushed, in drippings from meat loaf. Combine with 1/2 cup sour cream, 1 Tbsp. flour and mushrooms. Heat just to boiling.

Mrs. John Day (Florelee)

 For quick and handy seasoning while cooking, keep on hand a large shaker containing six parts salt and one of pepper. Other spices may be added as you prefer.

EASY MEAT LOAF TOPPER

3 Tbsp. brown sugar
1/4 cup ketchup
1/4 tsp. nutmeg
1 tsp. dry mustard
Bacon, 2 slices cut in half and
    laid diagonally on top of
    loaf

Mix together all ingredients and brush over top of meat loaf, then cover with bacon. When bacon begins to cook, baste meat loaf with remaining sauce. You may wish to double the amount.

Mrs. Don Stehr (Janet)

PARTY ENCHILADAS

Makes 12 enchiladas

1 lb. ground beef
1 medium onion, chopped
1 (15-1/2-oz.) can refried beans
1/2 tsp. salt
1/4 tsp. pepper
1 cup salad oil
12 corn tortillas
1-1/2 cups grated cheese, half
    cheddar and half Monterey
    Jack

Sauté ground beef and onion until meat is brown and onion is soft. Drain off fat. Stir in beans, salt and pepper. In another skillet, heat oil until hot enough to sizzle when splattered with water. Quickly dip each tortilla in hot oil just until softened. Place about 1/3 cup meat mixture on each softened tortilla; top with about 2 Tbsp. grated cheese mixture and roll tightly. Arrange enchiladas seam side down in large baking dish. Pour cheese sauce over all. At this point the casserole may be refrigerated if desired. Bake uncovered in 350° oven for 25-35 minutes or until sauce is bubbly. Garnish with olives and sour cream if desired.

SPICY CHEESE SAUCE
1/4 cup butter
1/4 cup flour
1/2 tsp. salt
2 cups milk
1 (10-1/2-oz.) can enchilada
    sauce
4 drops Tabasco
2 cups grated cheese, half
    cheddar and half
    Monterey Jack

Melt butter over low heat in heavy saucepan. Blend in flour and salt. Cook over low heat, stirring until mixture is smooth and bubbly. Remove from heat. Stir in milk and enchilada sauce, heat to boiling, stirring constantly. Boil for 1 minute. Remove from heat; add Tabasco and grated cheese. Stir until cheese melts.

Mrs. Doug Frantz (Dianne)

WILD RICE BARON

Serves: 12-16

2 cups raw wild rice*
4 cups water
2 tsp. salt
2 lb. ground round
1 lb. fresh mushrooms
1/2 cup chopped celery
1 cup chopped onion
1/2 cup butter
1/4 cup soy sauce
2 cups commercial sour cream
2 tsp. salt
1/4 tsp. pepper
1/2 cup slivered almonds
   (some for garnish)

Gently cook wild rice, water and salt for 45 minutes. Drain if necessary. Brown ground beef. If too lean, grind suet with it or add more butter. Rinse mushrooms and cut off ends of stems. Slice. Sauté mushrooms, onions and celery in butter for 5-10 minutes. Combine soy sauce, sour cream, salt and pepper. Add cooked wild rice, browned hamburger, mushrooms, onions and celery mixture and almonds. Toss lightly. Place rice mixture in a slightly buttered 3 quart casserole. Bake in 350° oven for about 1 hour, uncovered. Add more water if needed and season to taste. Stir several times. Garnish with slivered almonds. *Uncle Ben's Long Grain and Wild Rice may be substituted, to lower cost.

Mrs. Joe Hardy (Ruth)

SHERRIED BEEF

Serves: 8

3 lbs. stew meat (or cubed
   sirloin)
1 can water chestnuts
1 cup sherry (optional)
2 cans golden mushroom soup
1 large can mushroom pieces,
   drained
1 envelope Lipton
   Onion Soup Mix
Wild rice (to be served over)

Combine stew meat, water chestnuts, sherry, soups and mushrooms. Simmer 3-5 hours. Serve over wild rice.

Mrs. David Bules (Carolyn)

CURRIED BEEF AND RICE DINNER

Serves: 6

1 lb. ground round steak
2 medium onions, chopped
2 Tbsp. bacon drippings
1 to 1-1/2 cups dry long-grain regular rice
2 cans beef consommé
1 can mushrooms, undrained
2 tsp. curry powder
Butter, salt, pepper to taste
Sour cream, to garnish

Cook onions slowly in bacon drippings until they begin to wilt, then add meat and sear. Butter a large pyrex baking dish and mix well all ingredients, except sour cream. Mixture will appear soupy, but rice absorbs moisture. Cover, bake at 325° for 45 to 60 minutes. At mid-point of cooking time, stir gently. When completely done, stir lightly, dish up and place generous portions of sour cream on each serving.

Mrs. Brent Chapel (Jan)

DEVILED STEAK

Serves: 6

2 lbs. sirloin steak cut 2" thick
2 Tbsp. prepared mustard
2 tsp. lemon juice
Seasoned salt
1/4 cup ketchup
1/4 cup water
1/4 cup olive or salad oil
2 Tbsp. wine vinegar
2 Tbsp. soy sauce
3 Tbsp. plum or cherry jam
3 Tbsp. brown sugar
1/8 tsp. coarse pepper
Few drops of Tabasco sauce

Combine prepared mustard and lemon juice. Spread mustard mixture onto both sides of the steak. Sprinkle generously with seasoned salt. Combine other ingredients and heat to boiling. Pour sauce over steak and allow to stand two hours or longer, turning occasionally. Grill over charcoal. Baste with sauce as the steak is grilled or save sauce and pour over the steak before serving.

Mrs. Paul Allen (Joan)

 When cooking rice, add a spoonful of vinegar or the same amount of lemon juice, and it will be light, fluffy and separated.

EXTRAORDINARY BEEF DISH

Serves: 8

4 lbs. beef tenderloin, choice
(allow 1/2 lb. per serving)

Leave tenderloin in whole piece. Place in 500° oven for 30 minutes. Use meat thermometer. 30 minutes should cook beef to medium stage. Cut into thick slices and serve over Oven Baked Rice. Pass Superb Mushroom Sauce Diane.

OVEN WILD RICE
1-1/2 cups wild rice
1/2 cup butter
3-3/4 cans (10-oz.) consommé,
undiluted
Water chestnuts, if desired
Sliced mushrooms, if desired

Soak wild rice overnight in generous amount of water. Melt butter in pyrex dish. Add drained rice and stir. Add consommé (beef or chicken). Let stand until ready to bake. This mixture will be runny. Bake 1-1/2 hours at 325°. Add water chestnuts and mushrooms if desired.

SUPERB SAUCE DIANE
1/2 cup butter, melted
3/4 lb. mushrooms, sliced
1-1/2 cups green onions, sliced
2 tsp. mustard
1 Tbsp. lemon juice
1 Tbsp. Worcestershire sauce
1 tsp. salt
1/4 cup parsley, chopped

Sauté the green onions and mushrooms in the melted butter with mustard for 5 minutes. Add remaining ingredients and cook an additional 5 minutes. Serve hot.

Joan Allen

SHISH-KA-BOB MARINADE

1/2 cup salad oil
1/4 cup soy sauce
1/2 cup red wine
2 Tbsp. powdered ginger
Garlic
2 Tbsp. ketchup
1/2 tsp. pepper
5 shakes Worcestershire sauce

Combine all ingredients. Marinate steak pieces 12-24 hours. Use sirloin tip cut into cubes with onion, cherry tomatoes, green pepper, mushrooms and pineapple. Charcoal kabobs and brush with marinade. Serve over rice.

Danette Tucker

RAH RAH ROAST

Serves: 6-8

4 lb. rump roast, boneless
1 bottle Catalina French
    dressing (8 ozs.)
1 onion, sliced (large)
1 cup celery, diced
1 Tbsp. instant parsley flakes
1 pkg. Kraft brown gravy mix
1/2 cup dry red wine

Season meat with salt and pepper. Place in deep bowl. Combine dressing, onions, celery, parsley flakes and wine. Pour over meat. Cover and refrigerate overnight. Turn occasionally. Drain meat and reserve marinade. Brown meat in small amount of marinade and gravy mix. Pour over meat and cook at 300° for about 2-1/2 to 3 hours. Turn occasionally if possible.

Mrs. Robert Emery (Sandra)

SWEDISH MEAT BALLS

1 lb. ground round
1/2 lb. ground pork
1-1/2 cup soft bread crumbs
    (3 slices)
1 cup half and half
1/2 cup onion, chopped
1 Tbsp. margarine
1 egg
1/4 cup parsley, finely chopped
1-1/2 tsp. salt
1/4 tsp. ginger
Dash of pepper
Dash of nutmeg
2 Tbsp. margarine
2 Tbsp. flour
3/4 cup canned beef broth
1/4 cup cold water
1/2 tsp. instant coffee

Soak crumbs in cream for 5 minutes. Cook onion in margarine until tender. Combine meats, crumb mixture, egg, onion, parsley and seasonings. Beat until fluffy (about 5 minutes). Form into 1-1/2 inch balls. (For easier shaping, wet hands when necessary). Brown balls in 2 Tbsp. margarine, not too many at once. Remove meatballs from pan. Stir flour into drippings. Add broth, water, coffee heat and stir until gravy thickens. Return meatballs to gravy—cover and cook slowly for 30 minutes. Serve as main dish with brown beans or rice or serve as hors d'oeuvres.

Mrs. Robert Shuttee (Betty)

MEXICAN CASSEROLE

Serves: 6-8

1 Tbsp. oil
1/2 cup onion, chopped
2 cloves garlic, minced
1 lb. lean ground beef
1 (28-oz.) can stewed tomatoes
1 pkg. taco seasoning mix
1 (4-oz.) can diced green chilies
1 (2-1/2-oz.) can chopped
   black olives
2 (7-8-oz.) pkgs. cheese
   flavored tortilla chips,
   lightly crushed
1/2 lb. Mozzarella cheese,
   shredded
1 pt. sour cream
1/2 cup (2 oz.) cheddar cheese,
   shredded

Preheat oven to 350°. Heat oil in large pan over medium heat. Add onion and garlic and sauté until translucent. Add meat and cook until browned, stirring frequently. Blend in tomatoes, taco seasoning, chilies and olives and simmer about 10 minutes. Grease 9"x13" baking dish. Layer half of chips over bottom. Add all meat mixture, then Mozzarella and sour cream. Top with remaining chips. Bake until heated through, about 30 minutes. Sprinkle with cheddar cheese and continue baking until cheese melts. Let stand 5 minutes before serving. Note: Cook the meat mixture and pour in pans lined with greased foil. Freeze and then wrap well. They thaw quickly and then casserole can be put together. Will make two 8" square pans, if desired.

Mrs. John Taylor (Sue)

TACO CASSEROLE

Serves: 6-8

2 lbs. lean ground beef
2 envelopes taco sesoning
1 can chili beans (large or
   small, amount to taste)
1 small pkg. Doritos
1 lb. sharp cheddar cheese,
   grated

Brown meat thoroughly and drain all fat. Add taco seasoning mix according to package directions. Mix in 1 can chili beans (do not drain). Grease 2 qt. casserole. Spread a layer of meat-bean mix, a layer of Doritos and a layer of cheese, alternating layers and ending with a layer of cheese. Bake at 425° for 20 minutes or until cheese melts.

Mrs. Dale Anderson (Judy)

SUSIE'S BAR-B-QUE SAUCE

Yield: Makes 1-1/2 quarts

32 oz. bottle ketchup
2 cups water
1/2 cup packed brown sugar
3 Tbsp. Worcestershire sauce
1 tsp. garlic salt
2 Tbsp. vinegar
2 dashes Tabasco
1 tsp. dry mustard
1 tsp. chili powder
2 tsp. liquid smoke
1/4 tsp. cayenne pepper
1 tsp. coarse ground black
*   pepper*
2 tsp. "Woody Cook-in Sauce"

Let all this simmer in a sauce pan for 30-45 minutes. Pour into quart jars and keep in refrigerator.

Mrs. Phil Edwards (Susie)

BARBECUE SAUCE

1-1/2 lb. butter
1 pint ketchup
1 pint vinegar (Apple cider)
1 Tbsp. Tabasco
1 small bottle Worcestershire
*   sauce*
1 Tbsp. brown sugar
1 Tbsp. onion juice
1-1/2 cloves garlic, finely
*   chopped*
Dash of red and black pepper
2 Tbsp. salt
1/2 cup water

Bring all ingredients to a boil. Makes about 2 quarts. May be stored for later use. Good on chicken and pork.

Karol Hite

SMOTHERED STEAK

Serves: 6

1-1/2 lb. beef round steak,
    about 3/4" thick
1/4 cup flour
1 tsp. salt
1/4 tsp. pepper
2 Tbsp. cooking oil
2 medium onions, sliced
1 can (10-oz.) beef broth or
    consommé
1 Tbsp. vinegar
1 clove garlic, minced
1 bay leaf
1/4 tsp. dried thyme, crushed

Cut meat into serving sized pieces. Combine flour, salt and pepper. Pound into meat. Brown meat in oil. Top with onion slices, stir in remaining ingredients. Bring to a boil and then reduce heat to a simmer. Cover and cook slowly for one hour. Remove bay leaf and serve.

Mrs. Robert Jantzen (Colleen)

STUFFED ROUND STEAK

Makes 8 roll-ups

2 lbs. boneless round steak
2 Tbsp. butter or margarine
1/2 cup celery, chopped
1/4 cup onion, chopped
2 cups bread crumbs
Dash of salt & pepper
1 Tbsp. water
3 Tbsp. vegetable oil
1 can cream of mushroom soup,
    undiluted
2 tsp. Worcestershire sauce
1 clove garlic, minced
1/2 cup water

Cut steak into 8 equal pieces, approximately 1/4" thick. Melt butter in skillet, sauté celery and onion till tender. Remove from heat and stir in bread crumbs, salt, pepper, 1 Tbsp. water. Place 1/8 mixture on each steak and roll up. Secure with toothpick. Dredge each in flour and brown in hot oil. Combine soup, Worcestershire sauce, garlic and 1/2 cup water. Stir and pour over steak rolls. Cover and simmer 1-1/2 hours or until tender.

Linda Dunlap

SUKIYAKI

Serves: 8-10

3-4 lbs. beef sirloin or
    tenderloin, sliced Chinese
    style (thin diagonal strips)
1-1/2 cup celery, sliced
    diagonally
1-1/2 cup green onions, cut
    diagonally, including tops
1-3 white dry onions, sliced thin
1-1/2 cups fresh mushrooms
    (4-oz.) sliced thin
2 (8-1/2-oz.) cans bamboo
    shoots
1 (8-1/2-oz.) can water
    chestnuts

Brown meat in oil 1/2 at a time. Remove meat to chafing dish. Add 1/2 sauce to skillet. Cook onions and celery in skillet for 3 minutes. Add shoots and mushrooms and water chestnuts and cook 3 minutes. Add green onions and cook 1 minute. Add meat and rest of sauce. Stir gently until well heated. Serve immediately over steaming rice.

SAUCE
3/4 cup soy sauce
3/4 cup water
1/2 cup dry sherry
6 Tbsp. sugar
1-1/2 tsp. Accent

Put ingredients in pan and warm until sugar is dissolved over medium heat.

Nan Brim

GERMAN BEEF BIRDS

Serves: 6

1 beef round steak (about 2 lbs.)
6 smoked sausage links
2 Tbsp. salad oil
1 tsp. salt
1 medium sized onion, sliced
1 can (16-oz.) tomatoes
2 tsp. caraway seeds
1 can (16-oz.) sauerkraut

Pound steak to 1/4 inch thickness. Cut into 6 serving pieces. Place a sausage link on each piece of steak and roll like a jelly roll. Fasten with wooden picks or skewers. Brown meat slowly in salad oil. Pour off drippings. Season with salt. Add onion, tomatoes, caraway seeds and liquid from sauerkraut, reserving sauerkraut to add later. Cover tightly and cook slowly for one hour. Add sauerkraut and continue to simmer until heated through.

Mrs. Ray Downs (Linda)

GREAT MID-WEST ESPECIALE

Serves: 6-8

1 lb. Jimmy Dean Taco Meat
    (or ground beef plus taco
    seasoning)
2 cups cooked Minute Rice
1 zucchini, sliced
1 green pepper, sliced
1 bunch green onions (about
    6-8) with tops, sliced
2 medium tomatoes, peeled
    and diced

CHEESE SAUCE
1 can cheddar cheese soup
1 (8-oz.) carton sour cream
1 clove minced garlic (or
    1/2 tsp. garlic powder)
Crushed corn chips

Brown meat, drain fat, set aside. Cook rice while meat is browning. Use slicing blade in processor (or slice) zucchini, pepper and onion. Remove blade and add tomatoes. Toss lightly. Layer in 2 quart casserole: rice, vegetables, meat, cheese sauce, corn chips. Bake 30 minutes at 350°.Complement this dish with warm tortilla chips and picante sauce.

Mrs. Robert Hicks (Charla)

PORK

HAM & BROCCOLI ROLL-UPS

Serves: 6

6 thin slices of cooked ham
1 bunch fresh broccoli, or
    1 pkg. (10-oz) frozen
    broccoli spears, cooked
    and drained
1/2 cup mayonnaise
3 Tbsp. flour
1/2 tsp. salt
1/8 tsp. pepper
1-1/2 cups milk
1/3 cup cheddar cheese, grated
Dry bread crumbs

Roll ham slices around broccoli spears. Place rolls in shallow casserole. In small sauce pan, combine mayonnaise, flour, salt and pepper. Gradually stir in milk. Cook over low heat, stirring constantly, till thickened. Blend in cheese. Pour sauce over rolls. Sprinkle with bread crumbs. Broil until bubbly.

Mrs. Robert Jantzen (Colleen)

CHEESE SAUSAGE SOUFFLÉ ROLL

Serves : 6-8

CHEESE SOUFFLÉ MIXTURE
4 Tbsp. butter
1/4 cup flour
1/2 tsp. salt
Dash of pepper
1 cup milk
1-1/2 cup sharp cheddar
cheese, shredded
4 eggs, separated

SAUSAGE FILLING
12 oz. bulk pork sausage
1/2 cup fresh mushrooms,
sliced
1/4 cup onion, chopped
1/4 cup green pepper, chopped
1/2 cup dairy sour cream

Preheat oven to 350°. Grease a 15"x10" jelly roll pan. Line bottom and sides with waxed paper. Grease paper. In a small saucepan, melt butter. Blend in flour, salt and pepper. Add milk, stir constantly over medium-high heat until mixture thickens and bubbles. Remove from heat and add cheese. Stir until melted. Set aside. In a large bowl, beat egg whites with electric mixer on high speed until stiff peaks form. Set aside. In a small bowl, beat egg yolks with mixer on high until thickened and lemon colored (about five minutes). Gradually stir cheese mixture into egg yolks. Fold 1 cup egg white mixture into cheese mixture. Slowly pour egg yolk mixture over remaining egg whites and fold together gently. Pour mixture into jelly roll pan. Bake 25 minutes or until soufflé is puffed and browned. While soufflé is cooking, combine sausage, mushrooms, onion, and green pepper in a medium skillet. Cook over medium heat until sausage is done and vegetables are tender. Drain. Place sausage mixture in a medium bowl. Stir in sour cream and set aside. Place a piece of foil larger than the soufflé on a flat surface. When soufflé is done, turn out of pan onto foil immediately. Remove wax paper. Spread sausage filling on soufflé. Lift soufflé from short end and roll up. Slice and serve immediately.

Mrs. Steve Roney (Janie)

PARTY HAM

Serves: 16

5 lbs. ham, shaved
1/2 cup celery, chopped
1/2 cup onion, chopped
1 clove garlic or 1/2 tsp. garlic
    powder
3 Tbsp. parsley flakes
1 bay leaf
1/2 tsp. thyme
1/4 tsp. allspice
1 cup water
3 Tbsp. Worcestershire sauce
1 Tbsp. vinegar
2 cups Ketchup

Sauté celery and onion in butter till clear. In same pan add rest of ingredients (except ham) and simmer 1/2 hour. Add shaved ham and heat 15 minutes. Serve from heated chafing dish on warmed buns.

Mrs. Dennis Brown (Linda)

HAM AND POTATO SCALLOP

Serves: 4

4 cups cooked potatoes,
    peeled and sliced
2 cups cooked ham, cubed
1 can (16-oz.) small boiled
    onions, drained
2 cups milk
3 Tbsp. instant-type flour
    (Wondra)
2 Tbsp. butter or margarine
1/2 tsp. salt
1/8 tsp. pepper

Make 2 layers each of the potato slices, ham and onions in an 8 cup baking dish. Combine milk, flour, butter or margarine, salt and pepper in a small saucepan. Cook, stirring constantly, until sauce thickens and boils 1 minute. Pour over layers. Bake at 350° for 40 minutes, or until bubbly hot. Sprinkle with finely cut chives, if desired.
Variation: 1 cup whole sliced green onions may be used in place of canned onions. Good with a fresh vegetable dinner of fried okra, sliced tomatoes, black eyed peas.

Mrs. Larry Dobbs (Ruth)

HAM AND CHEESE SOUFFLÉ

(Great for brunch with fruit salad & cinnamon rolls)

Serves: 8-10

3/4 cup ham, coarsely ground
5 slices bread, buttered and
    cubed
3/4 lb. American cheese,
    grated
1/2 tsp. seasoned salt
4 eggs, beaten
2 cups milk

Put half of bread and ham in buttered 9"x13" pyrex dish. Sprinkle with cheese. Continue to layer bread, ham and cheese. Sprinkle with seasoned salt. Mix eggs and milk. Pour over top. Refrigerate overnight or 1 to 2 hours in advance. Bake at 350° for 1 hour. Let stand for 5 minutes before serving.

Mrs. Jim Nicholas (Ila)

OUR EASTER PARADE HAM LOAF

Serves: 20

3 eggs, slightly beaten
1 (13-oz.) can evaporated milk
1 (10-3/4-oz.) can tomato soup
1 cup cracker crumbs
3 lbs. smoked ham, ground
3 lbs. fresh pork, ground

Combine eggs, milk, tomato soup and cracker crumbs. Add to ground meats and mix thoroughly. Pack into two 9"x5" loaf pans. Bake at 325° for 2 hours.

"WITH ALL THE FRILLS UPON IT"
EPICUREAN SAUCE
1 pt. whipping cream
3/4 cup mayonnaise
1/2 cup horseradish
2 tsp. salt
4 tsp. prepared mustard
1/4 cup minced parsley

Whip cream until stiff. Fold in other ingredients until well blended. Chill.

Mrs. Frank Marquis (Barbara)

CIDER JELLY GLAZED HAM

12-14 lb. whole ham, cooked
1-1/3 cup cinnamon-Cider jelly
Whole cloves
Watercress or other greens
Spiced whole red crab apples

Place ham fat side up in a shallow baking pan. Bake at 325° for 2-1/2 to 3 hours. 1/2 hour before ham is done, remove from oven. Remove drippings. Cut away rind. Score ham diagonally with a sharp knife. Stud top of ham with whole cloves. To glaze the ham, spoon 2/3 cup jelly onto ham. Return ham to oven for 10 minutes. Spoon remaining jelly onto ham and return to oven for 20-25 minutes. Garnish with watercress or other greens and serve hot or cold with spiced crab apples and cider-cinnamon sauce.

Mrs. Wally Hite (Karol)

CIDER CINNAMON SAUCE

Serves: 6

6 Tbsp. cinnamon-cider jelly
1 Tbsp. cornstarch
1/4 cup orange juice
2 Tbsp. lemon juice
Dash salt
2 Tbsp. raisins or currants

Melt jelly over low heat. Mix cornstarch with orange and lemon juice; add to jelly with remaining ingredients. Bring to a boil and cook for 2-3 minutes, stirring constantly until thickened. Serve warm or cold with glazed ham.

Karol Hite

TOPPING FOR HAM LOAF OR HAM

2 cups brown sugar
1/2 cup vinegar
2 Tbsp. dry ground mustard

Combine and bring to a boil. Baste ham loaf several times during baking.

Ann Frazee Riley

HORSERADISH SAUCE

Yield: Approximately 3/4 cup

1/4 cup horseradish
1-1/2 Tbsp. vinegar
1 Tbsp. prepared mustard
1/2 tsp. salt
4 drops Worcestershire sauce
Dash of Cayenne pepper
Paprika
1/2 cup whipping cream,
    whipped

Combine first 7 ingredients. Then fold by hand into whipped cream.

Charlotte Kennedy

HAM MUSTARD SAUCE

Yield: Approximately 1-3/4 cups

1 Tbsp. French's prepared
    mustard
1/2 cup sugar
1/4 cup butter
1/4 cup vinegar
Salt to taste
2 whole eggs or 3 yolks
1/2 can tomato soup

Mix and cook until thick, stirring constantly.

Mrs. John Russell (Mary Jean)

SWEET-SOUR MUSTARD SAUCE

Yield: Approximately 3/4 cup

1 can Coleman's dry mustard
1/2 cup white vinegar
1/2 cup sugar
1 egg

Combine dry mustard and white vinegar and soak overnight. Next day add 1/2 cup sugar and 1 egg and cook over hot water until thick. This keeps indefinitely in refrigerator. Great with ham.

Eleanor Hornbaker

BROWN SUGAR GLAZE

3/4 cup brown sugar
1/4 cup water
1/4 cup vinegar
2 tsp. dry mustard

Combine ingredients and bring to a boil. Baste loaf every 15 minutes during baking.

Charlotte Kennedy

SWEET AND SOUR PORK

Serves: 6

1 lb. lean boneless pork
2 green peppers
4 pineapple slices
1/2 cup cornstarch
3 cups vegetable oil
1/2 carrot (for color)

MARINADE
1/2 tsp. salt
1/2 tsp. soy sauce
1 Tbsp. cornstarch
1 Tbsp. cold water
1 egg, lightly beaten

SEASONING SAUCE
6 Tbsp. vinegar
1/4 to 1/2 cup sugar
1/2 cup ketchup
1/2 cup cold water
2 Tbsp. cornstarch
2 tsp. salt
2 tsp. sesame oil

Pound pork with back of cleaver to tenderize; cut into 1" squares. Soak with marinade at least 1/2 hour or as long as possible. Cut green pepper into halves, remove seeds and membranes and cut into 1" squares. Cut pineapple same size. Prepare seasoning sauce. Peel carrot and cut diagonally, parboil for 1 minute. Rinse immediately in cold water till carrots are cold. To cook: heat 3 cups of oil, while oil is heating, coat each piece of pork in 1/2 cup cornstarch. When oil is ready, fry pork about 3 minutes or until brown and done. Remove pork and drain off oil, stir fry the green pepper for 2 minutes. Add carrots then add pineapple, stirring constantly. Add the seasoning sauce, stir well. Stir until thickened. Turn off heat. Add the pork, mix well and serve immediately.

Mrs. Paul Baker (Nikki)

PORK TENDERLOIN

Serves: 4

2 (2-lb.) pork tenderloins
Salt and pepper
Dry mustard
2 Tbsp. butter
1/4 tsp. rosemary
1/4 cup butter
1/2 cup currant jelly
1 cup cream
1 Tbsp. flour

Rub the tenderloins with salt and pepper and dry mustard and brown in 2 Tbsp. butter in skillet. Place in a covered casserole. Sprinkle with rosemary, 1/4 cup butter and currant jelly. Cover and bake for 45 minutes in 300° oven. Add the cream mixed with the flour and bake 15 minutes longer.

Mrs. Gary Hansen (Patti)

ITALIAN CHOPS CASSEROLE

Serves: 4-6

8 veal, pork or lamb chops
1/2 cup flour
1/2 tsp. salt
Dash of pepper
2 Tbsp. butter
2 Tbsp. olive oil
1/2 cup dry white wine
1 bouillon cube, dissolved
    in 1 cup hot water
1 can cream of mushroom soup
1 clove garlic, minced
2 Tbsp. parsley
Dash rosemary, crushed
3 potatoes, sliced
1/2 lb. sliced mushrooms
1 onion, sliced

Dust chops with flour combined with salt and pepper. Brown in heated butter and olive oil. Drain. In same pan add wine, bouillon, mushroom soup, garlic, parsley and rosemary. Heat. Layer potatoes, mushrooms, onions and top with chops. Pour liquid over all. Cover and bake at 350° for 1-1/4 hours. If refrigerated, allow 15-20 minutes more baking time.

Mrs. John Wynne (Gail)

STUFFED PORK CHOPS

Serves: 4

4 thick pork chops
2 Tbsp. fat
1/2 cup chopped onions
1 cup chopped mushrooms
1 cup stuffing mix
1 Tbsp. chopped parsley
1/4 tsp. salt
1/4 tsp. sage or poultry
 seasoning
Fresh ground pepper to taste
2 Tbsp. sour cream
1/4 cup water

SOUR CREAM GRAVY
Pork drippings
1-1/2 cups water
3 Tbsp. flour
2 Tbsp. sour cream
Salt and fresh pepper to taste

Preheat oven to 350°. In skillet heat fat, add onion and sauté till transparent. Add mushrooms, and cook gently for about 2 minutes. Add stuffing mix, parsley and seasonings. Mix well. Add enough sour cream to moisten the mixture (you may want to add water too.) Cut a pocket in each chop and stuff with the stuffing mix. Secure with a toothpick. Sprinkle lightly with additional seasonings. Place in baking dish, add water and bake covered for 30 minutes. Remove cover and bake until brown, about 30 more minutes. Serve with gravy.

Pour drippings from the pan into a bowl. Add water to the pan and scrape loose all brown particles and place in another bowl. Skim fat from drippings and put 3 Tbsp. back into the pan. Stir in flour and brown well. Slowly add water from the bowl and the drippings. Cook until thickened. Add sour cream and heat gently while beating with a whisk. Do not let boil after sour cream has been added.

Linda Murdock Wilson

SAUSAGE AND RICE CASSEROLE

Serves: 8-10

2-1/2 lbs. pork sausage, fried
    and drained
4-5 green onions, chopped
1 medium bunch celery, leaves
    and all, chopped
1 green pepper, chopped
2 packages Lipton chicken
    noodle soup
4-1/2 cups water
1 cup brown rice
1 can water chestnuts

Cook soup and water together. Add brown rice and water chestnuts. Mix with sausage, green onions, celery and green pepper. Bake covered at 350° for 1-1/2 hours. Sprinkle top with shredded almonds.

Mrs. Bruce Harvey (Jana)

ALFREDO SAUCE

Serves: 4

1/2 lb. pasta
1 clove garlic, chopped
1 cup fresh mushrooms, sliced
1 stick butter (not margarine)
Salt and pepper to taste
1 cup cream
1 cup Parmesan cheese,
    grated

While pasta is cooking, sauté garlic and mushrooms in half of butter. Stir in remaining butter. Reduce heat and slowly add cream, stirring well. Add salt and pepper to taste. (Do not overheat or boil this cream mixture.) Add cheese by sprinkling and stirring into heated cream mixture. (Additional cheese will make the sauce thicker.) Serve over pasta immediately. This sauce is quick and easy and can be prepared in the time it takes to cook the pasta.

Variation: Remove the casings from 1 or 2 Italian sausages and mash them. Sauté sausage in a small amount of butter with mushrooms. Proceed as above. Clams may also be used.

Mrs. Larry Keeler (Sally)

SEAFOOD

CHARCOALED SHRIMP

1/2 lb. fresh mushrooms
1 lb. fresh shrimp (small to
    medium)
1/4 lb. green olives
1 (32-oz.) bottle ketchup
Horseradish to taste
Lemon juice, from 2 large
    lemons
Unpainted metal lath, see Note

Cut mushrooms in smaller sizes than shrimp. Shell shrimp but it is not necessary to devein them. Mix mushrooms, shrimp, olives, ketchup, horseradish and lemon juice and marinate in refrigerator for 24 hours. (Mix ketchup and horseradish and taste before pouring over shrimp. Horseradish flavor stays, does not cook out.) Put above mixture on metal lath over charcoal until shrimp is heated but not crusty, about 3-5 minutes. Note: Use non-galvanized metal lath which may be purchased at the lumber yard. If painted, burn paint off. Do not buy screen wire, it will melt!

Tom and Donna Rogers

BAKED SALMON CROQUETTES

Makes 8 patties

1 can (15-1/2-oz.) red salmon
1/4 cup butter or margarine
2 Tbsp. onion, finely chopped
1/3 cup flour
1 cup milk
1/2 tsp. salt
1/4 tsp. pepper
1 Tbsp. lemon juice
1 cup corn flakes, crushed

SAUCE
2 Tbsp. flour
2 Tbsp. butter
1/4 tsp. salt
1/8 tsp. pepper
1 cup milk
1 can (8-1/2-oz.) small peas,
    drained

Drain salmon. Melt butter in heavy saucepan over low heat. Add onion and cook until tender. Add flour, stirring until smooth. Cook 1 minute, stirring constantly. Gradually add milk. Cook over medium heat, stirring constantly, until thickened and bubbly. Stir in salt and pepper. Set aside. Remove skin and bones from salmon and flake salmon with a fork. Add lemon juice, 1/2 cup corn flakes, and white sauce, stirring well. Refrigerate mixture until chilled. Shape into croquettes. Roll in remaining corn flakes. Place on lightly greased baking sheet. Bake at 400° for 30 minutes. Sauce: Make a standard medium white sauce (using sauce ingredients). Add peas and serve over croquettes.

Mrs. John Day (Florelee)

CRUNCHY FRIED FISH

Serves: 6

2 lbs. fish fillets
Salt and pepper
1 cup flour
2 tsp. baking powder
1 tsp. salt
1 egg yolk
1 cup lukewarm water
1 Tbsp. salad oil
1 egg white, stiffly beaten
Salad oil

Dry fillets thoroughly; sprinkle with salt and pepper to taste. Combine dry ingredients in a bowl; drop egg yolk in center, add water and add 1 Tbsp. oil; stir well. Fold egg white into batter. Dip fillets in batter, and fry until golden brown on both sides in 1/4" oil heated to 370°. Drain on paper towels.

Mrs. John Day (Florelee)

COQUILLE ST. JACQUES

Serves: 6

6 Tbsp. butter
3 Tbsp. flour
1 tsp. salt
1/8 tsp. white pepper
2 cups light cream
1/4 cup onions, finely chopped
1/2 lb. scallops, sliced
1/2 cup mushrooms, sliced
3/4 lb. cooked shrimp
1/2 lb. crab meat
2 Tbsp. sherry
1 cup Swiss cheese, grated

Combine 4 Tbsp. butter with flour, salt and white pepper in skillet. Stir in cream, gradually. Simmer, stirring constantly, until sauce is smooth and thickened. Sauté onions in remaining butter in small skillet. Add scallops. Sauté for 5 minutes. Remove onions and scallops. Add mushrooms. Sauté for 3-5 minutes. Combine shrimp, scallops, onions, crab meat, mushrooms and sherry with sauce. Mix lightly. Place in individual baking dishes. Sprinkle with cheese. Bake at 400° for 15 minutes or until cheese browns.

Mrs. Mike Dickey (Mary)

SALMON SOUFFLE PIE

Serves: 4-6

1 cup fine cracker crumbs
(25 2" crackers)
1/4 cup butter, melted
1/4 tsp. dry dill weed or basil
1 can (7-3/4-oz.) salmon
1 cup cream-style cottage
cheese (small curd)
3 eggs, separated
1/2 cup heavy cream
2 Tbsp. flour
1/8 tsp. pepper
1 Tbsp. chopped chives
(fresh or freeze dried)
1 tsp. lemon juice
1/4 tsp. salt

Stir together cracker crumbs, melted butter, and dill weed. Press over bottom and sides of a buttered 9" glass pie plate. Reserve. Turn salmon (including liquid and bones) into a mixing bowl; add cottage cheese and egg yolks; beat until well-mixed. Stir in cream, flour, salt, pepper, chives and lemon juice. Beat egg whites until they hold stiff, straight peaks; fold into salmon mixture. Turn into reserved crumb crust. Bake on low rack in 350° oven for 35 minutes. Remove and let stand 5-10 minutes so center will finish setting. Serve at once.

Beverly Evans

BAKED SALMON OMELET

Serves: 14-16

1 (15-1/2-oz.) can salmon
1 dozen eggs, beaten
1/8 tsp. Tabasco sauce
1/2 cup flour
1/2 tsp. salt
1 tsp. baking powder
2 cups Monterey Jack cheese,
diced
1 pt. cottage cheese
1 (10-oz.) pkg. frozen chopped
spinach, thawed and
drained

Drain and flake salmon, reserving liquid. Add Tabasco and salmon liquid to beaten eggs. Sift together, flour, salt and baking powder. Blend into egg mixture. Add salmon, cheeses, and drained spinach. Mix well. Pour into buttered 9"x13" pan or two 8" square pans. Bake at 400° for 15 minutes. Reduce heat to 350° and bake 15 minutes longer.

Mrs. Larry Dobbs (Ruth)

SHRIMP FLORENTINE

Serves: 10

4 pkg. (10-oz.) frozen spinach
3 lbs. shrimp, cooked, shelled
  and deveined (do not overcook, would be better to
  undercook) (3 lbs. before
  cooking)
1/2 cup butter
1/2 cup flour
3 cups milk
1 cup dry white wine
1/2 cup onion, chopped
Salt, pepper and paprika
2 cups (8-oz.) cheddar cheese,
  shredded

Preheat oven to 350°. Spray large pyrex dish with Pam. Thaw and drain spinach well. Spread spinach in pan. Top with shrimp. In a saucepan, melt butter, stir in flour. Then gradually add milk, wine and onions. Cook, stirring constantly over low heat, until sauce bubbles and thickens. Add salt and pepper to taste and enough paprika for a rosy color. Pour sauce over shrimp. Sprinkle with cheese. Bake uncovered for 35 minutes or until bubbly. Note: To cook shrimp, boil 3-4 minutes, depending on size, just until flesh begins to turn white.

Mrs. Ray Downs (Linda)

SHRIMP AND ASPARAGUS ROUND UP

Serves: 8

2 large cans asparagus spears
1 small can water chestnuts,
  sliced
1 small can mushroom stems
  and pieces
1 small can ripe olives
1 large can small shrimp
1 cup longhorn cheddar cheese,
  grated
1 can mushroom soup
1/2 can water
10-12 crushed crackers
1 small can French fried
  onion rings

Butter a 1-1/2 quart pyrex casserole. Place a layer of asparagus, chestnuts, mushrooms, olives, shrimp and cheese in this order. Dilute soup with 1/2 can water and pour 1/2 of this on first layer. Repeat layers. Top with cracker crumbs. Bake for 30 minutes at 350°. Place onion rings on top and brown for an additional 2-3 minutes.
Variation: 2 eggs, boiled and sliced, may be added with asparagus layers or sliced on top as a garnish when ready to serve.

Mrs. Loren Atwood (Vera)

SHRIMP VICTORIA

Serves: 8-10

2-1/2 lbs. shrimp, raw, peeled
  and cleaned
2 small white onions, sliced
  into sixteenths & separated
1/2 cup butter
1/2 lb. fresh mushrooms, sliced
  (or substitute canned)
2 Tbsp. flour
1/2 tsp. salt
Dash chili powder
1 pt. sour cream
8-10 servings cooked rice

Sauté shrimp and onion in butter for 10 minutes or just until shrimp are tender. Add mushrooms and cook for 5 minutes more. Sprinkle in flour, salt and chili powder. Stir in sour cream and cook gently for 5 to 8 minutes, not allowing mixture to boil. Serve over rice.

Mrs. Ray Downs (Linda)

EGG AND CHEESE MAIN DISHES

CRUNCHY BRUNCH EGG CASSEROLE

Serves: 6

2 cups plain croutons
4 oz. Cheddar cheese,
  shredded
4 eggs, slightly beaten
2 cups milk
1/2 tsp. salt
1/2 tsp. prepared mustard
1/8 tsp. onion powder
1/8 tsp. pepper
Bacon, crumbled (optional)

In bottom of buttered pyrex dish combine croutons and cheese. Mix remaining ingredients except for bacon and pour over crouton mixture in casserole. If using bacon crumbles, add to top. Bake at 325° for 50-60 minutes. May be prepared several hours in advance or overnight.

Janet Stehr

COMPANY FOR BREAKFAST

Serves: 8-10

9 slices of bread
1/2 lb. sharp Cheddar cheese
1/2 lb. Swiss cheese
1 lb. bacon, browned and
*   drained*
3 cups milk
6 eggs

Cover 9" x 13" pan with bread. Grate both cheeses on top. Layer with browned bacon slices. Beat milk and eggs and pour into pan. Cover overnight in the refrigerator. Bake uncovered for 45 minutes at 350.°

Chris Smith

VEGETABLE QUICHE

Serves: 6

Pie crust
1 lb. fresh spinach, cooked
*   and drained*
1/2 cup green onion, chopped
1 clove garlic, minced
2 Tbsp. butter
1-1/2 cup (6-oz.) Swiss
*   cheese, shredded*
3 eggs, beaten
3/4 cup milk
1 tsp. salt
1 tsp. leaf basil, crumbled
1/2 tsp. celery salt
2 medium tomatoes, peeled
*   and thinly sliced*
1 Tbsp. bread crumbs
1 Tbsp. Parmesan cheese

Place pie crust into a 9" pie plate. Press excess water out of cooked spinach and chop finely. Sauté green onions and garlic in butter until golden. Add spinach. Cook until excess moisture evaporates —stirring constantly. Combine spinach mixture, cheese, eggs, milk, salt, basil, and celery salt in a large bowl; stir. Turn into pastry shell. Arrange thinly sliced tomatoes around edge. Bake in 425° oven for 15 minutes and then 350° for 20 minutes. Combine bread crumbs and Parmesan cheese in small bowl; sprinkle over tomatoes. Bake 10 minutes longer or until top is puffy and center moves slightly when moved. Let stand 10 minutes before serving.

Mrs. John Scott (Marsha)

Use a tuna fish can opened at both ends and you have a perfect mold for poaching eggs or making English muffins.

QUICHE AUX CHAMPIGNONS
(Quiche with Mushrooms)

1 unbaked 9'' pastry shell
1 egg yolk
1 cup grated Swiss cheese
Fresh mushrooms, sliced
4 eggs
1 Tbsp. flour
1-1/2 tsp. salt
Freshly ground pepper
Pinch nutmeg
1-1/2 cups (13-oz. can)
    evaporated milk
2 Tbsp. green parsley, chopped

Line unbaked pastry with foil. Fill shell with beans or rice. Bake blind (without filling) at 425° for 14 minutes. Remove from oven. Remove foil and beans from pastry. Brush shell with beaten egg yolk. Return to oven and bake 2 minutes longer. (This provides a seal for the crust and prevents it from becoming soggy when baked with filling.) Sprinkle pre-baked pastry with cheese and line with mushroom slices. At this point it can be refrigerated for 24 hours or baked immediately. Beat eggs until lemon colored. Stir in flour and seasonings. Add milk and parsley. Mix until well blended. Pour into pre-baked pastry lined with cheese and mushrooms. Bake quiche in upper third of oven at 325° for approximately 45 minutes. To test for doneness, insert a knife in center. If it comes out clean, the quiche is done. Do not overbake. For easier serving, allow quiche to cool for a few minutes so that custard can set before cutting.
Note: A combination of regular milk and cream may be used in place of the evaporated milk.

Mrs. Bill Green (Mary)

To remove excessive water from fresh mushroom slices so that quiche or other dishes don't become watery: lay mushroom slices between layers of paper toweling and roll lightly with a rolling pin.

MEXICAN CHEESE CASSEROLE

Serves: 6-8

2 cans green chilies (4-oz. each, drained; or, 3 large chilies, milder flavored)
1 lb. Monterey Jack cheese (grated)
1 lb. Cheddar cheese (grated)
4 egg whites
4 egg yolks
2/3 cup canned evaporated milk
1 Tbsp. flour
1/2 tsp. salt
1/8 tsp. pepper
2 tomatoes (medium, sliced)

Preheat oven to 325°. Remove seeds from chilies and dice. Combine grated cheese and chilies in large bowl. Turn into a well buttered, shallow 2 qt. casserole. In large bowl, beat egg whites at high speed until stiff peaks form. In small bowl, mix egg yolks, milk, flour, salt and pepper until well blended. Gently fold beaten egg whites into egg yolk mixture using a rubber spatula. Pour egg mixture over cheese in casserole and using a fork, ooze it through cheese. Bake 30 minutes. Remove from oven and arrange sliced tomatoes around edge of casserole. Bake another 30 minutes, or until a knife comes out clean. Garnish with a sprinkling of chopped green chilies.

Mrs. Bruce Harvey (Jana)

PANHANDLE CASSEROLE
(Cookbook Committees' favorite brunch)

1 lb. lean, hot sausage
3 cans green chilies (4-oz.) each, drained)
1 lb. Cheddar cheese, grated
1-1/4 lb. Monterey Jack cheese, grated
9 eggs, beaten
1 cup milk
2 Tbsp. flour

Brown sausage and drain between paper towels. Layer sausage with cheeses and whole chilies in a 9" x 13" glass baking dish. Combine eggs, milk, and flour until well blended. Blender makes this step easier. Pour liquid over layered mixture. For a festive brunch, decorate top with strips of green chilies in a lattice design. Sprinkle with paprika and bake at 350° for 40 to 45 minutes. Slice and serve.

Kay Nicholas

Serving Suggestion: Serve with fresh fruit salad and "Berry Best Muffins."

INDIVIDUAL EGGLETS

Serves: 4-6

6 Tbsp. butter
6 eggs
6 Tbsp. cheese, grated
6 Tbsp. crumbled bacon or
    Bac-o's
6 tsp. minced parsley
Salt and pepper to taste
Worcestershire sauce
Paprika
Tabasco

Spray a 6-cup muffin tin with Pam. Place 1 Tbsp. butter in each muffin cup. Gently break egg into each cup and sprinkle with 1 Tbsp. cheese, 1 Tbsp. cooked bacon and 1 tsp. parsley. Add salt and pepper, Worcestershire, paprika and Tabasco to taste. Bake at 350° for 15-20 minutes.

Karol Hite

WESTERN SOUFFLÉ

Serves: 8-10

2 sticks margarine
8 slices bread
5 eggs
1-3/4 cups milk
Green pepper, chopped
Onion, chopped
Ham, chopped
Salt and pepper, to taste
Grated cheese

Melt butter and pour into a 9" x 12" baking dish. Cut bread into cubes and place in dish. Beat eggs and add milk. Sprinkle chopped peppers, onion and ham over bread. Salt and pepper to taste. Cover with shredded cheese. Pour egg mixture over cheese. Cover with foil and refrigerate overnight. Bake at 325° for 35 minutes. Remove foil and bake 10 minutes more. Let stand a few minutes before cutting.

Gail Wynne

 When cooking eggs in the shell, it helps prevent cracking if you put a big teaspoon of salt in the water.

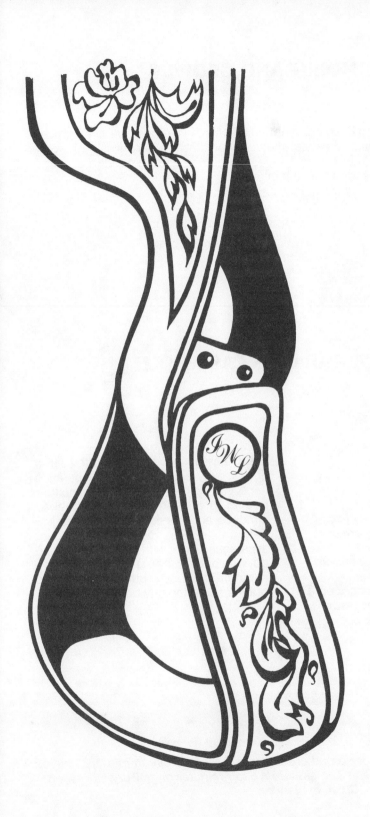

HOE'N AND GROW'N

VEGETABLES

"HOEIN' AND GROWIN' "

From Asparagus to Zucchini, whether steamed in lemon water or enhanced with a creamy almond sauce, these vegetables are sure to stir-up some great compliments to your menu. "Grown in the garden goodness"—your family and friends will really dig in!

ASPARAGUS CASSEROLE

Serves: 6-8

2 cans asparagus
2 Tbsp. butter
2 Tbsp. flour
3/4 cup light cream
3/4 cup asparagus juice
1 3-oz. pkg. chive cream
    cheese, diced
1/2 cup blanched almonds,
    chopped, or sliced
1/4 cup parsley, chopped
Salt and pepper to taste
1/4 cup bread crumbs
2 Tbsp. butter

Make a cream sauce: Melt butter, stir in flour, slowly add cream and asparagus juice, stirring over low heat until mixture begins to thicken. Add diced cheese, almonds and parsley, stirring over low heat until cheese dissolves. Pour over asparagus. Cover with bread crumbs and dot with butter. Cook in 400° oven for 15 minutes. This can be put together ahead of time, even the day before.

Mrs. Lee B. Thompson, Jr. (Ann)

 To make dry bread crumbs, cut 6 slices of bread into 1/2" cubes. Microcook in 3 qt. casserole 6 to 7 minutes or until dry, stirring after 3 minutes. Crush in blender.

BAKED ARTICHOKE HEARTS

Serves: 4

1 can artichoke hearts,
   drained and quartered
1/2 cup mayonnaise
1/2 cup Parmesan cheese
Dash of Tabasco
1 Tbsp. lemon juice
Garlic salt to taste
Paprika to taste

Combine all ingredients except paprika. Pour into buttered 1 qt. casserole dish. Sprinkle with paprika. Bake for 20 to 30 minutes at 350°.

Mrs. Steve Hendley (Mary Jo)

OKLAHOMA BAKED BEANS

Serves: 6-8

4 slices lean bacon, fried crisp
1/2 cup onion, chopped
1/4 cup green pepper, chopped
1/2 cup ketchup
1/4 cup brown sugar
1/4 cup Worcestershire sauce
1 tsp. barbecue seasoning
   (powdered)
1/2 tsp. liquid smoke
1 tsp. dry mustard
1 31-oz. can pork 'n beans,
   partially drained

In small skillet fry bacon, remove and set aside. Sauté onions and green pepper just until onion begins to become transparent. Drain on paper towels. In large bowl combine ketchup, brown sugar, Worcestershire, barbecue seasoning, liquid smoke and dry mustard. Skim liquid from top of beans while still in can and remove fatty pieces of pork. Combine beans, bacon, onion, and peppers with other ingredients. Pour in a 2 qt. buttered casserole and bake at 350° for 30-45 minutes.

Sherrel Jones

 When boiling corn on the cob, a little milk added to the water will sweeten and tenderize the corn.

SUMMERTIME BEETS

Serves: 2 to 2-1/2 cups

1/2 cup water or beet juice
1/2 cup cider vinegar
1 cup sugar (less if desired)
Pinch of salt
1 (16-oz.) jar Del Monte sliced
    beets, drained

Place the first 4 ingredients on medium heat and stir until sugar dissolves. Add beets. Let the juice get hot but not boiling (it shrivels them). Cook 3 to 5 minutes. Take off heat, but leave beets in juice until cool. Refrigerate for several hours. Keep juice in refrigerator and it can be used again. Note: If fresh beets are used, cook, peel, and add less sugar. Serve cool in the summertime.

Marion Nay

SWEET 'N SOUR BEETS

Serves: 8

3 #303 cans beets
1 cup sugar
2 Tbsp. cornstarch
1 cup vinegar (Tarragon or
    wine vinegar best)
4 whole cloves
3 Tbsp. ketchup
3 Tbsp. cooking oil
Dash salt
1 tsp. vanilla

Drain beets, reserve juice. Heat cooking oil, vinegar and ketchup. Combine sugar and cornstarch until well mixed. Stir sugar-cornstarch mixture into heated vinegar-oil mixture. Add vanilla and salt to taste. (Add enough water to reserved beet juice to make 1-1/2 cups juice.) Stir in beet juice. As mixture is heated and begins to thicken, stir in beets and cloves. Serve warm, or after cooling may be stored in refrigerator.

Mrs. Joe Vance (Wanda)

J-BAR BEAN BAKE

Serves: 12

1 30-oz. can pork and beans
1 15-oz. can red chili beans
    (drained)
1 8-1/2-oz. can small lima beans
    (drained)
1/4 lb. bacon (6 slices)
1/2 cup onion, chopped
1/2 cup ketchup
1/2 cup brown sugar
2 Tbsp. vinegar

Mix all beans and place in casserole. Fry bacon until brown. Remove from skillet, drain all but a small amount of grease. Fry onions. Add crumbled bacon and remaining ingredients. Pour over beans and mix. Bake at 350° for 1 hour, uncovered, in 8" x 11" (2 qt.) casserole which has been lightly greased.

Colleen Jantzen

EVERYONE'S FAVORITE BROCCOLI & RICE

Serves: 8

3/4 stick butter
1/2 cup onion, chopped
10-oz. pkg. frozen chopped
    broccoli, cooked
1 can cream of mushroom soup
2 cups cooked rice
8-oz. jar of Cheez Whiz

In heavy pan, melt butter and sauté onions. Add remaining ingredients one at a time, stirring to mix well. Add cheese. Pour into a greased 2-qt. baking dish. Bake at 300° for 30 minutes.
Note: Casserole can be made ahead and refrigerated or frozen.

Donna Messall's variation: Use 1/2 lb. grated or cubed Velveeta or Cheddar cheese along with 1/2 cup milk or cream in place of the Cheez Whiz.

Dee Everitt

BRUSSELS SPROUTS AND CASHEWS

(Enjoyed by those who don't usually care for brussels sprouts)

Serves: 4-6

3 cups water
2 chicken bouillon cubes
1/4 tsp. thyme
1/4 tsp. salt (or salt to taste)
2 lbs. fresh brussels sprouts (may
    substitute frozen)
'1/3 cup butter
3/4 cup dry-roasted cashew
    halves

Bring water to boil, add bouillon cubes, salt and thyme. When cubes have dissolved, add brussels sprouts. Cover pan. Cook over medium heat 12-15 minutes. Melt butter in small skillet. Add cashews and stir 3-4 minutes. Drain liquid from brussels sprouts. Pour butter and cashews over brussels sprouts. Serve.

Pat Reeves

GRANDMA'S SWEET AND SAUERKRAUT

Serves: 4-6

1/2 lb. bacon
2 onions, small to medium
30-oz. can (3-1/2 cups)
    sauerkraut
14 to 16-oz. can stewed
    tomatoes
1 cup brown sugar

Dice bacon and chop onion. Brown in heavy skillet and pour off grease. Add all other ingredients as listed and mix. Do not drain kraut or tomatoes. Place in 2-qt. baking dish. Bake for 1 hour at 350°, uncovered.

Mrs. Robert Harper (Sue)

RODE KOOL (Red Cabbage)

Serves: 4

1 medium-sized head red
    cabbage
1/4 cup vinegar
4-1/2 Tbsp. brown sugar
4 Tbsp. butter
1 tsp. salt
4 tart apples, quartered

Discard the outer leaves of the cabbage and shred finely. Cook cabbage with all other ingredients and 1 cup water, but use only 2 Tbsp. of the butter. Cook for 1/2 hour, stirring now and then and adding water if necessary. Add remaining butter before serving.

Mrs. Stu Meulpolder (Barbara)

CARROTS AU GRATIN

2 Tbsp. butter
2 Tbsp. flour
1 cup milk
1/2 tsp. onion, grated
1/2 tsp. salt
1/2 cup Cheddar cheese, grated
3-1/2 cups carrots, peeled,
    diced and cooked
1 tsp. celery salt
1 cup bread crumbs, sautéed
    in butter

Make a white sauce: In small sauce pan melt butter over medium heat. Add flour to butter and blend. Add milk, onion and salt. Cook until thick and smooth, stirring constantly. Stir in cheese. Alternate layers of carrots, sauce and celery salt in buttered casserole. Top with bread crumbs. Bake in 350° oven for 30 minutes.

Mrs. Lee Cromwell

GOLDEN CAULIFLOWER CASSEROLE

Serves: 8

1 medium sized cauliflower
5 small carrots, diced
1 small onion, chopped
2 Tbsp. butter, melted
3/4 cup milk
1/4 lb. (1 cup) grated cheddar
    cheese

Break cauliflower into flowerettes; arrange attractively with uncooked carrots in a greased 2-qt. casserole. Sprinkle on onion, salt, and paprika. Pour melted butter and milk over all and sprinkle with grated cheese. Cover and bake in a moderate oven (350°) for 45 minutes until vegetables are almost tender; remove cover and continue baking 15 minutes longer to brown lightly.

Ireta Hart

 When cooking cabbage, place a small tin cup or can half full of vinegar on the stove near the cabbage and it will absorb all odor from it.

CELERY WITH BUTTERED BREAD CRUMBS

Serves: 6

6 large hearts of celery or
    6 bulbs of fennel
8 Tbsp. unsalted butter
2 cups strong chicken broth
1-oz. plus 1 tsp. pernod or
    ricard
1 small clove garlic, bruised
1 tsp. whole fennel seeds
salt
Freshly ground pepper
1 cup soft bread crumbs

Cut celery into 1/2" slices. Combine celery, 3 Tbsp. butter and chicken stock in pan. Heat to boiling. Add 1 oz. pernod. Simmer until celery is tender-crisp. Drain. Rub shallow baking dish with garlic and 1 Tbsp. butter. Arrange celery in baking dish. Dot with 1 Tbsp. butter, salt, pepper and 1/2 tsp. fennel seeds. Sauté the bread crumbs in 3 Tbsp. butter—scatter over the celery. Bake at 350° for 35 to 40 minutes. (Omit last tsp. pernod if made with fennel bulbs.)

Mrs. Richard Davis (Elaine)

CORN CASSEROLE

Serves: 8

1 8-1/2-oz. pkg. cornbread mix
2-1/2 cups milk
1/2 cup vegetable oil
1 small onion, grated (optional)
1 can (17-oz.) cream style corn
1 can (17-oz.) whole kernel corn
1 Tbsp. sugar
1/2 tsp. salt
1 4-oz. can green chilies,
    chopped
4 eggs, beaten
2 cups Cheddar cheese,
    shredded

Combine cornbread mix, milk and oil; mix well. Stir in onion, corn, sugar, salt and chilies. Beat eggs and stir into mixture. Stir in 1-1/2 cups shredded cheese. Pour into a prepared 13" x 9" pan. Bake at 400° for 25 minutes. Sprinkle remaining 1/2 cup cheese over top. Continue baking 15-20 minutes.

Pat Reeves

WILD WEST CORN

Serves: 6-8

8-oz. pkg. cream cheese
1/2 cup milk
4-oz. can green chilies, diced
1 tsp. salt
2-oz. jar pimientos, drained
2 cans whole kernel corn,
    drained

Melt cream cheese and milk, stirring constantly. Add remaining ingredients. Pour into buttered 1-1/2-qt. casserole. Bake at 350° for 30 minutes uncovered. Variation: Shoe-peg corn can be used in place of whole kernel corn.

Mrs. Ralph Seals (Marcia)

CROWD PLEASIN' GREEN BEANS

Serves: 15-20

5 cans (16-oz.) whole
    green beans
2 cans cream of mushroom soup
2 cups sour cream
1 jar (4-oz.) pimiento
1 onion, grated
1 Tbsp. lemon juice
Rind of 1 lemon, grated
Lawry's Seasoned salt
Lawry's pepper
1 cup crushed seasoned
    croutons
1/2 cup Parmesan cheese

Place green beans in buttered 9" x 13" pyrex baking dish. Combine mushroom soup, sour cream, pimiento, onion, lemon juice and lemon rind. Pour over green beans. Sprinkle with Lawry's salt and pepper. Top with crushed croutons mixed with Parmesan cheese. Bake at 350° for 45 minutes.

Mrs. Fred Entriken (Sue)

SCALLOPED GREEN BEANS

Serves: 6-8

2 16-oz. cans green beans
1 can (10-3/4-oz.) cream of
    mushroom soup
1 small onion, chopped
4 strips bacon, fried and
    crumbled
1/2 cup American cheese,
    grated
Dash Tabasco sauce

Place beans in bottom of buttered 1-1/2 qt. casserole dish. Mix soup, onion, bacon, cheese and Tabasco. Pour soup mixture over beans. Bake in 350° oven for 20 minutes or until nicely browned and cheese is melted.

Beverly Evans

SAUTÉED GREEN BEANS WITH BUTTER & CHEESE

Serves: 6

1 lb. fresh green beans, crisp
    and snapped
1/4 cup butter
1/4 cup Parmesan cheese,
    freshly grated
Salt as required

Bring 4 qts. water and 1-1/2 Tbsp. salt to boil. Add snapped green beans. Heat on high until water returns to boil; then cook at a moderate boil. Do not cover. Boil until tender, but firm and crisp to bite, 6 to 12 minutes. Drain. Put beans into skillet with butter and lightly sauté over medium heat for 2 minutes. Add grated cheese and salt to taste. Transfer to a warm platter and serve immediately.
Dr. Chris Adelman
Great Falls, Montana

SWEET-SOUR GREEN BEANS

Serves: 8

1-1/2 cups cooking apples,
    cored and sliced with
    peeling left on
5 strips bacon
1/2 cup onion, chopped
3 Tbsp. brown sugar
3 Tbsp. cider vinegar
4 cups green beans, cooked
    and drained
2 tsp. parsley, chopped

Core and slice apples leaving peeling on. Cook bacon and drain. Pour most of grease out of skillet then sauté onions until brown. Remove from heat and blend in brown sugar and vinegar. Add green beans, apples and parsley. Heat all the ingredients. Serve immediately. Note: Do not use Red Delicious apples for cooking as they become mushy. Winesap, Johnathan and Granny Smith are good cooking varieties.

Betty Dillingham

TRUE GRITS

Serves: 12-15

4-1/2 cups boiling water
1-1/2 cups quick grits
1 tsp. salt
1 stick butter
1/2 lb. sharp longhorn cheese,
    grated
1/2 lb. mild longhorn cheese,
    grated
3 tsp. Lawry's salt
Worcestershire sauce, to taste
Tabasco, to taste

Cook grits in water and salt, according to box directions. Melt butter in cooked grits. Stir in cheeses to melt; add seasoning stirring well. Turn into buttered 13" x 9" pan and bake at 350° for 1 to 1-1/2 hours, till grits begin to brown. Can be frozen and baked later or refrigerated and baked later.

Mrs. Judy Halstead

FANCY GRITS

Serves: 12

1 qt. milk
1 stick margarine
1 cup grits
1 tsp. salt
1 tsp. pepper
1/3 cup additional margarine
1 cup New York sharp Cheddar
    cheese, grated
1/2 cup Parmesan cheese,
    grated

Bring milk almost to boiling. Add 1 stick margarine. Stir in grits. Cook until oatmeal consistency, about 5 minutes. Remove from heat. Add salt, pepper and additional margarine. Stir in cheddar cheese. Place in a buttered 2-qt casserole. Sprinkle with Parmesan cheese. Bake at 350° for 1 hour.

Mrs. Wallace Hite (Karol)

MARINATED MUSHROOMS

Serves: 6-8

1 lb. fresh mushrooms, sliced
    or quartered
2 Tbsp. soy sauce
1 tsp. pepper
1 clove garlic, crushed, or
    1/4 tsp. garlic powder
2 Tbsp. lemon juice
2 Tbsp. green onion, chopped
1 tsp. celery salt
1/4 cup vegetable oil

Combine all ingredients. Marinate at least 2 hours. Cook over medium heat. Serve as vegetable or over charcoaled steaks.

Mrs. John Wynne (Gail)

 For ease in washing a large amount of fresh mushrooms, use a salad spinner. Fill half full with water, add mushrooms, and spin. Repeat the process several times, then spin dry. This makes cleaning a pound of fresh mushrooms much easier.

MUSHROOMS 'N CREAM

Serves: 4-6

1 lb. mushrooms, sliced
1 Tbsp. butter
1/2 cup sour cream
1 Tbsp. flour
1/4 tsp. salt
Pepper, fresh ground to taste
1/2 cup grated Parmesan
    cheese
1/4 cup parsley, chopped

In heavy skillet sauté mushrooms in butter 2 minutes. Stir sour cream, flour, salt and pepper together and add to mushrooms. Heat until bubbly. Turn into shallow buttered baking dish, sprinkle with cheese and parsley and bake for 10 minutes at 425°.

Mrs. Jerry Shipley (Sally)

OKIE OKRA

Fresh okra, cut in 1/2" slices
    (allow 1 cup per person)
Salt to taste
Flour
2 to 3 Tbsp. bacon fat
    (per cup of okra)

Salt okra slices and shake in flour. Melt bacon fat in heavy skillet. Fry covered using low heat. Remove cover last 15 minutes. Okra is done when lightly brown, about 30 minutes. Variation: Corn meal may be substituted for flour or a combination of both may be used.

In Grandmother's day, bacon fat was used to fry okra and many still like this flavor. Frying uncovered in vegetable oil is also a favorite method of preparing okra in great plains kitchens of today. Selection tip: Look for fresh, young, small, tender pods. If pods are spotted or rubbery, do not use for frying.

Mrs. Terry Lewis (Barbara)

Mushrooms are best selected when caps are small and full underneath where cap joins stem.

SCALLOPED MUSHROOMS

Serves: 8

1-1/2 lbs. fresh mushrooms
1/4 cup butter
1/2 cup heavy cream
Salt, to taste
Red and black pepper
1-1/2 cups Monterrey Jack
    cheese, grated

Sauté mushrooms in butter for 5 minutes. Add cream and cook until liquid is almost gone, about 10 minutes. Add seasoning and pour into buttered casserole and cover with cheese. Bake at 400° just until cheese melts, about 10-15 minutes.

Sharon Iorio

OKRA GUMBO

Old Southern recipe from my great-grandmother

Serves: 6-8

2 cups okra, sliced
1 onion, chopped
1 can stewed tomatoes (2 cups)
2 Tbsp. bacon grease
Salt and pepper to taste

Mix all ingredients together in a pan and cook over medium heat until onions and okra are done, about 30-40 minutes. Can be served over cornbread or rice.

Diana Allen

JEANNETTE'S CREAMY COTTAGE POTATOES

Serves: 6-8

5 cups cooked potatoes, diced
2 tsp. salt
2 cups cottage cheese
1 cup sour cream
1/4 cup green onions, chopped
    including tops
1 small clove garlic, chopped
Butter
1/2 cup cheese, your choice,
    grated
Paprika

Combine all ingredients except grated cheese. Place in a 2-qt. buttered casserole. Dot with butter. Top with grated cheese. Sprinkle with paprika. Cook in 350° oven until it bubbles, approximately 30 minutes.

Mrs. E.B. Mitchell (Jean)

SWEDISH POTATOES

Serves: 4-6

6 large potatoes, peeled,
    boiled and mashed
3/4 cup light cream
Butter or margarine
Dash of pepper
2 tsp. salt
1 tsp. sugar
2 Tbsp. chopped chives
1-1/2 Tbsp. dill weed
1 pkg. frozen chopped spinach,
    partially cooked
    and drained

Mash potatoes, beat in cream. Add butter, salt, sugar and pepper. Whip until fluffy. Add chives, dill, and spinach. Place in greased casserole. Bake at 350° until hot, 15-20 minutes. Don't overheat. Good with fish.

Sue Harper

HITE'S DELIGHT
(Cheese Potato Sticks)

Serves: 4-6

4 large potatoes
1/4 cup butter
Salt
Onion salt
Paprika
1/4 cup Parmesan cheese,
    grated

Scrub potatoes thoroughly. Do not peel. Cut into strips slightly larger than for French frying. Soak in ice water for 30 minutes. Drain and dry. Preheat oven to hot (450°). Arrange a single layer of potatoes in a shallow greased baking pan. Brush with melted butter and sprinkle with salt, onion salt and paprika. Bake for 20 to 30 minutes, turning occasionally, until potatoes are crisp and brown on the outside but still tender on the inside. Sprinkle with Parmesan cheese, shaking the pan so that the potatoes are evenly coated. Serve hot.

Wally and Karol Hite

DILLY POTATO SAUCE

(Great over new spring potatoes.)

Serves: 6

2 Tbsp. butter
2 Tbsp. flour
1-1/2 tsp. salt
1 cup milk
1/2 cup mayonnaise
1/4 tsp. pepper
1 tsp. dill weed
1 tsp. onion, chopped
6 potatoes, cooked with jackets,
    peeled and sliced

Make a white sauce: In small sauce pan, over medium heat, melt butter. Add flour to butter and blend. Add milk and salt. Cook until thick and smooth, stirring constantly. Blend in mayonnaise, pepper, dill weed and chopped onion. Arrange cooked potato slices in shallow baking dish, cover with dilly sauce and bake for 30 minutes at 350°, or use as a sauce to pour over potatoes which have been pre-cooked, peeled and sliced.
Variation: Good over new potatoes which have been cooked in their jackets.

Jean Hill

MASHED POTATOES PARMESAN

(A Great Plains Tradition with an Italian Flair.)

Serves: 4

1 lb. boiling potatoes
3 Tbsp. butter
1/2 cup milk
1/3 cup Parmesan cheese,
    freshly grated
Salt to taste

Boil potatoes unpeeled in enough water to cover. Cook until tender. Drain and peel while hot. Begin whipping with electric mixer. In small sauce pan, melt butter and add milk. As milk is heated almost to the boiling point, pour into mixing bowl with potatoes and continue beating. While mixer is running sprinkle cheese into potato mixture. Add salt to taste. Amount of salt will vary as some Parmesan cheeses are already heavily salted. Whip until light and fluffy and serve piping hot.

Dr. Chris Adelman
Great Falls, Montana

ORANGE GLAZED SWEET POTATOES

Sweet potatoes, 6 medium (or enough for occasion)
Orange marmalade, to taste (8-oz. jar)
Butter, to taste

Boil sweet potatoes in their skins until almost tender. Peel and cut in thick lengthwise slices. Place in shallow buttered casserole in overlapping rows. Store in refrigerator until ready for baking. Salt and cover thickly with orange marmalade. Dot with butter and bake at 325° for 30-40 minutes or until potatoes are candied and brown.

Mrs. Gene Carrier

HARVEST POTATOES

Serves: 10

32 oz. frozen hash brown potatoes, thawed
1 can cream of chicken soup
8 oz. sour cream
8 oz. American cheese, shredded
1/2 cup margarine, melted
1-1/2 tsp. salt
1 medium onion, diced
TOPPING:
2 cups corn flakes, crushed
1/4 cup margarine, melted

Combine all ingredients in a greased 13'' x 9'' pyrex baking dish. Top with cornflake mixture. Bake at 350° for 45 minutes.

Mrs. Bob Anderson (Pat)

BACON CHEESE POTATOES

Serves: 6

4 large baking potatoes, peeled
    and sliced
1 large onion, chopped
1/2 cup celery, chopped
1/2 cup green pepper, chopped
2/3 cup margarine
6 slices bacon, cooked and
    crumbled
1 8-oz. pkg. American cheese or
    1 cup shredded Cheddar
    cheese or cheese of
    your choice

Place potato slices on large piece of heavy foil. Cover with onion, celery and green pepper. Season with salt, pepper and butter. Sprinkle with bacon and cover with cheese slices. Seal tightly. Bake at 350° for 1 hour. Also can be prepared on grill.

Variation: New potatoes with peeling intact may be used in place of baking potatoes.

Mrs. Gary Hansen (Patti)

FANCY FOREIGN PEAS

Serves: 12

1 lb. fresh mushrooms, sliced
3 Tbsp. butter or margarine
3 pkgs. (16-oz.) frozen peas
2 8-1/2-oz. cans water
    chestnuts, drained
    and sliced
2 8-1/2-oz. cans bamboo shoots,
    drained
2 10-3/4-oz. cans cream of
    mushroom soup
French fried onion rings,
    to taste

Sauté mushrooms in butter. Precook peas briefly. Mix all ingredients except onion rings. Pour into 11"x 13" buttered casserole and bake at 350° for 30 minutes. Crumble onion rings over top and bake 5 to 10 minutes longer. (Bean sprouts (16-oz. can) may replace the bamboo shoots.) May be made early in the day and refrigerated until 30 minutes before serving.

Mrs. Jerri Cook (Rita)

HOLIDAY PEAS

Serves: 4

1 box frozen peas
2 cups celery, chopped
1/2 cup onion, diced
3 oz. mushrooms
2 Tbsp. pimiento, chopped
1/2 tsp. salt
1/2 tsp. savory salt
1/4 tsp. pepper

Sauté celery and onion. Add remaining ingredients and heat thoroughly.

Virginia Semrad

ITALIAN STYLE PEAS

Serves: 4

1/2 cup water
1 8-oz. pkg. frozen peas
1/2 tsp. salt
1/4 tsp. garlic powder
2 Tbsp. olive oil
2 Tbsp. sugar
2 Tbsp. tomato paste

Mix all ingredients together. Bring to a boil, lower heat and simmer uncovered for 10-15 minutes.

Lori Carroll

AMBIDEXTROUS SOUFFLE (Spinach or Broccoli)

Serves: 8-10

2 pkgs. frozen spinach or
    broccoli
1 pkg. Lipton's onion soup
1/2 pt. sour cream

Thaw spinach or broccoli into ungreased casserole. Do not drain. Mix in soup and sour cream. Bake 350° for 30 minutes.
Mrs. J. Russell Swanson (Tina)

BAKED SPINACH CASSEROLE

Serves: 6

1 10-oz. pkg. frozen chopped
    spinach
3 eggs
3/4 cup flour
1 tsp. salt
Pepper
1 lb. small curd cottage cheese
2 cups Cheddar cheese,
    shredded

Cook spinach, drain, set aside. Beat eggs; add flour, salt, pepper and cottage cheese. Stir in spinach and Cheddar cheese. Blend well. Bake in 8" x 8" or 9" x 9" dish sprayed with Pam. Bake at 350°, covered, for 30 minutes. Uncover. Bake 30 minutes more. Cool 5-10 minutes.

Mrs. Dennis Iselin (Mary Helen)

SPINACH CASSEROLE

Serves: 4

1 pkg. frozen chopped spinach
3 oz. cream cheese and chives
    (or 1/2 tsp. chives)
1 can (10-3/4-oz.) cream of
    mushroom soup
1 egg, beaten
Bread crumbs or corn bread
    stuffing mix

Cook spinach according to directions and drain. Blend cream cheese and soup with beaten egg. Mix with spinach. Place in buttered 1-1/2 to 2-qt. casserole. Top with bread crumbs or corn bread stuffing mix. Bake at 350° for 45 minutes.

Joy Baker

ITALIAN ZUCCHINI

Serves: 4

8 zucchini, cut in 1" chunks
1 8-oz. can tomato sauce
2 Tbsp. olive oil
1/4 cup water
Salt and pepper, to taste
1/4 tsp. basil
2 cloves garlic

Combine all ingredients in sauce pan. Bring to boil and then lower to simmer. Cover and cook till zucchini is tender. Remove garlic before serving. (Tip: garlic cloves may be placed on toothpick for easy removal.)

Mrs. Buddy Carroll (Lori)

STUFFED SUMMER SQUASH

Serves: 8

4 summer squash, yellow
1/4 tsp. paprika
1/2 tsp. Worcestershire sauce
Dash cayenne
1/8 tsp. curry powder
Minced onion, to taste
1/4 tsp. salt
1 Tbsp. butter
1/4 cup Cheddar cheese,
    grated
1 2-oz. can mushrooms, drained

Wash squash; steam until barely tender. When cool, halve lengthwise and scoop out centers, leaving shell about 1/4" thick. Chop remaining pulp and add remaining ingredients. Refill shells. Bake in 400° oven till done, about 20 minutes.
Note: Squash may be steamed until tender, stuffed, then microwaved till warm and served immediately. Bread crumbs, chopped ham or other cooked meat, and almost any leftover may be added.

Mrs. Don Stehr (Janet)

CHEESE PLEASE SQUASH

Serves: 4-6

2 lbs. yellow squash (or a
    combination of yellow,
    zucchini and white
    summer squash), washed,
    pared and sliced
1 medium onion, chopped
1/2 cup sour cream
2 eggs, beaten
2 Tbsp. butter
2 Tbsp. sugar
1/2 cup Cheddar cheese,
    shredded
1 tsp. salt
Pepper
1 cup cracker crumbs
Slivered almonds (optional)

Cook squash and onion in small amount of water until tender. Drain and rinse. Add sour cream, eggs, butter, sugar, cheese, salt and pepper. Place in buttered 9" x 13" baking dish. Bake for 15 minutes at 350°. Remove from oven, cover with cracker crumbs and slivered almonds and bake an additional 15-20 minutes.
Peggy Munn's Variation: Increase cheese to 1-1/2 cups and use 1 cup milk in place of sour cream. Omit sugar and increase butter to 4 Tbsp. Mix 1/2 cup cracker crumbs with squash mixture and top with remaining 1/2 cup.

Mrs. Dennis Iselin (Mary Helen)

ZIPPY ZUCCHINI

Serves: 6

6 strips crisp bacon
1 Tbsp. butter
1/2 onion
1 tomato, chopped
4 medium zucchini squash,
    peeled
1 cup Cheddar cheese,
    shredded
Salt and pepper
Garlic powder, to taste
	Brown bacon and drain on paper towel. Reserve 1 Tbsp. fat in skillet. Add 1 Tbsp. butter and sauté 1/2 onion which has been cut into 1/4'' rings. Add chopped tomatoes. Grease casserole dish. Slice zucchini lengthwise. Layer squash, onion, crumbled bacon, tomato mixture and 1 cup shredded Cheddar cheese. Between layers add salt, pepper and garlic powder to taste. End layers with cheese on top. Bake covered at 350° for 20 minutes. Uncover; bake 20 minutes more.

Mrs. Doug Frantz (Dianne)

BAKED SQUASH SUPREME

Serves: 6

1-1/2 lbs. yellow squash, cut up
1 cup sour cream
1 can (10-3/4-oz.) cream of
    chicken soup, undiluted
1 small onion, chopped
1 large carrot, grated
4 Tbsp. butter, melted
1/2 pkg. Pepperidge Farm
    stuffing mix
	Cook squash in small amount of water until tender. Drain well and add remaining ingredients, except stuffing mix. Pour into well buttered 2 qt. casserole and bake at 350° for 30 minutes.
	Vivi Johnson's Variation: Use Cheddar cheese soup in place of cream of chicken soup. Place 1/2 of stuffing mix in bottom of well buttered casserole and remaining mix on top of squash mixture.

Mrs. Dennis Iselin (Mary Helen)

 A small flower from fresh dill weed lends an interesting flavorful garnish to squash.

ZUCCHINI PARMESAN

Serves: 6

3 large zucchini split lengthwise
(not peeled)
Butter or margarine
Lawry's Garlic Salt
Paprika
Parmesan cheese
Pepper

Spread squash with butter and sprinkle with garlic salt, pepper, Parmesan cheese and paprika. Bake on a baking sheet in a 350° oven for 30 to 40 minutes, until squash is done.

Mrs. Tim Traynor (Suzy)

RATATOUILLE

Serves: 8

1 small eggplant
3 or 4 medium zucchini
1 green pepper
1/3 cup olive oil
2 Tbsp. white vinegar
2 cloves garlic, crushed
1-1/2 tsp. salt
1 cup thin onion slices
3 medium tomatoes
2 Tbsp. sugar
1/2 tsp. dried basil leaves
1/2 tsp. dried oregano leaves

Peel eggplant, cut in 3/8 inch slices, then cut slices into strips about 3 inches by 1 inch. Cut zucchini into 1-1/2 inches by 1/4 inch sticks. Cut green pepper into 1/4" strips. Combine oil, vinegar, garlic and salt. In 3 qt. casserole, layer eggplant and zucchini and drizzle half of oil mixture over top. Layer onion and pepper next and add remaining oil mixture. Cover casserole. Bake at 350° for 45 minutes. Remove from oven; cover top with peeled, sliced tomatoes, sugar, basil and oregano. Bake uncovered 15 minutes longer.

Mrs. Jerry Shipley (Sally)

 Steam vegetables in lemon water for light aroma and flavor. Zucchini, broccoli, and fresh asparagus work well with this method. Add two tablespoons of lemon juice to water before steaming. A zest of lemon is a perfect garnish.

ZUCCHINI SURPRISE

2 zucchini, cut in chunks
(1 if it is large)
1/2 medium onion, chopped
6 oz. Monterey Jack cheese
shredded
6 oz. Cheddar cheese,
shredded
1 16-oz. can tomatoes, drained
1/2 tsp. salt
1/8 tsp. pepper

Cut up zucchini, onion and crumble the two cheeses in a buttered casserole dish. Add the can of tomatoes and stir. Add salt and pepper. Bake in 375° oven about 45 minutes until the zucchini is tender. You can substitute 1 can of zucchini rather than fresh.

Rosanne Dickinson

EGGPLANT PARMESAN

Serves: 6-8

1 large eggplant
2 eggs, slightly beaten
1-1/2 cups fine dry seasoned
bread crumbs
1/2 to 1 cup olive oil
2 15-oz. cans tomato sauce
with mushrooms
1-1/2 tsp. dried oregano leaves
1/2 tsp. salt
1/2 cup Parmesan cheese,
grated
1/2 lb. Mozzarella cheese,
thinly sliced

Pare and slice eggplant crosswise into 1/4" slices. Dip slices into beaten eggs and then into crumbs. Coat each slice completely. Heat enough oil to cover bottom of large skillet over medium heat. Fry eggplant until browned on both sides. Drain slices on paper towels. In buttered 8" baking dish, layer eggplant, tomato sauce, seasonings and cheeses, ending with Mozzarella. Bake at 350° for 25-30 minutes. Note: This is enough tomato sauce for 2 eggplants, if desired.

Mrs. Jerry Shipley (Sally)

 Eggplant slices for quick eating or special additions to casseroles may be brushed with melted butter and placed in 425 degree oven for ten minutes. Excess water may be removed before brushing with butter by placing eggplant slices between paper toweling and rolling lightly with a rolling pin.

MANY VEGETABLE CASSEROLE

Serves: 10-12

1 can (10-3/4-oz.) cream of
    mushroom soup, undiluted
1/2 to 3/4 cup Cheddar cheese,
    grated
Salt and pepper to taste
1 can (16-oz.) tiny LeSueur
    carrots, drained
1 can (16-oz.) green beans,
    drained
1 pkg. (16-oz.) frozen peas,
    cooked
1 can (8-1/2-oz.) water
    chestnuts, sliced and
    drained
1 can (8-oz.) mushrooms,
    drained
1 cup bread crumbs, sautéed
    in butter (optional)

Heat soup and add cheese. Stir until melted. Combine with vegetables and salt and pepper and place in a buttered 1-1/2 qt. baking dish. Top with bread crumbs, if desired. Bake at 350° for 30 minutes.

Jane Champlin

ESCALLOPED TOMATOES

Serves: 8-10

1/4 cup butter or margarine
1 small onion (chopped)
2 cups bread cubes (butter
    bread slices and cube,
    toast slightly in 350
    oven)
1 tsp. salt
1/4 tsp. pepper
1/2 tsp. basil
Bread crumbs, optional
2 14-1/2-oz. cans
    tomato wedges
4 tsp. sugar

Preheat oven to 375°. Sauté onion in butter until tender. Add bread cubes, salt, basil and pepper. Add sugar and tomatoes. Bake in 1-1/2 to 2 qt. casserole at 375° for 30 minutes or until hot and bubbly. May add bread crumbs over top if desired.

Mrs. Steve Frantz (Tana)

TOMATOES ROCKEFELLER

Serves: 36-48 slices

2 pkgs. cut frozen spinach
1 clove garlic, pressed
1/2 onion, chopped fine
2 sticks butter
1-3/4 cups bread crumbs
1/2 cup Parmesan cheese
1/2 tsp. Cayenne pepper
1/2 tsp. thyme
1 tsp. black pepper
1 Tbsp. Accent (optional)
3 eggs, beaten
12 fresh tomatoes, sliced
    1/2'' thick

Cook spinach according to directions. Add garlic, onion and butter to hot spinach. Stir in next 6 ingredients, let cool, then add beaten eggs. Using large spoon, heap spinach mixture on top of tomato slices. Bake on greased cookie sheet in 325° oven for 20 minutes.
Serving Suggestion: Wonderful garnish served individually—or use several slices as a hot appetizer for a pre-dinner treat.
Committee suggestion: Spinach may be topped with additional grated Parmesan cheese or pimento slice.

Joanna Champlin

CREAMY TURNIPS WITH DILL WEED

Serves: 6-8

5 cups turnips, peeled and
    sliced (about 4 medium)
1/2 tsp. sugar
1/4 tsp. salt

CREAM SAUCE:
4 Tbsp. butter
1-1/2 cup milk
2 Tbsp. flour
1/2 tsp. dill weed
1/8 tsp. salt

Place turnips in pan. Add enough water to barely cover turnips. Add sugar and salt to turnips. Cook 10-12 minutes (until just done, do not overcook) or you may wish to steam the turnips. Remove from heat, drain off liquid, cover to keep warm while making cream sauce.

CREAM SAUCE: Melt butter in small sauce pan. Stir in flour until well dissolved. Remove from heat momentarily while slowly pouring in milk. Stir well and return to heat, add dill weed and salt. Continue stirring over medium-low heat until sauce thickens. Transfer turnips to serving dish and pour cream sauce over them. This cream sauce is also very good over cooked cauliflower.

Pat Reeves

FRIED GREEN TOMATOES

Serves: 8

6 large, firm green tomatoes
1 cup cornmeal
Salt and pepper to taste
Bacon drippings or cooking oil

Slice tomatoes 1/4 inch thick. Season with salt and pepper. Coat with cornmeal. Add tomato slices to heated bacon drippings in skillet. Fry slowly, turning once. Variation: May want to use flour instead of cornmeal.

Colleen Jantzen

VEGETABLE AND WATER CHESTNUT CASSEROLE

Serves: 6-8

1 (16-oz.) can white corn, drained
1 (16-oz.) can French cut green beans, drained
1/2 cup celery, chopped
1/2 cup onion, chopped
1/4 cup green pepper, chopped
1/2 cup sharp cheese, grated
1/2 cup sour cream
1 (10-1/2-oz.) can cream of celery soup
1 (8-1/2-oz.) can water chestnuts
Salt and pepper to taste

TOPPING:
Crumbled cheese crackers, to taste (approximately 3/4 cup)
1/4 cup butter, melted

Mix all ingredients together. Place in buttered 1-1/2 qt. casserole and sprinkle with topping. Bake at 350° for 45 minutes.

Jana Harvey

GARDEN VEGETABLE BAKE

Serves: 8

2 zucchini, sliced
1 small cauliflower, broken
   into flowerettes
1 small green pepper, sliced
2 yellow squash, sliced
1 small onion, sliced
2 tomatoes, sliced
1/3 cup vegetable oil or less
Salt and pepper to taste

Layer sliced vegetables in buttered casserole. Sprinkle oil over top and season with salt and pepper. Cover tightly with foil. Bake at 350° for 35 minutes. Should be firm, not mushy.

Gretchen Young

CHRISTMAS CASSEROLE

Serves: 6-8

1 pkg. (10-oz.) frozen
   cauliflower
1 pkg. (16-oz.) frozen peas
1 can (8-oz.) sliced mushrooms
1-1/2-oz. chopped pimiento
1/2 lb. sharp Cheddar cheese,
   grated

SAUCE:
1 can (10-3/4-oz.) cream of
   mushroom soup, heated
1 can milk

Cook cauliflower and peas according to package directions. Make 2 separate layers of vegetables in buttered 9" x 12" glass baking dish, with mushrooms, pimientos and cheese mixture between the layers. Pour heated sauce mixture over this. Heat thoroughly at 250° for approximately 30-45 minutes and serve. Can be made ahead and frozen.

Elaine Davis

 Shapes from cheese slices and pimiento add appropriate designs and a festive touch to any favorite vegetable casserole.

THREE VEGETABLE CASSEROLE

Serves: 10-12

2 pkgs. (16-oz.) frozen
    green beans
2 pkgs. (16-oz.) frozen
    green peas
2 pkgs (16-oz.) frozen
    lima beans
2 or 3 green peppers, cut in
    strips
Juice of 1 large lemon
Salt and pepper to taste

SAUCE:
1 cup mayonnaise
1/4 cup Parmesan cheese
1 cup heavy cream, whipped

Pre-heat oven to 325°. Cook frozen vegetables separately according to directions. Place in buttered casserole in three layers with green pepper strips between each layer. Salt and pepper each layer and sprinkle with lemon juice. Add mayonnaise to cheese. Fold in whipped cream. Pour on top of vegetables. Bake approximately 30 minutes, until browned. This is very rich.

Mrs. Jon Ford (Jane)

VEGIE CHEESE SAUCE

1 8-oz. pkg. of cream cheese
3/4 cup milk
1/2 cup Parmesan cheese
1/2 tsp. garlic salt
1/2 tsp. salt

Soften cream cheese. Gradually add milk to softened cheese. Heat on low and stir in Parmesan cheese. Add seasoning. (An egg whisk works best for stirring, if you have one.)
Note: Great on broccoli and a variety of vegetables.

Mrs. Paul Fossett (Suzanne)

 Chicken broth adds a flavorful and low calorie seasoning in place of butter on vegetables.

RICE WITH SOUR CREAM AND CHILIES

Serves: 4-6

1 cup rice, uncooked
1 can (4-oz.) chopped green
   chilies
1-1/4 cups dairy sour cream
1/2 lb. sharp Cheddar cheese,
   shredded
Salt and pepper to taste
2 Tbsp. butter

Cook rice according to package directions. Combine rice, chilies, sour cream and 3/4 of the cheese, salt and pepper. Mix lightly but thoroughly. Place in buttered 2-qt. casserole. Sprinkle with remaining cheese. Dot with butter. Bake in preheated oven uncovered at 350° for 30 minutes or until golden brown on top.

Mrs. Jerry Shipley
Mrs. Carol Barrack

COMPANY SAUERKRAUT

Yield: 2 quarts

1 qt. kraut, drained
1/2 cup green peppers, diced
1/2 cup green onions, diced
1/2 cup celery, diced
1-1/2 cups sugar
1-1/2 cups vinegar

Mix drained kraut, onion, pepper and celery. Boil remaining ingredients and pour over kraut. Let ripen in refrigerator for 48 hours. Serve with roast pork, turkey and barbequed meats.

Mrs. Richard Risley (Kathy)

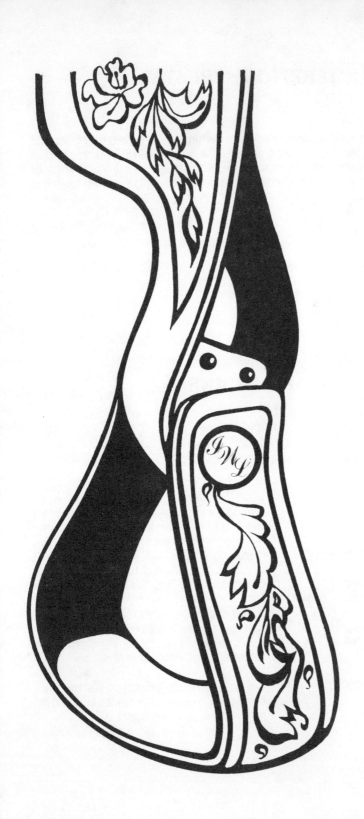

TERRITORY TREATS

DESSERTS

"TERRITORY TREATS"

Even before statehood, Oklahoma Territory families enjoyed that good old fashioned fellowship of a church social or a barn raising. You don't have to raise a barn to share these taste-tempting treats with your friends or neighbors. These rip-snortin' desserts are guaranteed to become favorites in your territory, too!

APPLE CAKE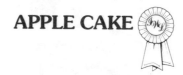

Serves: 16

3 cups sifted flour
1 tsp. soda
1 tsp. cinnamon
2 cups sugar
3 eggs
1-1/4 cups vegetable oil
1 tsp. vanilla
1/4 cup orange juice
2 cups unpared apples, grated
    or finely cut
1 cup walnuts, chopped
1 cup flaked coconut

Sift flour, soda, and cinnamon onto waxed paper. Combine sugar, oil, eggs, vanilla, and orange juice in large bowl. Beat until well blended. Stir in flour mixture until mixed well. Fold in apples, walnuts, and coconut. Spoon into well greased and floured tube pan. Bake at 325° for 1-1/2 hours. Cool on wire rack for 15 minutes. Remove cake from pan to serving plate with a raised edge. Puncture cake with toothpick or fork. Spoon hot buttermilk sauce over warm cake several times until all is absorbed.

BUTTERMILK SAUCE:
1 cup sugar
1/2 cup buttermilk

Cook, stirring constantly, over medium heat until mixture comes to boil. While hot, spoon over warm cake.

Mrs. Bruce Harvey (Jana)

APPLE DAPPLE CAKE

3 eggs
1-1/2 cups salad oil
2 cups sugar
3 cups flour
1 tsp. salt
1 tsp. soda
2 tsp. vanilla
3 cups apples, chopped
1 cup pecans, chopped

Mix eggs, oil, and sugar. Combine flour, salt, and soda and add to egg mixture. Add vanilla, apples, and nuts. Pour into greased 8-inch or 9-inch tube pan. Bake at 350° for 1 hour. While cake is still hot, pour hot topping over it in the pan and let cool. Remove cake from pan when completely cool.

TOPPING:
1 cup brown sugar,
    firmly packed
1/4 cup milk
1/2 cup margarine

Combine all ingredients and cook for 2-1/2 minutes. Pour immediately over cake in pan.

Ann Frazee Riley

RAW APPLE CAKE

2 cups sugar
2 eggs
1/2 cup salad oil
2 cups flour
2 tsp. soda
1/2 cup pecans, chopped
1 tsp. vanilla
4 cups apples, chopped
    (Winesap)
2 tsp. cinnamon
1/8 tsp. salt

Mix sugar, eggs and salad oil together. Add remaining ingredients and mix thoroughly. Pour in greased and floured 9"x12" pan and bake at 350° for 45 minutes.

TOPPING
6 oz. cream cheese, softened
4 Tbsp. butter (real)
1 cup powdered sugar
1/2 tsp. vanilla

Mix softened cream cheese with remaining ingredients. Spread on cooled cake.

Pat Diel

BELIEVE IT OR NOT CAKE

Serves: 12

2/3 cup butter, softened
1-1/2 cups sugar
3 eggs
1 tsp. vanilla
1/2 cup unsweetened cocoa
2-1/4 cups sifted flour
1 tsp. baking soda
2/3 cup sauerkraut, rinsed
    and chopped
1 cup beer

Cream butter and sugar together; beat in eggs and vanilla. Combine dry ingredients (cocoa, flour, and soda) and stir into wet mixture. Stir in sauerkraut and beer. Grease and flour two 8-inch round pans or one 9 x 11-inch oblong pan. Bake at 350° for 40 minutes.

FROSTING:
8 oz. German sweet baking
    chocolate
6 oz. cream cheese
2 Tbsp. cream (half & half)
2 cups powdered sugar, sifted
1/4 tsp. salt
1 tsp. vanilla

Melt chocolate in double boiler until just melted. Remove from heat and blend in cream cheese and light cream. Beat in powdered sugar and salt and vanilla.

Pat Reeves

CARROT CAKE

Serves: 15

2 cups cake flour, sifted
2 cups sugar
2 tsp. baking soda
2 tsp. cinnamon
4 eggs
1 tsp. salt
1 cup cooking oil
3 cups shredded carrots
1 tsp. vanilla

Combine flour, sugar, soda, cinnamon, salt and oil. Beat in eggs one at a time. Beat in carrots and vanilla. Pour into two greased 9" cake pans or a 9 x 13-inch loaf pan. Bake the 9" ones at 350° for 30 minutes. Bake 1 hour when using loaf pan.
Icing: Cream butter with cream cheese. Add sugar, vanilla and pecans. Beat until well blended. Spread between layers and over cake, or on top of 9 x 13-inch pan.

ICING:
1 stick butter
8 oz. cream cheese, softened
1 box powdered sugar
1 cup pecans, chopped
1 tsp. vanilla

Mona Payne

KATHY'S CARROT CAKE

Serves: 16-20

1-1/2 cups salad oil
2 cups sugar
2 cups flour
3 cups carrots, grated
1/2 cup walnuts, chopped
1 tsp. salt
4 eggs
2 tsp. soda
4 tsp. cinnamon
2 tsp nutmeg

ICING:
8 oz. softened cream cheese
1 stick butter, softened
1 lb. powdered sugar
3 tsp. vanilla
1 cup coconut (optional)
3 small boxes raisins (optional)
1/2 cup nuts

Mix oil, sugar, flour, and carrots. Add all other ingredients. Mix well. Pour into greased, floured pan 9 x 13-inch. Bake at 350° for approximately 50 minutes. Icing: Mix well and spread on cake.

Nan Brim

DATE CAKE

Serves: 8-12

1 lb. dates
1 lb. candied cherries
1 lb. candied pineapple
2 lbs. pecans
8 eggs
2 cups flour
2 Tbsp. baking powder
1 tsp. salt
2 cups sugar
2 tsp. vanilla

Cut dates and pineapple in almond-sized pieces. Cut cherries in half and chop nuts. Sift 1 cup of the flour over the fruit. Sift remaining flour with baking powder and salt. Beat eggs, sugar and vanilla together. Add dry ingredients and stir in fruit and nuts. Bake in 3 loaf pans, greased and floured. Bake at 275° for 1-1/2 hours. Place pan of water in bottom of oven underneath cakes. Cool on racks; saturate with rum and wrap in aluminum foil. Store in cool place.

Mrs. Earl Mitchell (Jean)

BETTY'S BUTTERMILK CAKE

3 cups sugar
1/2 cup butter
1/2 cup shortening
4 cups cake flour
1 tsp. salt
1 tsp soda
1/2 tsp. baking powder
2 cups buttermilk
1 Tbsp. vanilla
1 tsp. almond flavoring
6 egg whites

Cream sugar, butter, and shortening. Sift cake flour 3 times, the last time adding salt, soda, and baking powder. Add the flour alternately with the buttermilk mixed with vanilla and almond flavoring. Beat in 6 egg whites, one at a time, beating approximately 5 minutes after each egg. Pour into 3 greased and floured 9-inch cake pans. Cook 15 minutes at 350°, then 15 minutes more at 325°. Watch carefully. This is good with coconut cream frosting. This cake is a bit of trouble to make, but elegant and well worth the trouble.

COCONUT CREAM FROSTING:
1 cube margarine, softened
8 oz. cream cheese, softened
1 box powdered sugar
1 cup coconut
1/2 cup pecans, chopped
1 tsp. vanilla

Use large mixing bowl and electric mixer. Whip margarine and cream cheese together scraping bowl often. When mixture is light and fluffy, slowly add sifted powdered sugar. Add vanilla and beat well. Stir in coconut and pecans or sprinkle on top.

Mrs. Joe McDermott (Betty)

HEAVENLY CHEESECAKE

1 stick butter, melted
1-3/4 cup graham cracker
    crumbs, ground
Dash cinnamon
1/4 cup pecans, ground
3 eggs, beaten
2 (8-oz.) packages cream
    cheese, softened
Pinch salt
1 cup sugar
2 tsp. vanilla
1/2 tsp. almond extract
1-1/2 pt. (3 cups) sour cream

Mix butter, graham cracker crumbs, cinnamon, and pecans together and press into spring-form pan. Save 3 Tbsp. mixture to sprinkle on top. Mix eggs, cream cheese, salt, sugar, vanilla, and almond extract well until smooth. Add sour cream and blend all together. Pour in pan and sprinkle crumbs on top. Bake at 375° for 35 minutes or until just set. Cool at least 5 hours. May be served plain or with favorite fruit topping.

Mrs. Bill Word (Janie)

GRANDMOTHER'S CHEESECAKE

Serves: 12-14

1 cup all-purpose flour
1/4 cup sugar
1 tsp. lemon peel, grated
1 tsp. orange peel, grated
1-inch piece vanilla bean or
*   1/4 tsp. vanilla*
1/2 cup unsalted sweet butter
1 egg yolk
5 (8-oz.) packages cream
*   cheese, softened*
1-3/4 cups sugar
3 Tbsp. flour
1-1/2 tsp. lemon peel, grated
1-1/2 tsp. orange peel, grated
1-inch piece vanilla bean or 1/4
*   tsp. vanilla*
5 eggs
2 egg yolks
1/4 cup whipping cream

Combine 1 cup flour, 1/4 cup sugar, 1 tsp. lemon peel, and orange peel. Split 1-inch piece vanilla bean; scrape out seeds. Add seeds to flour mixture. Cut in butter until mixture resembles coarse crumbs. Add 1 egg yolk; stir until all flour is moistened. Gather dough into ball; refrigerate, wrapped in waxed paper, 90 minutes. Roll dough on lightly floured surface 1/8-inch thick; trim to 10-inch circle. Reserve pastry trimmings. Press pastry circle into bottom and 1/2 inch up side of 9 x 3-inch buttered springform pan. Refrigerate 1 hour. Heat oven to 400.° Bake pastry until light brown, about 20 minutes. Cool on wire rack 15 minutes. Beat cream cheese, 1-3/4 cups sugar, 3 Tbsp. flour, 1-1/2 tsp. lemon, and orange peel in large mixer bowl on medium speed until light and fluffy, about 10 minutes. Split 1-inch piece vanilla bean; scrape out seeds. Add seeds to cream cheese mixture. Beat in 5 eggs and 2 egg yolks, 1 at a time, on medium speed, about 5 minutes. Stir in cream. Increase oven temperature to 500.° Roll out reserved pastry trimmings on lightly floured board; cut into strips 2 inches wide. Pat strips up side of pan, pressing dough lightly to baked crust. Pour filling into prepared crust. Bake 15 minutes. Reduce oven temperature to 200.° Do not open oven door. Bake until cheesecake is firm in center, about 50 minutes. Turn off oven; leave cheesecake in oven with door slightly open 1 hour. Remove; cool completely on wire rack. Refrigerate at least 2 hours; remove side of pan before serving. This cheesecake is well worth the effort. Better if vanilla bean is used. Use food processor. Hope you enjoy it—after all, how many calories could it have??
Ann Frazee Riley

TUXEDO CHEESE CAKE

Exquisite black and white delight, worth every effort.

CRUST: *(9" springform pan)*
1-1/2 cups crushed Pepperidge
    Farm chocolate nut
    cookies (Any chocolate
    chip cookie with nuts
    would do)
5 Tbsp. butter, melted
1/4 cup granulated sugar

1. Preheat the oven to 350.°
2. Place the crumbs in a mixing bowl and add the butter and sugar. Blend well.
3. Press the crumb mixture onto the bottom and partly up the sides of a greased 9-inch springform mold. Smooth the crumb mixture along the bottom to an even thickness.
4. Bake for 10 minutes in a 350° oven. Cool before filling.

FILLING:
4 squares (4-oz.) unsweetened
    chocolate
1 tsp. vegetable shortening
2 lbs. cream cheese
2 tsp. vanilla extract
1-1/2 cups granulated sugar
6 large eggs, lightly beaten
2 cups light cream, or 1 cup
    heavy cream and 1 cup
    milk

1. Preheat the oven to 450.°
2. Melt the chocolate with the shortening in the top of a double boiler.
3. Meanwhile, in a large mixing bowl, beat the cream cheese and vanilla until light and fluffy.
4. Slowly add the sugar, then the eggs. Beat just until well blended. Stir in cream.
5. Place about 3 cups of the cream cheese mixture in a separate bowl and add the melted chocolate. Blend.
6. Pour the plain cream-cheese mixture into the prepared crust. Add the chocolate mixture by dabbing spoonfuls on top in about 3 different spots. Use a knife or spatula to swirl the chocolate mixture through the white mixture in a zigzag motion, in effect marbling the cake.
7. Bake for 15 minutes at 450,° then reduce the oven temperature to 300° and bake for an additional hour. Allow the cake to cool in the oven to room temperature. Chill.

Please Note: Cooking time as applied to a large cheese cake varies each time a cake is prepared. Oven temperature may have to be lowered and cooking time increased from 10 to sometimes as long as 20 minutes. If cake begins to crack during cooking, a small pan of hot water may be added to oven rack below the cheese cake. This pan should be removed for the slow cooling process. Sometimes cake may be left in oven to cool for a full hour or more. Finish cooling on wire rack before refrigerating. This cheese cake may be well wrapped and frozen. It is important to remember to allow for slow defrost time. It is suggested to remove from freezer, let stand at room temperature for 2 hours, and then place the cheese cake in the refrigerator for 4 to 6 hours.

Mrs. Stephen Jones (Sherrel)

ANGEL FOOD CAKE

1-1/2 cups egg whites
1 cup cake flour, sifted
1 cup less 2 Tbsp. sugar
3/4 cup sugar
1/4 tsp. salt
1-1/2 tsp. cream of tartar
1 tsp. vanilla

1. Add salt and cream of tartar to egg whites and beat 25 strokes with wire whisk (egg whites will be frothy).
2. Gradually add the 3/4 cup sugar in 6 separate additions, beating 15 strokes after each addition. When all the sugar is added, beat mixture until it stands in firm peaks. Beat in vanilla. Add flour and sugar less 2 Tbsp. and sift together 4 times. Add the sugar and flour mixture; folding in gently, blend. Pour carefully into angel food cake pan (ungreased). Bake in a 375° oven for 30 minutes. Turn pan upside down over small necked bottle and let cake hang until cool. Not a fine textured cake, but yummy good and moist.
3. To make chocolate angel food, use above ingredients, but instead of 1 cup cake flour, sift together 3/4 cup cake flour and 1/4 cup cocoa.

Tottie Kennedy

THE HERSHEY BAR CAKE

8 (1-oz.) Hershey bars
2 sticks margarine
2 cups sugar
4 eggs
2-1/4 cups flour
1/2 tsp. soda
1 cup buttermilk
3/4 cup Hershey chocolate
    syrup
1 tsp. vanilla

Melt Hershey bars in double boiler. Cream margarine, sugar, and eggs. Beat. Add flour and soda alternately with buttermilk. Add chocolate syrup, melted Hershey bars, and vanilla. Bake 1-1/2 hours in greased and floured tube pan at 350°. Serve plain or with whipped cream.

Beverly Evans

 Use cocoa instead of flour when preparing pan for chocolate cake.

"OKLAHOMA CRUDE" CAKE

2 sticks butter
4 Tbsp. cocoa
2 cups sugar
1 Tbsp. vanilla
4 eggs
1-1/2 cups flour
1 cup coconut
1-1/2 cups pecans, chopped
9 oz. jar marshmallow creme

Melt butter and add cocoa, sugar, vanilla and eggs, beating while adding eggs. Combine flour, coconut and pecans and add to butter mixture. Beat 2 minutes and pour into greased 9" x 13" oblong pan. Bake at 350° for 35-40 minutes. Remove from oven and spread marshmallow creme on while cake is still hot. Cool before icing.

ICING:
1 stick butter
6 Tbsp. milk
3-1/2 Tbsp. cocoa
1 to 1-1/2 boxes powdered
    sugar

Combine butter, milk and cocoa. Heat until butter is melted. Remove from heat; add powdered sugar and beat well. Spread on cooled cake, carefully making sure marshmallow creme does not show through chocolate icing.

Lynn Diel

JUST EVERYBODY'S FAVORITE CHOCOLATE SHEET CAKE

2 sticks margarine
1/2 cup water
4 Tbsp. cocoa
2 cups flour, sifted
2 cups sugar
2 eggs, beaten
1 tsp. soda
1 cup buttermilk
1/4 tsp. salt

Heat together margarine, water and cocoa, stirring constantly until margarine is melted. Pour over flour and sugar; add eggs, soda, buttermilk and salt. Bake in greased jelly roll pan at 350° for 25 minutes. Frost while warm.

FROSTING:
1 stick margarine
4 Tbsp. cocoa
6 Tbsp. milk
1-lb. pkg. powdered sugar
1 tsp. vanilla
1 cup nuts, chopped

About five minutes before cake is done, melt margarine, cocoa and milk, stirring constantly. Pour this mixture over powdered sugar, vanilla and nuts. Mix well and frost warm cake.
Variation 1 tsp. cinnamon may be added to cake, frosting or to both.

The Cookbook Committee

DEAR ABBY'S OWN CHOCOLATE CAKE

A brown and white delight.

CAKE:
4 squares unsweetened
   chocolate
1/2 cup butter or margarine
1 cup water
2 cups cake flour, sifted
1-1/4 tsp. baking soda
1 tsp. salt
2 eggs
1 cup dairy sour cream
2 cups sugar
1-1/2 tsp. vanilla

Grease two 8-inch round layer cake pans. Flour lightly. Combine 3 squares of chocolate, butter, and water in top of double boiler. Heat over simmering water until chocolate and butter melt; remove from heat. Cool. (May also be done in a microwave for 3 minutes on high.) Sift flour, soda, and salt into large bowl. Beat eggs with sour cream until blended in a medium-sized bowl. Beat in sugar and vanilla; stir in cooled chocolate mixture. Beat into flour mixture, half at a time, just until smooth. Batter will be thin. Pour evenly into prepared pans. Bake 350° for 40 minutes or until center springs back when lightly pressed with fingertips. Cool in pans on wire racks. Loosen around edges with knife and turn out onto racks.

FROSTING:
2 egg whites
3/4 cup sugar
1/2 tsp. cream of tartar
Dash of salt
2-1/2 tsp. cold water
1 tsp. vanilla

Combine egg whites, sugar, cream of tartar, salt, and water in the top of a large double boiler. Beat until blended. Place top over simmering water. Cook, beating constantly with an electric or rotary beater, about 7 minutes, or until mixture stands in firm peaks. Remove from water and stir in vanilla. Melt remaining 1 square of chocolate with 1 Tbsp. butter or margarine in a cup set in hot water. Stir until smooth. Drizzle around top edge of cake, letting mixture drip down sides.

Note: Can be used on other cakes as well.

Mrs. John Day (Florelee)

Use a potato peeler when wanting to shave chocolate bars or to make chocolate curls.

OATMEAL CAKE

1 cup quick cooking oatmeal
1-1/4 cups boiling water
1 stick margarine
1 cup white sugar
1 cup brown sugar
2 eggs
1-1/2 cups flour, sifted
1 tsp. soda
1 tsp. cinnamon
1/2 tsp. salt

Mix oatmeal, boiling water and margarine together and let stand for 20 minutes. Add sugars, eggs, flour, cinnamon, soda and salt. Bake at 350° for 30 minutes.

FROSTING:
6 Tbsp. margarine
1/4 cup evaporated milk
1/2 cup sugar
1/2 cup coconut flakes
1/2 tsp. vanilla
1/2 cup pecans, chopped

Mix together and boil for 1 minute. Have prepared when cake comes from oven.

Mrs. George Howard Wilson, Sr. (Myrna)

POPPYSEED CAKE

1 cup shortening
2-1/2 cups sugar
6 eggs, separated
1/4 tsp. soda
1/4 tsp. salt
3 cups flour
1 tsp. vanilla
1 tsp. butter flavoring
1 tsp. almond extract
Soak Overnight:
1 cup buttermilk
1 Tbsp. poppyseed

Mix sugar, egg yolks and shortening. Mix in remaining ingredients, except egg whites. Beat egg whites and fold into other mixture. Bake in well-greased and floured tube pan. (Do not use bundt pan.) Bake 1 hour at 350°, not more than 1 hour and 10 minutes.

GLAZE:
1/2 cup orange juice
1-1/2 cups powdered sugar
1 tsp. vanilla
1 tsp. butter
1 tsp. almond extract

Combine glaze ingredients. Pour over cake immediately after taking out of oven. Loosen sides and middle so glaze will run down. Cool 15 minutes and remove from pan.

Hidy Eby

PICNIC CAKE

1/2 cup margarine
1 cup brown sugar
3 eggs
1 tsp. vanilla
2 cups flour
1 tsp. salt
1 tsp. soda
1-1/2 cups buttermilk or
    sour milk
1 cup oatmeal (quick brand)
16 oz. pkg. butterscotch chips
1/2 cup pecans

Cream margarine, sugar and eggs. Add vanilla. Stir in flour, salt and soda. Add oatmeal and buttermilk. Pour in prepared 9 x 13-inch pan with chips and nuts. Bake at 350° for 35-40 minutes.
*I sometimes add shredded coconut to top or drizzle with some remaining icing if I have it on hand.

Mrs. Richard Risley (Kathy)

PUMPKIN CAKE ROLL

Serves: 8

3 eggs
1 cup sugar
2/3 cup pumpkin
1 tsp. lemon juice
3/4 cup flour
1 tsp. baking powder
2 tsp. cinnamon
1 tsp. ginger
1/2 tsp. nutmeg
1/2 tsp. salt

Beat eggs at high speed of mixer for 5 minutes. Gradually beat in sugar, pumpkin and lemon juice. Stir together flour, baking powder, cinnamon, ginger, nutmeg and salt. Add to other mixture. Spread in greased and floured 15x10-inch pan (cookie sheet with side or jelly roll pan). Top with 1 cup of nuts. Bake at 375° for 15 minutes. Turn out immediately onto towel sprinkled with powdered sugar. Starting at narrow end, roll towel and cake together. Cool and unroll.

FILLING:
1 cup powdered sugar
6 oz. cream cheese, softened
4 Tbsp. butter
1/2 tsp. vanilla
1 cup pecans

Combine ingredients and beat until smooth. Spread on inside of roll. Reroll. Cover and chill.

Mrs. Joe Jones (Sarah)

COCONUT SOUR CREAM CAKE

1 box white cake mix
1/4 cup oil
3 eggs
1 (8-oz.) carton sour cream
1 cup cream of coconut

Mix cake mix, oil, eggs, sour cream, and cream of coconut. Bake in greased and floured cake pan (9 x 13-inch) for 30 minutes at 350°.

FROSTING:
1 (8-oz.) pkg. cream cheese,
    softened
1 box powdered sugar
2 Tbsp. milk
1 tsp. vanilla
1 can shredded coconut

Blend powdered sugar into softened cream cheese. Add milk and vanilla. Spread icing on cooled cake. Sprinkle coconut over iced cake.

Peggy Harmon

ITALIAN CREAM CAKE

Serves: 16

1/2 cup shortening
1 stick margarine
2 cups sugar
5 eggs, separated
1 cup buttermilk
2 cups flour
1/2 tsp. salt
1 tsp. soda
1 Tbsp. vanilla-butternut
    flavoring
2 cups coconut
1 cup pecans, chopped
1/2 cup maraschino cherries,
    chopped

Cream shortening, margarine, and sugar. Add egg yolks, one at a time, and cream well. Add buttermilk slowly, alternating with dry ingredients (flour, salt, and soda), to shortening mixture. Stir in flavoring. Add coconut, pecans, and cherries. Fold in stiffly beaten egg whites. Bake in 3 greased cake pans at 350° for 40 minutes. Frost when cool.

ICING:
1 stick margarine
1 (8-oz.) cream cheese, softened
1 cup pecans, chopped
1 box powdered sugar
1 tsp. vanilla-butternut flavoring

Mix all ingredients together.

Mrs. Jim Lovell (Linda)

STRAWBERRY SHORTCAKE

1 cup sugar
1/2 cup shortening
1 egg
1 tsp. vanilla
2/3 cup milk
1 cup flour
1 tsp. baking powder
1 qt. strawberries, sliced
1/2 pt. whipped cream

Cream sugar and shortening. Add egg, vanilla, milk, flour and baking powder. Bake in prepared 13" x 9" pan at 350° for 30-45 minutes. Serve with fresh strawberries and whipped cream. If serving a group, two 8-inch, round layer pans may be used, placing berries and whipped cream between layers and on top for an attractive look.

Mrs. Bob Wooldridge (Martha)

SPICE CAKE

1 cup raisins
1-1/2 cups water
1-1/2 cups sugar
2 eggs
2 cups flour
1 tsp. vanilla
1/2 cup shortening
1 tsp. cinnamon
1/2 tsp. nutmeg
1/2 tsp. ground cloves
1/4 tsp. salt
1-1/4 tsp. soda

Boil raisins in water. (Save 1 cup of raisin water for liquid in cake.) Let water cool. Cream shortening and sugar. Add eggs. Beat well. Add remaining ingredients, including raisin water and beat at high speed for 2 minutes. Pour in greased and floured 9 x 13-inch pan and bake at 350° for 40-45 minutes.

FROSTING:
1 cup brown sugar
1/4 cup milk
2 Tbsp. butter
Pinch salt
2 cups confectioner's sugar

Bring first four ingredients to a boil. Add confectioner's sugar.

Mrs. Dennis Brown (Linda)

RUM CAKE

2 cups sugar
1 cup Crisco
4 eggs
1 cup buttermilk
3 cups flour
1/2 tsp. baking powder
1/2 tsp. salt
1 tsp. vanilla

Blend sugar and Crisco. Add eggs (one at a time). Add buttermilk. Mix well. Sift flour, baking powder, and salt; then add to cream mixture. Add vanilla. Bake 325° for 1 hour in heavily greased and floured bundt pan. Cool in pan for 15 minutes. Punch holes in cake with long fork.

GLAZE:
1-1/2 cups sugar
3/4 cup water
5-1/2 Tbsp. rum

Mix together sugar and water and boil for 2 minutes. When cool, add rum. Prepare while cake is baking. Pour over top. Let sit for 45 minutes. Remove cake from pan and cover with lid.

Mrs. Don Diehl (Pat)

LEMON GLAZE

(Use this icing for lemon cakes, pound cakes or yellow bundt cakes.)

2 cups powdered sugar
Juice from 2 lemons or
    4 Tbsp. reconstituted
    lemon juice

Combine ingredients. While cake is hot, poke holes with fork and pour icing over top.

Diana Allen

CREAM CHEESE-PECAN ICING

1/2 cup (1 stick) butter, softened
1 (8-oz.) pkg. cream cheese,
    softened
1 (16-oz.) box powdered sugar
1 tsp. vanilla
1 cup pecans, chopped

Combine butter and cream cheese and add powdered sugar. Mix until smooth. Stir in vanilla. Stir in pecans. Good on white, yellow, spice and carrot cake.

Pat Reeves

CHOCOLATE PECAN PIE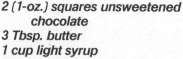

Makes: one 9-inch pie

2 (1-oz.) squares unsweetened
chocolate
3 Tbsp. butter
1 cup light syrup
3/4 cup sugar
1/2 tsp. salt
3 eggs, slightly beaten
1 tsp. vanilla
1 cup pecans, chopped
1 9-inch pie shell, unbaked
Whipped cream

In double boiler (or microwave), melt chocolate and butter together. In separate pan combine corn syrup and sugar and simmer 2 minutes. Add chocolate mixture and cool. Add salt to egg. Slowly dribble syrup mixture into eggs, while stirring. Blend in vanilla and nuts. Pour into shell. Bake 35 minutes at 325.° Top with whipped cream.

Mrs. Bill Word (Janie)

SUMMER CHOCOLATE PIE

"A rich and chocolatey no-bake filling"

Makes: one 8-inch pie

1/4 lb. butter
3/4 cup sugar
1 tsp. vanilla
1 square unsweetened
chocolate, melted
2 eggs

Beat butter until very light and fluffy. Add sugar. Beat well. Add chocolate and vanilla. Continue beating and add eggs, one at a time, beating 3 minutes after each egg. Pour into pie shell and chill in refrigerator until set. Top with whipped cream.

Colleen Harris

BUTTERMILK PIE

Makes: one 9-inch pie

1 9-inch unbaked pie shell
3 eggs, well beaten
2 cups sugar
2 Tbsp. flour
1 cup buttermilk
1 stick margarine
1 tsp. vanilla
nutmeg

Sift together sugar and flour and add to eggs. Add buttermilk, margarine and vanilla. Pour into pastry shell and sprinkle top very lightly with nutmeg. Bake at 450° for 10 minutes; then reduce to 350° and bake 45 minutes longer.

Mary Evans

CHOCOLATE OATMEAL PIE

Makes: 9-inch pie

2 eggs
1 cup sugar
1/4 tsp. salt
1 cup light corn syrup
2 Tbsp. butter or margarine
1 tsp. vanilla
1/2 cup coconut
1/2 cup quick oats
1/2 cup semi-sweet chocolate
    pieces
1 unbaked 9-inch pie shell

Beat eggs until thick and lemon colored (about 3 minutes). Continue beating and add sugar, salt, corn syrup, butter and vanilla. Stir in coconut, oats and chocolate pieces. Pour into pie shell. Bake 350° for 50-55 minutes. Pie will be very dark. Cool completely before serving. Serve with Cool Whip.

Mrs. Edward Bank (Dorothy)

CRANBERRY PIE

Serves: 6-8

2 cups fresh cranberries
1-1/2 cups sugar
1/2 cup water
2 egg yolks, beaten
2 tsp. flour
1 tsp. vanilla
1 tsp. butter
1 baked 9-inch pie shell

Cook sugar and water to a syrup. Add cranberries until they begin to pop. Let cool slightly and add flour and egg yolks. Slowly add this to cranberry mixture. Cook 3 minutes or until thickened. Add butter and vanilla. Pour into pie shell. Top with meringue. Bake 12-15 minutes at 350° Very festive dessert for Christmas.
Mrs. W. W. Musser (Bea)

 Meringue will not shrink if you spread it on the pie so that it touches the crust on each side before baking. Filling should always be cool before covering with meringue.

LEMON CHESS PIE

Makes: 9-inch pie

2 cups sugar
1 Tbsp. flour
1 Tbsp. cornmeal
4 eggs, beaten
1/4 cup butter, melted
1/4 cup milk
2 Tbsp. lemon rind, grated
1/4 cup lemon juice

Combine sugar, flour and cornmeal in a large bowl. Toss lightly with a fork. Add remaining ingredients. Beat with rotary beater until smooth and thoroughly blended. Pour into unbaked 9" pie shell. Bake at 350° for 35-40 minutes, or until top is golden brown.

Danette Tucker

MILLIONAIRE PIE

Serves: 6-8

1 9-inch baked pie crust or
    1 9-inch graham cracker
    crust
2 cups powdered sugar
1/2 cup margarine
1 egg
1/4 tsp. salt
1 tsp. vanilla
1 cup whipped cream (or Dream
    Whip or Cool Whip)
1 cup drained crushed
    pineapple
1/2 cup chopped nuts

Cream sugar and margarine. Add egg, salt, and vanilla. Beat until fluffy. Spread on crust. Fold pineapple and nuts into whipped cream. Spread on top of sugar mixture. Chill.

Mrs. Richard Eck (Myrna Kay)

 To prevent crust from becoming soggy with cream pie, sprinkle crust with powdered sugar.

SHIRLEY BELLMON'S PECAN PIE

3 eggs
1 cup white corn syrup
1 cup brown sugar
1 pie shell, unbaked
1 cup pecans, whole

Beat eggs. Add corn syrup and brown sugar to eggs; mix well. Pour this mixture into pie shell. Sprinkle with pecans. Bake at 325° for 1 hour.

History: When Daddy was Governor, Mother served pecan pie for dessert. She would bake one or two dozen and store them in the pantry. When you opened the pantry door, it would knock you out. Only last year—13 years later—did I eat a piece of pecan pie. Of course, it was made from this recipe; it is the best.

Mrs. John Wynne (Gail)

FANCY PECAN PIE

Makes: 9" pie

1 9-inch pie shell, unbaked
3 eggs, beaten
1/2 cup sugar
1/2 cup dark corn syrup
1/2 cup light corn syrup
1/2 tsp. vanilla
1/3 cup butter, melted
1/2 cup pecans, halved
1/2 cup pecans, broken

Beat the first 6 ingredients together with rotary egg beater. Mix in 1/2 cup broken pecan pieces. Pour into pie shell. Place 1/2 cup pecan halves on top of mixture. Bake at 325°-350° for 40-50 minutes or until mixture is set.

Mrs. Bob Young (Gretchen)

PINEAPPLE PIE FILLING

Makes: 9-inch pie

1 cup sugar
1 egg, beaten
1/2 stick butter, softened
1 Tbsp. cornstarch
1 (20-oz.) can pineapple,
    crushed

Mix all ingredients; pour into unbaked pie shell. Bake 25 minutes at 350°.

Note: Use creative coconut crust for a tropical treat. See page 228.

Mrs. Jesse Beck (Cecelia)

SOUR CREAM APPLE PIE

Makes: 8-inch pie

1 egg, beaten
1-1/2 cups sugar
1 cup sour cream
1/2 tsp. cinnamon
4 Tbsp. flour
4 cups fresh apples (Granny
    Smith or McIntosh apples)
1/2 cup brown sugar
1 Tbsp. margarine
8" unbaked pie shell

Combine egg, sugar, sour cream, cinnamon, 3 Tbsp. flour and apples. Pour into pie shell. Mix brown sugar, 1 Tbsp. flour and margarine and cover apple mixture. Bake at 350° for 1 hour.

Mrs. Don Diehl (Pat)

SOUR CREAM RAISIN PIE

Makes: 8-inch pie

1 cup raisins, cooked
1 cup sugar
1/4 tsp. cinnamon (may
    vary with taste)
1/4 tsp. cloves
1 Tbsp. flour
1 cup sour cream
2 egg yolks, beaten
Salt
8" baked pie shell

Cook raisins in small amount of water; reserve juice. Mix dry ingredients in sauce pan. Add sour cream, raisins and egg yolks. Cook until thick. If too thick, add a little raisin juice. Pour into pie shell. Top with meringue. Bake 12-15 minutes at 350°

Mrs. W. W. Musser (Bea)

STRAWBERRY PIE

Makes: 9-inch pie

1 9-inch pie shell, baked
1 cup sugar
3 Tbsp. cornstarch
3 Tbsp. strawberry jello
1 cup water
1 large basket strawberries
    (2 pints)
Whipped cream

Mix sugar, cornstarch and jello in a saucepan. Gradually add water. Cook over low heat until clear and thick. Cool. Place sliced strawberries in pie shell. Pour glaze over strawberries. Top with whipped cream.

Mrs. Dale Anderson (Judy)

CREAMY STRAWBERRY PIE IN COCONUT CRUST

Makes: 9-inch pie

2 pts. fresh strawberries
3/4 cup sugar
1 envelope gelatin, plain
1/2 cup water
2 Tbsp. lemon juice
1 cup whipping cream, whipped

Thinly slice 1-1/2 pts. strawberries, reserving 1/2 pt. Combine with sugar; set aside until sugar dissolves. Soften gelatin in water. Stir over low heat until dissolved. Combine gelatin, strawberries, and lemon juice. Fold in whipped cream. Chill until mixture mounds when dropped from spoon. Pour filling into coconut crust. Chill at least 4 hours and garnish with remaining strawberries.

Judy Puerta

CREATIVE COCONUT CRUST

Makes: 9-inch crust

2-1/2 cups flaked coconut
1/2 cup melted butter

Combine coconut and melted butter and press into 9-inch pie pan. Bake at 300° for 30-35 minutes or until golden brown. Cool. Add your favorite filling, such as pineapple, banana, etc. Use your imagination for unique flavor combinations.

Judy Puerta

CRUNCH TOPPING FOR PIES

Yield: 1 pie topping

3/4 cup flour
1/4 tsp. salt
1/4 cup sugar
1/4 cup brown sugar
1/3 cup butter, softened

Blend all of these ingredients until crumbly. Put filling in unbaked shell and top with above blended ingredients. Bake at 400° for 30-35 minutes. This is especially good on apple or cherry.

Mrs. Ken Boyle (Pam)

BRANDIED CHOCOLATE CRUST

Makes: 9" pie crust

1 (8-1/2-oz) pkg. thin chocolate
    wafers
1/4 cup margarine, softened
3 Tbsp. brandy

Blend chocolate wafers to fine crumbs. combine crumbs, margarine and brandy and mix well. Press mixture to bottom and side of a 9" pie plate. (Recommended with Tumbleweed Pie Filling.)

Linda Downs

PIE CRUST

Yield: 5 crusts

4 cups flour, unsifted
1 Tbsp. sugar
2 tsp. salt
1-3/4 cups vegetable
    shortening
1 Tbsp. white or cider vinegar
1 large egg
1/2 cup water

Mix flour, sugar and salt in a large bowl. Add shortening and mix until crumbly with pastry blender. In small bowl, beat together with fork, 1/2 cup water, vinegar, and egg. Mix into dry ingredients until moist. You can shape with your hands. Divide into 5 individual portions; shape each into a flat circle or round patty. Store in plastic bags. Chill 1/2 hour before rolling into crusts. If you want to freeze them, great, but roll the dough flat before freezing. This dough can be handled a lot and still be flaky and tender.

Mrs. John Taylor (Sue)

RICH AND BUTTERY PIE CRUST

Makes 5 small crusts

5-1/2 cups flour
1/2 tsp. salt
1 lb. margarine
1 egg yolk
1 tsp. vinegar
3/4 cup water (approx.)

Combine flour, salt and margarine with pastry blender until well blended. This mixture should be crumbly. Mix liquid ingredients together, and slowly add to crumb mixture. Form into balls and roll out as desired. This crust may be frozen, but it is best to prepare in pie plates and then freeze. Once frozen, layers of wax paper may be placed between pie shells; then, shells and pans may be stacked and wrapped together to save freezer space.

Pam Boyle

VERY FLAKY PASTRY

Makes: one 9-inch double crust or
two 8-inch single crusts

2-1/4 cups sifted flour
1 tsp. salt
3/4 cup plus 2 Tbsp. shortening
(Must use Crisco. Do not
use butter, margarine or
salad oil.)
1/3 cup ice water

Mix flour and salt. Cut shortening in with pastry blender until consistency of coarse meal. Sprinkle ice water over mixture and mix only enough for mixture to cling together. Divide dough into two balls. Roll out between waxed paper. Do not add any additional flour. Chill in pie plate for 1-2 hours.
Baked Pie Shell: 400° for 12-15 minutes. Prick shell before baking or sprinkle with dried beans while baking to prevent air bubbles from forming.
Unbaked: Fill and bake according to recipe.

Donita Mitchell

 For flaky, light pastry use half cake flour with half all-purpose flour in your favorite pastry recipe.

GRANDMA'S CHERRY PUDDING

2 Tbsp. shortening
1 cup sugar
1 cup flour
1 tsp. baking powder
1/2 cup milk
1 tsp. vanilla
1 can pitted cherries, undrained
3/4 cup sugar

Mix shortening, sugar, flour, baking powder, milk and vanilla. Spread in greased loaf pan. Bring cherries and 3/4 cup sugar to a boil and pour over batter. Bake at 350° until brown, about 40 minutes.

Mrs. Bill Batchelder (Jackie)

DATE PUDDING

1 cup dates
1 cup nuts (English walnuts)
1 cup sugar
1 tsp. baking powder
1 Tbsp. flour
2 Tbsp. milk
2 eggs, beaten separately

Cut dates into small chunks. Put flour, baking powder and sugar in mixing bowl. Add dates and mix till the dates are evenly distributed. Break up nuts, leaving them in fairly large pieces, and use only English walnuts. Add to above mixture. Beat egg yolks and whites separately. Add yolks and fold whites in last. Success in baking: Put in small, ungreased baking dish, and set this in a pan of hot water. Bake on lower rack of oven for 45 minutes at about 250.° When properly baked the pudding will be the consistency of thick honey when cold. Be very careful not to overbake.

Mrs. Tom Sailors, Jr. (Ruth Ann)

 Put a layer of marshmallows in the bottom of a pumpkin pie, then add the filling. You will have a nice topping as the marshmallows will come to the top.

OKLAHOMA BREAD PUDDING
WITH WHISKEY SAUCE

Serves: 8-10

1 cup whipping cream
3/4 cup milk
8-1/2 oz. stale French or
　　Italian bread, cut into
　　1/2 inch slices
4 egg yolks
1 cup sugar
1/2 cup dark raisins
2 tsp. vanilla
3 egg whites
3 Tbsp. sugar

Pour cream and milk over bread in large bowl. Beat egg yolks and 1 cup sugar in medium-sized bowl until light. Stir in raisins and vanilla. Gently stir egg-yolk mixture into bread mixture. Let stand 10 minutes. Beat egg whites in small mixer bowl until foamy. Gradually beat in 3 Tbsp. sugar. Beat until stiff but not dry, and fold into bread mixture; pour into buttered 2 qt. soufflé dish. Place dish in baking pan. Pour boiling water into pan 1/3 up the side of soufflé dish. Bake until top is puffed and golden and knife inserted in center comes out clean, about 1 hour at 350°Cool on wire rack. Spoon into serving dish and serve with whiskey sauce.

SAUCE:
3 egg yolks
1/2 cup sugar
1 cup hot whipping cream
1/3 cup hot milk
1 tsp. vanilla
1 Tbsp. bourbon

Beat egg yolks and sugar in sauce pan until light. Stir in cream and milk. Cook over low heat, stirring constantly, until mixture thickens and coats back of spoon, about 15 minutes. Stir in vanilla; cook, stirring constantly for 10 minutes. Stir in bourbon; cook, stirring constantly 5 minutes. Cool. Serve warm or at room temperature.

Mrs. Larry Dobbs (Ruth)

CHOCOLATE FONDUE

A great way to start your next shindig when accompanied with sherry.
For a final touch to the evening, serve with brandy or port.

12 oz. chocolate chips
1/2 cup sugar
2 Tbsp. butter
1 cup whipping cream,
　　do not whip
1 tsp. vanilla

In double boiler, melt chocolate chips. Add sugar and butter. Slowly stir in whipping cream and vanilla. Heat three minutes. Serve with mandarin oranges, apples, pineapple, bananas, angel food cake, and marshmallows.

Mrs. Ray Downs (Linda)

232

ORANGE CHOCOLATE MOUSSE

Serves: 6-8

6 oz. semi-sweet chocolate
2 Tbsp. Kahlua
1 Tbsp. orange juice
2 egg yolks
2 eggs
1 tsp. vanilla
1/4 cup sugar
1 cup heavy cream

Melt chocolate in Kahlua and orange juice over very low heat. Meanwhile put egg yolks, eggs, vanilla, and sugar in blender. Blend 2 minutes at medium high speed. Add heavy cream and blend another 30 seconds. Add melted chocolate mixture and blend until smooth. Pour into bowl or small individual cups. Refrigerate.
Committee suggests serving with whipped cream and an orange zest.

Mrs. Don Stehr (Janet)

SINFUL PUDDING

1 cup flour
1 stick margarine
2/3 cup dry roasted peanuts, chopped
8 oz. cream cheese, softened
1/3 cup smooth peanut butter
1 cup powdered sugar
1 cup Cool Whip
1 pkg. chocolate instant pudding
1 pkg. vanilla instant pudding
3 cups milk
1 tsp. vanilla

Mix flour, margarine, and peanuts and pat into 13 x 9-inch pan and bake at 350° for about 20 minutes until light brown. Let cool. Mix cream cheese with peanut butter and powdered sugar and add Cool Whip. Put this mixture on the baked crust. Prepare each pudding with 1-1/2 cup milk and 1/2 tsp. vanilla. Layer each over cheese mixture. Spread remainder of 9 oz. carton of Cool Whip over pudding layer. Sprinkle with 1/3 cup chopped dry roasted peanuts. If desired, peanut butter can be omitted from the cream cheese layer and pecans substituted for the peanuts.

Florelee Day

PLUM PUDDING (Modern Style)

Just plum good!

1 can purple plums
1 pkg. gingerbread mix,
   Pillsbury
1/2 tsp. salt
1/2 cup nuts
1 cup light raisins

SAUCE:
1/4 cup sugar
2 Tbsp. cornstarch
Plum syrup (to make 1-1/2 cup)
1 Tbsp. lemon juice

Drain plums; reserve juice. Mix cake as directed on package. Cut plums in pieces and add to cake mixture. Prepare bundt or angel food cake pan (well greased and floured). Bake at 375° for 1 hour or less. Loosen edges and let stand 30 minutes to cool. Combine sauce ingredients and cook until boiling, stirring constantly. Boil 1 minute. Add lemon juice. Serve hot over pudding.

Sparkey Gordon

POT DE CRÈME

Serves: 6

1 (6-oz.) pkg. Nestle's
   Chocolate bits
1 egg
2 tsp. crème de menthe
1 Tbsp. sugar
2 or 3 tsp. black coffee
Pinch of salt
1 cup coffee cream

Put first six ingredients in blender; scald cream and add. Blend on low speed for 1 minute and pour into pot de crème or demitasse cups. Refrigerate until firm and top with whipped cream.

Karol Hite

 If the juice from your apple pie runs over in the oven, shake some salt on it, which causes the juice to burn to a crisp so it can be removed.

APPLE BETTY

5-6 cups sour apples*
    (peeled and sliced)
1/3 cup orange juice
1 cup sugar
3/4 cup flour
1 tsp. cinnamon
1/2 tsp. nutmeg
Dash of salt
1/2 cup butter

Put sliced apples in 9-inch pie plate. Pour orange juice over apples.

Topping: Blend sugar, flour, cinnamon, nutmeg, salt, and butter with a pastry cutter. Crumble over apples and mash down. Bake at 375° for 45 minutes or until apples are done and topping is brown.

*Use cooking apples, Winesap or Jonathan for best flavor.

Mrs. Robert Jantzen (Colleen)

APPLE DUMPLINGS

Serves: 12

2 to 2-1/2 cups flour
2 tsp. baking powder
1 tsp. salt
3/4 cup shortening
1/2 cup milk
4-6 cooking apples (peeled,
    cored & cut into eights)
Sugar
Ground cinnamon
Ground nutmeg
Butter or margarine

SYRUP:
2 cups sugar
1/4 tsp. cinnamon
1/4 tsp. nutmeg
2 cups hot water
1/4 cup melted butter or
    margarine
Cream (optional)

Combine flour, baking powder, and salt. Cut in shortening until mixture resembles coarse meal. Gradually add milk, stirring to make a soft dough. Roll dough into 1/8" thick rectangle on a lightly floured surface; cut into 5" squares. Place 3-4 pieces of apple on each square. Sprinkle each with 2 tsp. sugar, cinnamon, and nutmeg to taste; dot with butter. Moisten edges of each dumpling with water; bring corners to center; pinch edges to seal. Place dumplings, 1" apart in a lightly greased, shallow baking dish. To make syrup: Combine sugar, cinnamon, nutmeg, hot water, and butter. Stir to dissolve sugar. Pour syrup over dumplings. Bake at 375° for 35-45 minutes or until golden.

Mrs. John Wynne (Gail)

"BETTER WITH BOURBON" MINCE-APPLE CRISP

Serves: 8

3 lbs. tart cooking apples
1/2 cup sugar
1/2 tsp. ground cinnamon
1/4 tsp. ground nutmeg
2 tsp. lemon juice
1/2 cup mincemeat
1/2 cup bourbon
1/3 cup honey
1 cup coarsely chopped walnuts
1/4 cup butter, softened
1/2 cup firmly packed light
     brown sugar
3/4 cup sifted flour
1 cup heavy cream, whipped

Preheat oven to 375.° Peel and core the apples and slice 1/4" thick. Use enough of the apples to get eight cups of slices. Combine the sugar with cinnamon and nutmeg. Mix the apples with the sugar-spice mixture and the lemon juice in a large bowl. Set aside. Stir mincemeat, bourbon, and honey together. Add 1/2 cup of the nuts. Set aside. To make the topping, cream the butter with brown sugar, add the flour and the remaining 1/2 cup of nuts. Mix well, using your fingers if necessary. The mixture should be crumbly.

Butter an 8x8x2-inch baking dish or a one-and-a-half-quart shallow casserole. Arrange a layer of apples in the bottom. Add a layer of the mincemeat mixture. Repeat layers until the dish is full, ending with apples. Sprinkle sugar-nut mixture over the top. Bake for 40-55 minutes, or until the apples are tender when tested with a toothpick and the syrup begins to bubble. Serve with whipped cream.

Marion Collier

BAKED FUDGE

Serves: 8

4 eggs, well beaten
2 cups sugar
1/2 cup flour
1/2 cup cocoa
1 cup melted butter
1 cup chopped pecans
2 tsp. vanilla
1/2 tsp. salt

Beat eggs and dry ingredients until well blended. Mix in butter. Stir in remaining ingredients. Pour in 9x9-inch pan. Set in another pan of boiling water. Bake at 325° for 45 min. or until set like custard. Do not overbake. Cool and cut into 2" squares. Serve with whipped cream.

Mrs. John Wynne (Gail)

BLUEBERRY DELIGHT

Serves: 8-10

2 sticks margarine, melted
2 cups flour
1 cup chopped pecans
8 oz. cream cheese
1 (8-oz.) container Cool Whip
1/2 box powdered sugar
1 cup sugar
2 Tbsp. cornstarch
1 cup water
1 Tbsp. lemon juice
2 cups fresh or frozen
   blueberries

Mix first three ingredients. Pat into 9x13-pan. Bake 30 minutes at 350° Cool.

Mix cream cheese, Cool Whip, and powdered sugar and spread over cooled crust.
Cook sugar, cornstarch, water, lemon juice, and blueberries until thickened and cool. Spread over cream cheese filling. Also good with strawberries.

Mrs. Stephen Chambers (Mary Suzan)

RASPBERRIES 'N CREAM

Serves: 6

2 cups whipping cream
1 cup sugar
2 Tbsp. gelatin
1/2 cup cold water
2 cups sour cream
1 tsp. vanilla
Raspberries (strawberries,
   blueberries or other
   berries are equally
   as good)

Soak gelatin in cold water. In medium saucepan, heat whipping cream and sugar; add dissolved gelatin to hot mixture. When mixture thickens, remove from heat and stir in sour cream and vanilla. Refrigerate until set. Serve with fresh or frozen raspberries. If cream is scooped into individual dishes, spoon berries over top—or if cream is set in attractive serving dish, arrange berries across the top or around the edge.

Pat Reeves

LINDA WILSON'S CHOCOLATE ROLL & CHOCOLATE SAUCE

Serves: 10

5 eggs (yolks & whites
   separated)
1 cup sugar
6 oz. semi-sweet chocolate
   chips
3 Tbsp. cold water
Semi-sweet chocolate bars,
   grated
Powdered sugar
1 cup whipping cream
1 tsp. vanilla

In mixer, beat egg yolks and 3/4 cup sugar until thick. Melt chocolate chips in 3 Tbsp. cold water. Fold chocolate into egg mixture. Fold in stiffly beaten egg whites. Oil jelly roll pan (11" x 16"). Oil sheet of waxed paper (both sides) and place in pan bottom. Spread chocolate mixture evenly on it and bake 350° for 15 minutes. Remove from oven and cover with damp cloth. Chill in refrigerator for 1 hour. Remove cloth and dust with grated chocolate and powdered sugar. Cover with wax paper and invert on board or cookie sheet. Lift off jelly roll pan and wax paper. Whip cream adding remaining sugar and vanilla. Spread cream on chocolate mixture and roll up like a jelly roll (roll on long side). Sprinkle with grated semi-sweet chocolate. Store in refrigerator. Serve with chocolate sauce.

Mrs. Doug Frantz

CHOCOLATE SAUCE

4 squares semi-sweet chocolate
1 stick butter
4 Tbsp. water
2 eggs
2 cups powdered sugar
2 tsp. vanilla

Melt chocolate and butter in double boiler with 4 Tbsp. water. Beat eggs well, add powdered sugar and vanilla. Add to hot mixture and cook 3 minutes. Serve over chocolate roll.

Mrs. Doug Frantz (Dianne)

KAHLÚA MOUSSE

Serves: 10

1/2 cup sugar
1/2 cup water
2 eggs
Pinch salt
2 Tbsp. cognac
6 oz. chocolate chips
3 Tbsp. Kahlúa
1-1/2 cups whipping cream

Heat sugar and water slowly until sugar is completely melted. In blender place eggs, salt, and chocolate. Blend (low speed) adding sugar syrup in a slow steady stream. Blend until smooth. Cool. Add cognac and Kahlúa. Beat whipped cream until thickened, but pourable. Stir into chocolate mixture. Put in large crystal bowl or individual cups. Chill. (Sprinkle chocolate shot or shaved chocolate on top.) Freezes well.

Mrs. Harold Gasaway (Virginia)

LEMON ROLL

4 eggs, separated
1/4 cup sugar
1 tsp. lemon extract
1 Tbsp. oil
1/2 cup sugar
2/3 cup sifted cake flour
1 tsp. baking powder
1/4 tsp. salt
Powdered sugar
Coconut

FILLING:
1 (14-oz.) can Eagle Brand milk
1/3 cup lemon juice
2 tsp. lemon rind
5 drops yellow food color
1 (4-oz.) Cool Whip

Beat egg yolks until light and lemon colored. Gradually add 1/4 cup sugar, beating constantly. Stir in oil and lemon extract; set aside. Beat egg whites until foamy; gradually add 1/2 cup sugar. Beat until stiff, but not dry. Fold yolk mixture into egg whites. Combine flour, baking powder and salt and fold into egg mix. Grease jelly roll pan; line with wax paper. Bake at 375° for 10-12 minutes. Mix filling in order listed. Sift powdered sugar on tea towel. Immediately when cake is done, turn cake into powdered sugar. Peel off waxed paper. Starting at narrow edge, roll cake seam down. Unroll cake —spread with 1/2 creamy filling; re-roll and spread filling on all sides. Combine coconut, water, and color and sprinkle on cake. Refrigerate 1 to 2 hours before serving. Serve with Cool Whip.

Mrs. Paul D. Fossett II (Suzy)

CARAMEL ORANGES

Serves: 8-12

15 large navel oranges
1/2 oz. Grand Marnier or
orange liqueur
1 cup sugar
1/4 cup slivered almonds,
slightly toasted
Whipped cream

Remove peeling from 4 oranges. Cut peeling thin or grate off rind. Peel oranges, catch juice. Pour 1/2 cup juice in measuring cup. (Add concentrated orange juice if not enough). Slice rest of oranges and arrange in large glass bowl. Sprinkle with liqueur. Refrigerate. Combine sugar, orange juice and peeling and bring to a slow boil until straw colored. Pour over orange slices. Sprinkle with almonds and cover with whipped cream.

Cindy Benge

PUMPKIN SQUARES

Serves: 12

24 single graham crackers,
crushed (about 1-3/4 cups)
1/3 cup sugar
1/2 cup butter or margarine,
melted
2 eggs
3/4 cup sugar
1 (8-oz.) package cream cheese,
softened
1 (16-oz.) can pumpkin
3 egg yolks
1/2 cup sugar
1/2 cup milk
1/2 tsp. salt
2 tsp. ground cinnamon
1 envelope unflavored gelatin
1/4 cup cold water
3 egg whites
1/4 cup sugar
1 cup whipping cream, chilled
1 Tbsp. sugar
1 tsp. vanilla

Heat oven to 350°. Mix crackers and 1/3 cup sugar. Stir in melted butter; pat in buttered baking dish, 13" x 9." Beat 2 eggs, 3/4 cup sugar, and cream cheese until light and fluffy. Pour over crust. Bake 20 minutes. Beat pumpkin, egg yolks, 1/2 cup sugar, milk, salt, and cinnamon in top of double boiler. Cook over boiling water, stirring frequently until thick, about 5 minutes. Sprinkle gelatin on water in small saucepan. Stir over low heat just until dissolved. Stir into pumpkin mixture. Cool. Beat egg whites until foamy. Gradually beat in 1/4 cup sugar. Beat until stiff and glossy. Gently fold beaten egg whites into pumpkin mixture. Pour over baked crust. Refrigerate. Just before serving, beat whipping cream and 1 Tbsp. sugar in chilled bowl until stiff. During last minute of beating, add vanilla. Cut into squares, garnish with whipped cream or Cool Whip.

Mrs. Gail Nausbaum (Myrtle)

PEACH COBBLER

Serves: 4-6

3/4 cup flour
3/4 cup milk
Pinch of salt
1/2 cup sugar
1/2 cup brown sugar
1/4 tsp. cinnamon
2 tsp. baking powder
1/2 cup butter
2 cups fresh peaches, peeled
    and sliced
1/2 cup sugar

Sift together flour, salt, cinnamon, and baking powder. Mix in sugars. Stir in milk and beat. Melt butter in 9x9-inch baking dish. Pour batter over melted butter. Do not stir. Pour peaches mixed with 1/2 cup sugar over this. Do not stir. Bake 350° for 1 hour.
Can use canned peaches if desperate.

Mrs. John Wynne (Gail)

BLYTHE SPIRIT
(Also called STRAWBERRY PECAN ICE CREAM)

Serves: 3 quarts

6 eggs
3-1/4 cups sugar
4 pts. half and half
2 cups milk
2 pkgs. strawberries, large
    (well thawed)
3 Tbsp. vanilla
3/4 tsp. salt
8 oz. pecan pieces

Mix eggs until light. Add one pint half and half. Add sugar. Put all other ingredients into bowl and mix thoroughly. Add to freezer and freeze.

Sharon Blythe

 When freezing ice cream, remember that the finer the chunks of ice, the finer the grain of ice cream.

CHOCOLATE MINT ICE CREAM

Makes: 2 quarts

2 eggs
3 cups whipping cream
1 cup milk
1/2 cup sugar
1/4 cup light corn syrup
1 tsp. vanilla
1/4 tsp. salt
1/3 cup green creme de menthe
Green food coloring (optional)
2 squares (2-oz.) semi-sweet
   chocolate, shaved

In mixing bowl beat eggs on high speed till light, about 4 minutes. Add whipping cream, milk, sugar, light corn syrup, vanilla, and salt. Stir till sugar is dissolved. Add creme de menthe. Stir in green food coloring, if desired. Pour into 2 qt. ice cream freezer. Add additional milk till 2/3 full, if necessary. Freeze. Remove dasher. Stir in chocolate. Cover. Pack with additional salt and ice, using 1 part rock salt to 4 parts ice. Let ripen 3 hours

Danette Tucker

BUTTERFINGER ICE CREAM

Makes: 2 quarts

3 eggs
2 cups sugar
Salt, pinch
1-2 tsp. vanilla
3 pts. half and half
8-10 Butterfinger candy bars,
   chopped
Milk

Beat eggs and sugar together. Add salt, vanilla, half and half and Butterfingers. Pour in 1/2 gallon ice cream freezer. Fill with milk and freeze.

Mrs. Bob Brim (Nan)

CRANBERRY ICE

Serves: 12-14

1 qt. cranberries
2 cups sugar
Water
1/2 pkg. cherry, lemon or
   lime Jello

Cover cranberries with water and cook until tender and soft. Strain. Add sugar to warm mixture until dissolved and then add enough water to make 6 cups. Pour over 1/2 package Jello, and freeze.

Betty Dillingham

LEMON SHERBET

Serves: 6-8

3 cups milk
1-1/2 cups sugar
Juice of 3 lemons
Rind of 1 lemon
Pinch of salt
1 egg white, beaten stiff

Add sugar and salt to milk. Add lemon juice, rind and egg white last. The milk thickens a little when lemon juice is added. Freeze like ice cream.

Mrs. Joe Champlin (Jane)

CHOCOLATE SAUCE FOR ICE CREAM

2 squares Bakers semi-sweet
    chocolate
2 Tbsp. butter
2/3 cup sugar
1/2 cup evaporated milk,
    undiluted
1 tsp. vanilla
1/4 cup cooking sherry
    (optional)

Melt chocolate and butter over low heat, then stir in sugar and milk. Cook over low heat until sugar has dissolved and sauce has thickened. Add vanilla and sherry.

Pamela Buller

FROZEN DESSERT

Serves: 8

3/4 cup chopped pecans
3/4 cup flaked coconut, toasted
3/4 cup brown sugar
1/2 cup butter, melted
1/2 gal. butter brickle ice cream

Press 3/4 of mixture of nuts, coconut, brown sugar and butter in 9" x 9" greased pyrex pan. Chill. Soften ice cream and spread over crust. Top with remaining mixture. Freeze.
Serving Suggestions: Top with Cool Whip and pour chocolate sauce over Cool Whip. Everyone loves it and its so easy.

Judy Anderson

GRANITE OF CABERNET
(Sherbet)

Serves: 8-10

3/4 cup water
1 cup sugar
1 fifth Cabernet Sauvignon
   (California Bordeaux wine
   may be substituted)
Juice of 1 lemon
Juice of 1 orange

Bring sugar and water to boil. Be sure it is dissolved. Stir slightly at first. Simmer 1 minute; then pour the syrup into a metal bowl. Cool. Combine it with the wine and juices, stir it well and pour in a long flat dish. Freeze for at least 4 hours. Every 30 minutes stir with a fork. As it freezes, you will form shavings like snow. Pile the snow into wine glasses or sherbets and add a sprig of mint.

Jean Mitchell

CHOCOLATE CHIP TORTONI

1/2 cup toasted slivered
   almonds, chopped
2 egg whites
1/4 cup sugar
2 cups whipping cream, whipped
1/3 cup powdered sugar
2 Tbsp. instant coffee
2 egg yolks
2 tsp. vanilla
1/2 cup semi-sweet
   chocolate chips
1 tsp. butter

There are five steps to this recipe. 1. Toast almonds in slow oven and chop. Set aside. 2. Beat egg whites till foamy; add sugar. 3. Whip cream until stiff. Mix powdered sugar and instant coffee, then fold into cream. 4. Beat egg yolks and vanilla together. Then fold egg and cream mixtures together. Set this mixture in freezer until it starts freezing around the edges. 5. In double boiler, melt chocolate chips with butter. Cool to warm. When first mixture is icy, add a spoonful to chocolate to make a sauce. Then add the chocolate mixture to whipping cream mixture. As it mixes, the chocolate breaks into small pieces. Fold in the almonds. Spoon into cupcake papers or small paper cups and freeze.

Mrs. Earl Mitchell (Jean)

OKLAHOMA ICE CREAM

Makes: 1 gallon

6 eggs
1 cup sugar
1 can Eagle Brand milk
1 pt. half and half
3 Tbsp. vanilla
Milk
Fruit (optional)

Beat eggs till foamy. Add sugar, Eagle Brand, cream and vanilla. Mix well. Pour in freezer can. Finish filling can with milk. You can add 4 cups mashed fruit at the same time milk is added. My favorite is bananas and pecans.

Source: "Recipes from the Campaign Trail." A campaign brochure from my father's 1968 U.S. Senate Campaign. It contained several of my mother's recipes, as well as "Henry Bellmon's recipe for 'Good Government.'"

Mrs. John Wynne (Gail)

FROZEN LEMON PUDDING

Serves: 6-8

3 eggs, separated
1/4 cup lemon juice
Rind of half lemon, grated
1/8 tsp. salt
1/2 cup and 1 Tbsp. sugar
1 cup whipping cream
1 cup graham cracker or
  vanilla wafer crumbs

Combine egg yolks, lemon juice, rind, salt and sugar. Cook and stir until smooth. Cool. Combine cooled mixture with stiffly beaten egg whites and whipped cream. Pour over 1 qt. crumb-lined casserole and freeze.

Sara Earnest

 To prevent quick melting of homemade ice cream, add 1 Tbsp. unflavored gelatin. (Dissolve gelatin in 1/4 cup water, and add to milk.)

TUMBLEWEED PIE

Makes: 1 10'' pie

1 10-inch graham cracker or chocolate cookie crust

Prepare and bake crust.
Cookbook Committee recommends useing Brandied Chocolate Crust.

FILLING:
1/2 gal. vanilla ice cream
2 jiggers Kahlúa
4 jiggers Amaretto
Chopped almonds or pecans

SAUCE: Put ice cream in blender with liqueurs and blend. Pour in pie crust and freeze overnight. When serving, thaw 20 minutes, cut each piece and sprinkle with chopped almonds or pecans. Garnish with coconut, chocolate shavings or hot fudge sauce.

Mrs. Dick Allen (Diana)

COFFEE SUNDAE PIE

Makes: 9'' pie

18 Oreo cookies or chocolate wafers, crumbled
1/2 cup butter or margarine, melted
2 squares unsweetened chocolate
1/2 cup sugar
1 Tbsp. butter
2/3 cup evaporated milk
1 qt. coffee ice cream or chocolate marble
1 cup whipping cream, whipped or Cool Whip
Pecans, chopped

Add melted butter to cookie crumbs and pat into a 9'' pie pan and chill. Melt chocolate over low heat (watch carefully). Add sugar, butter, and mix. Slowly add evaporated milk. Stir until mixture thickens. Cool. Spread coffee ice cream over crust. Freeze. Pour cooled chocolate mixture over ice cream and freeze. Lastly, top with whipped cream, nuts and return to freezer until ready to serve. Simply delish! Rich—not too large servings.

Mrs. Richard Kennedy (Tottie)

FROZEN PEANUT BUTTER PIE

Serves: 8

4 oz. cream cheese
1 cup confectioners' sugar
1/3 cup peanut butter (nutty)
1/2 cup milk
8 oz. heavy cream, whipped
9" graham cracker crust,
    baked and cooled
Note: Finely chopped peanuts
    make a nice addition to
    the crust

Beat cheese until fluffy. Beat in sugar and peanut butter. Slowly add milk, blending thoroughly. Fold in whipped cream. Pour into crust. Freeze until firm. Serve while frozen, allowing 5-8 minutes after cutting before serving. Will keep smooth about a week, if kept frozen. Garnish with finely chopped peanuts before serving. This specialty is served in the restaurant of the House of Representatives in Washington, D.C.

Betty Behring

FROZEN STRAWBERRY SQUARES

Serves: 10-12

2 cups flour
1/2 cup brown sugar
1 cup nuts
1 cup oleo, melted

FILLING:
4 egg whites
2-2/3 cups sugar
2 (10-oz.) pkgs. frozen
    strawberries
4 Tbsp. lemon juice
2 cups cream, whipped

Combine flour, brown sugar, nuts and oleo. Spread in shallow pan and bake at 350° for 20 minutes, stirring occasionally. Cool. Sprinkle 1/2 of crumbs in 13" x 9" greased pan.
Filling: Beat egg whites until frothy. Add sugar, thawed berries and lemon juice. Beat 10 to 12 minutes. Fold in whipped cream. Spoon over crumbs and top with remaining crumbs. Freeze 6 hours. Can be made with fresh berries and Cool Whip.

Mrs. Dale Anderson (Judy)
Mrs. John Taylor (Sue)
Mrs. Richard Davis (Elaine)

RASPBERRY FREEZE

Serves: 8-10

1 12-oz. pkg. frozen raspberries
2 egg whites, beaten stiff
3/4 cup sugar
2 Tbsp. lemon juice
1 cup whipping cream, whipped
Vanilla wafer crumbs

Beat frozen raspberries in mixer for 20 minutes. Food processor may be used for shorter time. Process until smooth and light. Beat 2 egg whites stiff. Beat sugar and lemon juice into egg whites. Fold in whipped cream. Fold all into raspberries. This may be frozen at this stage and served in sherbets. Or crush vanilla wafers and line a 2 qt. cake pan. Spread with raspberry mixture and sprinkle more crumbs on top. Freeze. Slice and serve.

Mrs. Earl Mitchell

CARAMEL ICE CREAM PIE

Serves: 8

9-inch baked pie shell
1-1/2 pt. chocolate ice cream
1-1/2 pt. butter pecan ice cream
1 cup pecans, coarsely chopped

Soften chocolate ice cream and spread into pie crust. Freeze until firm. Then spread softened butter pecan ice cream on top of chocolate. Refreeze.

RUM-BUTTERSCOTCH
    SAUCE:
1 cup brown sugar, packed
1/3 cup light cream
1/4 cup light corn syrup
1/4 cup butter
1/2 tsp. vanilla
1/2 tsp. rum extract

To make sauce, combine first four ingredients, boil 1 or 2 minutes, stirring constantly. Remove from heat and add vanilla and rum extract. Cover and chill. When cool, drizzle ice cream pie with 1/4 to 1/2 cup of sauce and then sprinkle top with pecans. Refreeze. To serve, set out about 20 minutes, then cut into wedges and serve with additional sauce.

Margaret Wright

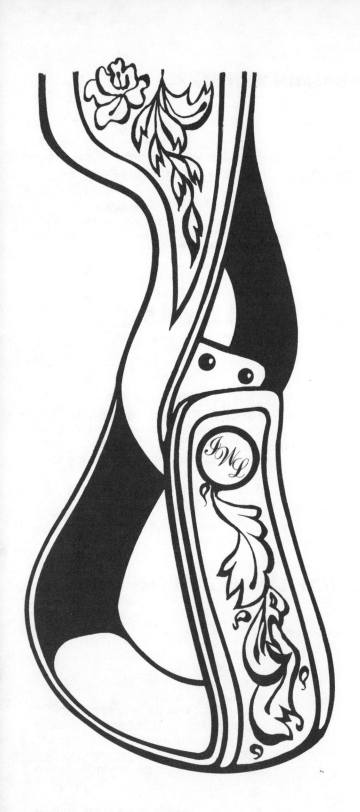

CAN'T SAY NO
COOKIES AND CANDY

"CAIN'T SAY NO"

Just as Aiddo Annie couldn't say no to fellas in the musical "Oklahoma," no one will be able to say no to these delightful confections. From creamy candies to crisp golden cookies these recipes are sure to please.

COOKIES

CHOCOLATE COOKIES

Yield: 2-3 dozen

1 can Eagle Brand milk
1 stick margarine
1 (12-oz.) pkg. chocolate chips
1 cup flour, sifted
1 cup chopped pecans
1 tsp. vanilla

Mix Eagle Brand, margarine, and chocolate chips; place in microwave for 2 minutes to melt or melt over boiling water, stirring until dissolved. Add flour, pecans, and vanilla to melted chocolate. Cool 10 minutes. Drop by teaspoon on greased cookie sheet. Bake at 350° for 7-10 minutes.

Mary Helen Iselin

DUTCH HANDKERCHIEFS

Yield: 24-30 (Not ever enough!)

DOUGH:
2 cups flour
1 cup butter
1/4 cup water

FILLING:
1 egg white
1 cup sugar
1 tsp. almond flavoring

Mix dough as for pie; roll very thin; cut into four inch squares.
Filling: Beat egg white until stiff; fold in sugar and flavoring. Put one teaspoon in center of each square. Fold corners to center. Bake on lightly greased cookie sheet until lightly browned, in 350° oven.

Barbara Meulpolder

CENCI

Yield: 48

3 cups flour, sifted
3 eggs
1/2 cup sugar
4 Tbsp. butter or margarine,
    melted
2 Tbsp. Marsala wine or rum
1 tsp. vanilla
Vegetable oil (enough for
    deep fat frying)
6 Tbsp. olive oil
1/2 cup powdered sugar

Place flour in a mound on a pasta board and make a well in the center. Put eggs, sugar, butter, wine and vanilla in well. Mix ingredients in the well together with fork working outward little by little to absorb almost all the flour. Use enough to make a pliable dough. Heat vegetable oil and olive oil in a deep fat fryer until hot. Roll out dough to 1/8" thickness. Cut into 1" x 2" rectangles. Drop in hot oil and fry until golden brown. Drain on paper towels. Sprinkle with powdered sugar and serve cold.

Lori Carroll

CARROT COOKIES

Yield: 3-4 dozen

3/4 cup sugar
3/4 cup shortening
1 egg
1 cup cooked, mashed carrots
1 tsp. vanilla
2 cups flour
1/2 tsp. salt
2 tsp. baking powder

Cream sugar and shortening. Add egg and mix well. Add carrots and vanilla. Sift together flour, salt, and baking powder. Add to sugar mixture. Drop by teaspoon onto greased cookie sheet. Bake at 375° for 10 minutes.

FROSTING:
1 cup powdered sugar
2 tsp. orange rind, grated
2 Tbsp. orange juice
1 tsp. butter

Cream all ingredients. Spread frosting on cooled cookies.

Colleen Jantzen

CORN FLAKE COOKIES

Yield: 60

1 cup white sugar
1 cup brown sugar
1 stick oleo
1 stick butter
2 eggs
1 tsp. vanilla
2 cups flour, sifted
2 tsp. baking soda
1/4 tsp. salt
2 cups Old Fashioned Oats
1 cup coconut, shredded
2 cups Corn Flakes

Cream together sugar, brown sugar, oleo and butter. Add eggs and vanilla. Sift flour, baking soda, and salt together then gradually add to mixture. By hand, stir in oats, coconut, and corn flakes. Roll into teaspoon-size balls and place on greased cookie sheet. Bake at 375° for 8-10 minutes. Let cool a few minutes before removing from pan.

Jane Boyer

GLYNDEN'S BEST EVER COOKIES

Yield: 60-72

1/2 cup margarine
1/2 cup shortening
3/4 cup sugar
3/4 cup brown sugar, packed
2 eggs
2 cups oats
3/4 cup coconut, shredded
1 tsp. vanilla
2 cups flour, sifted
1 tsp. baking soda
1/4 tsp. baking powder
1 cup chocolate chips
1/2 cup nuts, chopped

Mix margarine, shortening, sugar and brown sugar well. Add eggs and mix well. Blend in oats and coconut. Add vanilla. Sift flour, baking soda and baking powder together. Gradually add to the rest, mixing well. Stir in chocolate chips and chopped nuts. Drop from teaspoon onto lightly greased cookie sheet. Bake for 7-10 minutes at 350°. This recipe can be baked ahead and frozen.

Marsha Scott

OKIE BOLLEN
(Delightfully Dutch)

Yield: 30

2 cups flour, sifted
1/4 cup sugar
3 tsp. baking powder
1 tsp. salt
1 tsp. nutmeg or mace
1/4 cup Wesson or Mazola oil
3/4 cup milk
1 egg
Citron or raisins may be added

Sift together flour, sugar, baking powder, salt, and nutmeg or mace. Add oil, milk, egg and citron or raisins. Drop by teaspoonfuls into hot fat or oil at 375°. Fry until golden brown. Drain on absorbent paper. Roll warm puffs in cinnamon-sugar mixture.

Barbara Meulpolder

PEANUT BUTTER COOKIES WITH CHOCOLATE KISSES

Yield: 24-36

1/2 cup shortening
1/2 cup sugar
1/2 cup brown sugar, packed
1/2 cup peanut butter, smooth
1 egg
1-3/4 cups flour, sifted
1 tsp. baking soda
1/2 tsp. salt
2 Tbsp. milk
1 tsp. vanilla
36 chocolate candy kisses,
    more or less

Before starting, unwrap kisses and set aside. Cream shortening, sugar, and brown sugar. Add peanut butter and egg. Sift flour, baking soda, and salt together. Gradually add to mixture. Add milk and vanilla. Blend well. Shape into balls using a rounded teaspoon for each. Roll balls in sugar and place on an ungreased cookie sheet. Bake for 10-12 minutes at 375°. Remove from oven and top each cookie immediately with a candy kiss, pressing down firmly so cookie cracks around edge.

Esther Bouziden

CREAM CHEESE COOKIES

Yield: 96

3 sticks butter (room
    temperature)
2 (3-oz.) pkgs. cream cheese
    (room temperature)
2 cups powdered sugar
2 tsp. vanilla
2 Tbsp. lemon juice
4 tsp. grated lemon peel
2 cups finely chopped pecans

Cream together butter and cream cheese until light and fluffy. Gradually add sugar and beat hard. Stir in vanilla, lemon juice and peel. Add flour, mixing well. Stir in nuts. Push small amount of dough from teaspoon onto ungreased baking sheet. Bake at 300° for 20-25 minutes until delicately browned. While hot, roll in powdered sugar. Recipe can be frozen after baking.

Claudell Thomas

MOLASSES COOKIES

Yield: 48

3/4 cup shortening
1 cup sugar
1/4 cup molasses
1 egg
2 cups flour, sifted
2 tsp. baking soda
1/2 tsp. ground cloves
1/2 tsp. ginger
1/2 tsp. salt
1/2 tsp. cinnamon

Melt shortening in a 3 or 4-qt. saucepan over low heat. Remove from heat and let cool. Add sugar, molasses, and egg. Beat well. Sift together flour, baking soda, cloves, ginger, salt and cinnamon. Add to first mixture. Mix. Chill; then form in one inch balls, and roll in sugar. Place on a greased cookie sheet about 2 inches apart. Bake at 375° for 8 minutes. Cookies should be chewy and not done in middle. Recipe can be baked ahead and frozen. Great to serve with a fruit salad.

Jo Brown

CALIFORNIA GOLD BARS

Yield: 16

1 cup brown sugar, packed
1 cup margarine
1 egg
1 tsp. vanilla
1-3/4 cups flour, sifted
1 cup nuts, chopped
1/2 cup apricot jam

Beat brown sugar, margarine, egg and vanilla, until smooth and creamy. Stir in flour and nuts. Spoon half of batter in a greased 9'' square pan. Batter is thick so you may have to spread it with your fingers. Spread jam evenly over batter. Cover jam with remaining batter. Bake at 325° for 50 minutes. Cool 10 minutes before cutting.

Esther Bouziden

DUTCH SANTA CLAUS COOKIES

Yield: 84

2 cups brown sugar
1-1/2 cups butter
3-1/2 cups flour, sifted
1 tsp. cinnamon
1/2 tsp. nutmeg
1/2 tsp. cloves
1 tsp. baking powder
1 egg, beaten
1 scant tsp. salt

Cream butter and brown sugar. Add remaining ingredients. This makes a very stiff dough. Mold cookies on a Santa Claus Cookie Board or form into a roll as for refrigerator cookies and slice when thoroughly chilled. Bake at 350° for 10-12 minutes. Recipe can be frozen after baking.

The sixth of December is celebrated as St. Nicholas' Birthday and is kept much as we keep Christmas. The Dutch insist that our idea of Santa Claus (St. Nick) originally came from Holland. The wooden shoes are placed beside the fire on St. Nicholas Eve and fat carrots or a bunch of hay are placed beside the shoes for St. Nicholas' horse. St. Nicholas is careful to punish the naughty and to reward the good. There is a special cookie for this time of year called the Santa Claus Cookie.

Barbara Meulpolder

"SLICE A SUGAR" COOKIE

Yield: 100

1 cup sugar
1 cup powdered sugar
1 cup margarine (2 sticks)
1 cup oil
2 eggs
4-1/2 cups flour, sifted
1 tsp. baking soda
1 tsp. cream of tartar
1 tsp. salt
1 Tbsp. vanilla extract
1 tsp. almond extract

Mix sugar, powdered sugar, margarine and oil. Add eggs. Cream well. Sift flour, baking soda, cream of tartar and salt. Gradually add to mixture. Add vanilla and almond extracts to mixture. Refrigerate for about an hour. (The dough can be rolled into a log, wrapped in wax paper and stored in the refrigerator up to two weeks. Just slice and bake as much as you want.) Drop by small balls onto cookie sheet. Press lightly with a fork. Bake for about 10 minutes at 375.° They should not be too brown. After baking, cookies can be frozen.

Sue Harper
Bobbie Stoner

SUGAR COOKIES

Yield: 4-6 dozen

1 cup sugar
1/2 cup butter, softened
1/2 cup shortening
1 egg
2 cups flour, sifted
1/2 tsp. cream of tartar
1/2 tsp. baking soda
Dash of salt
1 tsp. vanilla
Butter
Sugar

Cream sugar, butter and shortening together. Add egg. Sift flour, cream of tartar, baking soda and salt together. Add flour combination gradually to mixture. Add vanilla. Drop from teaspoon onto an ungreased cookie sheet. Spread a little butter onto bottom of small glass and dip into sugar. (Repeat between each cookie.) With glass, press down slightly on each cookie. Bake for 10 minutes at 350.° Cool. Cookies will not be brown when done.

Vicki Sturgis

SANDTARTS

Yield: 48

1 lb. softened butter
3-1/2 cups flour, sifted
6 Tbsp. sugar
2 cups chopped pecans
2 tsp. vanilla
Powdered sugar

Cream together softened butter, flour, and sugar until blended. Add nuts and vanilla and mix well. Chill mixture one hour. Roll into walnut sized balls. Bake for 6-8 minutes at 350° on ungreased cookie sheets. Roll in powdered sugar three times. Recipe can be baked ahead and kept for a long time in a covered container.

Jo Barnes

PECAN CUPS

Yield: 60

SHELL:
1 cup margarine or butter
1 (8-oz.) pkg. cream cheese
Dash of salt
2 cups flour, sifted

FILLING:
2 eggs, beaten
1-1/2 cups brown sugar, packed
2 Tbsp. melted butter
1-1/2 cups pecans, chopped
1/2 tsp. vanilla

To make shells, beat butter, cream cheese, and salt until fluffy. Add flour and continue to mix. Put dough in refrigerator until firm enough to handle. After chilling, form dough into little balls and press into bottom and sides of small lightly buttered muffin tins.
For filling, mix all ingredients and pour into shells. Bake at 350° for 30 minutes. Note: Tiny muffin tins make dainty bite sized pieces.

Carolyn Bules
Pat Diehl

PECAN CLUSTERS

Yield: 3-4 dozen

1/4 cup butter
1/2 cup sugar
1 egg
1-1/2 tsp. vanilla
1-1/2 sq. unsweetened
   chocolate, melted
1/2 cup flour
1/2 tsp. salt
1/4 tsp. baking powder
2 cups pecans, whole

Mix together butter and sugar. Add egg and vanilla. Mix in melted chocolate. Sift dry ingredients together and add to chocolate mixture. Stir in the pecans. Drop by teaspoon onto greased cookie sheet. Bake at 350° for 10 minutes.

Colleen Jantzen

LEMON CLOUDS

Yield: 4-6 dozen

2 cups margarine
2/3 cup powdered sugar
2 cups unsifted flour
1-1/3 cups unsifted cornstarch

LEMON ICING:
6 Tbsp. margarine
1 box powdered sugar
Lemon juice for consistency
Lemon rind (optional)

Cream margarine and sugar. Sift in flour and cornstarch. Mix well. Drop by small teaspoonful on ungreased cookie sheet about one inch apart. Bake for 15 minutes at 350°. Do not brown. Cool and ice. To prepare icing, cream margarine and powdered sugar, adding lemon juice for consistency. Lemon rind may be added if desired. This recipe may be baked ahead and frozen.

Myrna Kay Eck

 Place a piece of apple in the brown sugar jar. It will keep the sugar from drying out and lumping. Try the same cure for too dry cookies.

GERMAN CREAM CHEESE BROWNIES

Yield: 2 dozen

*1 pkg. Baker's German Sweet
    Chocolate*
3 Tbsp. butter

Step 1: Melt chocolate and butter in double boiler, stirring occasionally. Set aside to cool.

*1 (3-oz.) pkg. Philadelphia
    cream cheese*
2 Tbsp. butter
1/4 cup sugar
1 egg
1 Tbsp. flour
1/2 tsp. vanilla

Step 2: Cream butter and cream cheese until soft; gradually add sugar. Stir in egg, flour and vanilla until well blended. Set aside.

2 eggs
3/4 cup sugar
1/2 cup flour
1/2 tsp. baking powder
1/4 tsp. salt
1 tsp. vanilla
1/4 tsp. almond extract
1/2 cup nuts, chopped

Step 3: Beat eggs until fluffy; then gradually add sugar. Mix dry ingredients and fold into egg mixture. Add vanilla and almond extract. Blend in cooled chocolate mixture and nuts. Measure 1 cup chocolate mixture and set aside. Spread remaining chocolate mixture into greased 9" pan. Pour cheese mixture on top. Drop remaining chocolate batter onto cheese mixture by spoonfuls and swirl just to marble. Bake at 350° for 35-40 minutes. Cool, cut into bars and refrigerate until served.

Judy Halstead

PETITE CHEESE CAKES

Yield: 2 dozen

*2 (8-oz.) pkgs. cream cheese,
    softened*
3/4 cup sugar
2 eggs
2 Tbsp. lemon juice
1 tsp. vanilla
24 vanilla wafers
1 (12-oz.) can cherry pie filling

Beat cream cheese, sugar, eggs, lemon juice, and vanilla until light and fluffy. Line muffin tins with crinkle cups. Place a vanilla wafer in bottom of each filler, then fill 2/3 full. Bake at 375° for 15-20 minutes. Top with cherry pie filling and chill. Recipe can be frozen.

Tottie Kennedy

CHRISTMAS BARS

Yield: 48

1 cup butter
1 cup sugar
2 cups flour, sifted
1 tsp. cinnamon
1 egg yolk, beaten
1 egg white
1/4 cup chopped walnuts
1/4 cup chopped almonds
Light Karo syrup
Green cherries
Cinnamon candies

Mix butter, sugar, flour, cinnamon and egg yolk together. Press on large cookie sheet with thumbs. Beat egg white slightly and spread on mixture. Sprinkle chopped nuts on top. Bake at 350° until light brown on corners. Cut diagonally and decorate with green cherries dipped in white Karo and cinnamon candies (redhots). Arrange cherries and candies to look like a holly leaf.

Nan Brim

PEANUT BUTTER BROWNIES

Yield: 16

1/2 cup butter or margarine
1/2 cup sugar
1/2 cup dark brown sugar, packed
1 egg, beaten
1/3 cup peanut butter
1/2 tsp. vanilla
1 cup 3 Minute Oats
1 cup flour, sifted
1/2 tsp. baking soda
1/4 tsp. salt

FROSTING:
1 cup powdered sugar
1/2 cup peanut butter
6 Tbsp. milk or cream

Grease and flour a 9" x 9" pan. Cream butter, sugar and dark brown sugar. Add egg, peanut butter and vanilla. Mix well. By hand, stir in oats, flour, baking soda and salt. Bake for 25 minutes at 350° For frosting, combine powdered sugar, peanut butter and milk. Frost brownies while hot. Let cool before cutting. This recipe can be baked ahead and frozen. Double recipe if using a 9 x 13 pan.

Mary Dickey

PEANUTTY BREAK-UPS

Yield: 3 dozen

1 (11-oz.) pkg. pie crust
    mix—dry
1 cup brown sugar, packed
1 egg, beaten
1 tsp. vanilla
1 cup salted-dry roasted
    peanuts
1 cup butterscotch chips

Put all ingredients in a large mixing bowl and mix by hand, as for a pie crust. Dough will be stiff. Turn out on a board, or cabinet and knead until workable. Press by hand into a greased large cookie sheet and spread about 1/3" thin. Bake at 400° for 10-12 minutes. Turn entire sheet (uncut) onto cabinet or rack for cooling. When completely cool, break-up into serving size pieces.
Tip: Pie crust sticks work well. Spread 1/3" to 1/4" inch for crispier break-ups.

Kathy Risley

FRUIT BARS

Yield: 2 dozen

FILLING:
2-1/2 cups sliced fresh fruit
    (your choice)
1/2 cup sugar
2 Tbsp. cornstarch
3/4 cup water

CRUNCH MIXTURE:
3/4 cup butter
1 cup brown sugar, packed
1-3/4 cups flour, sifted
1/2 tsp. salt
1/2 tsp. baking soda
1/2 tsp. ground cinnamon
1-1/2 cups rolled oats

Grease a 9" x 13" pan. Prepare filling first by combining fruit, sugar, cornstarch and water in a saucepan. Stir over medium heat until mixture is thickened. Set aside and cool. Combine butter and brown sugar. Sift flour, salt, baking soda, and cinnamon together. Add to butter and brown sugar. Mix well, then stir in oats. Press half of crunch mixture in pan. Bake for 5 minutes at 400°. After baking crust, spread filling over top. Pat remaining crunch mixture over filling and bake for 15-20 minutes at 400°.

Mrs. Luther Payne

OATMEAL CARMELITAS

Yield: 16

1 cup flour, sifted
1 cup quick-cooking oats
3/4 cup brown sugar, packed
1/2 tsp. baking soda
1/4 tsp. salt
3/4 cup margarine, melted
1 cup chocolate chips
1 cup chopped nuts
3/4 cup caramel ice cream
    topping
3 Tbsp. flour
    OR
32 Kraft caramels
5 Tbsp. milk or cream

Grease a 9" x 9" pan. Combine flour, oatmeal, brown sugar, baking soda, salt, and margarine. Press half of mixture into pan. Bake for 5 minutes at 350°. Sprinkle chocolate chips and nuts over baked crust. Either 1. mix topping and flour, or 2. melt caramels with milk. Drizzle either mixture over chocolate chips and nuts. Sprinkle remaining crust mixture over caramel topping. Bake for 15 minutes at 350°.

Judy Anderson
Pauline Fossett

LEMON SQUARES

Yield: 16

CRUST:
1 stick margarine
1 cup flour, sifted
1/4 cup powdered sugar

Cream margarine, flour, and powdered sugar. Pat mixture into an ungreased 8" x 8" pan. Bake for 15 minutes at 350°.

TOPPING:
1/2 fresh lemon rind, grated
2 eggs, slightly beaten
2 Tbsp. lemon juice
1 cup sugar
2 Tbsp. flour
1/4 tsp. baking powder
1/4 cup powdered sugar

Mix lemon rind with eggs, lemon juice, sugar, flour, and baking powder. Put mixture on top of crust and bake for an additional 20-25 minutes at 350°. After baking, while still hot, lightly dust with powdered sugar.

Carolyn Bules

SOFT NESTLE COOKIES

Yield: 6-8 dozen

1 cup shortening
3/4 cup brown sugar, packed
3/4 cup sugar
2 eggs
1 tsp. baking soda
1-1/2 tsp. hot tap water
2-1/4 cups flour, sifted
1 tsp. salt
1 (6-oz.) pkg. chocolate chips
1/2 cup chopped nuts (optional)

Cream shortening, brown sugar, and sugar. Add eggs and beat mixture until fluffy. Dissolve baking soda in water then add to mixture. Sift flour with salt, and gradually add to mixture. Add chocolate chips and 1/2 cup chopped nuts, if desired. Drop by teaspoonfuls onto lightly greased cookie sheet and bake at 350° for 10 minutes.

Mona Payne

COCONUT REFRIGERATOR COOKIES

Yield: 2-3 dozen

2 cups flour, sifted
1/8 tsp. salt
1/4 tsp. cinnamon
1-1/2 tsp. baking powder
1/2 cup margarine
1 cup sugar
1/4 cup brown sugar, packed
1 egg or 2 yolks, beaten
1/2 tsp. lemon extract
1 cup coconut, flaked
    or shredded

In large mixing bowl, mix together flour, salt, cinnamon, and baking powder. In a separate bowl, cream margarine, sugar, and brown sugar. Add eggs, vanilla, and lemon extract to sugar mixture; then blend in coconut. Constantly blending, add sugar mixture to flour mixture slowly. Shape dough in 1-1/2" rolls and wrap in wax paper or foil. Chill several hours, overnight, or freeze. When ready to bake, cut in 1/8-1/4 inch slices. (Thin slices are crisper.) Bake on oiled cookie sheets. Bake at 350° for 8-10 minutes. Cookies should be golden brown and cooled on racks. Recipe can be frozen before baking or after.

Kathy Risley

CARAMEL GERMAN
CHOCOLATE BROWNIES

Yield: 2 dozen

1 pkg. German Chocolate
　　cake mix
3/4 cup butter, softened
1/3 cup evaporated milk
3 cups chopped nuts
45 caramels, melted
1/2 cup evaporated milk
1 (12-oz.) pkg. chocolate chips

Mix cake mix, butter, 1/3 cup evaporated milk, and 2 cups of the nuts together. Press half of mixture in a greased and floured 9" x 13" pan. Bake at 350° for 8 minutes. Melt caramels with 1/2 cup milk in a sauce pan over low heat. Sprinkle chocolate chips and one cup nuts over baked mixture. Drizzle melted caramels over chips and nuts. Place remaining batter on top. Bake for an additional 20 minutes at 350°.

Sharon McCune
Submitted by Beverly Evans

CANDY

CHOCOLATE COVERED FONDANT

1/2 cup butter
1 lb. pecans, chopped
1 can Eagle Brand condensed
　　milk
1 to 1-1/4 box powdered sugar
1 tsp. vanilla
1 can coconut (optional)
2 (6-oz.) pkgs. chocolate chips
1/4 lb. paraffin

Melt butter, pour over pecans and set aside. Combine milk, powdered sugar, vanilla, and coconut (if desired). Add buttered pecans to this mixture and form small balls. Chill. Melt chocolate chips and paraffin in double boiler or microwave. Keep warm. Dip chilled fondant balls into chocolate mixture. Mixture for centers may be divided and flavored separately with different flavors (i.e., maple, peppermint, lemon, orange, etc.).

Mrs. Fred Blythe (Sharon)

CARAMEL CORN

Yield: 1-1/2 gal.

5 qts. popped corn
1 cup roasted and shelled
*   peanuts*
2 cups brown sugar
2 sticks butter, softened
1/2 tsp. cream of tartar
2 tsp. soda

Combine brown sugar, butter and cream of tartar; boil for 5 minutes. Remove from heat and add soda. Pour over corn and nuts and spread on 2 cookie sheets and bake 40 minutes in a 200° oven. Stir and break up into chunks.

Exa Clayton

CARAMEL CANDY

Makes: 1-1/2 lbs.

1 cup sugar
1 cup white Karo syrup
1/2 pt. heavy cream
1/4 lb. butter
1/2 cup nuts
1-1/2 tsp. vanilla

Cook sugar, corn syrup, butter and half of the cream until it boils. Add remaining cream and vanilla. Cook over low heat, stirring constantly, until thick. Add nuts and pour into buttered 9" x 9" pan and cool and slice.

Mrs. Bruce Thomas (Betsy)

CRANBERRY SURPRISE
Wow! A different taste experience!

1 lb. pkg. almond bark
1 lb. pkg. fresh cranberries

Melt almond bark in microwave on low or in double boiler. Drop dry, fresh cranberries into melted bark a few at a time. Remove to wax paper, individually, and let harden. Delicious as hors d'oeuvres, candy or a snack.

Wanda Wright

CREAMY BON BONS

2 sticks butter or margarine
1 (8-oz.) pkg. cream cheese
1 Tbsp. vanilla
2-1/2 boxes powdered sugar
  (sifted)
2 cups creamy peanut butter
1 (12-oz.) pkg. chocolate chips
  (semi-sweet)
1 section paraffin wax

Have butter, cream cheese, and peanut butter at room temperature. Cream together (food processor may be used). Add vanilla and beat. Add sugar gradually and stir. When mixed well, shape into balls and place on a piece of wax paper on a cookie sheet. Insert toothpick in each ball and chill in ice-box about 1 hour. Melt chocolate chips and wax in double boiler. Dip chilled balls into melted mix. Place on wax paper and remove toothpicks. Store in ice-box until ready to eat.

Carolyn Bules

DATE LOAF CANDY

Yield: Two 1-foot logs

2 cups white sugar
1 (5.33-oz.) can Carnation
  evaporated milk
1 (8-oz.) box dates, chopped
1 cup pecans, chopped

Cook sugar and milk to soft ball stage, stirring constantly with a wooden spoon. Remove from heat and add dates. Return to heat and cook to hard ball stage. Remove from heat, add nuts, and cool for 5 minutes. Beat with wooden spoon until creamy and stiff. Knead in wet cloth towel, then roll into 2 one-inch diameter logs. Wrap in wax paper and refrigerate. Committee Variation: For a softer nut roll, do not add nuts to candy. Shape rolls with well buttered hands. Roll logs in nuts. Wrap and chill.

Mona Payne

CREAM CANDY

Makes: 3 lbs.

3 cups sugar
2 cups cream (thick)
1 cup white syrup
2 tsp. vanilla
Pinch of salt
1 cup nuts

Over very low heat, simmer sugar, cream, and white syrup slowly, stirring occasionally, for 1 hour until soft ball stage. Remove from heat and beat. Add vanilla, salt, and nuts. Pour into buttered, greased pan. Slice when nearly cooled.

Pat Diehl

DRIED APRICOT CANDY

Makes: 24 candies

1 lb. dried apricots
1 pkg. shredded coconut, ground
1 orange rind, grated
Juice of 1 orange
1 cup sugar

Combine apricots, coconut, and orange rind. Add juice which has been sweetened with sugar. Make into small balls and roll in granulated sugar.

Mrs. Frank Carter

DUTCH OVEN DELIGHT

Makes: over 5 lbs.

1 lb. butter or margarine
1 (16-fl. oz.) can evaporated milk
3/4 cup dark Karo syrup
7 cups sugar
3 cups nuts, chopped
1-1/2 tsp. vanilla

Combine all ingredients except nuts and vanilla in an ovenproof container. Bake uncovered at 250° for three hours, stirring often. Let cool 30 minutes. Beat with an electric mixer for 10 minutes. Add the nuts and the vanilla. Pour into a buttered pan. Let cool and cut.

Ann Frazee Riley

OKLAHOMA BROWN CANDY (Aunt Bill's)

*Great with strong-arm helpers in the kitchen.

Yield: 6 lbs.

6 cups sugar
2 cups whole milk or cream
1/4 tsp. soda
1/4 lb. butter or margarine
1 tsp. vanilla
1 to 2 lbs. pecans

Pour 2 cups sugar into heavy aluminum or iron skillet and place over low heat. Begin stirring with a wooden spoon and keep sugar moving so that it does not burn. It will take approximately 1/2 hour to melt sugar completely. At no time let it smoke or cook so fast that the sugar turns dark. It should be the color of light brown sugar syrup. As soon as you have the sugar starting to heat in the skillet, pour remaining 4 cups sugar and milk or cream into a deep, heavy kettle. Set over low heat to cook slowly while you are melting sugar in skillet. As soon as all sugar is melted, begin pouring it into kettle of boiling milk and sugar, keeping it on very low heat, while stirring constantly. The real secret to mixing these ingredients is to pour a very fine stream from the skillet. Continue cooking and stirring until mixture forms firm ball (245°) when dropped into cold water. Remove from heat and immediately add soda, stirring vigorously as it foams up. Add butter, allowing it to melt as you stir. Let cool for 20 minutes. Add vanilla and beat (using a wooden spoon) until mixture is thick and heavy, having a dull appearance instead of a glossy sheen. Add pecans and mix. Turn into a large pan and cut into squares when cooled slightly. Candy keeps moist and delicious indefinitely. It is most attractive when decorated with a sprig of holly, candied cherries or pecan halves.

Note: A long time favorite of many Oklahomans, "Aunt Bill's Brown Candy" was first published in *The Daily Oklahoman* in April, 1938.

JINX'S PEANUT BUTTER FUDGE

Makes: 2 lbs.

2 cups sugar
1 small can evaporated milk
1 cup peanut butter
1 cup marshmallow cream

Combine sugar and milk. Cook to soft ball stage. Remove from heat and add peanut butter and marshmallow cream. Mix thoroughly and spread in 8-inch pan. When cool, cut into squares. Preparation time—25 minutes.

Rosanne G. Dickinson

OPERA ROLL

Difficult production, but rave reviews.

Makes: 4 rolls or 95-100 slices of candy

FONDANT:
2 cups sugar
1 cup water
1/4 tsp. cream of tartar
2 Tbsp. butter
1 tsp. vanilla

OUTER LAYER:
1 cup brown sugar
1 cup white sugar
1 cup Karo syrup
1/2 cup butter
2 cups cream
Pecan halves

Butter sides of heavy pan. Combine sugar, water, and cream of tartar. Stir over medium heat until sugar is dissolved. Boil mixture until it forms a soft ball (do not stir). Let fondant cool in pan until lukewarm. Pour onto a chilled platter. Work in butter and vanilla. Knead with hands until soft and creamy. Form into four long rolls, approximately 1" x 12". Outer Layer: In a heavy pan, combine outer layer ingredients, reserving 1 cup cream, and bring to a boil. Add remaining 1 cup cream slowly so boiling does not stop. Stir mixture every 3 minutes. Cook until it forms a firm ball. Cool until lukewarm then beat until creamy. Pour into two 13" x 9" buttered pyrex pans and let cool completely. Cut the caramel in half lengthwise, making 4 rectangles of caramel. In center of each, place 1 roll of fondant. Roll caramel around fondant, pinching ends to hold in place. Press pecan halves on all sides. Slice into 1/2-inch slices (round) to serve.

Bernice Kuzel

MICROWAVE PEANUT BRITTLE

Makes: 1 lb.

1 cup raw peanuts
1 cup sugar
1/8 tsp. salt
1/2 cup Karo syrup
1 Tbsp. margarine
1 tsp. vanilla
1 tsp. baking soda

Combine first 4 ingredients and stir. Cook in microwave on high for 4 minutes. Stir candy and turn the dish. Return to microwave and continue to cook on high for 4-1/2 minutes. Remove and add margarine and vanilla. Stir and microwave for 1-1/2 minutes. Remove; add baking soda. Mix well. Pour out onto foil (foil need not be buttered). Let cool before cracking.

Mrs. Joe Bolin (Pat)

PEANUT BRITTLE

Makes: 2 lbs.

2 cups sugar
1/2 cup water
1 cup light Karo syrup
2 cups raw peanuts
Dash of salt
1 tsp. butter
1 tsp. soda (heaping)
1 tsp. vanilla

Combine sugar, water, and Karo syrup in a heavy, large sauce pan and boil to hard ball stage. Remove from heat; add raw peanuts, salt, and butter (mixture will be quite thick). Return to fire and boil until mixture is golden brown. Remove from heat; add soda and vanilla. Stir to blend. Mixture will bubble. Pour onto well buttered surface and smooth with buttered hands until thin, working fast. (You might need a helper at this point.) Crack when cooled.)

Gail Wynne
Janie Word

 If it's important to you to get walnut meats out whole, soak the nuts overnight in salt water before you crack them.

GRAMMY LUCY'S MILLION DOLLAR FUDGE

Makes: 5 lbs.

5 cups sugar
5.3 oz. Carnation evaporated
milk
1/3 lb. butter
24 oz. chocolate chips
1 (8-oz.) jar marshmallow cream
1 lb. pecans

Combine sugar, evaporated milk and butter. Boil 8 minutes. Remove from heat and add chocolate chips and marshmallow cream. Beat until well blended. Add nuts and pour into well-greased pan. Cool and cut into squares.

Mrs. Bud Layton (Lucille)

SUZYBELLE'S PRALINES

Makes: 3 lbs.

4 cups brown sugar
1/2 cup cream
2 Tbsp. butter
2 cups pecans

Combine brown sugar, cream and butter. Bring to a boil and boil for 3 minutes without stirring. Test for soft ball: when hot mixture forms into ball in cold water test remove from heat. Stir in pecans. Pour candy onto a greased surface in clusters (put newspaper on counter; then waxed paper, sprayed lightly with Pam).

Carolyn Bules

TOFFEE

1 lb. butter (not margarine)
1/4 cup water
2 cups sugar
6 oz. pecans, chopped
10-3/4 oz. milk chocolate bar

Spread nuts in jelly roll pan. Break apart chocolate bar and set aside. Cook butter, water and sugar, stirring constantly until 300° (Mixture will be a rich caramel color.) Spread over nuts. Sprinkle chocolate on top. Spread chocolate with knife when soft. Cool and break into pieces.

Robin Sigler

PECAN CHEWS

Makes: 100 bite size pieces

2 cups sugar
1-1/2 cups white Karo syrup
1 cup light brown sugar
1 (14-1/2-oz.) can evaporated
   milk
1 cup whipping cream
1/2 lb. butter
1 cup water
2 cups pecans, broken
1/4 tsp. salt

Combine first 7 ingredients and cook to soft ball stage (238°), stirring frequently. This will take approximately 1 to 1-1/4 hours. Remove from heat; add pecans and salt. Pour into buttered 10" x 15" jelly roll pan. Cool. Cut into squares and wrap individually in Saran wrap. Store candy in a tight container and a cool place, and it will keep for months.

Mrs. Joe McDermott (Betty)

REESE CUP CANDY

Yield: 5 dozen

2 cups powdered sugar
2 sticks oleo
1 (12-oz.) jar peanut butter
12 oz. chocolate chips
1/2 bar paraffin wax

Combine powdered sugar, oleo, and peanut butter and shape into balls. Refrigerate about one hour. Melt chocolate chips and paraffin in double boiler and keep hot. Insert toothpicks into chilled balls and dip into melted mix. Store in refrigerator.

Peggy Harmon's crispy and crunchy variation: Substitute crunchy peanut butter and add up to 3 cups rice Krispies.

Sally McKnight

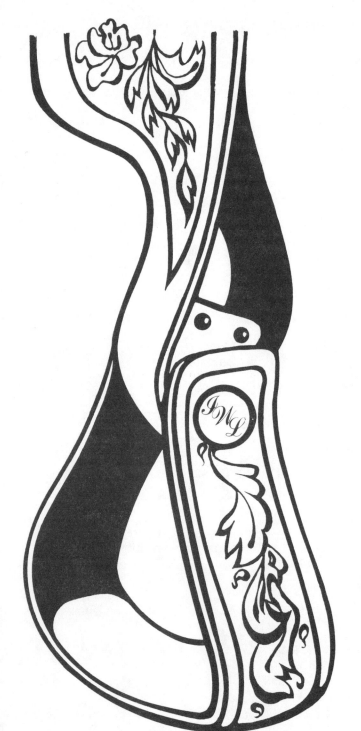

FANCY FIXIN'S
GOURMET

"FANCY FIXINS' "

Flavors from near and far provide a variety of menus from several gourmet clubs who share some of their favorites with us.

SPRING LUNCHEON
For Eight

Bloody Mary
Hot Fruit Compote
Ham Empañadas   **Stuffed Eggs Mornay**
Strawberry Sorbet
Almond Butter Bars
Coffee

BLOODY MARY

6 jiggers vodka
6 drops Tabasco
6 dashes Worcestershire sauce
6 Tbsp. lemon juice
1/2 tsp. salt
1 tsp. pepper, freshly ground
1/4 tsp. monosodium glutamate
2 tsp. sugar
2 (12-oz.) cans vegetable juice
*   (V-8)*

Stir well and pour into ice filled glasses. Garnish with fresh celery stalk.

HOT FRUIT COMPOTE

Serves: 8

12 macaroons, crumbled
4 cups canned fruits, drained
    (peaches, pears, apricots,
    pineapple, or cherries)
1/2 cup almonds, slivered
    and toasted
1/4 cup brown sugar
1/2 cup sherry
1/4 cup butter, melted

Butter a 2-1/2 qt. casserole. Cover bottom with macaroon crumbs. Then alternate fruit and macaroons in layers, finishing with macaroons. Sprinkle with almonds, sugar, and sherry. Bake in 350° oven for 30 minutes. Serve hot. Add melted butter.

HAM EMPAÑADAS

Makes: 18 empañadas

SOUR CREAM PASTRY:
1 cup flour, sifted
1/4 tsp. salt
1/2 cup (1 stick) butter
1/2 cup dairy sour cream

Combine sifted flour and salt in a mixing bowl. Cut in butter with pastry blender until crumbly. Stir in sour cream. Gather dough into a ball. Wrap and refrigerate.

FILLING:
1 cup ham, cooked and ground
4 green onions, chopped
1 (4-oz.) can chilies, drained
    and chopped
1/4 cup dairy sour cream

Filling: Combine ham, onions, chilies, and sour cream in a medium-sized bowl. Roll out sour cream pastry on a flour sur- to a 1/8-inch thickness. Cut out 4-inch rounds. Put 1 Tbsp. ham filling on each round. Moisten edge and fold to make half circles and crimp to seal. Place on cookie sheet and prick with tines of fork. Bake in moderate oven (375°) for 15 minutes or until golden brown. Cool on wire rack. Serve warm. These may be made ahead and frozen before baking.

STUFFED EGGS MORNAY

Serves: 8

8 Tbsp. (1 stick) butter, softened
1 tsp. salt
1/2 cup flour
Pinch cayenne
1/4 tsp. white pepper
3 cups hot milk
2 oz. Swiss cheese, shredded
6 Tbsp. Parmesan cheese,
   grated
16 eggs, hard cooked
1/2 lb. mushrooms, minced
2 Tbsp. parsley, chopped
1/2 tsp. leaf tarragon, crumbled
1 cup (2 slices) fresh bread
   crumbs
2 Tbsp. butter, melted

1. Put 4 Tbsp. of the butter in container of electric blender with salt, flour, cayenne pepper, and 2 cups of hot milk. Cover; whirl for 30 seconds. Pour into large saucepan; add remaining hot milk and cook over medium heat, stirring constantly until sauce is thickened and bubbles, about 2 minutes.
2. Add Swiss cheese and 4 Tbsp. of the Parmesan. Cook, stirring constantly, until cheese is melted; remove from heat. Cover.
3. Cut eggs in half, lengthwise. Empty yolks into bowl; reserve the whites.
4. Heat 4 more Tbsp. of the butter in a small skillet. Sauté mushrooms for about 5 minutes, or until mixture is almost dry, stirring occasionally. Stir in parsley and tarragon.
5. Mash egg yolks with 1/2 cup of sauce; add the mushrooms. Fill whites with the mushroom mixture.
6. Spread a thin layer of sauce in a shallow baking dish and arrange the stuffed eggs in the sauce, stuffing side up. Spoon remaining sauce over.
7. Toss bread crumbs with remaining 2 Tbsp. Parmesan and melted butter. Sprinkle over eggs.
8. Cool, cover, and refrigerate until needed.
9. Bake in moderate oven, 350°, for 30 minutes.

STRAWBERRY SORBET

3 pts. fresh strawberries
2 cups sugar
Juice of 3 oranges
Juice of 3 lemons
1/3 cup Grand Marnier

Marinate whole berries in other ingredients 12-24 hours. Drain juice and serve whole berries.

ALMOND BUTTER BARS

1 cup butter
1 cup sugar
1/4 tsp. salt
1 tsp. vanilla
1 egg yolk
2 cups flour, sifted
1 egg white
2 Tbsp. sugar
1 can slivered almonds

Cream butter and sugar. Add salt, vanilla, and egg yolk and beat well. Add flour. *Pat* and roll onto oiled cookie sheet. Beat egg white slightly and add 2 Tbsp. sugar. Spread over dough. Press almonds into dough. Bake at 275° for 45 minutes.

NOTES:

CRABMEAT SANDWICH LUNCHEON
For Eight

Open-faced Crab Meat Sandwiches

Asparagus Vinaigrette

Deep-fried Strawberries
With Vanilla Sauce Broadmoor

Coffee

OPEN-FACED CRAB MEAT SANDWICH

3 (6-oz.) cans King or
    Dungeness crab meat
3/4 cup lemon juice
2 (8-oz.) cream cheese
3/4 cup heavy cream
3/4 cup mayonnaise
3 Tbsp. grated onion
3 cloves garlic, minced
2 Tbsp. snipped chives
Worcestershire sauce, to taste
Tabasco, to taste
Salt, to taste
White pepper, to taste
8 English muffins, halved

In a bowl let crab meat, picked over and flaked, marinate in lemon juice for 1 hour. In another bowl cream together softened cream cheese, heavy cream, and mayonnaise. Stir in the grated onion, garlic, and chives. Add the drained crab meat and Worcestershire sauce, Tabasco, salt, and white pepper to taste. Divide the mixture among muffin halves and put under a preheated broiler till tops are bubbly and golden.

NOTES

ENGLISH MUFFINS

1 pkg. dry active yeast
1/2 cup warm water
1-1/2 cups scalded milk
2 tsp. salt
2 Tbsp. sugar
1/4 cup shortening
5-3/4 — 6 cups all purpose flour

Soften yeast in water. Combine next four ingredients, cool to lukewarm. Stir in 2 cups flour, beat well, add yeast, and mix. Add enough of the remaining flour to make a moderately stiff dough. Turn out on a lightly floured surface. Knead 8-10 minutes till smooth. Place in greased bowl. Cover and let rise till double (1-1/4 hours). Punch down, cover, and let rest 10 minutes. Roll to slightly less than 1/2-inch on lightly floured surface. Cut with 3-inch cutter. Re-roll edges. Cover and let rise till very light, about 1-1/4 hours. Bake on top of range on medium-high, greased griddle; turn frequently till done, about 30 minutes. Cool thoroughly. Split with fork, toast, and serve.

VINAIGRETTE SAUCE FOR ASPARAGUS

3/4 cup olive oil
1/4 cup lemon juice
Salt to taste
1/2 tsp. dry mustard
Freshly ground black pepper
1 Tbsp. chopped capers
1 tsp. sweet pickles, finely
        chopped
1/2 tsp. parsley, chopped
1/2 tsp. chervil, chopped
1/2 tsp. chives, chopped

Combine all ingredients well and chill. Pour over hot or cold asparagus and let stand 1 hour, turning asparagus once.

DEEP-FRIED STRAWBERRIES WITH VANILLA SAUCE BROADMOOR

4 cups half and half
1/2 cup sugar
2 inch piece vanilla bean, split
5 egg yolks, large
36 strawberries
2 cups all-purpose flour
1/4 tsp. sugar
1/4 tsp. salt
1-1/2 cups beer
5 egg whites, large
Cream of tartar, pinch
Salt, pinch
1/4 cup sugar
1-1/2 tsp. cinnamon

In a small sauce pan, scald half and half with sugar and vanilla bean. Discard the vanilla bean. In a bowl, beat egg yolks until they are light. Add the scalded cream mixture in a stream, continuing to beat. Transfer the custard to a heavy saucepan and cook it over low heat, stirring continually until it coats the spoon. Transfer the sauce to a chilled bowl and cover with a buttered round of wax paper. Chill it for 2 hours. Wash, hull, and dry thoroughly 36 strawberries. In a large bowl, combine flour, sugar, salt, and beer in a stream, beating continually. Beat the mixture until it is smooth. In a bowl, beat egg whites with cream of tartar and salt until they hold stiff peaks. Fold them gently but thoroughly into the beer mixture. Dip the strawberries into the batter, a few at a time. Fry them in hot oil in a deep fryer for 1-2 minutes, or until they are golden. As they are done, transfer the strawberries with a slotted spoon to paper towels to drain. Roll the fried strawberries in 1/4 cup sugar combined with 1-1/2 tsp. cinnamon. Divide the vanilla sauce among shallow dishes and top each serving with 6 of the strawberries.

PIONEER OKLAHOMA DINNER

For Eight

Chilled Cider
Filet of Quail Breast Fried
Biscuits and Cream Gravy
Country Style Fresh Green Beans
Cherokee Strip Cole Slaw
Relishes
Apple Crisp
Ice Cream
Coffee

FILET OF QUAIL BREAST FRIED

Serving: 2 breasts per person

Quail
1 egg, beaten
Milk
Flour
Salt
Pepper

Cut meat from breast of quail. (Use filet knife and cut along breast bone. Meat should come off easily.) Dip meat into mixture of beaten egg and milk. Next dip into flour and repeat this process. Salt and pepper. Pan fry in hot shortening. Brown on both sides. Quail are done when tender and brown. It doesn't take long to cook this way. Be careful not to overcook.

BISCUITS

2 cups flour, sifted all-purpose
3 tsp. baking powder
1/4 cup shortening
1/2 tsp. salt
2/3 to 3/4 cup milk

Cut shortening into sifted dry ingredients until crumbly. Make a well and add milk all at once. Stir quickly with fork only until dough follows fork around bowl. Turn dough onto lightly floured surface. Knead. Roll out and cut. Bake on ungreased sheet at 350° for 12-15 minutes.

COUNTRY STYLE FRESH GREEN BEANS

2 quarts fresh green beans
2 lbs. small new potatoes with
    jackets
Bacon, 5 slices
2/3 cup boiling water

Snap and wash beans. Scrub small new potatoes. Drain all but water that clings. Heat heavy pot and render 5 slices bacon until most fat is out but meat is not crisp. Remove bacon and leave fat. Add green beans (pan still uncovered). Stir beans often the first 10 minutes till well blanched (losing some bright green color). This is almost like frying them on medium heat. Sprinkle with salt. Place scrubbed new potatoes on top of beans. Add 2/3 cup boiling water. Place on tight cover. Cook about 45 minutes, stirring only once during cooking.

CHEROKEE STRIP COLE SLAW

1-1/2 lb. cabbage, chopped
1 cup whipping cream
1/3 cup vinegar
1 tsp. salt
2/3 cup sugar

Mix well and let stand in refrigerator before serving.

NOTES:

APPLE CRISP

Serves: 8

3 lbs. apples, pared and sliced
1/2 cup orange juice
1/2 cup brown sugar, packed
1/2 cup granulated sugar
3/4 Tbsp. orange rind, grated
1/2 tsp. nutmeg
1/2 tsp. cinnamon, heaping
1/4 tsp. salt
1/4 lb. butter or margarine
3/4 cup flour, sifted

Place apples in 9x9-inch buttered pan. Pour orange juice over them. Mix together all dry ingredients and cut in butter. Spread over apple mixture and bake for 1 hour at 350°. Serve with whipped cream or ice cream.

ICE CREAM

4 eggs, well beaten
6 cups milk
1-1/2 tsp. vanilla
2-1/2 cups sugar
4 cups heavy cream
1/2 tsp. salt

Add sugar gradually to beaten eggs, beating well after each addition. When mixture becomes very stiff, add remaining ingredients and mix thoroughly. Pour into gallon freezer. Freeze as directed on ice cream maker.

 Vanilla Bean adds a special touch to your favorite vanilla ice cream. Flavor is enhanced when bean is split and warmed in milk or allowed to marinate overnight in the refrigerator. Then, pod should be removed and seeds scraped into ice cream mixture before freezing.

FIESTA DINNER
For Ten

Margaritas
Sombrero Spread
Avocado and Shrimp Fiesta
Fiesta Soup
Orange and Vegetable Salad
Inland Paella
Zucchini Mexican Style
Cuban Water Bread
Barcelona Drunken Sponge
With Brandy Sauce

SOMBRERO SPREAD

1 lb. ground beef
1/4 cup onion, chopped
1/4 cup extra-hot ketchup
1-1/2 tsp. chili powder
1/2 tsp. Cavender's All-Purpose
  *Greek Seasoning**
1 (8-oz.) can (1 cup) red kidney
  beans (with liquid)
1/2 cup Cheddar cheese,
  shredded
1/4 cup stuffed green olives,
  sliced
1/4 cup onion, chopped
Tortilla chips or corn chips
*Cavender's seasoning can be
found in specialty shops and is
a blend of salt, black pepper,
cornstarch, garlic, MSG,
oregano, beef bouillon, parsley,
and five other secret spices.

Brown meat and 1/4 cup onion in skillet. Stir in ketchup, chili powder, and salt. Mash in beans. Heat through. Garnish with the cheese, olives, and 1/4 cup onion. Serve hot as a dip with Doritos or corn chips. (This works well in a chafing dish.)

AVOCADOS AND SHRIMP FIESTA

Serves: 10

1-1/2 lbs. small shrimp, cooked
1 pkg. Shrimp Boil*
1 stalk celery, minced
6 green onions, minced
5 avocados

VINAIGRETTE SAUCE:
3/4 tsp. Cavender's All-Purpose
*   Greek Seasoning*
1/2 tsp. dry mustard
1/3 cup vinegar
1 cup olive oil
*Shrimp Boil is a special
mixture of herbs and spices to
be added to water when boiling
shell fish.

Cook shrimp according to Shrimp Boil directions. Cool and peel. Combine shrimp, celery, and onions. Halve avocados and place shrimp mixture in each half. Top with vinaigrette sauce.

Put all ingredients into a bottle and shake to mix. Store at room temperature. Makes 1-1/2 cups.

FIESTA SOUP

Serves: 10

2 (10-oz.) pkgs. frozen,
*   cut asparagus*
1 cup canned chicken broth
4 egg yolks
2-1/2 cups milk
1 tsp. Cavender's All-Purpose
*   Greek Seasoning*
4 drops hot sauce
Parsley
Paprika

Combine asparagus and chicken broth; bring to a boil and cook, uncovered, for 8 minutes. Put in blender and blend well until smooth; add egg yolks and blend well. Return asparagus mixture to saucepan; stir in milk, salt, and hot sauce. Heat well, but do not boil. Top each serving with parsley and paprika.

PICO DE GALLO

Orange and Vegetable Salad

Serves: 10

*Leaf lettuce (broken into
bite-sized pieces)*
*2-3 oranges, peeled and
thinly sliced*
1 avocado, peeled and sliced
*1 small red onion, sliced in
thin rings*
1/2 green pepper, diced
1/2 c. pitted ripe olives
1 cucumber, thinly sliced
Creamy Chili Salad Dressing

Arrange on serving plates, or large salad bowl, if serving buffet style. Add dressing just before serving.

*CREAMY CHILI
SALAD DRESSING:*
2 Tbsp. red wine vinegar
3/4 cup olive oil
*1 tsp. Cavender's All-Purpose
Greek Seasoning*
*Green chilies, diced or chopped
(one half 3-4-oz. can
El Paso or one fourth
3-4-oz. can Del Monte)*
1 egg

Creamy Chili Salad Dressing: Whirl all ingredients in blender until smooth. Chill.

CUBAN WATER BREAD

*1 cake compressed yeast or
1 pkg. dry yeast*
1 Tbsp. salt
1 Tbsp. sugar
*2 cups lukewarm water (very
warm for dry yeast)*
About 6 cups all-purpose flour
About 2 Tbsp. cornmeal
Melted butter

Dissolve yeast, salt, and sugar in lukewarm water in large bowl. Gradually stir in flour, adding only until mixture refuses to absorb more. (You may need no more than 5-1/2 cups). Knead dough on floured board until slightly elastic, 3-4 minutes. Transfer to greased bowl; brush top lightly with a little oil or melted butter, and cover with damp cloth. Place in warm spot to rise until double in bulk. Butter a baking sheet and sprinkle with cornmeal, shaking off excess. Punch dough down, turn onto floured dough board, and divide into thirds. Shape into long, narrow loaves; place on prepared

continued...

baking sheet, and with sharp knife, make several shallow diagonal cuts across tops. Brush lightly with melted butter; allow to rise, about 45 minutes. Brush with cold water. Place in a cold oven. This is important. Set oven at 400° and bake until bread is nicely browned, about 40 minutes. Brush loaves twice with cold water during last 20 minutes of baking. The loaves should be deliciously crisp.

INLAND PAELLA

Serves: 10

3 Tbsp. olive oil
10 chicken breast halves or
    10 chicken thighs
4 medium onions, chopped
3 cloves garlic, crushed
2 cups rice, uncooked
3-4 hot smoked link
    sausages, sliced
5 cups beef or chicken broth
    or bouillon
Pinch saffron
Salt and pepper to taste
1-1/2 lbs. fresh shrimp, boiled
    and cleaned
1/2 (10-oz.) pkg. frozen peas,
    cooked barely tender
1 (4-oz.) jar pimientos, drained

Heat oil in large skillet and brown chicken. Remove to large, lightly-greased casserole and set aside. Add more oil to skillet and sauté onions and garlic until onions are golden and tender. Add rice and sauté until golden. Add to casserole. Fry all grease out of sausage slices; add them to casserole. Pour 4 cups of bouillon in which saffron has been dissolved over the mixture. Add salt and pepper, cover, and bake at 325° until chicken is done, about 1 hour. During cooking, check to see if rice has absorbed all bouillon; if it has, add remaining cup. Continue adding bouillon if necessary; rice should be cooked through but not mushy. Just before paella is done, add shrimp. When fully done, sprinkle top of casserole with cooked peas and pimientos cut in strips.

ZUCCHINI MEXICAN STYLE

Serves: 10

6 cups zucchini, grated
1 medium onion, thinly sliced
*   and separated into rings*
1 cup celery, thinly sliced
1 medium carrot, grated
1 green pepper, cut in strips
1/3 cup vegetable oil
1/3 cup commercial taco sauce
2 tsp. prepared mustard
1/4 tsp. basil leaves, diced
1/2 tsp. Cavender's All-Purpose
*   Greek Seasoning*
4 tomatoes, cut into wedges

Sauté first 5 ingredients in hot oil in skillet for 5 minutes, stirring occasionally. Stir in taco sauce, mustard, basil, salt, and pepper. Add tomatoes; cook 5 minutes.

BARCELONA DRUNKEN SPONGE

4 eggs, separated
1-3/4 cups granulated sugar
1 Tbsp. orange rind, grated
1/2 cup plus 1 Tbsp. orange
*   juice, freshly squeezed*
3 Tbsp. butter, melted
1-1/3 cups all-purpose flour,
*   sifted*
1/2 tsp. baking powder
1/2 tsp. ground nutmeg
1/4 tsp. salt

BRANDY SAUCE:
Boil 1/4 cup sugar and 1/4 cup water together for 6 minutes. Cool slightly; stir in 1/4 cup brandy. Pour over cake at once.

NUTMEG WHIPPED CREAM:
Whip 1/2 pt. heavy cream with 1/2 tsp. ground nutmeg and 1/4 cup sugar.

Beat egg whites; gradually add 3/4 cup sugar, beating until stiff peaks form. Refrigerate. Beat egg yolks with remaining cup of sugar until light and fluffy. Beat in orange rind and juice, then butter. Sift together flour, baking powder, nutmeg, and salt. Fold into eggs by hand. Now fold beaten eggs whites into batter. Turn into ungreased 9-inch tube pan and bake at 325° for 1 hour, or until cake tests done. Invert pan and cool. Turn out onto serving plate. Carefully pour brandy sauce over top and allow to stand 2-3 hours. To serve, spread nutmeg whipped cream over top.

EASTER DINNER
For Eight

Roman Artichoke Hearts
Mount of Olives Surprise
Chicken Jerusalem
Garden of Gethsemane Vegetables
With Vermouth Dip
Leavened Bread
Sweet Lemon Yogurt Cake
Coffee

ROMAN ARTICHOKE HEARTS

1 (14-oz.) can artichoke hearts, drained, rinsed, drained again, and patted dry
1 (3-oz.) pkg. cream cheese
3 Tbsp. chives, chopped
2 Tbsp. butter, softened
2 Tbsp. sour cream
Salt and pepper
1/4 cup Parmesan cheese
Paprika

Soften cream cheese. Mix cream cheese with sour cream, butter, and chives. Sprinkle with salt and pepper. Fill artichoke hearts with cream cheese mixture. Sprinkle liberally with Parmesan cheese. Microwave full power for 3 minutes, turning once. Sprinkle with paprika. Serve warm with cocktail fork. This recipe fills 6-8 artichoke hearts, which is about the average number of artichoke hearts that come in a 14-oz. can.

MOUNT OF OLIVES SURPRISE

1 large jar of large stuffed green olives
1 (8-oz.) pkg. cream cheese, softened
Chopped pecans

Roll olives in cream cheese, then in pecans until completely covered. Serve well chilled. Can be made a day or two ahead.

CHICKEN JERUSALEM

Serves: 8

4 chicken breasts, boned and
  split
Salt and pepper
1 stick butter
Paprika
2 (10-3/4-oz.) cans cream of
  chicken soup, undiluted
1 cup Madeira wine
2 (14-oz.) cans artichoke hearts
2 small cans sliced mushrooms
8 servings of rice

Sprinkle chicken with salt, pepper, and paprika. Brown well in butter. Transfer to a greased oven-proof casserole. Pour chicken soup and wine in remaining drippings. Stir to a smooth gravy. Add artichoke hearts and mushrooms. Pour sauce over chicken. Bake in covered casserole at 350° for 1 hour and 15 minutes. Serve on rice.

SWEET LEMON-YOGURT CAKE

1 cup (1/2-lb.) butter or
  margarine
2 cups sugar
6 eggs, separated
2 tsp. lemon peel, grated
1/2 tsp. lemon extract
3 cups cake flour
1 tsp. soda
1/4 tsp. salt
1 cup yogurt
2 Tbsp. brandy (or substitute
  more yogurt)

Beat butter and 1-1/2 cups of the sugar with an electric mixer until creamy. Add egg yolks, lemon peel, and lemon extract. Beat until thick and pale yellow. Sift the flour; measure and sift again with the soda and salt. Into the creamed butter mixture alternately mix the flour and the yogurt (and brandy, if used). Beat the egg whites until soft peaks form; then gradually add the remaining 1/2 cup of sugar, beating until glossy. Fold batter into beaten egg whites and pour into a greased 10-inch tube pan. Bake in a 350° oven for 45 minutes or until done. Cool 15 minutes in pan, then turn out on a rack. Serve this Greek cake, unfrosted, with ice cream.

FRENCH FRIED BRUSSELS SPROUTS WITH VERMOUTH DIP

VERMOUTH DIP:
1 cup dry vermouth
2 Tbsp. onion flakes
1 cup Hellman's mayonnaise
2 Tbsp. dried parsley
1 Tbsp. frozen or dried chives
2 tsp. horseradish
2 (10-oz.) pkgs. frozen brussels
*   sprouts*
Salt and pepper

EGG BATTER:
2 eggs, beaten
4 tsp. cooking oil
Flour
1-1/2 cups bread crumbs
Salad oil for deep fat frying

Boil brussels sprouts in salted water until semi-tender (do not over-cook). Drain at once. Chill well. This may be done early in the day.

VERMOUTH DIP:
Pour vermouth into small saucepan. Add onion. Heat over moderate flame until reduced to 1/4 cup liquid. Stir vermouth into mayonnaise. Add parsley, chives, horseradish. Chill well. This may also be done early in the day.

Preparation for Deep Fat Frying:
Preheat fat to 370°. Sprinkle sprouts with salt and pepper. Beat eggs with 4 tsp. cooking oil. Dip sprouts into flour. Pat off any excess flour. Then dip sprouts into egg mixture, then into bread crumbs. Fry in batches until medium brown. Between batches of frying, the finished sprouts may be kept warm in a warm oven (140° to 200°). This part of the recipe is the most time consuming; allow at least 30 minutes. Best eaten as soon as frying is completed. Serve dip in individual bowls at the table. I have also fried other fresh vegetables in this manner, such as broccoli, cauliflower, mushrooms, etc. Boil the broccoli and cauliflower in the same manner as the sprouts. No parboiling for the mushrooms; fry whole or half, whichever you prefer.

CREOLE DINNER
For Ten

Shrimp Rémoulade
Creole Gumbo
Hearts of Palm Salad
With Vinaigrette
Chicken Rochambeau
French-style Green Peas
Cherries Jubilee
Coffee

SHRIMP RÉMOULADE

Serves: 10-12

6 cups boiled shrimp, peeled
2 cups Rémoulade Sauce;
   below
6 cups lettuce, shredded

Blend the shrimp with the rémoulade sauce, being careful not to break them. Chill in the refrigerator. To serve, put 1/2 cup shredded lettuce on each of 10 plates. Spoon the shrimp onto the lettuce and serve.

RÉMOULADE SAUCE:
1-1/2 cups ketchup
1 tsp. powdered mustard
2 Tbsp. horseradish
1 Tbsp. Worcestershire
4-5 drops Tabasco sauce
2 Tbsp. green onions, minced
2 Tbsp. celery, minced
2 Tbsp. parsley, minced

Combine all ingredients. Makes 2 cups.

CREOLE GUMBO

Serves: 10

3/4 stick butter
2 cups green onions, chopped
3 crabs (top shell discarded,
    cut in 4 pieces)
2 cups okra, sliced
1 cup white onions, chopped
2 cups raw shrimp, peeled
2 cups raw oysters
1 cup tomato pulp, chopped
2 cups tomato juice
1-1/2 qts. fish stock (below)
3 Tbsp. butter
3 Tbsp. flour
1 Tbsp. filé (sassafras)
Salt, pepper and cayenne
3 cups rice, cooked

Melt butter and sauté green onions, okra, white onions, and crabs. In a separate pot put the shrimp, oysters, tomatoes, and tomato juice with 1-1/2 qts. of fish stock and bring to a boil. Let boil for a minute, then add to the first pot. In a small skillet cook the butter and flour together until brown. Blend this brown roux with the filé and some of the gumbo liquid and add to the gumbo. Add salt, pepper, and cayenne to taste. Simmer for 1-1/2 hours. To serve, pour 3/4 cup of gumbo into each bowl over 1/4 cup rice. To serve 6 larger portions, pour 1-1/2 cups of gumbo into each bowl over 1/2 cup rice.

FISH STOCK:
10 lbs. fish heads and bones
or
2 lbs. fish fillets
3 onions, sliced
2 stalks celery
2 bay leaves
3 sprigs parsley
2 Tbsp. salt
4 qts. water

Add all ingredients, including the water, to a large soup pot. Simmer for 4 hours, skimming the scum off the top from time to time. Strain. Makes 2 qts.

HEARTS OF PALM SALAD

Serves: 10-12

6 cups lettuce leaves, chopped
12 slices tomato, halved
6 cups hearts of palm, cut into
*   1-inch pieces*
3 cups vinaigrette sauce (below)

Put 1/2 cup chopped lettuce on each of 10 chilled salad plates. Cover each with 1/2 cup hearts of palm and garnish with 2 half slices of tomato. Chill. Pour 1/4 cup vinaigrette sauce over each salad and serve.

VINAIGRETTE SAUCE:
1 tsp. salt
1/2 tsp. white pepper, finely
*   ground*
1 tsp. dry powdered mustard
2/3 cup vinegar
2 cups olive oil

Put all ingredients into a bottle and shake to mix. Store at room temperature. Makes 3 cups.

CHICKEN ROCHAMBEAU

Serves: 10

5 chickens, 2-1/2 lbs. each or
10 deboned chicken breasts
Salt and ground white pepper
2 sticks butter
10 slices ham, cooked
2-1/2 cups Brown Rochambeau
*   Sauce (below)*
2 cups Béarnaise Sauce
*   (below)*
2 cups Hollandaise Sauce
*   (below)*

Wash and dry the chickens and rub inside and out with salt, pepper, and butter. Put in a shallow baking pan and into a preheated 350° oven for 1-1/2 hours, or until completely cooked. Split the chickens in half and remove the bones and return to a low oven to keep warm. Put the ham slices in a saucepan with the Brown Rochambeau Sauce and simmer for a few minutes. Put a slice of ham on each plate and spoon on some of the brown sauce. Top the ham with 1/2 boned chicken and cover chicken with Béarnaise Sauce.

continued...

BROWN ROCHAMBEAU SAUCE:

3 Tbsp. butter
1 cup onions, chopped
3 Tbsp. flour
1/3 cup vinegar
2 Tbsp. sugar
2 cups chicken stock
Salt and ground white pepper

Sauté the chopped onions in the butter until they begin to color. Add flour and cook until brown. Blend in the vinegar, then the sugar. Add chicken stock and season to taste with salt and pepper. Simmer for 20 minutes. Makes 2-1/2 cups.

BÉARNAISE SAUCE:

1/4 cup white onion, minced
2 Tbsp. tarragon leaves, minced
1/4 cup tarragon vinegar
2 Tbsp. parsley, chopped
2 cups warm Hollandaise Sauce
    (below)

Put the onion, tarragon leaves and tarragon vinegar in a pot and reduce the liquid completely. Cool slightly and blend in the Hollandaise Sauce. Makes 2 cups.

HOLLANDAISE SAUCE:

2 cups melted butter, warm
8 egg yolks
2 Tbsp. lemon juice
2 Tbsp. tarragon vinegar
3/4 tsp. paprika
Salt and cayenne pepper to
    taste

Beat the egg yolks together with lemon juice and vinegar and pour the mixture into the top of a double boiler. Cook on low heat stirring constantly, never letting the water in the double boiler come to a boil. Continue cooking until the mixture thickens. Remove from heat and beat in the warm melted butter, a little at a time. Keep warm but not hot.

FRENCH-STYLE GREEN PEAS

Serves: 10-12

2/3 cup ham, chopped
6 Tbsp. butter
1 cup green onions, chopped
1 cup lettuce leaves, chopped
2 bay leaves
5 cups canned baby peas in
    packing water
1 cup additional water
4 Tbsp. butter
4 Tbsp. flour
Salt and ground white pepper

Sauté ham in butter for a minute; then add green onions, lettuce and bay leaves. Continue cooking until vegetables are limp. Add peas and packing water and extra water. Bring to a boil. In a skillet melt butter and add flour. Stir and cook for 2 minutes. Blend flour and butter mixture with some of the liquid and add to the peas. Season to taste with salt and pepper. Cook until liquid thickens and serve.

CHERRIES JUBILEE

Serves: 10-12

2 qts. vanilla ice cream
6 cups canned Bing cherries
2-3 cups brandy

Scoop the ice cream out onto 10 dessert dishes. Put the cherries and brandy into a metal mixing bowl and heat over a flame until brandy is hot but not boiling. Ignite the brandy with a match and mix the cherries, while flaming, for a brief moment in the bowl. Spoon the cherries and brandy (still flaming) over the ice cream and serve.

FRENCH DINNER
For Six

Kir

Purée of Asparagus Soup
With Tarragon

Stuffed Pork Rolls in Cream Sauce

Applesauce With Orange

Green Salad
With Vinaigrette Dressing

Hard French Rolls

Assorted Cheeses

Pear Tart

KIR

5 parts dry white wine
1 part Cassis syrup

Mix chilled white wine with Cassis syrup —or serve with ice.

SOUPE TOURANGELLE AUX ASPARGES

(Purée of asparagus soup with tarragon)

Serves: 6

2 lbs. fresh asparagus
Salt
2 cups milk or unsweetened
evaporated milk
3 large, full branches of tarragon
or about 1 tsp. dried
tarragon
1 cup full-bodied white wine
Black pepper, freshly ground
6 Tbsp. butter
6 Tbsp. flour
6 cups chicken bouillon
2 Tbsp. fresh tarragon or 1 tsp.
dried tarragon

Peel the asparagus to remove the scales and put aside a few of the finest tips to decorate the soup. Cut the tenderest part of the asparagus into quarters and then into thin sticks to facilitate the cooking. Boil in a large quantity of salted water for 12 to 15 minutes until tender. Drain thoroughly and pass through a food mill to make a purée. (A sieve may be used.) Then return to the saucepan with the milk, set over moderate heat, and simmer, stirring until smooth. If using fresh tarragon, roughly chop the leaves. Put the tarragon into a saucepan with the white wine, add some freshly ground black pepper, bring to a simmer, and simmer for 20 minutes. The liquid should reduce by evaporation to about a tablespoon. Set aside. In an enameled saucepan set over moderate heat, melt 4 Tbsp. butter. Stir in the flour, and cook, stirring for a few seconds. Add the chicken bouillon, simmer several minutes, and add the asparagus purée. Pour a cup of soup into the saucepan containing the reduced wine and tarragon. Stir over heat; then pour through a sieve back into the soup. Bring to a boil; taste and correct the seasoning. Blend 2 Tbsp. fresh or 1 tsp. dried tarragon into the remaining butter and stir into the soup. If the reserved asparagus tips are large, cut them into halves or quarters lengthwise and garnish each serving with two or three pieces.

PAUPIETTES DE PORC A LA TOURANGELLE
(farcie a l'oignon et au fromage)

Small rolls of pork, stuffed with onions and cheese, in cream sauce

Serves: 6

1/3 cup vegetable oil
5 medium-sized yellow onions
  (2 cups chopped)
6 pork scallops, about 3 x 5 to
  be rolled
Salt
Black pepper, freshly ground
6 Tbsp. Dijon mustard
1 Tbsp. fresh oregano, minced
  or 1 tsp. dried
6 very thin slices imported
  Swiss cheese
4 Tbsp. butter
Bouquet garni of Thyme,
  1/2 bay leaf, oregano

Warm 2 or 3 Tbsp. of the oil in a heavy-bottomed, ovenproof skillet with a lid. Add the chopped onions; cook them very gently, stirring occasionally, until they are tender and lightly colored (about 15 minutes). Remove them with a slotted spoon, set aside, and season with salt and pepper. (Do not clean the pan.) Flatten the pork between pieces of waxed paper with a heavy bottle, the side of a cleaver, or a rolling pin, to make them as thin as possible. Sprinkle them with salt and pepper. Brush each scallop with mustard and sprinkle lightly with oregano. Reserving 1 cup of onions for later, spread each scallop with a thin layer of onions and cover with a slice of cheese. Roll up the scallops into paupiettes and secure them with toothpicks or tie them with string. (It is easier to brown them if you use string.) Preheat oven to 350.°Put the paupiettes into the pan in which the onions were cooked, adding more oil, if necessary, and brown them on all sides over moderate heat, about 15 minutes. Remove the meat to a plate and clean the skillet. Melt the butter in the skillet, and add the meat, the remaining onions, and the bouquet garni. Cover with a piece of waxed paper, put the lid on the skillet, and place in preheated oven. Cook 45 minutes to 1 hour, according to the tenderness of the meat. The meat will be done when it is easily pierced with a sharp knife. Put the paupiettes on a warmed serving dish, discarding the string or toothpicks. Spread the onions around the meat and keep the platter warm while making the sauce.

CREAM SAUCE

2 Tbsp. flour
1/4-1/3 cup heavy cream
Juice of 1 lemon, strained
1 cup beef bouillon, fresh
    or canned
Salt
Black pepper, freshly ground
1-1/2 Tbsp. parsley, chopped

Put the flour in a small saucepan and gradually stir in the cream to make a smooth paste. Stir in the strained juice of the lemon and set aside. Pour the bouillon into the skillet in which the meat was cooked, and set over heat. Let boil half a minute, scraping the bottom to deglaze. Pour 4 or 5 Tbsp. of the bouillon into the flour mixture and mix well; then pour back into the skillet and simmer, stirring constantly while the sauce thickens. Taste, and correct the seasoning. Cover the paupiettes with the sauce and serve them sprinkled with chopped parsley.

APPLESAUCE WITH ORANGE

Serves: 6

2 lbs. apples
Juice of 1/2 lemon
1 orange

Core and quarter, but do not peel apples. Put apples, lemon juice, and 1/2 cup water in heavy pan; cover and cook till applesauce. Add a bit of sugar, if you like. Stir. Serve warm or cold with 1/2 slice of orange.

VINAIGRETTE DRESSING

4 Tbsp. lemon juice, red wine
    vinegar, or Tarragon
    vinegar
2 tsp. Dijon mustard
Salt and freshly ground pepper
6 Tbsp. oil

Combine all ingredients, except oil, in blender or food processor. Blend thoroughly; then slowly add oil.

PEAR TART

Serves: 8-16

1 lemon, cut in very narrow
    strips
2 Tbsp. crystallized ginger, diced
6 fresh pears, peeled, cored,
    cut in half, sliced thin

TOPPING:
1 cup sugar
2 Tbsp. flour
1 stick cold butter

Boil lemon rind in small amount of water for 10 minutes and set aside. Combine topping ingredients in blender and blend until they look like oatmeal. Prepare crust and place in 12 inch tart pan. Do not bake. Put half of topping mixture in tart shell. Cover with sliced pears; cover with remaining topping. Sprinkle lemon peel and ginger on top. Bake at 400° for 45 minutes or until pears are tender and top is bubbly.

TART CRUST

Makes: 2 crusts

1-3/4 cups flour
1-1/4 sticks butter, well chilled
2 Tbsp. shortening, well chilled
1 tsp. salt

Put flour and salt in bowl of food processor, run three seconds to mix. Add chilled butter, sliced into 1/2-inch patties. Add the chilled shortening. Run for 10 seconds. Add 1/2 cup ice water, minus 2 Tbsp., to the mixture while food processor is running. Stop as soon as the mixture forms a ball. Shape into balls. Put into refrigerator for 30 minutes. Grease pan before rolling the crust. An easy way to roll crust is between two pieces of wax paper. It is important to keep this cold. After rolling the crust and placing in pie pan, chill in refrigerator while making the filling.

NEW ENGLAND DINNER

for Twelve

Sherry
With Apples

Cream of Zucchini Soup

Garlic Toast Rounds

Baked Salmon With Wine Sauce

Fresh Asparagus
With Lemon and Butter
Cranberry-Orange Relish
Green Salad
With Vinaigrette Dressing

Popovers

Indian Pudding

Coffee

CREAM OF ZUCCHINI SOUP

1 lb. fresh zucchini
1 small onion, quartered
1 cup chicken broth
1 tsp. salt
1/4 tsp. pepper
1/2 tsp. sweet basil
2 cups half and half
1/4 tsp. curry powder

Trim and slice zucchini thickly. Combine in saucepan the prepared zucchini, onion, broth, salt, pepper, and basil. Bring to boil and simmer until soft. Empty into container of blender or food processor and purée. Gradually add 1/2 cup of half and half and blend until smooth. Add curry and remaining cream and return to saucepan to heat. Or if serving cold, refrigerate for several hours in suitable container.

WHOLE SALMON BAKED IN FOIL

1 7-10 lb. salmon, cleaned
3/4 cup dry white wine
1/4 tsp. dried thyme leaves
1/2 tsp. dried basil
1/4 tsp. dried tarragon
1/4 tsp. dried rosemary
Celery leaves from a small stalk
1 small onion freshly minced
2 slices lemon with peel
Salt

Leave the salmon whole or remove the head. Rinse under cold running water and place on paper towels to dry. Place the wine in a saucepan and add the remaining ingredients, except the salt. Let the mixture simmer, uncovered, one-half hour without boiling. Preheat oven to 375°. Place the fish lengthwise on a long sheet of foil; bring up the edges and pour the wine mixture over the fish. Sprinkle with salt. Completely enclose the fish, crimping the foil to seal the edges tightly. Place the foil-wrapped fish in a large baking pan and transfer to the oven. Bake until the fish flakes easily when tested with a fork, about two hours. Serve with Hollandaise sauce or with a white wine sauce.

WHITE WINE SAUCE

1/2 cup butter
2 shallots, finely minced
6 Tbsp. flour
Liquid in which salmon was
*   baked*
Equal parts dry white wine and
*   boiling water*
1/2 cup heavy cream
Salt
Pepper, freshly ground
2 egg yolks

While the salmon is baking, melt the butter in a saucepan and add the shallots. Cook until transparent but not brown. Using a wire whisk, stir in the flour until it is well blended. Cook over low heat three minutes. Let stand until fish is done. When the fish is removed from the oven, use a large spoon to dip out the juices and add to the butter mixture in the saucepan, stirring constantly over moderate heat. Continue stirring vigorously and add enough wine and boiling water to make five cups of liquid. Cook the liquid, stirring, until thickened and smooth. Add the cream and season with salt and pepper. Strain through a fine sieve. Just before serving, reheat and add the egg yolks lightly beaten with a little of the hot sauce. Cook two minutes over low heat, but do not let boil.

GARLIC TOAST ROUNDS

Brown and serve dinner rolls
Butter
Garlic powder
Lemon juice
Parmesan cheese

Slice brown and serve rolls vertically and lay out on cookie sheets. Mix butter, lemon juice and garlic powder to taste; brush on rolls. Sprinkle with Parmesan cheese. Cook in 200° oven for approximately 30 minutes. Watch closely.

CRANBERRY-ORANGE RELISH

1 lb. cranberries, fresh
2 large oranges, thin-skinned,
**   seedless**
2 cups sugar

Wash cranberries under cold running water and pat dry with paper towels. Cut oranges into quarters. Then put cranberries and orange quarters (skins and all) through the coarsest blade of a food processor into a deep glass or ceramic bowl. Add sugar and mix well with a wooden spoon. Taste and add more sugar if desired. Cover with plastic wrap and let relish stand at room temperature for about 24 hours to develop flavor before serving. (Tightly covered, the relish can safely be refrigerated for 2 to 3 weeks.)

VINAIGRETTE DRESSING

1/3 cup lemon juice
1 tsp. Dijon mustard
1 tsp. anchovy paste
Salt
Freshly ground pepper
1 cup salad oil

Combine first five ingredients in food processor or blender. While processing, add salad oil. Then add any of the following, if desired: 1/2 cup minced parsley, 1 tsp. capers, hand chopped pimientos, 2 chopped hard-cooked eggs, sliced black olives.

POPOVERS

Serves: 6

1 cup milk
1 cup flour
1 Tbsp. vegetable oil
2 eggs
1/2 tsp. salt

Place all ingredients in mixing bowl. Stir with spoon until dry ingredients are moist. Disregard lumps. Pour into six cold, greased custard cups, half full. Place in *cold* oven. Set oven for 450°, timer for 30 minutes. Don't peek. When bell rings, serve glorious popovers to startled guests.

INDIAN PUDDING

2 cups milk, scalded
1/2 cup corn meal
1/2 cup dark molasses
1 tsp. salt
1/2 cup sugar
1 tsp. ginger
2 oz. rum
1 egg, beaten
2 cups milk

Mix corn meal with a little milk and add to scalded milk in top of double boiler. Cook and stir until thick. Add remaining ingredients except last 2 cups milk, and pour into shallow buttered casserole. Gently add 2 cups milk. Do not stir. Bake 2-1/2 hours at 300°. Serve hot with vanilla ice cream.

UNO NOLT'E EN MILANO

(A night in Milan)

Italian Style Salad

A fine selection of PASTAS and SAUCES

Italian Bread

Wine

Spumoni and Cappucino

BROWN DERBY SPAGHETTI SAUCE

Serves: 12-16

2 large onions, chopped
2 large cloves of garlic, chopped
1-1/2 lbs. ground beef
2 bay leaves
1 tsp. oregano
1 tsp. cumin
1 (4-oz.) can chopped ripe olives
1 (4-oz.) can chopped green chilies
4 (8-oz.) cans tomato sauce
3 squares semi-sweet chocolate
2 (4-oz.) cans mushroom stems and pieces
1 large bottle red chili sauce

Sauté onions and garlic until clear in a small amount of butter. Add meat and bay leaves and brown. Add all other ingredients except mushrooms and red chili sauce. Simmer 1/2 hour. Add mushrooms and chili sauce and simmer several hours.

Mrs. Tim Traynor (Suzy)

 Enid-Phillips Chorale tip for serving pasta in large quantities...Cook pastas in small amounts just until tender. Remove from heat immediately and rinse thoroughly in cold water to stop process. Keep large amounts of pre-cooked pasta in cold water in the refrigerator until ready to serve. To heat flash pasta into boiling water for just a minute and drain before serving.

WHITE CLAM SAUCE

4 cans minced clams
1 cup butter
5 cloves garlic
Lawry's garlic salt
1 Tbsp. lemon juice
1 Tbsp. onion, grated
Parsley, chopped
Chives
White pepper
1/2 pt. heavy cream
Corn starch

Pour clams, including juice, into saucepan. Add butter and let melt. Add remaining ingredients, except cream and corn starch, and let simmer 15 minutes. Add cream with corn starch and let thicken slightly. Serve over fresh pasta.

PASTA:
3 egg yolks
1 whole egg
2 Tbsp. water
1 tsp. olive oil
1/2 tsp. salt
1-3/4 cup unsifted flour,
    approximately

Combine all ingredients in food processor until dough is formed. Knead slightly and roll through pasta machine. Add 1/4 cup spinach for green pasta or 2 Tbsp. tomato paste, eliminating oil, for rosy pasta.

Sue Ellen Singer

SUELLEN'S WONDERFUL CHEESE SAUCE

3 Tbsp. butter
1-1/2 Tbsp. flour
1 cup half and half
1/2 cup chicken broth
Salt to taste
Pepper to taste
Nutmeg to taste
1/3 cup Belle Paese, grated
1/3 cup Gorgonzola, grated
1/3 cup Fontina, crumbled
1/2 cup Parmesan, grated

Melt butter in medium saucepan. Stir in flour. Slowly add half and half with broth. Add salt, pepper, and nutmeg to taste. Cook and stir until mixture starts to thicken. Add the Belle Paese, Gorgonzola, and Fontina. Cook and stir until thickened. Grated Parmesan is best added by tossing with pasta and sauce. If sauce is to be maintained, Parmesan may be stirred in; however, additional cream or milk may be needed to get right consistency.

Mrs. Richard Singer

"Spur of the moment Spumoni"
Spumoni *can be a spur of the moment trick with a selection of ice-creams from your favorite ice-cream parlor. Italian style is enhanced with a combination of flavors and fruits frozen together. After a feast of home-made pasta, a small serving of (fancy ice-cream) is just the right touch!*

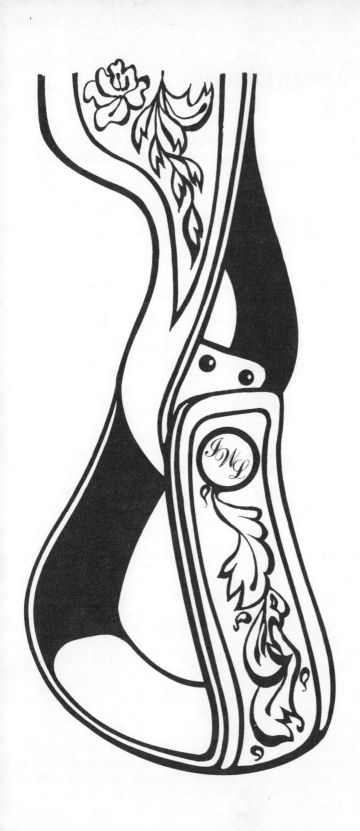

SLIM·PICKIN'S
LOW-CAL

"SLIM PICKINS'"

The pickins' don't have to be slim, but with these delightful recipes calorie cutting can be more fun. These special selections will enhance your next attempt at slim pickins'.

ALMOND MILK

Serves: 1

4 ice cubes
3/4 cup water (may use
*   skim milk)*
1/2 small banana
2 oz. blanched almonds
1/2 tsp. vanilla
1 tsp. honey

Mix in blender and serve immediately.

APRICOT FIZZIE
A fun and frivolous treat!

Serves: 3-4

1-1/2 cups apricot nectar
3 cups diet 7-Up
Crushed ice

Pour 7-Up over nectar and stir once. Pour over cracked ice and garnish with kiwi slice and fresh mint. You can use other juices for a variety in flavors. Sixty calories to sip and savor! Serve immediately, as fizz will be lost if you try and save it.
*To make single serving, just use 1/3 nectar to 7-Up ratio.

Sherrel Jones

STRAWBERRY ICE CREAM

2 cups buttermilk
1-1/2 cups strawberry jam
   (diet variety)

Stir milk into jam. Pour into refrigerator trays. Freeze firm. Cut up frozen mixture. Place in a chilled mixing bowl. Whip with electric mixer until fluffy. Return to trays. *Cover* and freeze firm. Garnish with fresh strawberries. Makes about 1 quart.

Margaret Binion

HERB ROASTED CHICKEN BREASTS

Serves: 4

2 whole breasts, split and boned
3-1/2 Tbsp. butter, melted
1 Tbsp. onion, chopped fine
1 Tbsp. garlic, chopped fine
1 tsp. thyme, crumbled
1/2 tsp. salt
1/2 tsp. pepper
1/2 tsp. rosemary, crumbled
1/4 tsp. ground sage
1/8 tsp. marjoram, crumbled
Dash hot pepper sauce
Parsley garnish

Wipe each breast dry. Mix remaining ingredients, except parsley garnish. Turn breasts in herb sauce to coat thoroughly. Tuck edges of breast under to form compact shape, about 1-1/2" thick. Place in dish, skin side up. Roast in pre-heated 425° oven, basting occasionally, just until done (do not overcook), about 14 minutes. Brown skin by turning on broiler for a few minutes. Each serving equals 237 calories. Remove to warm platter, spoon juices over and garnish with parsley.

Judy Halstead

BAKED GREEN TOMATOES

2 large green tomatoes
3 whole green onions, chopped
1 Tbsp. whipped margarine
2 Tbsp. Parmesan cheese

Cut tomatoes in half. Cover with onions. Place in shallow casserole and add the margarine and cheese. Bake at 350° until the tomatoes are soft and the onion brown.

Mrs. Stephen Jones (Sherrel)

BUTTERMILK SHERBET

Serves: 12

1 qt. buttermilk
12 oz. frozen orange juice
    concentrate

*You may choose any of the
following to replace the orange
juice in this tempting sherbet
recipe.

1-1/2 cups dietary strawberry
    preserves
12 oz. frozen lime ade or
    lemon ade
12 oz. pkg. frozen raspberries
    with artificial sweetener
    to taste
1-1/2 cups peach preserves or
    jam (dietetic)

Beat buttermilk and any of the varieties of fruit you wish together. Freeze till firm. You may put individual servings in paper cups or molds. A combination of flavors gives a rainbow effect.
*Be creative with this calorie counting favorite: Add a banana or other fresh fruit to give variety to a taste you will probably be enjoying a lot. You will find your non-dieting family enjoying this one. Serve sherbet J.W.L. Tearoom style in a scooped out orange or lemon half, and garnish with a mint leaf.

The Tearoom Special

ITALIAN SAUCED FISH

Serves: 8

2 (16-oz.) pkgs. flounder fillets,
    thawed
1/2 cup spaghetti sauce with
    mushrooms (canned)
2 Tbsp. onion, finely chopped
4 oz. shredded Mozzarella
    cheese

Pat fish dry with paper towels. Arrange fillets in single layer in appropriate serving dish. Sprinkle with salt. Mix spaghetti sauce and onion. Pour over fillets. Cover and microwave on high for 7-8 minutes or until fish flakes easily with fork. Sprinkle with cheese. Return to range until cheese melts. Let stand 5 minutes before serving.

Mary Dickey

CARROONIES

Lots of chewing for hunger craving dieters

Yield: 2 dozen

3 egg whites
1/2 cup powdered sugar
   (optional)
2 Tbsp. cornstarch
1/4 tsp. salt
1/2 tsp. almond extract
1/3 cup almonds, chopped
   or slivered
2 cups shredded carrots
2 cups packaged flaked coconut

Beat egg whites until almost stiff. Stir in dry ingredients and almond extract. Add almonds, carrots and coconut. Drop by teaspoonfuls, 1/2-inch apart, onto greased cookie sheets. Bake at 300° for 18 to 20 minutes, or until lightly browned. Remove to wire rack and cool.
Lynda Nelson's variation: Add 1/4 cup grated orange peel to egg white mixture.

Sherrel Jones

CHARCOALED FISH

Serves: 8-10

8-10 bass fillets or other fish
   of your choice, the more
   fresh the catch...the more
   fantastic the flavor!

MARINADE:
1 stick margarine, melted
1 cup lime juice
2 Tbsp. Worcestershire sauce
1/4 cup dry white wine
Paprika
Sliced fresh mushrooms

Prepare fish. Make marinade: Melt margarine and add other ingredients. Place fillets in shallow dish or plastic bag and marinate at least 2 hours in the refrigerator. Build fire of charcoal and Mesquite wood. When coals are a medium low, place fish in fish grates or specially prepared foil.* Place fish on fire skin side down. Sprinkle heavily with paprika, and baste often with sauce to keep moist. Do not turn if using foil. Cook 20 to 25 minutes. Remove with spatula as fish will flake apart easily. Fish grates can be sprayed with Pam for ease in removing fish. Add mushrooms to remaining marinade and cook while fish are on grill. Serve over fish.
*Make your own fish grate from heavy duty foil with numerous holes punched in it.

Jo Ann Nicholas

CUCUMBER DRESSING

Makes: 1-1/4 cups

1/2 cup cucumbers, chopped
1-1/2 tsp. instant minced onions
1 tsp. horseradish
1/2 tsp. salt
1 (8-oz.) yogurt, unflavored

Beat all ingredients with rotary beater. Refrigerate leftover dressing. 10 calories per tablespoon.

Mary Dickey

NO-BAKE CHERRY CHEESECAKE

1-1/4 cups graham cracker
    crumbs
3 Tbsp. butter or margarine,
    softened
1/4 tsp. cinnamon
1/4 tsp. nutmeg
2 eggs, separated
1 cup water
2/3 cup sugar
2 envelopes unflavored gelatin
1/3 cup non-fat dry milk
1/4 tsp. salt
2 tsp. orange peel, grated
3 cups (24-oz.) creamed
    cottage cheese
3 Tbsp. sugar
1 cup red maraschino cherries
12 maraschino or fresh cherries,
    for decorating
1/2 cup frozen blueberries
    for decorating

Blend together crumbs, butter, and spices; firmly press into an even layer on bottom of springform pan. In small saucepan, beat egg yolks slightly, stir in water. Add sugar, spices, gelatin, dry milk, and salt; mix well. Cook and stir over medium heat until mixture thickens slightly and gelatin dissolves. Add orange peel and cool slightly. In blender combine cheese and about 1 cup gelatin mixture and blend until smooth. In large bowl, combine cheese mixture and remaining gelatin mixture. Chill until mixture mounds slightly when stirred with a spoon. Beat egg whites until stiff; gradually fold in 3 Tbsp. sugar. Beat until stiff peaks form. Fold into cheese mixture. Pour half into prepared pan; chill until firm. Sprinkle cherries over cheese layers. Pour remaining cheese mixture over cherries. Chill until firm (about 3 hours). Decorate center in 3" diameter with blueberries surrounded by cherries.

Mrs. Richard Karam (Hannah)

DIABETIC APPLESAUCE COOKIES

Yield: 4-6 dozen

1/2 cup butter
1-1/2 tsp. liquid sweetener
1 tsp. vanilla
1 tsp. baking soda
1 cup unsweetened applesauce
1 egg, beaten
2 cups flour, sifted
1/2 Tbsp. salt
1/2 Tbsp. cinnamon
1/2 tsp. nutmeg
1/2 tsp. cloves
1 cup nuts, chopped
1 cup raisins

Cream butter, vanilla and sweetener. Stir in baking soda to applesauce and egg. Combine this with butter and sweetener mixture. Gradually add dry ingredients and blend well. Add nuts and raisins. Drop by spoonfuls onto greased cookie sheet. Bake at 375° for about 10 minutes. Cookies should be light brown.

Sally Keeler

NO GAIN APPLE SPICE CAKE

Yield: 4 servings

4 slices slightly dry white bread
2/3 cup non-fat dry milk powder
1 Tbsp. cinnamon
1 tsp. baking soda
4 eggs
20 drops Sweeta
1 Tbsp. vanilla extract
4 Tbsp. vegetable oil
2 apples, chopped finely
1 cup applesauce, unsweetened

Place bread, one slice at a time, in blender and make into crumbs. Put crumbs in bowl and add milk, cinnamon, and baking soda. Beat eggs in mixer until very thick (about 10 minutes); add Sweeta, vanilla extract and vegetable oil. Gently fold in apples. Bake in non-stick 8" or 9" pan at 350° for 25 minutes. Top with warm applesauce.
Note: Each serving equals 1/2 cup milk, 1 bread, 1 egg, 1 Tbsp. vegetable oil, 1 apple.

Carolyn Bules

PRAIRIE PEP-UP

Serves: 2

2 cups skimmed milk
1 Tbsp. vegetable oil
2 pkgs. Sweet and Low
3 tsp. brewer's yeast
4 Tbsp. lecithin
crushed ice

Very high energy drink! Put all ingredients in blender. Slowly add crushed ice and blend.

TUNA BROCCOLI CASSEROLE

Yield: 8-10

4 eggs
1 cup buttermilk
2 (6-1/2 or 7-oz.) cans tuna
1/2 tsp. salt
1 lb. (2 cups) creamed cottage
    cheese (small curd)
2 (10-oz.) pkg. frozen chopped
    broccoli, thawed
    and drained
1/4 cup onion, chopped
1 medium tomato, thinly sliced
1/2 cup (4-oz.) mozzarella
    cheese, shredded

Beat eggs and buttermilk in large bowl. Add tuna, salt, cottage cheese, broccoli and onion. Turn into 2 well-greased 9" pie plates or into one 13" x 9" baking dish. Bake at 350° for 35 minutes. Top with sliced tomato and mozzarella cheese and continue to bake 10 minutes longer until set.

Mary Dickey

STRAWBERRY ICE

2 qts. fresh strawberries
1 cup honey
2 cups cold water
2 Tbsp. lemon juice
Artificial sweetener to taste

Pour honey over hulled and washed berries. Mash and let stand for 30 minutes. Put in a blender or force through a sieve. Add water and lemon juice, and artificial sweetener to taste. Freeze.
Variation: Use fresh peaches and well coat with additional freshly squeezed lemon juice.
Serving suggestion: Serve in a special dish and garnish with fresh fruit and mint leaves.

NO-NOODLE LASAGNE

Serves: 9

1 lb. ground beef, lean
1 (15-oz.) can tomato sauce
1-1/2 tsp. garlic salt
1 tsp. basil leaves
1 tsp. oregano leaves
1 (12-oz.) carton cottage cheese (dry)
1/4 cup grated Romano cheese
1 egg
1-1/2 lb. zucchini, cut lengthwise into 1/4-inch slices
2 Tbsp. flour
1 (4-oz.) pkg. mozzarella cheese, shredded
1/4 cup grated Romano cheese

Heat oven to 350°. Cook and stir meat in large skillet until brown. Drain off fat. Stir in tomato sauce, garlic salt, basil leaves and oregano leaves; heat to boiling. Reduce heat and simmer uncovered until mixture is consistency of spaghetti sauce, about 10 minutes. Use baking pan 9" x9" x2", with non-stick finish or spray with Pam. Mix cottage cheese, 1/4 cup Romano cheese and the egg. Layer half each of zucchini, flour, cottage cheese mixture, meat sauce and mozzarella cheese, repeat. Sprinkle 1/4 cup Romano cheese on top. Bake uncovered 45 minutes. Let stand 20 minutes before serving. Cut into squares.

Mary Dickey

SOCIOLOGIST'S SUGARLESS SODA BREAD

3 cups whole wheat flour
1/2 tsp. salt
2 tsp. baking soda
1 egg, beaten
1-1/2 cups buttermilk
1/3 cup molasses
3 Tbsp. margarine, melted

Mix the flour, salt, and baking soda together, In a separate container mix egg, buttermilk, molasses, and melted margarine. Mix together with a heavy wooden spoon. Shove into a greased 9"x 5"x 3" loaf pan. Let stand 20 minutes. Bake 45 minutes at 350°. Check with cake tester for doneness. Whole wheat, no sugar, no yeast increases VIRILITY and VITALITY!

Dennis L. Porter

TRIM TIPS

Skin chicken parts when preparing chicken with a sauce and you'll save many calories.

Use commercially prepared low-cal foods when you can. The juice pack fruits are excellent additions to a dieter's pantry.

Keep munchies of fresh raw vegies in easy reach in the refrigerator... hopefully by the time you chew several carrot sticks, the urge to pull additional goodies from your refrigerator will have subsided.

and

Tape a picture of a VERY FAT person on your refrigerator...or think more positively and simply tape...(size 7) signs in your nibbling spots.

Include at least one food with each meal which can be eaten in an unlimited quantity such as lettuce, celery, cabbage, broccoli, spinach, cauliflower, mushrooms, cucumber or green peppers.

Make your food colorful and as attractive as possible to increase your pleasure while slimming.

Reserve a portion of your meal for a later-in-the-day snack.

Search out Low-cal cookbooks to give as much variety and enthusiasm as possible to your efforts.

Get plenty of sleep, particularly during the first weeks of a diet, as the extra rest will help you to be more alert and less irritable.

Avoid using your dieting success to gain a reward of ANY FOOD... instead, do something which requires physical activity or fun.

Dilute fluids whenever possible with water. Apple cider when diluted with water and garnished with a lemon slice and cinnamon stick can still warm you on a winter evening. Lots of fluids are a must to a dieter.

Substitute low-cal choices whenever possible, i.e., skim milk for whole milk, diet margarine for butter, and especially well-blended cottage cheese is a great replacement for sour cream.

Season fresh vegetables with a small amount of chicken broth instead of butter.

Experiment with herbs, spices, and extracts to add flavor without calories.

Adopt a slogan for yourself such as "sleek and slim" for a positive outlook.

Use a champagne glass or special dish to serve a slim snack...it will be much more enjoyable to you.

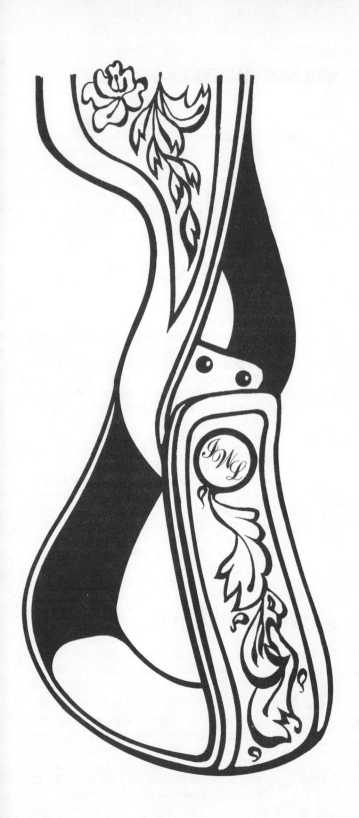

CELLAR DWELLERS

PICKLES AND PRESERVES

CELLAR DWELLERS

In years past home-canned fruits, vegetables, jams and jellies, pickles and preserves were often stored in the root cellar to help preserve freshness and stay cool. Foods were grown to sustain the family throughout most of the year. Garden fresh nowadays is a luxury and well appreciated. Preserving freshness to be savored in another season or to share as a gift for a special occasion is a treat. Selections await your pleasure and are guaranteed not to stay in the cellar for long!

APPLE BUTTER

Yield: 4 pints

4 lbs. apples (Jonathan,
Winesap, or other
well-flavored apples)
2 cups water or cider
1/2 cup sugar per cup of pulp
2 tsp. cinnamon
1 tsp. cloves, ground
1/2 tsp. allspice

Wash, stem and quarter apples. Cook slowly until soft in water or cider. Put through fine strainer and add sugar. Add cinnamon, cloves and allspice. Cook over low heat, stirring constantly until sugar is dissolved. Then cook rapidly, stirring frequently until it sheets from a spoon or drop a small amount on a plate— when no rim of liquid separates around the edge, it is done. (Use the latter method.) Reduce heat as butter thickens. (Use very large heavy pan as it splatters. Pull up a chair—it takes a long time. I usually make two batches at once.) Pour into boiling-hot sterilized jars. Seal and process in boiling water bath for 10 minutes.

Mrs. Jerry Shipley (Sally)

PICKLED PEACHES

Yield: 1 quart

1 cup vinegar, white
2-1/4 cups sugar
1 stick cinnamon
1/2 tsp. whole cloves
12 small peaches or 6 large

Peel peaches. Boil vinegar, sugar, cinnamon and cloves for 10 minutes. Then drop in peaches and cook until peaches are tender (not too long). Pour peaches and juice into pre-sterilized jars. Put on lids and rings and let them seal.

Joan Adelman

PINE COT MARMALADE

Yield: 10 (6 oz.) glasses

1 lb. dried apricots
1 #2 can sliced pineapple
Sugar

Wash apricots. Let stand overnight in water to cover and in the morning, stew in same water until tender. Cut pineapple in thin strips. Cut apricots in pieces; measure and add 1/2 cup sugar for each cup fruit and juice. Cook in oven in shallow baking dish at 250° until thick and transparent, 1-1/2 to 2 hours. Stir after 30 minutes and then every 15 minutes. To test thickness and transparency, spoon a little into sauce dish and observe when cool. Seal in hot, sterilized glasses.

Marion Collier

PEACH JAM
(Can use frozen fruit if you don't have fresh.)

Yield: 1 quart

4 cups or 3 12-oz. boxes
    frozen sliced peaches,
    thawed and crushed
1/4 cup lemon juice
4-1/2 cups sugar
1 bottle Certo fruit pectin

Place fruit in very large saucepan. Place over high heat, bring to a full rolling boil, and boil hard 1 minute, stirring constantly. Remove from heat, and stir in Certo. Skim off foam with metal spoon. Then stir and skim for 5 minutes. Cool slightly to prevent fruit from floating. Ladle into glasses. Cover at once with 1/8 inch hot paraffin.

Cherry Anderson

HOMEGROWN CHILI SAUCE

Yield: 6 pints

8 lbs. ripe tomatoes
4 medium green peppers,
   coarsely chopped
4 medium sweet red peppers,
   coarsely chopped
2 jalapeño peppers, finely
   chopped
3 cups celery, coarsely chopped
3 cups onion, coarsely chopped
2 cups granulated sugar
1 cup light-brown sugar, firmly
   packed
2 Tbsp. salt
2 cinnamon sticks
3/4 tsp. ground cloves
1 Tbsp. mustard seed
1 Tbsp. celery seed
3 cups cider vinegar
4 to 6 Tbsp. cornstarch

Pour boiling water over tomatoes to cover. Let stand several minutes. Peel, remove stems, and chop.
Prepare peppers: Remove seeds, ribs, and chop. In 12-qt. kettle combine chopped tomato, peppers, celery and onion with both kinds of sugar and salt. Stir over medium heat until sugar is dissolved. Boil uncovered 45 minutes. Add spices, boil uncovered 30 minutes longer, stirring occasionally. Add vinegar. Boil 1 hour longer. Sterilize jars, leaving in hot water until ready to fill. Depending on consistency desired, add some of the boiling liquid to cornstarch to form a thick paste; add to the boiling sauce and boil 5 minutes longer. Remove and discard cinnamon sticks. Complete one jar at a time. Ladle hot chili sauce into jars, filling within 1/2" of top. Cap at once as manufacturer directs.

Wendell Strickland

GRANDMA RIKLI'S STRAWBERRY PRESERVES

Yield: 4-1/2 pints

3 cups strawberries
3 cups sugar

Combine berries and sugar and let stand a few minutes in a large kettle. Place on low heat. When boil starts around edge, take wooden spoon and move around. Do not stir much when boil begins again. Time 20 minutes. Remove from stove. Take off foam with wax paper. Pour into flat pyrex dishes and leave overnight. Put into jars and seal with hot wax.

Mrs. Jim Nicholas (Ila)

GRANDMA BULES' PEAR BUTTER

3 lbs. pears, peeled (or 4 cups
    prepared fruit)
1 lemon, grated and juiced
1-1/2 cups (1 large can)
    crushed pineapple
1 box Sur-Jel or Pen-Jel
5-1/2 cups sugar
1 box paraffin squares (melted)

Cook pears until soft (approximately 10-15 minutes) at a low temperature (simmer). After fruit has softened, mash with a potato masher. Add pineapple, lemon and juice and Sur-Jel or Pen-Jel. Bring to a hard boil, then add sugar. Cook again to a hard boil. Cook for 5-10 minutes. Test to see if ready to pour into pre-sterilized jars by putting a small amount into a bowl, let cool and check to see if it is runny or has set up. If ready to set up, turn off heat and let cool for 1-2 minutes. Skim off foam and pour into jelly glasses. Cover top of Pear Butter with 1/4" paraffin. If you are short on pears, canned pears can be used.

Carolyn Bules

OKLAHOMA SANDPLUM JELLY

Earliest kitchen memories of many an Oklahoman include the pickin' of sandplums for jelly makin'. Each family watched for a plum thicket to get the pickin's before everybody else discovered the plums were ripe. Jelly the color of an Oklahoma sunrise being the coveted reward for scratches gotten in the thicket. Sandplum Jelly is still a tradition on the Oklahoma Range...the tart red plums make the sampling just as pleasurable as the memories.

5-1/2 cups prepared plum juice
7-1/2 cups sugar
1 box fruit pectin

To prepare plum juice: Wash plums, cover with cold water and boil until plums are soft and skins pop. Press through jelly bag, strain and measure. (At this point, juice may be frozen for later use.)
To prepare jelly: Mix plum juice with pectin and bring to a boil, stirring constantly. Add sugar, continue stirring and boil hard for one minute. Pour in sterile jars. Let set for one minute and skim off top. Seal with new lids. Let jelly cool slowly as sudden temperature change can cause jar to explode. The foamy jelly skim makes a fun treat for little helpers as well as a tasty memory of jelly making time!

Jon and Jane Ford

PICKLED OKRA

Yield: 5 pints

2 lbs. small, tender okra
5 pods red or green peppers
5 cloves garlic, peeled
1 qt. white vinegar
6 Tbsp. pickling salt (or plain,
    not iodized, salt)
1 Tbsp. celery seed
5 pint jars

Wash okra and pack in hot sterilized jars. Place one pepper pod and one clove of garlic in each jar. Bring vinegar, salt, and celery seed to boil. Pour over okra. Seal. (If pepper pods are unavailable, use 1/4 tsp. crushed dried hot red pepper for each jar.)

Mrs. Bill Green (Mary)

RUBY'S DILLED OKRA

Yield: 2 quarts

3 lb. okra
3 cups white vinegar
6 Tbsp. canning salt
3 cups water
Dill seed (or weed)
Garlic
Mustard seed (optional)
Jalapeño peppers, fresh
    (optional)

Pack into pint jars: 3-4 inch long, whole pods of okra, leaving crown and a bit of the stem on each. Add 1 clove of garlic to each jar. Bring to boil: water, vinegar, salt and dill seed. Pour hot over packed okra. Seal. Optional: Ingredients may be added for hotter or spicer flavor.
Note: For easy increase, simply add 1 cup water, 1 cup vinegar, and 2 Tbsp. salt for each pound of okra.

Pam Faubian

PICKLED BEETS (Aunt Eunice's Pickled Beets)

Fresh beets, cooked and peeled
2 cups apple cider vinegar
3 cups water (include juice
    from cooked beets)
1 cup sugar
Salt and pepper to taste

Cook beets until tender. Peel. Bring vinegar, water, sugar, salt and pepper to boil. Place cooked beets in the brine. Heat through. Remove beets and pack in hot, sterilized jars. Pour hot vinegar solution over beets. Seal.

Mrs. Bill Green (Mary)

PICALILLI

Makes: 6 1/2 pint jars

2 qts. green tomatoes
2 cups onions, chopped
2 cups celery, chopped
2 cups green pepper, chopped
2 Tbsp. cinnamon
1 Tbsp. cloves
2 cups cabbage, chopped
1/4 cup salt
1/2 cup mustard seed
4 cups vinegar
4 cups sugar
1 tsp. allspice

Wash tomatoes—do not peel. Cut out bloom ends. Chop until fine. Add salt— let stand 24 hours. Drain well. Combine with remaining ingredients. Boil until thick. Reduce heat and cook 1 hour, stirring frequently. Pour into sterilized jars and seal.

Mrs. David Bules (Carolyn)

CORN RELISH

Yield: 6 pints

2 qts. cut corn (1-1/2 doz. ears)
1 qt. cabbage, chopped
1 cup sweet red pepper, chopped
1 cup sweet green pepper, chopped
1 cup onions, chopped
1 Tbsp. celery seed
1 Tbsp. salt
1 Tbsp. turmeric
2 Tbsps. dry mustard
1 Tbsp. mustard seed
1 cup water
1 qt. vinegar
1 to 2 cups sugar

To prepare corn, boil 5 minutes, cut from cob. Combine with remaining ingredients and simmer 20 minutes. Bring to boiling. Pack, boiling hot, into sterilized jars, leaving 1/8 inch head space. Adjust cap. Great with red beans and cornbread.

Mrs. Larry Dobbs (Ruth)

WATERMELON PRESERVES

Yield: 6

1 medium watermelon
1 Tbsp. cloves
1 Tbsp. allspice
2 sticks cinnamon
2 lemons, sliced
5 lbs. sugar

Peel skin from the rind of watermelon. Leave 1/8 inch of the red meat on the rind. Slice marmalade style. This is easy in a processor. Put in a large container. Put cloves and allspice in cloth bag. Put this in rinds along with a stick of cinnamon, lemons and sugar. Cook until very thick. Put in sterilized jars, and seal.

Mrs. David Bules (Carolyn)

LIME PICKLES

Yield: 6 pints

7 lbs. cucumbers
2 cups lime
2 qts. vinegar
1 tsp. celery seed
9 cups sugar
1 tsp. mixed pickling spice
1 tsp. turmeric powder

Slice cucumbers and cover with lime and 2 gallons of water. Let soak 24 hours. Rinse and cover with fresh water for 3 hours; then drain and put in vinegar, celery seed, sugar, mixed pickling spice and turmeric powder. Let stand overnight. Heat for 35 minutes, pickles and all, before sealing in sterilized jars.

Mrs. Robert Jantzen (Colleen)

BREAD & BUTTER PICKLES

Yield: 4 quarts

4 qts. cucumbers, sliced but
    not pared
5 small onions
2 cloves garlic
1/3 cup salt
2 qts. ice
4-1/2 cups sugar
1-1/2 tsp. turmeric
1-1/2 tsp. celery seed
2 tsp. mustard seed
3 cups vinegar

Soak cucumbers, onions, garlic, salt and ice for 3 hours. Mix sugar, turmeric, celery seed, mustard seed, vinegar, and bring to a boil. Drain cucumber mixture, add to spice mixture and let boil 5 minutes. Place in jars and seal.
Suggestion: Heat thoroughly, but do not boil for crispier pickles.

Mrs. Jim Lovell (Linda)

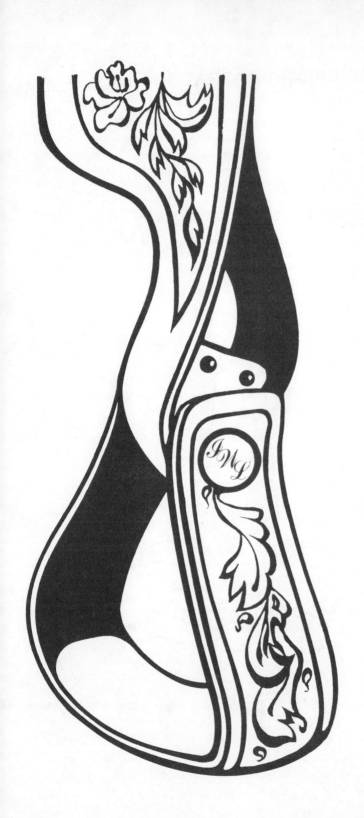

KIDS KORRAL

KID'S SPECIALTIES

"KIDS KORRAL"

You and your little wranglers will enjoy rustling up these recipes. Several will provide a rainy-day project, while others are especially fun without a lot of sugar. Even the most stubborn eaters will enjoy these nutritious treats.

FLYING SAUCER SICLE SAVER

Let your little "Moon Men" design and color their own flying saucer from an inexpensive paper plate. When the design is complete, punch a small hole in the center and insert your favorite popsicle. This drip-saver shield will save a lot of stained elbows and sticky legs.

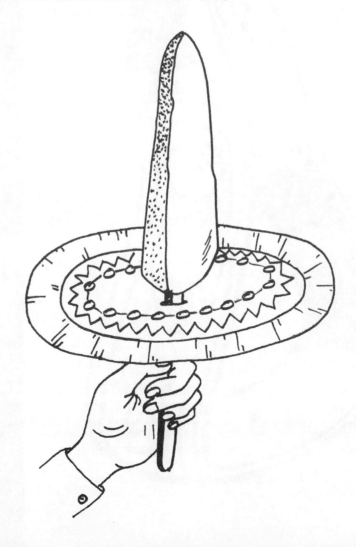

LOVE IN THE LUNCH BOX!

Napkin Notes: Write a note or message on your child's napkin. Smiling faces and words of encouragement create special memories to savor along with the lunch!

A RIDDLE A DAY...include pages from an inexpensive riddle or joke book... keeps the doldrums away!

YOU ARE MY SUNSHINE !!!

CHILDREN'S HOUSE PLAYDOUGH

This recipe is a favorite standby of Cimarron Children's House, and is graciously shared with us by one of the school's founders. This playdough has served dozens of little wranglers over the years, and keeps well at room temperature!

3 cups flour
1-1/2 cups salt
2-3 tsp. cream of tartar*
6 Tbsp. cooking oil
3 cups water

*Alum may be used in place of
cream of tartar.

Mix dry ingredients together in heavy sauce pan. Stir until well blended. Pour in liquid ingredients. Stir well. Cook and stir over medium heat until a large ball forms around the stirring spoon. Let cool. Take out and knead until pliable. If a color is desired, add food coloring to the water before mixing with the dry ingredients.
Linda Gungoll

327

ENERGY CANDY

1/4 cup molasses
1/4 cup honey
1/2 cup peanut butter
1 cup powdered milk
1/2 cup seedless raisins
    (optional)

Mix all ingredients well in a bowl and form into a ball. Add more powdered milk if necessary. Knead on a board until stiff. Shape into individual bite-size balls. Roll in brown sugar, if desired. Let stand for a couple of hours until hardened or put in refrigerator. Be sure to use powdered, not crystalline, dry milk. Great for after-school snacks!

*Busy and energetic young athletes will enjoy making this one to have on hand for extra energy during their next big sports event!

Lynn Diel

SANTA APPLES

Makes: 8 servings

8 medium sized cooking apples

SYRUP:
6 cups water
2 cups sugar
1 cup red hots candy
1 tsp. red food coloring

FILLING:
8 oz. cream cheese, softened
2 Tbsp. milk
1/4 cup chopped pecans

HEADS:
8 large marshmallows
8 large red gum drops
16 whole cloves

BODIES:
Toothpicks
32 tiny marshmallows
Spray type whipped cream
* (optional)*
Green maraschino cherries
Lettuce leaves (frilly loose leaf
* for base)*

Combine syrup ingredients and boil over medium heat until candy and sugar are melted. While syrup is cooking, prepare apples. Peel and core each. Add them to syrup and cook until done. Turn frequently until each apple takes on a nice red color. Do not overcook as apples should be firm for making Santas. Remove from heat. Cool. Refrigerate apples in syrup overnight, turning occasionally. Drain apples on paper towels within one hour of serving time. Prepare filling: Whip cream cheese with milk and nuts. Fill core area of apple.

Place marshmallow on top for head. Place two cloves for eyes and a small slice of gumdrop for mouth. Mouth will stick easier if marshmallow is moistened slightly. A large gumdrop should be placed on top for hat. Tassel can be made from additional piece of marshmallow or dollop of whipped cream.
Place toothpicks with small marshmallows speared on them in sides of body for arms. A green maraschino cherry slice can make glove on the end.
Additional cloves may be placed down front of body for buttons. Garnish with additional whipped cream and serve on doilies. Keep in refrigerator until ready to serve.

Mrs. Jim Caton (Marge)

FRACTIONAL FUDGE COOKIES

An easy no-bake recipe that is great for experience in working with fractions in a classroom where an oven is not available.

1/2 cup margarine (1 stick)
2 cups sugar
1/4 cup cocoa
2 tsp. dry milk added to 1/2 cup water...OR 1/2 cup milk
1 tsp. vanilla
1/2 cup peanut butter
3 cups 1-Minute Oats
1/2 cup chopped nuts (optional)

Pre-measure all ingredients for ease in combining mixtures without over cooking. Combine margarine, sugar, cocoa, and milk or (water-dry milk mixture) in a saucepan. Bring to a boil over medium heat, stirring constantly as mixture will scorch easily. Boil for 1 minute. Remove from heat and stir in peanut butter and vanilla. Mix well and gradually add oatmeal and nuts if desired. Work fast before mixture sets up and drop by spoonfuls onto wax paper. Cool and enjoy eating after arithmetic!

*Depending on class size and lesson of the day, this recipe may be divided in half or even doubled. This is also easy to take ingredients to prepare as they need not be refrigerated.

Mona Payne

MONSTER COOKIES

Big Batch-Crowd Pleasers

Serves: 80

12 eggs
2 lbs. brown sugar
4 cups white sugar
1 lb. margarine
3 tsp. vanilla
3 tsp. white corn syrup
1 (3-lb.) jar peanut butter
8 tsp. baking soda
1 (16-oz.) pkg. mini chocolate chips
18 cups quick cooking oatmeal
1 (16-oz.) pkg M & M's

In a dishpan, combine ingredients in the order listed, adding one at a time. Mix thoroughly between each addition. Using a small ice cream scoop or tablespoon, place mound of dough on greased cookie sheet—flatten. Bake at 350° for 10-12 minutes. Cool before removing from sheet. Can make half of recipe and use mixer for creaming first ingredients and then transfer to dishpan to mix in rest by hand.

Beverly Evans

FIRESTICKS

2-1/2 cups sugar
1 cup Karo syrup
1/2 cup water
1 tsp. red food coloring
1 tsp. cinnamon oil

Combine sugar, syrup and water. Cook until thermometer reads 295°F. Add red food coloring and cinnamon oil. Pour onto well buttered cookie sheet. Let harden, then crack with end of knife.

Pam Boyle

JUMPIN' JIMMINEY JELLO COOKIES!

3 small pkgs. jello
3 envelopes of unflavored
    gelatin
4 cups hot water

Combine all ingredients and pour into a 9" x 13" pan. Place in refrigerator until hard. Cut into squares or your favorite shapes.
*These are especially nice for satisfying the cookie baking urge in the heat of summer.

Carolyn Bules

MUSCLE-MAN MUNCHIES
Wheat Germ Crackle Cookies

Serves: 36

3/4 cup margarine
1/2 cup brown sugar, packed
1 egg, beaten
1 cup flour, sifted
1 cup wheat germ
1 tsp. ginger
1/2 tsp. cinnamon
1-1/2 tsp. baking powder
1/8 tsp. salt
1 cup flaked coconut

Cream butter and sugar. Add beaten egg and cream thoroughly. To sifted flour add, wheat germ, ginger, and cinnamon. Blend baking powder and salt into flour mixture. Stir flour mixture into creamed sugar mixture with a large mixing spoon. Add coconut and mix well. If dough is sticky, add a small amount of flour. Chill dough for one hour. Form dough into balls the size of walnuts and roll in sugar. Place on greased cookie sheets. Bake at 350° for 10-12 minutes.

Kathy Risley

PEANUT BUTTER BARS

Fun for all "kids in the kitchen!"

Yield: 32

1 pkg. graham crackers, crushed
3 cups powdered sugar
1 cup peanut butter, smooth
    or crunchy
2 sticks margarine, melted
1 (12-oz.) pkg. milk chocolate
    chips

In mixing bowl, put crushed graham crackers, powdered sugar, and peanut butter. Melt margarine and pour over cracker mixture. Mix well. Press into an ungreased 13" x 9" pan. Melt chocolate chips and pour over crust. Chill. Cut into bars.

Kathy Risley

PEANUT BUTTER COOKIES

Yield: 3 dozen

1-1/2 cups flour, sifted
1 tsp. baking soda
Dash of salt
1/2 cup shortening
1/2 cup brown sugar, packed
1/2 cup sugar
1/2 tsp vanilla
1/2 cup peanut butter
1 egg

Sift flour, salt, and baking soda together. Beat egg slightly, combine with shortening, sugar, brown sugar, and peanut butter. Gradually add flour mixture. Add vanilla. Form into balls and place on lightly greased cookie sheet. Press lightly with fork. Bake for 10 minutes at 375.° Recipe can be baked ahead and frozen.
*PEANUT BUTTER BEARS: To make bears and other shapes, form dough into various sizes of balls and ropes. Arrange on cookie sheets to make desired shapes; flatten slightly with your hand. Peanut Butter Bears are a real treat to make and to eat!

Carolyn Bules

PUZZLE COOKIES FOR CHILDREN

A favorite roll out cookie dough can be used in creating a unique spelling or mix and match activity. Geometric shapes can be cut apart for eager little eaters to put together before gobbling them up. Letters can spell names or difficult words from the next day's word list. What a yummy lesson!

ICE CREAM MUFFINS
Super for little do it your selfers.

Yield: 6 regular or 12 miniature

1 cup vanilla ice cream, softened
1 cup sifted self-rising flour

Preheat oven to 350°. Put paper liners in muffin tin. Combine softened ice cream with flour in medium sized bowl; stir until moistened, do not overmix. Fill liners 3/4 full. Bake for 20 minutes or until inserted toothpick comes out clean. Very good with honey-butter (see bread section).

Pat Reeves

RAINBOW ADE

For easy identity of their own drink and a quick lesson in mixing colors, add various drops of food color to your favorite lemonade. Play a color guessing game…"What do you get with yellow and red?"

RAINBOW ICE

Freeze a variety of colorful ice cubes for a cool and colorful treat. A Cherry Kool-Ade cube in your next glass of lemonade. Add a variety of cubes for a rainbow effect. These cubes can be made super healthy by freezing cranberry juice, grape juice, orange juice, or even colored apple juice. A variety of colors in the same glass are a special treat!

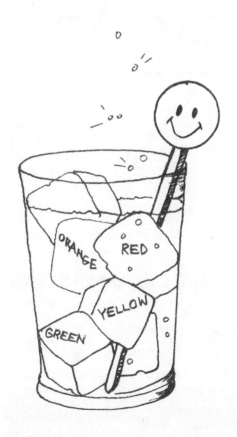

FRUITY BANANA DRINK

Serves: 2

1 medium size banana
1/3 cup fruit juice (orange,
    apple, pineapple)
Ice-cubes
Ice cream (optional)

Cut banana into chunks and combine with other ingredients in blender. More ice may be added if you want a thicker drink. Ice cream may be blended in or dropped in top when serving.

Pat Reeves

ORANGE JULIUS

1 (6-oz.) can frozen orange
    juice concentrate
1 cup milk
1 cup water
1/2 cup sugar
1 tsp. vanilla
Ice cubes

Combine ingredients in blender. Pour in glasses and serve.

Ann Frazee Riley

KOOL-AID PUNCH
(Home room mother's delight)

48 small servings

2 (.21-oz.) pkgs. raspberry
    Kool-aid
2 (.21-oz.) pkgs. strawberry
    Kool-aid
4 cups sugar
1-1/2 qts. water
2 qts. ginger ale
1 (12-oz.) can frozen orange
    juice concentrate
1 (6-oz.) can frozen limeade
    concentrate
1 (7-1/2-oz.) bottle frozen
    lemon juice

Mix Kool-aid powder with sugar and water. Add fruit concentrate. When ready to serve, add ginger ale and pour over crushed ice. This is refreshing to children as well as adults.

Florelee Day

TICKLISH TEA

1 cup ginger ale
1 cup orange juice

Pour the ginger ale and the orange juice into a teapot, or a pitcher, if you don't have a teapot. Stir a few times. You can add a few ice cubes if you like. Serve in teacups and watch your friend giggle when the bubbles burst in his nose.

SURPRISE CUPCAKES

Makes: 24 cupcakes

1 pkg. chocolate cake mix
(German Chocolate
is great)
8-oz. cream cheese, softened
1 egg
1/3 cup sugar
Dash of salt

Prepare cake mix as directed on box for muffins. Fill cups 2/3 full.
Prepare surprise filling: Blend cream cheese, sugar, salt, and egg thoroughly. Drop filling mixture by teaspoon into top of each cupcake. Bake at 350° for 15 to 20 minutes.

Pam Boyle

FUNNY BUNNY SALAD

This bunny has just come out of the garden.

Place crisp lettuce leaf on plate.

On top of it, place upside down, 1 chilled pear half.

2 raisins make the eyes.

1 red cinnamon candy makes the nose.

2 blanched almonds make the ears.

A ball of cottage cheese makes his tail.

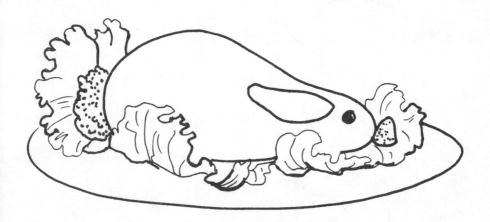

FRILLY MILLY SALAD

Fun for Children or Mom

Half a hard-cooked egg for the head

Fresh or canned peach half for the body

Small celery sticks or carrot sticks make the arms and legs

Grated yellow cheese for the hair

Piece of cherry or a redhot for the mouth

Raisins for the eyes, nose, shoes and buttons

Ruffled leaf lettuce for the skirt

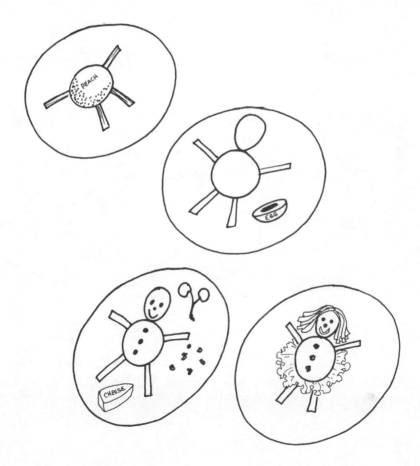

CURIOUS GEORGE SANDWICH

A favorite character becomes a whole wheat treat!

*Whole wheat bread (you can
    use dark rye for top portion)*
*Favorite filling (start with a
    reliable such as cheese
    or peanut butter for
    picky eaters)*
*Sweet red pepper slice or a thin
    slice of tomato for mouth*
2 raisins for eyes
*2 cucumber slices for ears (may
    use cheese or radish
    slices also)*

Cut partially frozen bread slices with cookie cutter and spread filling between. Pumpernickle or rye may be used for the contrasting top portion of face. Place both sections together on plate and add eyes, mouth and ears. This is guaranteed to give your reluctant brown bread eaters some "monkey business!"

CAT-WICH

FILLING:
*Cream cheese, pimiento
    cheese, egg salad or
    another favorite*
6 pretzels for whiskers
Olive slices for eyes
Tomato slice for mouth
Cheese for ears and nose

Cut bread with round cookie cutter. Spread with your choice of filling. Decorate with eyes, ears, whiskers, etc. The possibilities for making other animals in this manner are unlimited.

EASY PIGS IN BLANKETS

Serves: 4

Pork sausage links
Refrigerated prepared biscuits

Brown sausage in skillet. Drain and cool. Roll each biscuit flat; wrap around a sausage. Bake on cookie sheet at 450° for 10-12 minutes or until brown. Serve warm.

Mrs. Stu Meulpolder (Barbara)

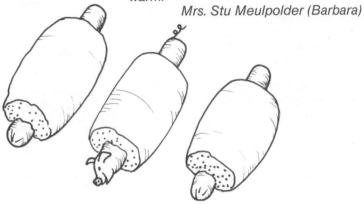

GHOSTY TOASTY

2 slices bread
1 Tbsp. butter
3 Tbsp. coconut

Toast the two slices of bread. Then spread them with butter. Put the coconut on a plate, spread it around, and put the buttered toast face down in it.
If there is some coconut left on the plate after you have done this, sprinkle what's left over on the toast.

PRONTO PIZZA MAN

1 slice white bread
Ketchup
Grated Mozzarella cheese
1 green stuffed olive, sliced
Green pepper slice or yellow
    cheese slice
Wiener or sausage slice

Cut crust from bread and make circular shape. Roll flat with rolling pin. Spread a thin layer of ketchup on top. Sprinkle with Mozzarella cheese. Garnish with olive slices for eyes, wiener slice for nose, and a sliver of green or red pepper for mouth. Variations of ingredients for eyes, nose, and mouth may be used. These may include mushroom slices, onion pieces, and lunch meat. Place Pizza Man in a 450° oven for 3 to 5 minutes. Face will vary according to ingredients on hand.
Variation: Make a Jack-O-Lantern Pizza for Halloween! Use a green pepper stem.

POCKETWICH
Curried beef pita

Serves: 8-10

1 lb. ground beef
1 diced onion
1 garlic clove, halved
1 Tbsp. curry powder*
1 medium zucchini, diced
1/2 cup water
1-1/4 tsp. salt
1/2 tsp. sugar
1/4 tsp. pepper
1 medium tomato, diced
1 (9-oz.) pkg. pita bread

Cook beef, onion, garlic and curry powder until meat is browned and onion tender. Add zucchini, water, salt, sugar and pepper. Heat to boiling. Reduce heat to low; cover and simmer 15 minutes or until zucchini is tender. Stir in tomato; heat through. Cut pocket bread in half, heat for 5 minutes. Spoon mixture in pockets.
*Add curry according to taste.

Mrs. Glenn Devoll (Susie)

RUDOLPH SANDWICHES

Brown bread slices (whole
    wheat, pumpkin, etc.)
1 8-oz. pkg. cream cheese,
    softened
Maraschino cherries, halved
Pretzels for antlers
Raisins for eyes
Crushed pineapple (optional)

Whip cheese with 2 Tbsp. of crushed pineapple or cherries to add flavor. Cut bread slices into small triangles. (Each side of triangle should be about 2-1/2 to 3-inches.) Place filling between bread. Put a small dab of cheese at one point of triangle to secure a cherry half for nose. Do the same to secure raisins for Rudolph's eyes. Then insert pretzels into filling along top of head to make antlers. *This is a special, not so sweet treat for your sugar-filled Christmas season.

Cimarron Children's House

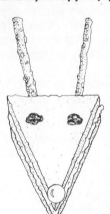

ROLY POLY ROUNDUPS

Bread slices, very fresh

FILLING:
Peanut butter
Egg salad
Cream cheese or pimiento
    cheese, etc.

Trim bread slices to remove crusts. Roll bread flat with a rolling pin. (Kids can do this.) Spread filling on top. You may even use mayonnaise and add a slice of ham or your favorite lunch meat. A leftover slice of bacon from breakfast combined with cream cheese makes a tasty spread, too. Roll up and secure with a tooth pick and small olive or pickle. Eat it round or cut in small pinwheel slices for little folks!

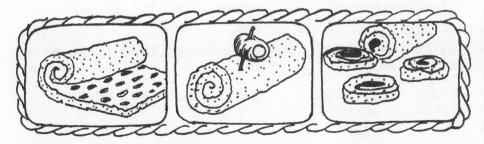

SUPERMAN STEAK

Make a super beef patty to house lots of special ingredients. A mini meat-loaf to include extra nutritious ingredients such as wheatgerm, spinach, carrots, with lean ground beef. Grill or pan fry and add cheese and ketchup with "Superman" logo. Make several and keep in freezer for Mom's night out. With or without bun, a little muscle man's treat.

SWEETHEART SANDWICHES

Makes: 2 servings

Heart-shaped cookie cutter
8 slices bread
2 Tbsp. butter
2 Tbsp. red jelly

Spread one side of each slice of bread with butter. Cut out a heart from each slice of bread with cookie cutter. Spread four of the heart shapes with jam or jelly. Make sandwiches of a slice with jelly and a slice with butter. Takes 15 minutes.

CELERY CANOES

Celery canoes can accommodate nutritious cargo:
Peanut butter with "Banana Men,"
Egg Salad with "Olive Men,"
Tuna and ham salad with "Pickle Men,"
Pimiento cheese with "Carrot Men,"—

and pineapple cream cheese filling with Fruit Men made from apples, orange wedges, pears, pecans or strawberries—creative little additions packed with nutrition to accompany a favorite soup (Tomato Lake).

FUNNY FACE FRANKS

Yield: 8 sandwiches

8 franks
16 slices of bread
8 slices American cheese
Butter, melted
Ketchup

For each funny face sandwich, split a frank in half lengthwise. Make a cheese sandwich and cut with a cookie cutter into a 2-1/2-inch circle. Wrap frank halves around sandwich and fasten with wooden picks. Place on buttered cookie sheet. Brush bread and franks with melted butter. Make a face on the bread with ketchup. Bake in 400° oven for 5 minutes.

Kids Committee

BUTTERY CARAMEL CORN

4-5 qts. popped corn
1-1/2 cups sugar
1/2 cup white syrup
2 sticks butter or margarine
1 tsp. vanilla

Mix sugar, syrup and butter and heat to 300° Watch carefully—it burns easily. Add vanilla and pour over popped corn.

Mrs. Ken Boyle (Pam)

BEEF JERKY

1 2-lb. round steak
1 Tbsp. salt
1 Tbsp. onion powder
1 tsp. garlic powder
1/2 tsp. pepper
2 drops Tabasco sauce
2 Tbsp. Worcestershire sauce

Remove bone and all fat from steak. Put meat in freezer for 20 minutes for ease in slicing into 1/8 to 1/4-inch strips. Slice with the grain. Combine all ingredients to make the marinade. Place meat strips and mixture in a shallow dish with enough water to cover meat. Refrigerate overnight. Drain strips on toweling and place on wire racks of oven so that they do not touch one another. Cover bottom of oven with large sheet of foil to catch drips. Bake at lowest possible setting (200°) for 4 or 5 hours. It is helpful if oven door is left slightly open. Cook until meat is black and cracks when bent, but it should not break. This jerky can be kept in sealed plastic bags or jars for up to 6 months without refrigeration.
*On an economic note! Homemade beef jerky without harmful preservatives costs only 1/10th of the price of the store bought variety.

Blake Evans

TRAIL MIX

1 (15-oz.) box seedless raisins
1 (12-oz.) can Spanish peanuts
1 (11.5-oz.) milk chocolate chips

Preparation time: 2-1/2 minutes...or however long it takes to open the packages!
Serves 12 children at 3:30 in the afternoon.

Mrs. Jon Ford (Jane)

EGGY PANCAKES

Serves: 4-6 pancakes

3 eggs
1/8 tsp. salt
1/2 cup sugar or less
1/2 cup flour
1/4 cup milk
Increase milk according to desired results: More milk will give you a thinner crêpe-like cake, while less milk will give you a thicker cake.

Beat eggs. Beat in remaining ingredients in order. Use small skillet over medium heat, add enough oil to moisten bottom of skillet. Pour small amount of mixture (about 3-4 Tbsp.) into center of skillet, turn pancake over when edges appear cooked and begin to ruffle even though center is moist; continue to cook 1 more minute. (These are so sweet you can eat them with just butter. The children might want to use honey.)
*A great way for not so eager egg eaters to partake of nature's most nearly perfect food!

Pat Reeves

CRAZY CORN

Great treat for a long winter evening of old movies.

Yield: 1 gallon

1 cup sugar
1/2 cup oleo
1/2 cup light Karo syrup
1/2 tsp. salt
1/2 tsp. vanilla
4 qts. popped corn
1 cup pecan halves

Combine first 5 ingredients. Bring to boil and boil for 5 minutes. Mix popped corn and pecan halves in large roaster pan and stir in the cooked mixture. Bake at 250° for 1 hour (in the roaster pan). Stir every 15 minutes. Remove from oven and stir to cool.
*Perfect Christmas gift for Girl Scouts to prepare!

Ila Nicholas

GRANOLA BARS

Yield: 30-35 bars

3-1/2 cups oats, quick
  or uncooked
1 cup raisins
1 cup chopped nuts
2/3 cup margarine, melted
1/3 cup honey, corn syrup,
  or molasses
1 egg, beaten
1/2 tsp. vanilla
1/2 cup brown sugar, packed
1/2 tsp. salt

Toast oats in ungreased shallow baking pan at 350° for 15-20 minutes. Combine toasted oats with remaining ingredients and mix well. Press firmly into well greased 15-1/2" x 10-1/2" jelly roll pan. Bake at 350° for 20 minutes. Cool and cut into bars. Recipe can be baked ahead and frozen.
*Great for mailing to your favorite college student....These keep well and are terrific travelers!

Toni Dekock

GRANOLA

5-1/2 cups rolled oats
1 cup Sesame seeds
1 cup Sunflower seeds
1 cup almonds (slivered or bits)
1 cup wheat germ
1 cup dry skimmed milk
1 cup Safflower oil
1 cup Organic honey
1-1/2 tsp. vanilla
1 cup raisins
1 cup coconut, if desired

In large bowl, mix first six ingredients and coconut. In separate bowl, stir oil, vanilla and honey. Pour oil mixture over oat mixture and blend well. Spread on 2 cookie sheets and bake at 250° for 1 hour or longer. Stir with wooden spoon every 15 minutes. When cooling, also stir to keep it from packing. When cool, add raisins. Store in tight container and it can also be frozen.

Lee Anne Simpson

Rename an old standby such as trail mix or granola to "Moon Man Munch" to generate new enthusiasm for a nutritious snack.

YUMMY POPCORN

A slightly cinnamon snack.

2 Tbsp. sugar
1/8 tsp. cinnamon
1/8 tsp. nutmeg
1/4 cup butter, melted
2 qts. salted popcorn

Combine sugar, cinnamon and nutmeg in bowl. Melt butter and pour over popcorn and then sprinkle spice mixture through popcorn.
*Great to prepare and serve on that first frosty evening in the fall. Perfect with a cup of warmed apple cider!

Pamela Buller

ALL PROTEIN CRUNCH GRANOLA

1/2-3/4 cup honey
1/2 cup oil
1 Tbsp. vanilla
1/2 tsp. salt
1/2 cup sesame seeds
1 cup soy grits
1 cup wheat germ
7 cups rolled oats

In large saucepan, heat oil, honey and vanilla until mixture is thin. Turn off heat and stir in remaining ingredients in order given. Make sure each ingredient is coated with honey mixture. Put in Dutch oven, cake pans, etc., and pre-heat oven to 350.° The cereal will begin to toast in about 15 minutes. Once it has started to brown, check and stir at least every 5 minutes. It's best toasted lightly to a golden color. Let cool before storing.

Nan Brim

GREAT GRANOLA IDEAS
Serve with milk as a cereal or eat it dry as a super snack. Stir it into your favorite bread or cookie recipe or sprinkle on top of apple pie or your favorite cobbler.

NOTES:

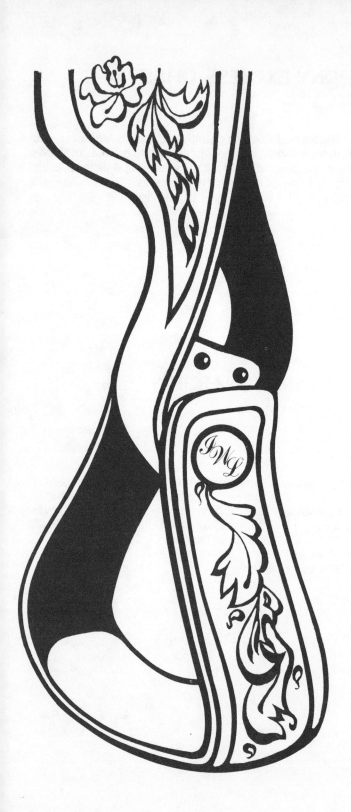

PONY EXPRESS-OHS
QUICK OR EASY

"PONY EXPRESS-OHS!"

It's oohs and aaahs! Whether company's comin' and time is limited or you just want to spend more time away from the kitchen, these express methods and ideas provide even the busiest cook with a variety of delicious foods. From day-before delights to quick tricks in the microwave, you could even have time for a Can-Can in the kitchen, not to mention lots of applause.

CINNAMON FRUIT

Serves: 10

1 large can pineapple chunks, drained
1 large can pear halves, drained
1 large can peach halves, drained
1 can apricot halves, drained
1 jar of maraschino cherries, drained
1/2 cup nuts, chopped

TOPPING
2 cups fruit juice
3 Tbsp. cornstarch
1/2 cup brown sugar
1 tsp. cinnamon
1/2 cup margarine

Arrange fruit in a 2 qt. glass baking dish. Save the juice. Cook the ingredients for the topping until thick. Pour topping over fruit and sprinkle with nuts. Bake at 350° for 45-60 minutes.

Ann Frazee Riley

HAYSTACKS

Serves: 30

1 (12-oz.) pkg. butterscotch
    chips
2 cups chow mein noodles
    1 cup salted cocktail nuts

Heat butterscotch chips in double boiler or microwave until completely melted. Add chow mein noodles and nuts and stir until each piece is coated. Drop from spoon onto waxed paper. Cool.

Diana Allen

QUICK CHOCOLATE CAKE FOR CHOCOHOLICS

18.5 oz. pkg. devils food cake
    mix with pudding
1/2 cup warm water
1/4 cup corn oil
4 large eggs, slightly beaten
1 cup commercial sour cream
1 Tbsp. vanilla
1-1/2 cups semi-sweet
    chocolate pieces (Nestle's)

Mix dry cake mix, water, oil, eggs, sour cream and vanilla at low speed. Scrape bowl constantly and beat until moistened. Beat at medium speed for 2 minutes. Stir in chocolate pieces. Pour into greased and floured 10" tube pan. Bake at 350° for 50-55 minutes. Cake will crack. Cool for 10 minutes. Then turn cake on a wire rack. Can be lightly iced or served plain.

Beverly Evans

SIMPLE PEACH COBBLER

6-8 peaches, peeled and diced
1/4 cup sugar
1/4 cup water
1 cup flour
2 tsp. baking powder
1/2 tsp. salt
1 cup sugar
1 egg, beaten
1/2 cup butter

Place peaches in 13" pyrex baking dish. Sprinkle with 1/4 cup sugar and 1/4 cup water. Mix flour, baking powder, salt, 1 cup sugar and egg until crumbly. Sprinkle over top of peaches and add 1/2 cup butter in thin slices over top of peaches. Bake at 350° for 40 minutes. Serve plain or with ice cream.

Mrs. George Wilson, Sr. (Myrna)

"COME ON OVER" CAKE

2-1/4 cups sifted flour
2 tsp. baking soda
1/2 tsp. salt
1 (14-oz.) can prepared vanilla
    frosting
1 egg
1 lb. can peaches, sliced
    (undrained—22 slices, 1/2
    cup juice)
1/2 cup coconut, shredded
1/2 cup pecans, chopped
1/2 cup brown sugar, packed

Prepare 13" x 9" pan. Sift flour, soda, and salt. Add 1-1/2 cups frosting, egg, peaches, and juice to flour mixture. Beat 2 minutes at medium speed. Pour into cake pan and sprinkle remaining ingredients on top, except remaining icing. Bake at 350° for 40-45 minutes. Cool and drizzle remaining frosting on top (thinned with cream).

Mrs. Richard Risley (Kathy)

CHOCOLATE ANGEL FOOD DESSERT

Serves: 15

4 eggs, separated
1/2 cup sugar
1 (6-oz.) pkg. semi-sweet
    chocolate chips
1 pt. cream, whipped
1 large angel food cake

Beat egg whites with sugar until stiff. Beat egg yolks. Melt chocolate chips. To this add beaten egg yolks, fold in egg whites and whipped cream. Tear angel food cake into pieces. Place 1 layer cake pieces in 9" x 13" pan. Cover with 1/2 of the chocolate. Then another layer of cake pieces and cover with chopped nuts, if desired. Chill. Cut into squares to serve.

Danette Tucker

PEANUT CLUSTERS

1-1/2 lb. almond bark
12 oz. semi-sweet chocolate
    chips
4-5 cups salted peanuts

In double boiler melt the almond bark and chocolate chips. Add peanuts. Drop spoonfuls onto waxed paper to cool.

Jana Harvey

CRUNCHY PEACH COBBLER

Serves: 6-8

4 cups or 6 fresh peaches,
    peeled and sliced
1 cup sugar
1 Tbsp. lemon juice
1 (14-oz.) pkg. oatmeal
    muffin mix or
1 pkg. muffin mix and 3/4 cup
    quick oats
1/4 tsp. nutmeg
1/2 cup butter or margarine

Combine peaches, sugar and lemon juice. Turn into greased 8″ square pan. In medium mixing bowl combine muffin mix and nutmeg, cut in butter or margarine until coarse crumbs. Spoon over peaches. Bake at 375° for 40-45 minutes. Serve warm or cold with ice cream.

Mrs. Robert Emery (Sandra)

VANILLA BARS

Serves: 2 dozen

1 (18-1/2-oz.) box yellow
    cake mix
1 stick butter, melted
1 egg
1 cup chopped pecans (optional)
1 (8-oz.) pkg. cream cheese,
    softened
2 eggs
1 lb. box of powdered sugar
1 tsp. vanilla

Combine cake mix, butter, one egg, and nuts. Mix well and pat into a 9 x 13-inch pan. Combine cream cheese, two eggs, powdered sugar, and vanilla. Mix at low speed and pour over crust. Bake at 300° for 55 minutes. Cool and cut into squares. Recipe can be frozen after baking.

Susie Edwards

TEXAS GOLD BARS

Yield: 3 dozen

1 (18-1/2-oz.) pkg. yellow
    cake mix
3 eggs
1 stick oleo, melted
1 (16-oz.) box powdered sugar
1 (8-oz.) pkg. cream cheese
1/2 to 1 cup pecans
1/2 to 1 cup shredded coconut

Combine cake mix, one egg, and melted oleo. Pat mixture in a jelly roll pan. Combine sugar, two eggs, and cream cheese; spread over crust. Sprinkle nuts and shredded coconut over top. Bake for 40-45 minutes at 325°. When cool, cut into bar size. This recipe can be baked ahead and frozen.

Irene Conway

M-M-M-MOUSSE AU EASY

1 cup milk
2 pkgs. German Sweet
    chocolate
1/2 cup sugar
1/2 cup cocoa
1 large pkg. cream cheese
    (8-oz.)
2 large containers Cool Whip
    (8-oz. each)

Combine in small sauce pan over medium heat; milk, chocolate, sugar and cocoa. If you stir the sugar and cocoa together, it will dissolve more quickly. When the chocolate is melted, this mixture should be combined with the cream cheese in a large mixing bowl. Beat this well and scrape bottom and sides of mixing bowl a few times to be sure all lumps are dissolved. When this mixture looks like a rich chocolate syrup, add the Cool Whip and mix well. Do not over beat, but scrape bottom and sides of bowl to make sure your mousse is well-blended.
Serving Ideas: Put in Clear glass bowl and garnish with whipped cream and chocolate shavings.
Double Chocolate Pie. Put in a chocolate cookie crumb crust and keep in freezer until one hour before serving. Optional: For an elegant spur of the moment trick, garnish with real whipped cream and a candied violet.

Sherrel Jones

EASY PINEAPPLE CREAM PIE

1 (20-oz.) can pineapple
    (crushed) and juice
1 can Eagle Brand milk
1 cup pecans (chopped)
1 large Cool Whip
1 Tbsp. lemon juice
2 8-inch pie shells, baked or
    24 tart shells

Bake two pie shells or 24 tart shells. Mix ingredients. Put in shells. Refrigerate.
* Great in Creative Coconut Crust. See dessert section.

Mrs. David Eck (Kathy)

PECAN PATTIES

Serves: 1 dozen

1 6-oz. pkg. semi-sweet real chocolate morsels, milk chocolate or combination of each
1-1/2 cups pecans, coarsely chopped

Melt chocolate in microwave on medium. Add nuts—stir until well coated. Drop in clusters on waxed paper. Cool until set.

Diana Allen

MINTED PEARS
(A light and different dessert.)

Serves: 4

1 16-oz. can pear halves, with syrup
1/4 cup creme de menthe for each cup syrup

Drain pears. Heat syrup and add 1/4 cup creme de menthe to each cup syrup. Pour hot syrup over pears, cover and chill several hours.
Variation: Shave or grate dark chocolate over tops just before serving.

Mrs. Jerry Shipley (Sally)

STRAWBERRY PIE

2 egg whites, beaten stiff
2/3 cup sugar
1 (10-oz.) pkg. strawberries (frozen)
2 Tbsp. lemon juice
2 cups Cool Whip

Beat egg whites. Add sugar slowly. Add strawberries and lemon juice. Beat 5 minutes at high speed. Fold in 2 cups Cool Whip.

CRUMB LINING:
1-1/2 cups flour
1/2 cup brown sugar
1/2 cup pecans, chopped
1/2 cup margarine, melted

Mix together and spread on a cookie sheet. Bake 350° for 10 minutes. Cool. Crumble. Press into 9-inch pie plate. Reserve 1/4 cup of crumbs for topping. Fill pie plate with strawberry filling and place reserved crumbs on top. Freeze 3-4 hours.

Mrs. Jerry McCune (Sharon)

QUICK CHILI RELLENOS

Serves: 4

6 oz. Monterey Jack cheese,
   shredded
1 can (4-oz.) green chilies
5 eggs
1/2 cup self rising flour
8 oz. Cheddar cheese,
   shredded

Crumble Monterey Jack cheese in bottom of buttered 9" baking dish. Spread drained green chilies on top. Beat eggs and add flour. Pour over Jack cheese and top with Cheddar cheese. Bake at 375° for 30 minutes.
Serving Suggestion: Top with black olive slices, or for a brunch, top with cooked sausage.
Variation: Omit flour and serve as a dip with Triscuits. Use whole green chilies, slice Monterey Jack cheese and stuff inside green chilies.

Rosanne Dickinson

ASPARAGUS PARMESAN

Serves: 5-8

2 cans Green Giant asparagus
2 Tbsp. butter
1/2 cup mayonnaise
1/4 tsp. salt
1/8 tsp. white pepper
1/8 tsp. dry mustard
Juice of 1/2 large lemon
1/2 cup buttered bread crumbs
1/3 cup Parmesan cheese

Place asparagus in greased 8-inch casserole. In a saucepan, melt butter. Heat just until brown. Add mayonnaise, seasonings, and lemon juice. Pour over asparagus. Sprinkle bread crumbs and cheese on top. Bake at 375° for 10-15 minutes until top is brown. Recipe may be doubled or tripled.
Note: Fresh asparagus may be used if steamed briefly before placing in casserole dish.

Mrs. Jon Ford (Jane)

CRISPY HERB BREAD STICKS

Yield: 16 servings

4 hot dog buns, halved and
**   sliced lengthwise**
1 stick butter
1 Tbsp. basil
1/2 Tbsp. tarragon

Slice buns (each bun will make 4 sticks similar to a long watermelon slice). Melt butter and add basil and tarragon. Brush on buns and bake in low oven, 200° for 2 to 3 hours. Great with spaghetti or a salad luncheon.

Mrs. Jesse Beck (Cecilia)

CAULIFLOWER BROCCOLI SALAD

1 large head cauliflower
1 bunch broccoli
1 bunch green onions
1 large green pepper
1-1/2 cups celery, chopped
3/4 cup green olives with
**   pimiento or ripe olives**
Cherry tomatoes
Italian dressing

Cut into pieces and marinate with Italian dressing.

Jana Harvey

IN A HURRY CHEESE BREAD

Yield: 6 servings

1/2 cup milk
1 egg, beaten
1-1/2 cups Bisquick
2 Tbsp. chopped parsley, (dried)
1 Tbsp. onion, minced
1 cup Cheddar cheese,
**   shredded**
1/4 cup butter or margarine,
**   melted**

Combine milk and egg. Add Bisquick, parsley, onion and 1/2 cup cheese. Pour into a greased 8" or 9" round pan. Sprinkle remaining 1/2 cup cheese on batter. Pour melted butter over top. Bake at 350° for 25 minutes or until golden brown.

Linda Downs

EASY GREEN BEAN CASSEROLE

Serves: 10-12

2 (16-oz.) cans whole green
 beans, drained
1 (16-oz.) can peas, drained
1 onion, thinly sliced
1 can (10-3/4-oz.) cream of
 celery soup
1 can (10-3/4-oz.) cream of
 mushroom soup
1 (8-oz.) jar Cheez Whiz
4 soda crackers, crushed

Layer 1 can beans, peas, 1/2 onion, 4 oz. Cheez Whiz, soups, 1 can beans, 1/2 cup onion, and 4 oz. Cheez Whiz in a 2-qt. casserole dish. Top with cracker crumbs and bake at 350° for 50 minutes. Variation: Use Pepperidge Farm stuffing mix for crumb topping.

Naoma Barnard

FAVORITE FRIED POTATO PATTIES

(A yummy use for a dab of leftover mashed potatoes, corn or frozen peas)

Serves: 4 potato patties (approximately 4″ in diameter)

1 cup leftover mashed potatoes
1 egg
1/2 cup flour
1/4 tsp. baking powder
1/4 cup whole green onions,
 chopped (or more to taste)
Salt and white pepper, to taste
Vegetable oil

Mix all ingredients together. Drop by spoonsful into hot oil in heavy skillet. Fry 3-4 minutes on each side until crisp golden brown. Remove and drain between paper towels to absorb excess oil. Serve warm. Chopped onions are a must. Variation: You may also add 1 or 2 of the following optional ingredients: 1/2 cup chopped celery, 1/4 cup sliced black olives, 1/3 cup drained whole kernel corn, 1/4 cup diced green pepper or 1/4 cup chopped pimiento. So good you will find yourself making extra mashed potatoes just to have leftovers.

Sherrel Jones

BETTER CHEDDAR POTATOES

Serves: 6

6 large potatoes, peeled
1 onion, chopped
1 can (10-3/4-oz.) cream of
    mushroom soup
1 can (10-3/4-oz.) Cheddar
    cheese soup
1-1/4 cups milk
Paprika to taste

Slice potatoes and mix with onion. Place in buttered 9" x 13" casserole dish. Combine soups and milk and pour over potatoes. Sprinkle with paprika. Bake at 350° for 1-1/2 hours.

Mrs. Steve Hendley (Mary)

EASY CHEESEY POTATOES

Serves: 6-8

1/2 cup onion, chopped
2-3 Tbsp. vegetable oil
1 (10-3/4-oz.) can cream of
    celery soup
1 (3-oz.) pkg. cream cheese
1 (12-oz.) pkg. frozen
    hash browns, thawed
1/2 cup cheddar cheese,
    shredded

Sauté onions in oil until tender. Stir in undiluted soup and cream cheese. Stir until hot and creamy. In 1-qt. casserole, make layers of potatoes, soup mixture* and cheddar cheese, ending with cheddar cheese. Cover and bake at 400° for 45 minutes.
*I sometimes add diced green pepper with soup mixture.

Kathy Risley

FRUITY COFFEE CAKE

1 large can refrigerated biscuits
6 or 8 medium peaches
    or apples
1-1/2 cups sugar
1/2 tsp. nutmeg
1/2 tsp. cinnamon
1/2 tsp. allspice
1/4 cup melted butter
    or margarine

Place biscuits in buttered pan. Butter tops and sprinkle with 1/2 cup sugar mixed with spices. Combine 1 cup sugar and melted butter with fruit. Pour mixture over biscuits. Bake at 350° for 30-40 minutes. Turn out immediately onto large serving plate. Eat while hot. Nuts may be added if apples are used.

Mrs. Marion Sheets (Ila)

HEATH ICE CREAM PIE

Serves: 8

9-inch graham cracker pie shell
1/2 gal. vanilla ice cream
4 Heath toffee candy bars

SAUCE:
1-1/2 cups sugar
1 cup evaporated milk
Salt, dash
1/4 cup butter
2 Heath candy bars
1/4 cup light corn syrup

Spoon half of softened (but not melted) ice cream into pie shell. Sprinkle 4 crushed Heath bars on top. Cover with remaining ice cream. Freeze.

Combine sugar, milk, butter, and salt. Boil one minute. Remove from heat. Stir in 2 crushed Heath bars. Cool slightly. Spoon over individual pie wedges. Remaining sauce may be refrigerated.

Mrs. E. Evans Chambers III (Judy)

PEANUT BUTTER PIE

1/2 cup crunchy peanut butter
1 (8-oz.) pkg. cream cheese
1/2 cup milk
1 cup confectioner's sugar
1 (8-oz.) Cool Whip

Blend first 4 ingredients well. Fold in Cool Whip. Pour into a 9" graham cracker crust. Refrigerate 4-6 hours before serving. Garnish with additional Cool Whip and chopped peanuts. Freezes well.

Amy Cromwell

CHERRY PIE FILLING SALAD

Serves: 8-10

1 can Cherry Pie filling
1 can Eagle Brand milk
1 9-oz. container Cool Whip
1 cup pineapple chunks
1/2 cup nuts

Mix all together and chill.

Mrs. Larry Dobbs (Ruth)

Committee variation: Omit Eagle Brand milk, and use 2 cups drained crushed pineapple.

EASY FRESH VEGETABLE SALAD

Do ahead great to keep on hand in summer time.

*Cauliflower flowerets
(2 to 3 cups)
Broccoli flowerets (2 to 3 cups)
Cherry tomatoes, 1 pt., cleaned
and stems removed
Black ripe olives (whole
and pitted)
Viva Wishbone dressing,
Italian or Vinaigrette*

Cook cauliflower and broccoli separately until still crunchy (approximately 3 minutes). Drain well. Combine all ingredients with your choice of dressing and marinate overnight. Serve in large glass bowl. This makes a lovely buffet salad.
Jana Harvey's variation: Add chopped green pepper and green onions to taste.

Mrs. Herman Hackett (Gail)

QUICK CRABMEAT SOUP

Serves: 4

*1 can tomato soup
1 can consommé
1 pt. half and half coffee cream
1 can green pea soup
1 can crabmeat
1/2 cup sherry*

Simmer all ingredients together for 1/2 hour. Add 1/2 cup sherry and serve.
Note: Bisque can be made by placing all ingredients in blender, and blending well before heating.

Diana Allen

MUSHROOM AND ASPARAGUS SOUP

Serves: 4

*1 can cream of mushroom soup
1 can cream of asparagus soup
White pepper and salt to taste
Cream or milk
1 Tbsp. sherry*

Combine soup and cream or milk in pan over low heat, adding enough cream to achieve desired consistency. Heat thoroughly, stirring well. Add sherry, pepper, and salt to taste. Mix well and serve.
Note: Company soup for a gourmet meal.
Elaine Gage

DIFFERENT TUNA SALAD

Serves: 4-6

1 can tuna (large or small,
    drained)
1 cup carrots, grated
1 cup finely chopped celery
1/4 cup grated onion
3-oz. can shoestring potatoes
Mayonnaise to taste

Mix first four ingredients. Just before serving, add shoestring potatoes and mayonnaise.

Mrs. S. Joe Bolin (Pat)

FAMOUS FAST SALAD

Serves: 4-6

1 (14-oz.) can artichoke hearts,
    drained, rinsed and cut
    in half
1/2 Bermuda onion,
    thinly sliced
1/2 lb. fresh mushrooms,
    sliced (or use canned
    mushroom slices)
1 small bottle garlic or Italian
    salad dressing
1 head iceberg lettuce, washed,
    torn and chilled
1 avocado, sliced

Marinate the first three vegetables in the salad dressing for one hour. Just before serving, toss marinated vegetables with lettuce. Add avocado slices and toss again lightly.

Linda Downs

PIZZA P.D.Q.

1 loaf Italian or French bread
1 10-oz. can pizza sauce
    with cheese
1/4 lb. salami, pepperoni or
    precooked sausage,
    thinly sliced
1 8-oz. pkg. Mozzarella cheese
1 or 2 Tbsp. Parmesan cheese

Split bread lengthwise; place on aluminum foil-lined cookie sheet, split side up. Spoon half the pizza sauce over cut sides of each piece of bread; arrange salami or pepperoni over bread, top with Mozzarella cheese and sprinkle with Parmesan. Bake at 400° for 15 minutes or until cheese melts. Add toppings as desired: cooked green pepper, onion, mushrooms, olives, anchovies, etc.

Mrs. Steve Roney (Janie)

PARTY CASSEROLE

Serves: 8

1 (6-oz.) pkg. Uncle Ben's Long
    Grain and Wild Rice
1 #2 can French Style green
    beans, drained
1 (10-3/4-oz.) can cream of
    celery soup
1/2 cup mayonnaise
    (no substitute)
1 (8-oz.) can water chestnuts,
    drained and sliced
1/4 cup chopped onion
2 cups cooked chicken, turkey,
    ham or tuna, diced
2 oz. chopped pimiento
1/2 cup slivered almonds
Paprika to taste

Cook rice as directed on package. Combine green beans, celery soup, mayonnaise, water chestnuts, onion, meat, pimiento and slivered almonds (reserving some almonds for the top of casserole). Sprinkle top with paprika. Bake 30 minutes at 350° in buttered 2-qt. casserole. This casserole can be assembled several hours ahead and refrigerated and cooked just before serving. (The cook-donor is partial to the ham version!)

Mrs. Laird Barnard (Naoma)

EASY LASAGNA

Serves: 8

1-1/2 lbs. ground beef
2 (1-1/2-oz.) pkgs. Lawry's
    Spaghetti Sauce Mix
Onion and garlic powder,
    to taste
2 (8-oz.) cans tomato sauce
1 cup water
2 cups canned tomatoes
1 (4-1/2-oz.) jar sliced
    mushrooms
1 small pkg. lasagna noodles
8 oz. Mozzarella cheese
1 cup cottage cheese, small curd
1 egg
Parmesan cheese, to taste

Brown beef and drain. Add sauce mix, onion and garlic powder, tomato sauce, water, tomatoes, mushrooms. Cook 1 to 1-1/2 hours on low heat, depending on your schedule. Can also be used in 15 minutes, if desired. Cook lasagna noodles as directed on package. Cover bottom of 9 x 13-inch dish with 1/2 meat mixture. Cover with slices of Mozzarella cheese. Cover with cottage cheese and egg mixture. Cover cottage cheese with noodles. Add remaining meat mixture, and cover with grated Parmesan cheese. Bake at 325° for 30 minutes. Let stand a few minutes before serving. Freshly grated Parmesan cheese adds a nice zest.

Mrs. Jim Nicholas (Ila)

CHICKEN BREASTS PARTY-STYLE

Serves: 8

8 chicken breasts, skinned and boned
8 strips bacon
1/4 lb. pkg. chipped beef or 1-5-oz. jar
1 (10-3/4-oz.) can cream of chicken soup
1 cup sour cream

Preheat oven to 275.° Wrap each chicken breast with a strip of bacon and secure with toothpicks. Place chipped beef in bottom of greased 9 x 13-inch pan. Top with chicken. Mix soup and sour cream and pour over chicken. Bake uncovered 3 hours. Low temperature method gives better results than higher temperature for shorter cooking period. May be prepared the day before and refrigerated until baking time.
Linda Down Variation: Use cream of mushroom soup in place of cream of chicken soup and increase sour cream to 2 cups.

Mrs. Jerry Mosley (Marlene)

QUICK BLENDER CRÊPES

Yield: 25 crepes

3 eggs
1/8 tsp. salt
1-1/2 cups milk
2 Tbsp. vegetable oil or melted butter
1 tsp. sugar (for dessert crêpes or blintz, page 107)
1-1/4 cups flour

Combine ingredients in blender jar; blend about 1 minute. Scrape down sides with spatula; blend for another 15 seconds or until smooth.
Brush heated pan with oil. Pour batter on the side and swirl so batter completely covers bottom in very thin layer. Cook crêpe until it is browned. Lift carefully and turn over gently.

Cookbook Committee

EASY CHICKEN CRÊPES

Serves: 8

1 (10-3/4-oz.) can cream of
    chicken soup
2 cups diced, cooked chicken
1 (8-oz.) can water chestnuts,
    sliced
1/4 cup white wine
Dash of salt, white pepper,
    paprika and Worcestershire
    sauce

BECHAMEL SAUCE
3 Tbsp. butter
3 Tbsp. flour
1 cup chicken or beef bouillon
1/2 cup cream
Salt and pepper to taste
1-2 egg yolks, optional
    (room temperature works
    best)

Prepare crêpes. These may be done ahead and layered between sheets of wax paper and refrigerated day before. For recipe see page 366. Mix all ingredients together in saucepan and heat. Fills 8 crêpes. Place in a buttered serving dish. Top with Bechamel Sauce. Place in 325° oven for 10-15 minutes until crêpes are heated. Bechamel Sauce could also be poured hot over the crêpes topped with mushrooms just before serving.

Bechamel Sauce: Melt butter over low heat. Stir in flour. Gradually stir in bouillon, cooking over medium heat until desired thickness. Blend in seasonings and cream. If using egg yolks, beat them well. Add a small amount of the heated sauce to the egg mixture, stirring constantly. Slowly add this egg mixture to remainder of sauce stirring as addition is made and cook over low heat for 1 minute longer. Other additions which could be made to the Bechamel Sauce or included in filling: sautéed onions, mushrooms, grated Swiss, Cheddar or Parmesan cheese, curry, dill, nutmeg, cayenne, chives, mustard, sherry, capers or horseradish. Slivered almonds may replace water chestnuts as well as sprinkled on top.

Committee Variation: You may want to add a stalk of crisp lightly steamed broccoli to the inside of the crêpe. Asparagus stalks work nicely also.

Mrs. Jon Ford (Jane)

DINNER IN A SKILLET

Serves: 6-8

2 lbs. ground beef
1 chopped onion
1 chopped green pepper
2 (16-oz.) cans hominy
2 (8-oz.) cans tomato sauce
1 cup sliced stuffed green olives
1 cup shredded cheddar cheese

Fry ground beef, onions and green pepper together over medium heat until meat is brown. Remove from heat and drain off fat. Add hominy and tomato sauce. Simmer until mixture is heated through. Turn off heat. Add olives and cheese. Cover and let stand until cheese melts, about 10-15 minutes.

Mrs. Bruce Harvey (Jana)

HAMBURGER CRUNCH

Serves: 8

1 lb. ground beef
1 small onion, minced
4 Tbsp. soy sauce
1/2 cup rice
1 (10-3/4-oz.) can cream of
    chicken soup
1 (10-3/4-oz.) can cream of
    mushroom soup
2-1/2 cups water
2 cups chow mein noodles
Salt and pepper to taste

Brown beef and onion. Place in a 3 qt. greased casserole with soy sauce, rice, soups, water, salt and pepper. Bake at 350° for 50 minutes. Sprinkle top with chow mein noodles the last 10 minutes of cooking time. Remove from oven and let stand 10 minutes before serving.

Mary Beth Wilson

COWBOY'S DELIGHT

Serves: 4-6

2 Tbsp. oil
1 lb. ground beef (lean)
1/2 cup celery, chopped
1/2 cup onion, chopped
1 (16-oz.) can red kidney beans
1 (16-oz.) can tomatoes
2 tsp. chili powder
1 tsp. salt
1/2 cup minute rice

Heat oil. Brown beef over medium heat. Add remaining ingredients and simmer for 30 minutes. Serve with hot bread or corn bread.

Mrs. Don Collins (Vivian)

GRILLED LEMON CHICKEN

Serves: 8-10

2 sticks butter
1 (32-oz.) bottle of ReaLemon
*   lemon juice*
2 cup-up fryers or favorite
*   chicken parts*
Garlic salt

Melt butter in large pan. Add entire bottle of lemon juice. Stir and let cool while preparing chicken. Skin and garlic salt each piece of chicken. Add chicken to lemon mixture. Try to cover each piece with juice. Cover and refrigerate overnight. Grill over charcoal. Great for picnics—it beats hamburgers—very easy. Cook 30-45 minutes.

Mrs. David Schram (Stefani)

Space saving tip: combine all ingredients into a large plastic bag for easy marinating.

TURKEY TREASURE
"An after Turkey Special"

Serves: 6-8

4 oz. medium cooked noodles
1 small onion, chopped
1 can cream of chicken soup
1/4 cup milk
1/4 tsp. salt
1-1/2 cups turkey, cooked
*   and diced*
1/4 cup green pepper, chopped
2 Tbsp. butter
1 cup sour cream
1/2 cup sliced olives
1/8 tsp. pepper
1/4 cup almonds, sliced

Combine all ingredients except almonds. Place in a buttered casserole or oblong pan. Sprinkle almonds on top. Bake at 350° for 30 minutes. Chicken, tuna or ham can be substituted for turkey.

Mrs. Jack Messal (Donna Neal)

CHERRY ICE CREAM

4 oz. dark sweet chocolate,
    coarsely chopped
1/2 cup canned pitted black
    cherries, drained
    and chopped
1-1/2 qt. French vanilla ice
    cream, softened
Peter Heering cherry liqueur

Fold chocolate and cherries into ice cream, blending evenly. Refreeze. To serve, scoop ice cream into individual serving dishes and top each with 1/2-1 Tbsp. of the cherry liqueur. Delicious dessert for the month of February.

Mrs. Dick Allen (Diana)

PUMPKIN ICE CREAM PIE

1 cup canned pumpkin
1/2 tsp. salt
1/2 cup brown sugar
1/4 tsp. nutmeg
1/2 tsp. cinnamon
1/2 tsp. ginger
1 qt. vanilla ice cream, softened
1-1/2 cups ginger snap crumbs
1/2 cup butter
1/4 cup powdered sugar

Make crust of ginger snap crumbs, butter and powdered sugar. Freeze. Mix pumpkin, ice cream, sugar, and spices with electric mixer. Pour into crust and sprinkle pie with pecans. Freeze.
Note: 1-1/4 tsp. pumpkin pie spice may be used in place of spices.

Mrs. Jerry Shipley

EASY CHOCOLATE PIE

1 small pkg. softened
    cream cheese
1 (3-oz.) pkg. instant
    chocolate pudding
1 cup milk
2/3 cup cold milk
1 baked pie shell or graham
    cracker crust

Cream the cheese, adding 1 cup milk gradually. Add instant pudding and mix. Add 2/3 cup cold milk. Whip until thick. Pour into baked pie shell or graham cracker crust. Let chill. Cover with Cool Whip. It's fast, easy and great.

Mrs. Peter Rooks (Nancy)

FROZEN STRAWBERRY PIE

(or Strawberry-Pecan Parfait)
"J.W.L. Tea Room Favorite"

Serves: 1 9"x 13" pie or 2 8" pies or 16 parfaits

1 (12-oz.) pkg. frozen
  strawberries
1 stick butter (1/2 cup)
2 eggs
1 tsp. vanilla
1-1/2 cups powdered sugar
1 large container Cool Whip
  (12-oz.)
2 cups pecans

Thaw strawberries. Melt butter. Beat together butter, eggs, vanilla and powdered sugar. Add strawberries, Cool Whip and blend. Stir in pecans. Pour mixture over a layer of graham cracker crumbs which have been sprinkled over the bottoms of two 8" pie pans or one 9"x 13" rectangular pan. If making a parfait simply spoon into parfait glasses. Freeze 4-6 hours, overnight is best.

Serving suggestions: For a special parfait, alternate layers of the strawberry-pecan mixture with layers of frozen strawberry sauce (made with partially thawed 12-oz. box frozen strawberries in heavy syrup. This can be done by mashing partially thawed strawberries with a fork and spooning between layers of the strawberry-pecan mixture).

For summer, garnish with fresh strawberries, and mint leaves.

Mrs. Stephen Jones (Sherrel)

NUTTY PIE

3 egg whites
3/4 cup sugar
3/4 cup graham cracker crumbs
1 tsp. baking powder
1 tsp. vanilla
1 cup chopped pecans

Beat egg whites at high speed until stiff, but not dry. Add sugar gradually, Continue beating until stiff. Mix baking powder with graham cracker crumbs. Then fold lightly into meringue. Add vanilla, then nuts. Bake in very well greased pyrex pan at 350° for 25-30 minutes. Let cool. Put whipping cream on top. Keep in refrigerator overnight or until time to serve.

Barbara Surface

NOTES:

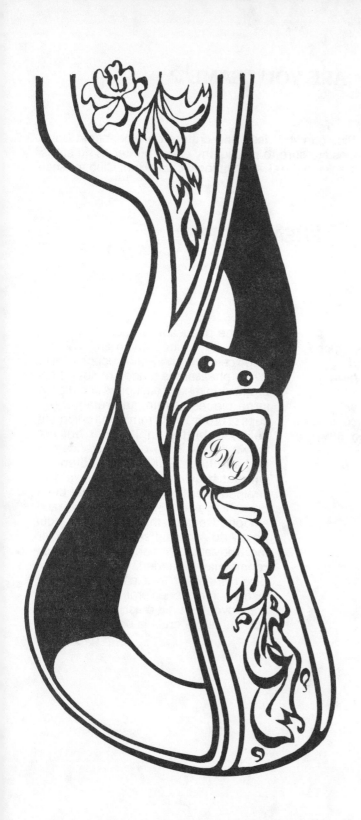

ARE YOU GAME?

SPORTMAN'S PLEASURE

ARE YOU "GAME"?

Many of us get a little "gun-shy" fixin' the critters our sportsmen bring home. These selections are sure to please any eager hunter as he stalks your kitchen. Many thanks to the Grand National Quail Hunt Club for sharing these selections.

PHEASANT PIE

Serves: 4

1 pheasant
2 medium size onion, diced
3 stalks celery, diced
Salt and pepper to taste
5 Tbsp. butter
3 heaping Tbsp. flour
Worcestershire sauce, to taste
Yellow food coloring, few drops
Pie crust
Mushrooms (optional)

Boil one pheasant in enough water to cover, with 1 diced onion and 1/2 cup diced celery, and salt and pepper to taste. When pheasant is tender, remove from broth, strip meat from bones and dice in large pieces. Strain, and retain three cups of broth. Sauté remaining onion and celery in butter until tender but not brown. Melt 4 Tbsp. butter in sauce pan and add flour. Stir until well blended without browning. While hot, add to strained pheasant broth which has been brought to a boil. Stir well until thick and smooth. Remove thickened broth from heat. Add Worcestershire and food coloring. Add sautéed onion and celery. Mushrooms may be added, if desired. Place diced pheasant in a pan or casserole dish, pour thickened broth over pheasant and cover with pie crust. Bake at about 450° until pie crust is brown and done.

Hilly Sailer

ANTELOPE STROGANOFF

Serves: 6-8

2-1/2 lbs. lean antelope meat
Meat tenderizer
Flour
Oil
1 cup celery, chopped
1 cup onion, chopped
1 cup potatoes, chopped
1 cup burgundy wine
1 cup orange juice
1/2 cup water
1 Tbsp. kitchen bouquet
Salt and pepper
1 pt. sour cream

Cut meat into thin strips. Put tenderizer on strips and dust with flour. Brown lightly in small amount of oil. After meat has browned, add rest of ingredients except sour cream. Cover and simmer 3-4 hours, stir occasionally, add more liquid if needed. Thicken with a little flour if necessary. Add sour cream about 2 minutes before removing from heat. Serve with peppered rice.

Shirley Nelson (Mrs. Craig)

BARBECUED BLACK BASS

Black Bass Fillets
Lemon-Pepper Marinade
Barbecue Sauce

Put fillets on cookie sheet or shallow dish side by side. Cover heavily with barbecue sauce on both sides. Sprinkle both sides with lemon-pepper until completely covered. Let fish marinate in refrigerator for 4 hours, occasionally brushing with barbecue sauce. Cook outside over hot coals until flaky. Baste with barbecue sauce while cooking and keep a thin film of lemon-pepper on fish until well cooked.

Cathy Cross (Mrs. Mike)

CHARCOALED DOVE

12 slices bacon
1 dozen breasts of dove
1/2 cup corn oil
3/4 cup lemon juice
1-1/2 tsp. Worcestershire sauce
1-1/2 tsp. salt
1/4 cup water

Clean and dry dove breasts. Combine remaining ingredients to be used as a marinade. Marinate birds at least 2 hours. Using a flat wire basket, arrange breasts which have been wrapped in bacon in a single layer. Close basket securely and arrange on spit over hot briquets to give medium heat. Barbeque 30 to 40 minutes. Baste often during this time.

Jo Ann Nicholas

CHARCOAL BROILED DOVE

6 bacon strips
5 beef bouillon cubes
4 cups water
12 breasts of dove
Optional: For a hickory smoked
flavor, add 2 Tbsp. Wright's
Liquid Smoke to water

Add beef bouillon cubes to water in sauce pan and bring to boil. Add liquid smoke (if desired) and dove breasts. Reduce heat to low and simmer for 20 minutes.
Remove and wrap each breast with one-half strip of bacon. Use toothpicks to hold bacon in place. Now place on charcoal grill to finish cooking. (Be sure to have a water bottle on hand to put out excessive flame up due to bacon drippings.)

Charles Grayson

To keep birds and fish fresh, prepare and clean. Place in milk cartons filled with water and freeze. This helps prevent freezer burn and is an aid to the traveler.

ROAST PHEASANT WITH BRANDY AND CREAM

Serves: 6

3 pheasants
1/2 cup brandy
2 cups heavy cream
8 shallots, thinly sliced
    (I use green onions)
1/4 cup butter
2 cups chicken bouillon
6 slices bacon
1/4 cup horseradish (not sauce)
1 tsp. salt
Freshly ground black pepper

Sauté shallots in butter in roasting pan for 5 minutes. Add pheasants and sauté until brown on all sides. Pour some brandy into a ladle and remaining over pheasants. Warm ladle over a match, light the brandy and flame pheasants. When flames die, add bouillon, salt and pepper. Place bacon over pheasants' breasts and roast uncovered in 375° oven for 45 minutes, basting frequently. Stir cream and horseradish into pan juices and continue roasting for 15 minutes, basting frequently. This can be used with quail or cornish hens. Serve with juices over wild rice.

Mrs. Don Stehr (Janet)

PHEASANT WITH MADEIRA

Serves: 6

6 pheasant breasts, skinned
Salt and paprika
Heavy cream
Flour
1/2 cup butter
1 cup Madeira wine
1/2 cup heavy cream
1/2 cup green grapes
1 can whole artichoke hearts

Sprinkle pheasant with salt and paprika. Dip in cream. Dust in flour and sauté lightly in 2 Tbsp. butter. Add the wine and cover with foil. Bake 1 hour and 15 minutes at 325° or until tender. Remove breasts from baking dish and set aside. Add 1/2 cup cream to the sauce remaining in baking dish, reheat. Stir in 1/2 cup green grapes, split and seeded, and artichoke hearts. Pour over breasts and serve with wild rice.

Mary Miller

BROILED PHEASANT

2 pheasants
1/4 lb. butter
2/3 bottle Heinz 57 Sauce
1/2 pint heavy cream
1 Tbsp. liquid smoke
Salt

Cut birds into quarters and age in refrigerator for 48 hours. Line broiler pan with foil. Melt butter in saucepan, add steak sauce slowly and blend thoroughly. Then add cream and liquid smoke. Lower heat. Puncture birds with a knife to allow basting sauce to penetrate. Lay pieces in pan and salt generously. Place under broiler flame and as meat begins to dry, baste with sauce every 5 minutes for 45 minutes, turning birds occasionally.

Judy Chambers

PHEASANT WITH WILD RICE

1 pheasant
1 can chicken broth
1 pt. light cream
1/2 cup wild rice
1 oz. sherry
1/2 onion, chopped
3 strips bacon
Salt and pepper
Vegetable oil
Flour

Season bird with salt and pepper, coat with flour. Fry in hot oil until golden brown, drain on paper towels. In another pot, make a thin sauce of broth and cream. Place bird in pot, cover with sauce and simmer on low heat. When almost done, add sherry. While bird is cooking, steam rice until tender and fluffy. Place in colander to drain and cool. Sauté onion and bacon in skillet and add to rice. Add rice mixture to pheasant pot and season with salt and pepper.

Diana Allen

QUAIL AND DRIED BEEF

4 Quail
1 or 2 pkgs. dried chipped beef
1 can cream of chicken soup
1 cup sour cream

Place beef in bottom of casserole, forming a bed for quail. Place quail on top of beef. Mix chicken soup and sour cream and pour over quail. Bake 1 hour at 350?
May be used for dove or chicken breasts.

Florelee Day (Mrs. John)

QUAIL IN MUSHROOMS

6 quail, whole or split in half
1/2 cup milk
1/4 cup flour
Salt and pepper
1/2 cup butter
1/2 lb. (1 cup) fresh mushrooms,
   sliced
2 cups sour cream

Dip quail in milk and dredge with flour seasoned with the salt and pepper. Melt butter in heavy skillet. Brown quail in hot butter and remove to casserole. Sauté mushrooms in the hot butter and spoon over quail. Cover quail and mushrooms with sour cream. Bake in 325° oven about 45 minutes, or until quail is tender. May also be used for dove and chicken.

Florelee Day (Mrs. John)

ROAST QUAIL

Quail
Butter
Salt
Freshly ground pepper
Tarragon leaf
Bacon slices

Place a pat of butter inside the cavity of each prepared quail, along with some salt, pepper and a leaf of tarragon. Wrap one slice of bacon around the outside of each bird after spreading butter over the skin. Arrange the quail on a rack in a roasting pan. Sprinkle with salt and pepper. Roast at 450° for 25 minutes, basting once during that time. Serve over wild rice.

Judy Chambers

STUFFED QUAIL

Serves: 4

8 quail
1 onion, diced
4 Tbsp. butter, melted
4 cups bread crumbs, toasted
1 can Cream of Mushroom Soup
2 eggs, beaten
Salt and pepper to taste
8 strips bacon

Sauté onion in butter, add bread crumbs, soup, eggs, salt and pepper. Stuff each quail with this mixture and wrap each bird with a strip of bacon. Secure with a toothpick. Bake with a small amount of water at 350° for 1 hour, 30 minutes.

Diana Allen

RAISIN-APPLE STUFFING FOR WILD GOOSE

2 cups unpeeled apples,
    chopped
2 cups rice, cooked almost
    tender
1 cup raisins
2 tsp. salt
1 tsp. sage
1/2 cup onion, chopped
2 cups bread cubes
1/3 cup butter
1/2 tsp. black pepper
1/3 cup hot water

Mix thoroughly, and stuff goose, allowing room for stuffing to expand. This will make enough stuffing for a 10 lb. bird.

Peggy Slack (Mrs. Kenneth)

ROAST MALLARD

Mallard
Dried bread
Water
Salt
1/2 tsp. ground sage
1 heaping tsp. butter
1 can mushroom chunks,
    with juice
Poultry seasoning

For each bird—crumble 1 quart of dried bread for dressing. Dice gizzards and hearts into quarter-inch cubes and place in sauce pan with 1/4 pt. water. Season with salt and sage. Add butter and boil 10 minutes. Pour over crumbled bread and add mushroom chunks and juice. Grease birds inside and out with butter. Season inside and out with salt or poultry seasoning, and lay birds on large sheet of aluminum foil. Spoon in dressing, but do not pack tightly. Wrap in the aluminum foil, rolling edges tightly but not puncturing foil. Place birds in shallow pan and put into oven which has been preheated to 400°. After 10 minutes (when birds begin to sizzle), reduce heat to 350°. Do not unwrap to brown, for this will dry the bird.

Hilly Sailer
Oklahoma City

RATTLESNAKE APPETIZERS

Skin rattlesnake and fillet all white meat. (Save the rattlers; they make excellent souvenirs.) Cut in small bite sized pieces. Roll in batter like chicken or fish. Salt, pepper and season with your favorite seasoning. Deep fat fry until golden brown.

Milton Garber

"DEEREST" CHILI

1 lb. ground venison
1 lb. ground beef
1 onion, chopped
1 (1-oz.) pkg. Williams Chili Seasoning
1 small pkg. pinto beans (cooked)
1 (46-oz.) can tomato juice

Brown venison, beef and onion in medium sized pot. Salt to taste. Drain. Add chili seasoning and tomato juice and simmer for 10 minutes. Then add beans and the liquid they cooked in, and simmer on very low heat for at least 2 hours, the longer the better.

Jackie Batchelder

VENISON OR ELK FILLETS

Serves: 8

8 (1" thick) Venison or Elk fillets
1/2 cup butter, softened
2 tomatoes, sliced
2 Tbsp. onion, grated
1 Tbsp. parsley, minced
1 cup mushrooms, diced
Salt and fresh ground pepper

Rub fillets with butter. Place in shallow pan under a hot broiler, close to flame for 5 minutes. Remove from oven and turn each fillet. Cap each fillet with 1 tomato slice, 1/4 tsp. grated onion, and a sprinkle of parsley. Salt and pepper to taste. Replace the fillets in the broiler for another 5 minutes. Remove to a hot platter and keep warm. Place the pan over low flame and sauté mushrooms in the drippings. Pour over fillets and serve.

Judy Chambers

VENISON MINCEMEAT

Yield: 6 quarts

1 qt. raisins
1-1/2 qt. meat broth
1/4 lb. ground suet
1 Tbsp. allspice
1 Tbsp. pepper
1 qt. sorghum
5 lbs. apples, chopped
Juice of 3 lemons
4 qt. sugar
2 lbs. currants
2 Tbsp. cinnamon
2 Tbsp. cloves
1 Tbsp. cloves
3 qt. ground venison, cooked
1 qt. cider vinegar

Combine all ingredients. Store in freezer.

Judy Holcomb

SWEET AND SIMPLE JERKY
Great take along for your favorite hunter!

1 lb. flank steak or sirloin

MARINADE:
1/3 cup soy sauce
1/3 cup sherry
1/3 cup sugar
1 Tbsp. "Bar-Coal" or
  liquid smoke

Trim fat from meat. Chill steak in freezer for 20 minutes to allow for ease in slicing very thin. Cut with the grain, if using flank steak. Place meat strips in a plate and sprinkle with marinade. Turn meat strips making sure to coat them well with marinade. The marinade ingredients may be warmed slightly in the microwave to help dissolve sugar. Transfer meat with marinade to a plastic bag and keep in the refrigerator overnight. Cover lower rack of oven with foil to catch drips. Lay steak strips across grids of upper rack and bake at 150° to 200° for 3 to 4 hours until dry and chewy. Store in tightly closed glass container.

Pat Reeves

INDEX

A

Alfredo Sauce............................167
All Protein Crunch Granola...............349
Almond Butter Bars......................277
Almond Milk............................308
Ambidextrous Souffle (Spinach or Broccoli)...195
Angel Food Cake........................215
Angel Wings............................110
"Ann's an Angel" Rolls..................123
Antelope Stroganoff.....................374
APPETIZERS, DIPS & SPREADS
  Bacon & Sausage Quichelets............15
  Baked Chicken Strips..................13
  Beer-Cheese Pinecones................13
  Bite-size Pepperoni Pizzas............14
  Bravo Avocado........................12
  Bronco Busters.......................14
  Calico Pecan Ball.....................16
  Candie's Goodies.....................15
  Cattlemen's Spread...................17
  Caviar...............................12
  Cheese Casserole Dip.................18
  Cheese Fondue........................16
  Cheese Onion Rounds..................18
  Cheesey Chutney Spread...............19
  Cheesies.............................17
  Chili Cheese Rolls....................20
  Chipped Beef Ball.....................23
  Clam Dip.............................18
  Cocktail Meatballs....................19
  Crab Pillows.........................22
  Crab Quiche..........................22
  Creamy Artichoke Bottoms.............21
  Cucumber Tea Sandwiches..............20
  Curried Chicken Appetizers............21
  Curry Connection.....................92
  Curry Dip............................24
  Dandy Dilly Dip.......................24
  Diana's Clam Dip.....................23
  French Fried Brussels Sprouts with
    Vermouth Dip.......................291
  Garlic Toast Rounds..................303
  Gazpacho............................25
  Green Onion Sandwiches..............25
  Ham Round Ups.......................29
  Hot Broccoli Dip.....................26
  Hot Clam Cheese Dip..................28
  Hot Crab Cocktail....................28
  Hot Crab Dip.........................27
  Hot Walnut 'n' Beef Dip..............26
  Hummas Bi Tahini.....................27
  Jeannine Bower's Hot Artichoke Spread....29
  Kir..................................296
  La Puerta Taco Dip...................29
  Mount of Olives Surprise.............289
  Mucho Grande Layers.................31
  Mushrooms Supreme..................31
  Party Pizzas.........................30
  Pickled Mushrooms...................30
  Plum Pleasures.......................32
  Potachos.............................32
  Rancho de Chimayo...................34
  Raspberry Soup.......................33
  Rattlesnake Appetizers...............381
  Roman Artichoke Hearts...............289
  Roney Egg Rolls......................34
  Ruth Bondurant's Salsa...............33
  Sausage Stuffed Mushrooms...........33
  Sausage Swirls.......................36
  Seasoned Pecans.....................36
  Sesame Chicken w/Honey Dip..........37
  Show Stopper Sandwiches.............35
  Shrimp Remoulade..............91, 292
  Shrimp Spread........................37
  Shrimply "Devine"....................38
  Smoked Ham Balls....................40
  Smoked Oyster Dip....................41
  Sombrero Spread.....................284
  Soy Chestnuts........................37
  "Square Dancers".....................39
  Stuffed Mushrooms w/Bacon...........36
  Sunny's Fabulous Cheese Dip..........35
  Super Spinach Dip....................39
  Supreme Salmon Spread...............40
  Swedish Nuts.........................38
  Sweet-Sour Smokies..................35
  Too Easy Tamale Dip..................38
  Walnut Cheese Spread................41
  Wild West Hot Dip....................41
  Zucchini Appetizers..................42
APPLES
  Apple Betty..........................235
  Apple Butter.........................318
  Apple Cake..........................208
  Apple Crisp..........................283
  Apple Dapple Cake....................209
  Apple Dumplings......................235
  Apple Raisin Stuffing.................380
  Apple Sauce with Orange..............299
  "Better w/Bourbon" Mince-Apple Crisp....236
  Diabetic Applesauce Cookies..........313
  No Gain Apple Spice Cake.............318
  Raw Apple Cake.......................209
  Santa Apples.........................329
  Sour Cream Apple Pie.................227
APRICOTS
  Apricot Bread........................96
  Apricot Fizzie.......................308
  California Gold Bars..................255
  Dried Apricot Candy..................267
  Pine Cot Marmalade...................319
ARTICHOKES
  Baked Artichoke Hearts...............179
  Creamy Artichoke Bottoms.............21
  Hot Artichoke Spread.................29
  Roman Artichoke Hearts...............289
ASPARAGUS
  Asparagus Casserole.................178
  Asparagus Parmesan..................358
  Asparagus Soup w/Tarragon...........297
  Cream of Asparagus Soup.............52
  Fiesta Soup.........................285
  Mushroom and Asparagus Soup.........363
  Shrimp and Asparagus Round-up.......171
  Vinaigrette Sauce for Asparagus......279
Aunt Bill's Brown Candy...............268
Aunt Eunice's Pickled Beets...........322
AVOCADO
  Avocado Cream Soup..................53
  Avocado Jello Salad..................72
  Avocado and Shrimp Fiesta...........285
  Avocado-Spinach Salad...............72
  Bravo Avocado.......................12
  Rancho De Chimayo...................34
  Shrimp with Avocados................90

B

BACON
  Bacon Cheese Potatoes...............194
  Bacon Flavored Green Beans..........76
  Bacon & Sausage Quichelets..........15
  Cauliflower Bacon....................74
  Potato Bacon Chowder................61
  Stuffed Mushrooms in Bacon..........36
Baked Artichoke Hearts...............179
Baked Beans...................179, 181

Baked Chicken Strips........................ 13
Baked Chicken, Sweet 'N Sour.............136
Baked Fudge................................236
Baked Green Tomatoes.....................309
Baked Salmon Croquettes.................168
Baked Salmon Omelet......................170
Baked Spinach Casserole..................196
Baked Squash Supreme....................198
BANANAS
  Banana Fruit Punch...................... 42
  Banana Oatmeal Muffins................106
  Blueberry Banana Bonanza............. 66
  Fruity Banana Drink.....................335
  Kona Inn Banana Bread................. 97
  Linda Wilson's Banana Dressing........ 92
BARBECUE
  Bar B Q Brisket.........................139
  Barbecue Sauce.........................155
  Barbecued Black Bass..................375
  Charcoal Broiled Dove..................376
  Charcoaled Dove........................376
  Charcoaled Fish.........................311
  Charcoaled Shrimp......................168
  Grilled Lemon Chicken..................369
  Outdoor Smoked Brisket................139
  Susie's Bar-B-Que Sauce...............155
Barcelona Drunken Sponge with
  Brandy Sauce...........................288
Batter for Chicken/Fish...................132
BEANS
  Bacon Flavored Green Beans........... 76
  Black Bean Soup........................ 53
  Grandmother Thole's Green Bean Soup.... 58
  J-Bar Bean Bake........................181
  Marinated Green Beans................. 75
  Mother's Bean Soup..................... 60
  Oklahoma Baked Beans.................179
  Tiffany's Bean Pot Soup................. 63
BEEF
  Bar B Q Brisket.........................139
  Beef Jerky..............................346
  Beef and Snow Peas....................144
  Cattlemen's Spread..................... 17
  Chipped Beef Ball....................... 23
  Deviled Steak...........................151
  Extraordinary Beef Dish................152
  German Beef Birds......................157
  Hot Walnut 'N Beef Dip................. 26
  Jerry's Veal Parmesan..................147
  Marinated Brisket.......................140
  Outdoor Smoked Brisket................139
  Rah Rah Roast..........................153
  Ruth's Brisket...........................140
  Sherried Beef...........................150
  Steak Soup............................. 63
  Shish-Ka-Bob Marinade.................152
  Smothered Steak........................156
  Stuffed Round Steak....................156
  Sukiyaki................................157
BEEF, GROUND
  Brown Derby Spaghetti Sauce..........305
  Cabbage Rolls..........................141
  Cheese Please Meat Loaf...............148
  Chili Con Carne......................... 56
  Chili Queen's Chili...................... 54
  Cocktail Meatballs...................... 19
  Cowboy's Delight.......................368
  Curried Beef and Rice Dinner..........151
  Dinner in a Skillet......................368
  Easy Lasagna..........................365
  Easy Meat Loaf Topper.................149
  Great Mid-West Especiale..............158
  Hamburger Crunch......................368
  Italian Cheese-It Casserole............142
  Italian Spaghetti Sauce................143

Kathryn Masteryanni's Spaghetti Sauce.....145
Lasagna..................................146
Meatballs Rosé..........................147
Meat Loaf Supreme......................148
Mexican Casserole......................154
No-Noodle Lasagna......................315
Party Enchiladas........................149
Pop Over Pizza..........................144
Rice Dressing (Hashwah)................145
Stuffed Squash (Kousa).................146
Swedish Meat Balls.....................153
Sweet & Simple Jerky...................382
Taco Casserole.........................154
Wild Rice Baron........................150
Beef Jerky...............................346
Beer Batter..............................132
Beer Bread..............................120
Beer & Cheese Pinecones............... 13
Beer Cheese Soup....................... 54
BEETS
  Pickled Beets..........................322
  Summertime Beets......................180
  Sweet 'n' Sour Beets...................180
Believe It or Not Cake...................210
"Berry Best" Muffins.....................103
"Best in the West" Waffles or
  Pancakes.............................108
Better Cheddar Potatoes.................361
"Better w/Bourbon" Mince-Apple Crisp......236
Betty's Buttermilk Cake..................212
BEVERAGES
  Almond Milk...........................308
  Apricot Fizzie.........................308
  Banana Fruit Punch.................... 42
  Bloody Mary...........................274
  Bourbon Slush......................... 43
  Bundle Tea Spiced Tea................. 43
  Champagne Punch...................... 44
  Coffee Frappe......................... 44
  Cranberry Tea......................... 45
  Creme De Menthe...................... 44
  Fruity Banana Drink...................335
  Golden Wassail........................ 45
  Hot Buttered Rum...................... 46
  Hot Buttered Rum 'n' Cream........... 46
  Hot Cinnamon Cider................... 46
  Indian Tea............................ 47
  Kahlua................................ 47
  Kir...................................296
  Kool-Ade Punch.......................335
  Legacy Wine Punch.................... 48
  Mint Julep............................ 48
  Oklahoma Joy Juice................... 47
  Open House Punch..................... 48
  Orange Julius.........................335
  Prairie Firewater...................... 49
  Prairie Pep-up........................314
  Punchy Sangria....................... 49
  Rainbow Ade..........................334
  Rainbow Ice...........................334
  Spiced Apple Cider.................... 49
  Ticklish Tea..........................336
  Vodka Orange Slush................... 49
  Weddin' Party Punch w/Sherbet........ 50
  Wedding Punch........................ 50
Biscuits.............102, 110, 133, 281, 286
Bite-size Pepperoni Pizzas............... 14
Black Bean Soup........................ 53
Blintzes................................107
Bloody Mary............................274
BLUEBERRY
  Blueberry Banana Bonanza............. 66
  Blueberry Delight......................237
  Blueberry Salad....................... 66
Blue Ribbon Bread......................110

Blythe Spirit. 241
Bon Bons. 266
Bourbon Slush. 43
Braised Chicken in Soy Sauce. 126
Brandied Chocolate Crust. 229
Bran Refrigerator Rolls. 113
Bravo Avocado. 12
Bread & Butter Pickles. 324
BREADS, QUICK
　　Apricot Bread. 96
　　Biscuits
　　　　Angel Wings. 110
　　　　Biscuits. 281
　　　　Chicken Fried Biscuits. 133
　　　　Cuban Water Bread. 286
　　　　Grandmother's Angel Biscuits. 102
　　　　Sour Cream Biscuits. 102
　　Cheese Onion Rounds. 18
　　Cheesies. 17
　　Crispy Herb Bread Sticks. 359
　　Czech Caraway Seed Loaf. 97
　　Garlic Toast Rounds. 303
　　In a Hurry Cheese Bread. 359
　　Kona Inn Banana Bread. 97
　　Lemon Nut Bread. 99
　　Mexicali Cornbread. 98
　　Muffins
　　　　Banana Oatmeal Muffins. 106
　　　　Berry Best Muffins. 103
　　　　Chocolate Chip Orange Muffins. 104
　　　　Chocolate Muffins. 103
　　　　Ice Cream Muffins. 333
　　　　Muffins By the Pail Full. 104
　　　　Pure Bran Muffins. 105
　　　　Refrigerator Gingerbread Muffins. 105
　　　　Sausage Swirls. 36
　　　　Sociologist's Sugarless Soda Bread. . . . 316
　　PANCAKES, SYRUPS & BUTTERS
　　　　Best in the West Pancakes or Waffles. . . . 108
　　　　Blintzes. 107
　　　　Dutch Baby. 108
　　　　Eggy Pancakes. 347
　　　　French Orange Sauce. 109
　　　　German Pancakes. 106
　　　　Grandmother's Brown Sugar Syrup. 109
　　　　Janie's Buttermilk Pancakes. 107
　　　　Orange Honey Butter. 109
　　　　Pecan Butter. 109
　　　　Popovers. 98, 304
　　　　Pumpkin Bread. 99
　　　　Pumpkin Date Bread. 100
　　　　Strawberry Bread. 100
　　　　Whole Wheat Bread. 101
　　　　Zucchini Bread. 101
BREADS, YEAST
　　Angel Wings. 110
　　"Ann's An Angel" Rolls. 123
　　Beer Bread. 120
　　Blue Ribbon Bread. 110
　　Bran Refrigerator Rolls. 113
　　County Fair Egg Bread. 112
　　Cream Cheese Sweet Rolls. 111
　　Creole Doughnuts. 113
　　Crispy Herb Bread Sticks. 359
　　Cuban Water Bread. 286
　　Easy Butterscotch Pull-Aparts. 121
　　English Muffin Bread. 117
　　English Muffins. 279
　　Grandmother's White Bread. 114
　　Hannah's Rolls. 119
　　Herb Parmesan Bread. 120
　　Hobo Bread. 111
　　Honeyed Whole Wheat Bread. 112
　　In a Hurry Cheese Bread. 359
　　Judge's Favorite Coffee Cake. 118

Manna Bread. 122
Mother Templeman's Butter Horn Rolls. 119
Mother Wiles Rolls. 114
No Fail French Bread. 116
No-Knead Oatmeal Bread. 117
Pita Bread. 115
Randall's Roll-Ups. 123
Ruth's Raised Cinnamon Rolls. 121
Simple Cinnamon Pecan Bread. 122
Whole Wheat Egg Bread. 124
Braised Chicken in Soy Sauce. 126
Bran Refrigerator Rolls. 113
Brisket, Bar B Q. 139
Brisket, Marinated. 140
Brisket, Smoked. 139
BROCCOLI
　　Ambidextrous Souffle. 195
　　Cauliflower Broccoli Salad. 359
　　Chicken Divan. 135
　　Curried Broccoli Soup. 57
　　Everyone's Favorite Broccoli & Rice. 181
　　Ham & Broccoli Roll-Ups. 158
　　Hot Broccoli Dip. 26
　　Marinated Broccoli. 73
　　Tuna Broccoli Casserole. 314
Broiled Pheasant. 378
Bronco Busters. 14
Brown Derby Spaghetti Sauce. 305
Brown Sugar Glaze. 164
Brown Sugar Syrup. 109
Brussels Sprouts and Cashews. 182
Brussels Sprouts, Fried. 291
Bundle Tea Spiced Tea. 43
BUTTER
　　Orange & Honey Butter. 109
　　Pecan Butter. 109
Butterfinger Ice Cream. 242
Buttermilk Pancakes. 107
Buttermilk Pie. 223
Buttermilk Sherbet. 310
Butterscotch Pull-Aparts. 121
Buttery Caramel Corn. 345

C

CABBAGE
　　Cabbage Rolls. 141
　　Cabbage Soup. 58
　　Cherokee Strip Cole Slaw. 282
　　Company Sauerkraut. 206
　　Make Ahead Cole Slaw. 73
　　Rode Kool (Red Cabbage). 182
CAKES
　　Angel Food Cake. 215
　　Apple Cake. 208
　　Apple Dapple Cake. 209
　　Believe It or Not Cake. 210
　　Betty's Buttermilk Cake. 212
　　Carrot Cake. 210
　　Coconut Sour Cream Cake. 220
　　"Come on Over" Cake. 354
　　Date Cake. 211
　　Dear Abby's Own Chocolate Cake. 217
　　Fruity Coffee Cake. 361
　　Hershey Bar Cake. 215
　　Italian Cream Cake. 220
　　Just Everybody's Favorite Chocolate
　　　　Sheet Cake. 216
　　Kathy's Carrot Cake. 211
　　Lemon Roll. 239
　　Linda Wilson's Chocolate Roll
　　　　& Chocolate Sauce. 238
　　No Gain Apple Spice Cake. 313
　　Oatmeal Cake. 218
　　"Oklahoma Crude" Cake. 216
　　Picnic Cake. 219

Plum Pudding. 234
Poppyseed Cake. 218
Pumpkin Cake Roll. 219
Quick Chocolate Cake for Chocoholics. 353
Raw Apple Cake. .209
Rum Cake. 222
Spice Cake. 221
Strawberry Shortcake. 221
Sweet Lemon Yogurt Cake. 290
Calico Pecan Ball. 16
Calico Salad. 74
California Gold Bars. 255
Candie's Goody. 15
CANDY & CONFECTIONS
  Caramel Candy. .265
  Caramel Corn. 265
  Chocolate Covered Fondant. 264
  Chocolate Fondue. 232
  Cranberry Surprise. 265
  Cream Candy. 267
  Creamy Bon Bons. 266
  Date Loaf Candy. 266
  Dried Apricot Candy. 267
  Dutch Oven Delight. 267
  Energy Candy. 328
  Firesticks. 331
  Grammy Lucy's Million Dollar Fudge. 271
  Haystacks. 353
  Jinx's Peanut Butter Fudge. 269
  Microwave Peanut Brittle. 270
  Oklahoma Brown Candy (Aunt Bill's). 268
  Opera Roll. 269
  Peanut Brittle. 270
  Peanut Clusters. .354
  Pecan Chews. 272
  Pecan Patties. 357
  Reese Cup Candy. 272
  Suzy Belle's Pralines. 271
  Toffee. 271
CARAMEL
  Caramel Candy. .265
  Caramel Corn. 265
  Caramel German Chocolate
    Brownies. 264
  Caramel Ice Cream Pie. 248
  Caramel Oranges. 240
Carroonies. 311
CARROTS
  Carroonies. 311
  Carrots Au Gratin. 183
  Carrot Cake. 210
  Carrot Cookies. .251
  City Slicker Carrots. 81
  Kathy's Carrot Cake. 211
Cashew Chicken. .127
CASSEROLES
  Asparagus Casserole. 178
  Baked Salmon Omelet. 170
  Baked Spinach Casserole. 196
  Cheese Casserole Dip. 18
  Chicken Breasts Party-Style. 366
  Chicken Jerusalem. 290
  Christmas Casserole. 204
  Company for Breakfast. 173
  Corn Casserole. .184
  Crunchy Brunch Egg Casserole. 172
  Easy Cheesey Potatoes. 361
  Easy Green Bean Casserole. 360
  Easy Lasagna. 365
  Everyone's Favorite Broccoli & Rice. 181
  Garden Vegetable Bake. 204
  Golden Cauliflower Casserole. 183
  Inland Paella. 287
  Italian Cheese-It Casserole. 142
  Italian Chops Casserole. 165

Italian Sauced Fish. 310
Many Vegetable Casserole. 201
Mexican Casserole. 154
Mexican Cheese Casserole. 175
No Noodle Lasagna. 315
Panhandle Casserole. 175
Party Casserole. .365
Quick Chili Rellenos. 358
Sausage & Rice Casserole. 167
Spinach Casserole. 196
Taco Casserole. 154
Three Vegetable Casserole. 205
Tuna Broccoli Casserole. 314
Turkey Treasure. .369
Vegetable & Water Chestnut Casserole. 203
Cattlemen's Spread. 17
Cat-wich. 339
CAULIFLOWER
  Cauliflower-Bacon. 74
  Cauliflower Broccoli Salad. 359
  Golden Cauliflower Casserole. 183
Caviar. 12
Celery Canoes. 344
Celery w/Buttered Bread Crumbs. 184
Cenci. 251
Champagne Punch. 44
Charcoaled (See Barbeque)
CHEESE
  Beer-Cheese Pinecones. 13
  Beer Cheese Soup. 54
  Better Cheddar Potatoes. 361
  Calico Pecan Ball. 16
  Cheese Casserole Dip. 18
  Cheese Onion Rounds. 18
  Cheese Please Meat Loaf. 148
  Cheese Please Squash. 197
  Cheese Sauce. 306
  Cheese Sausage Soufflé Roll. 159
  Cheese Soup. 55
  Cheesey Chutney Spread. 19
  Cheesies. 17
  Chili Cheese Rolls. 20
  Chipped Beef Ball. 23
  Corn & Cheese Chowder. 55
  Easy Cheesey Potatoes. 361
  Ham & Cheese Soufflé. 161
  Hite's Delight. 191
  Hot Clam Cheese Dip. 28
  In a Hurry Cheese Bread. 359
  Italian Cheese-It Casserole. 142
  Mexican Cheese Casserole. 175
  Quick Chili Rellenos. 358
  Spinach Cheese Soup. 62
  Sunny's Fabulous Cheese Dip. 35
  Vegie Cheese Sauce. 205
  Walnut Cheese Spread. 41
  Wild West Hot Dip. 41
CHEESECAKE
  Grandmother's Cheesecake. 213
  Heavenly Cheesecake. 212
  No-Bake Cherry Cheesecake. 312
  Petite Cheese Cakes. 259
  Tuxedo Cheese Cake. 214
Cherokee Strip Cole Slaw. 282
CHERRIES
  Cherries Jubilee. .296
  Cherry Ice Cream. 370
  Cherry Pie Filling Salad. 362
  Grandma's Cherry Pudding. 231
  No-Bake Cherry Cheesecake. 312
CHICKEN
  Baked Chicken Strips. 13
  Braised Chicken in Soy Sauce. 126
  Cashew Chicken. 127
  Chicken Alberghetti. 127

Chicken Breasts in Lemon Cream. 128
Chicken Breasts Party-Style. 366
Chicken Cacciatore. 129
Chicken Divan. 135
Chicken Elizabeth. 128
Chicken Jerusalem. 290
Chicken Kapama (Greek). 130
Chicken-Mushroom Soup. 57
Chicken Parmesan. 130
Chicken Rochambeau. 294
Chicken Salad. 85
Chicken Salad Mold. 85
Chicken Tetrazzini. 131
Chinese Chicken. 129
Cranberry Stuffed Cornish Hens. 132
Curried Chicken Appetizers. 21
Curried Chicken w/Saffron Rice. 131
Easy Chicken Crepes. 367
Fried Chicken. 133
Gingered Peach Nuggets. 137
Gourmet Chicken in Mushrooms. 134
Grilled Lemon Chicken. 369
Herb Roasted Chicken Breasts. 309
Imperial Chicken. 134
Inland Paella. 287
Keeler's Favorite Beer Batter
    for Chicken or Fish. 132
Miss Bonnie's Fried Chicken w/Her Original
    Chicken Fried Biscuits. 133
Paradise Chicken Salad. 88
Parisian Chicken Dinner. 135
Parmesan Chicken w/Pasta. 137
Ranch House "Chickenchilada". 136
Sesame Chicken w/Honey Dip. 37
Sweet 'n' Sour Baked Chicken. 136
Children's House Playdough. 327
CHILI
Chili Cheese Rolls. 20
Chili Con Carne. 56
Chili Queen's Chili. 54
Chili Sauce. 320
Deerest Chili. 381
Quick Chili Rellenos. 358
CHINESE (See Oriental)
Chinese Chicken. 129
Chinese Stew. 56
Chipped Beef Ball. 23
CHOCOLATE
Baked Fudge. 236
Believe It or Not Cake. 210
Brandied Chocolate Crust. 229
Caramel German Chocolate Brownies. 264
Chocolate Angel Food Dessert. 354
Chocolate Chip Orange Muffins. 104
Chocolate Chip Tortoni. 244
Chocolate Cookies. 250
Chocolate Covered Fondant. 264
Chocolate Fondue. 232
Chocolate Mint Ice Cream. 242
Chocolate Muffins. 103
Chocolate Oatmeal Pie. 224
Chocolate Pecan Pie. 223
Chocolate Sauce. 238
Chocolate Sauce for Ice Cream. 243
Creamy Bon Bons. 266
Dear Abby's Own Chocolate Cake. 217
Easy Chocolate Pie. 370
Fractional Fudge Cookies. 330
German Cream Cheese Brownies. 259
Grammy Lucy's Million Dollar Fudge. 271
Hershey Bar Cake. 215
Just Everybody's Favorite Chocolate
    Sheet Cake. 216
Kahlua Mousse. 239
Linda Wilson's Chocolate Roll & Sauce. 238

M-M-M-Mousse Au Easy. 356
"Oklahoma Crude" Cake. 216
Orange Chocolate Mousse. 233
Peanut Butter Bars. 332
Peanut Butter Cookies w/Chocolate Kisses. . 253
Peanut Clusters. 354
Pecan Clusters. 258
Pecan Patties. 357
Quick Chocolate Cake for Chocoholics. 353
Reese Cup Candy. 272
Soft Nestle Cookies. 263
Summer Chocolate Pie. 223
Surprise Cupcakes. 336
Tuxedo Cheese Cake. 214
CHOWDER (See Soups)
CHRISTMAS
Christmas Bars. 260
Christmas Casserole. 204
Christmas Salad. 67
Dutch Santa Claus Cookies. 255
Golden Wassail. 45
Rudolph Sandwiches. 342
Santa Apples. 329
CIDER
Cider Cinnamon Sauce. 162
Cider Jelly Glazed Ham. 162
Hot Cinnamon Cider. 46
Spiced Apple Cider. 49
CINNAMON
Cinnamon Fruit. 352
Cinnamon Pecan Bread. 122
Cinnamon Rolls. 121
Hot Cinnamon Cider. 46
City Slicker Carrots. 81
CLAM
Clam Dip. 18
Diana's Clam Dip. 23
Hot Clam Cheese Dip. 28
White Clam Sauce. 306
COBBLERS
Crunchy Peach Cobbler. 355
Peach Cobbler. 241
Simple Peach Cobbler. 353
Cocktail Meatballs. 19
COCONUT
Carroonies. 311
Coconut Cream Frosting. 212
Coconut Refrigerator Cookies. 263
Coconut Sour Cream Cake. 220
Creative Coconut Crust. 228
Texas Gold Bars. 355
COFFEE
Coffee Frappe. 44
Coffee Sundae Pie. 246
COFFEECAKE
Fruity Coffeecake. 361
Judge's Favorite Coffeecake. 118
Cold Pickles. 324
COLE SLAW (See Salads, Cabbage)
"Come on Over" Cake. 354
Company for Breakfast. 173
Company Sauerkraut. 206
COOKIES, BARS
Almond Butter Bars. 277
California Gold Bars. 255
Caramel German Chocolate Brownies. 264
Christmas Bars. 260
Fruit Bars. 261
German Cream Cheese Brownies. 259
Granola Bars. 348
Lemon Squares. 262
Oatmeal Carmeletas. 262
Peanut Butter Bars. 332
Peanut Butter Brownies. 260
Peanutty Break-ups. 261

387

Texas Gold Bars. 355
Vanilla Bars. 355
COOKIES, DROPPED
Carroonies. 311
Carrot Cookies. 251
Cenci. 251
Chocolate Cookies. 250
Cream Cheese Cookies. 254
Diabetic Applesauce Cookies. 313
Fractional Fudge Cookies. 330
Glynden's Best Ever Cookies. 252
Haystacks. 353
Lemon Clouds. 258
Monster Cookies. .330
Muscle-Man Munchies. 331
Okie Bollen. 253
Peanut Butter Cookies. 332
Pecan Clusters. 258
Sandtarts. 257
Soft Nestle Cookies. 263
Sugar Cookies. 256
COOKIES, REFRIGERATOR
Coconut Refrigerator Cookies. 263
Dutch Santa Claus Cookies. 255
Jumpin' Jimminey Jello Cookies. 331
"Slice A Sugar" Cookie. 256
COOKIES, SHAPED
Corn Flake Cookies. 252
Dutch Handkerchiefs. 250
Molasses Cookies. 254
Peanut Butter Cookies w/Chocolate
Kisses. 253
Pecan Cups. 257
Petite Cheese Cakes. 259
Coquille St. Jacques. 169
CORN
Corn Casserole. 184
Corn & Cheese Chowder. 55
Corn Relish. 323
Cornbread Dressing. 138
Crazy Corn. 347
Mexicali Cornbread. 98
Wild West Corn. 185
Cornbread Dressing. 138
Cornflake Cookies. 252
Cornish Hens. 132
County Fair Egg Bread. 112
Country Style Fresh Green Beans. 282
Cowboy's Delight. .368
CRAB
Coquille St. Jacques. 169
Crab Louie. 86
Crab Pillows. 22
Crab Quiche. 22
Crabacado. 86
Crabmeat Sandwich Luncheon. 278-280
Hot Crab Cocktail. 28
Hot Crab Dip. 27
Open Faced Crabmeat Sandwich. 218
Quick Crabmeat Soup. 363
CRANBERRY
Cranberry Freeze. 67
Cranberry Ice. 242
Cranberry Orange Relish. 303
Cranberry Pie. 224
Cranberry Salad. 68
Cranberry-Stuffed Cornish Hens. 132
Cranberry Surprise. 265
Cranberry Tea. 45
Mellow Cranberry Salad. 70
Crazy Corn. 347
Cream Candy. 267
Cream Cheese Brownies. 259
Cream Cheese Cookies. 254
Cream Cheese-Pecan Icing. 222

Cream Cheese Sweet Rolls. 111
Cream of Asparagus Soup. 52
Cream Sauce. 299
Cream of Zucchini Soup. 301
Creamy Artichoke Bottoms. 21
Creamy Bon Bons. 266
Creamy Mushroom Salad. 76
Creamy Strawberry Pie in Coconut Crust. 228
Creamy Turnips w/Dill Weed. 202
Creative Coconut Crust. 228
Creme De Menthe. 44
Creole Dinner. 292-296
Creole Doughnuts. 113
Creole Gumbo. 293
CREPES
Crepe Twists. 87
Easy Chicken Crepes. 367
Quick Blender Crepes. 366
Crispy Herb Bread Sticks. 359
Crowd Pleasin' Green Beans. 185
Crunch Topping for Pies. 228
Crunchy Brunch Egg Casserole. 172
Crunchy Fried Fish. 168
Crunchy Peach Cobbler. 355
Cuban Water Bread. 286
CUCUMBERS
Bread & Butter Pickles. 324
Cold Pickles. 324
Cucumber Dressing. 312
Cucumber Tea Sandwiches. 20
Cucumbers in Sour Cream. 75
Curious George Sandwich. 339
CURRIED DISHES
Curried Beef Pita. .341
Curried Beef & Rice Dinner. 151
Curried Broccoli Soup. 57
Curried Chicken Appetizers. 21
Curried Chicken w/Saffron Rice. 131
Curry Connection. 92
Curry Dip. 24
Czech Caraway Seed Loaf. 97

D
Dandy Dilly Dip. 24
DATES
Date Cake. 211
Date Loaf Candy. .266
Date Pudding. 231
Pumpkin Date Bread. 100
Dear Abby's Own Chocolate Cake. 217
Deep-Fried Strawberries w/
Vanilla Sauce. 280
Deerest Chili. 381
DESSERTS: (See also CAKES, CANDY,
COBBLERS, COOKIES, ICE CREAM, ICES,
FROZEN DESSERTS, PIES, PUDDINGS,
SOUFFLES, MOUSSE. Pages 207-248.)
Apple Betty. 235
Apple Crisp. 283
Apple Dumplings. .235
Applesauce with Orange. 299
Baked Fudge. 236
Barcelona Drunken Sponge w/Brandy
Sauce. 288
Blueberry Banana Bonanza. 66
Blueberry Delight. .237
Caramel Oranges. .240
Cherries Jubilee. 296
Chocolate Angel Food Dessert. 354
Chocolate Fondue. 232
Cinnamon Fruit. 352
Frozen Fruit Salad. 70
Frozen Strawberry Squares. 247
Heath Ice Cream Pie. 362
Lemon Roll. 239

Mince Apple Crisp. 236
Minted Pears. 357
Pear Tart. 300
Pot de Creme. 234
Pumpkin Squares. 240
Raspberries 'n' Cream. 237
Strawberry Shortcake. 241
Deviled Steak. 151
Diabetic Applesauce Cookies. 313
Diana's Clam Dip. 23
Different Tuna Salad. 364
Dilly Potato Sauce. 192
Dinner in a Skillet. 368
DIPS (See Appetizers)
Doughnuts. 113
DRESSINGS (See Salad Dressings)
Cornbread Dressing. 138
Rice Dressing. 145
Dried Apricot Candy. 267
Dried Beef & Quail. 378
DUTCH
Dutch Baby. 108
Dutch Handkerchiefs. 250
Dutch Oven Delight. 267
Dutch Santa Claus Cookies. 255
Okie Bollen. 253

E

Easter Dinner. 289-291
EASY (See PONY EXPRESS-OHS Pages 351-372)
"Ann's An Angel" Rolls. 123
Asparagus Parmesan. 358
Cheese Onion Rounds. 259
Easy Butterscotch Pull-Aparts. 121
Easy Cheesey Potatoes. 361
Easy Chicken Crepes. 367
Easy Chocolate Pie. 370
Easy Fresh Vegetable Salad. 363
Easy Green Bean Casserole. 360
Easy Lasagna. 365
Easy Meat Loaf Topper. 149
Easy Pigs in Blankets. 170
Easy Pineapple Cream Pie. 356
Fruit Salad. 69
Italian Sauced Fish. 310
M-M-M-Mousse Au Easy. 356
Quick Chili Rellenos. 358
Quick Crabmeat Soup. 363
Simple Peach Cobbler. 353
Strawberry Ice Cream. 309
Too Easy Tamale Dip. 38
Egg Batter. 291
EGGS
Baked Salmon Omelet. 170
Company for Breakfast. 173
Crunchy Brunch Egg Casserole. 172
Egg Bread. 112
Eggy Pancakes. 347
Individual Egglets. 176
Panhandle Eggs. 175
Quiche Aux Champignons. 174
Roney Egg Rolls. 34
Stuffed Eggs Mornay. 276
Vegetable Quiche. 173
Western Souffle. 176
Eggplant Parmesan. 200
Elk or Venison Fillets. 381
Enchiladas. 149
Energy Candy. 328
English Muffin Bread. 117
English Muffins. 279
Escalloped Tomatoes. 201
Everyone's Favorite Broccoli & Rice. 181
Extraordinary Beef Dish. 152

F

Famous Fast Salad. 364
Fancy Foreign Peas. 194
Fancy Grits. 188
Fancy Pecan Pie. 226
Favorite Fried Potato Patties. 360
Fiesta Dinner. 284-288
Fiesta Soup. 285
Filet of Quail Breast Fried. 281
Firesticks. 331
FISH
Baked Salmon Croquettes. 168
Baked Salmon Omelet. 170
Barbecued Black Bass. 375
Charcoaled Fish. 311
Charcoaled Shrimp. 168
Clam Dip. 18
Coquille St. Jacques. 169
Crabacado. 86
Creole Gumbo. 293
Crunchy Fried Fish. 169
Diana's Clam Dip. 23
Hot Clam Cheese Dip. 28
Italian Sauced Fish. 310
Keeler's Favorite Beer Batter for Fish
or Chicken. 132
Salmon Souffle Pie. 170
Shrimp Florentine. 171
Shrimp & Asparagus Round Up. 171
Shrimp Victoria. 172
Smoked Oyster Dip. 41
Supreme Salmon Dip. 40
Whole Salmon Baked in Foil. 302
Flying Saucer Sicle Saver. 326
FONDUE
Cheese Fondue. 16
Chocolate Fondue. 232
Fractional Fudge Cookies. 330
French Dinner. 296-300
FRENCH
Cherries Jubilee. 296
Chicken Rochambeau. 294
Coquille St. Jacques. 169
Easy Chicken Crepes. 367
French Fried Brussels Sprouts. 291
French Onion Soup. 59
French Orange Sauce. 109
French Style Green Peas. 295
No-Fail French Bread. 116
Parisian Chicken Dinner. 135
Royal French Dressing. 94
Quiche Aux Champignons. 174
French Fried Brussels Sprouts
w/Vermouth Dip. 291
Fried Green Tomatoes. 203
Frilly Milly Salad. 338
FROSTINGS, GLAZES & ICINGS
(Pages 209-212 and 216-222)
FROZEN DESSERTS (Pages 241-248)
(See also ICE CREAM & ICES)
Caramel Ice Cream Pie. 370
Cherry Ice Cream. 370
Chocolate Chip Tortoni. 244
Coffee Sundae Pie. 246
Cranberry Freeze. 67
Frozen Dessert. 243
Frozen Fruit Salad. 70
Frozen Lemon Pudding. 245
Frozen Peanut Butter Pie. 247
Frozen Strawberry Pie. 371
Frozen Strawberry Squares. 247
Fruit Bars. 261
Heath Ice Cream Pie. 362
Pumpkin Ice Cream Pie. 370
Raspberry Freeze. 248

Strawberry Ice. 309
Strawberry Sorbet. 277
Tumbleweed Pie. .246
FRUITS (See VARIETIES)
Fruit Bars. 261
Fruit Compote. 275
FRUIT SALADS (See SALADS, FRUIT)
Fruit Salad. 69
Fruity Banana Drink. 335
Fruity Coffeecake. 361
FUDGE
Baked Fudge. 236
Grammy Lucy's Million Dollar Fudge. 271
Jinx's Peanut Butter Fudge. 269
Funny Bunny Salad. 337
Funny Face Franks. 345

G

GAME (Pages 373-382)
Antelope Stroganoff. 375
Barbequed Black Bass. 375
Broiled Pheasant. 378
Charcoal Broiled Dove. 376
Charcoal Dove. 376
Cranberry-Stuffed Cornish Hens. 132
"Deerest" Chili. 381
Pheasant Pie. 374
Pheasant with Madeira. 377
Pheasant with Wild Rice. 378
Quail & Dried Beef. 378
Quail in Mushrooms. 379
Raisin-Apple Stuffing for Wild Goose. 380
Rattlesnake Appetizers. 381
Roast Mallard. 380
Roast Pheasant w/Brandy & Cream. 377
Roast Quail. 379
Stuffed Quail. 379
Sweet & Simple Jerky. 382
Venison Mincemeat. 382
Venison or Elk Fillet. 381
Garden Vegetable Bake. 204
Garlic Toast Rounds. 303
Gazpacho. 25
GERMAN
Caramel German Chocolate Brownies. 264
German Beef Birds. 157
German Cream Cheese Brownies. 259
German Pancakes. 106
German Potato Salad. 79
Ghosty Toasty. 340
Gingerbread Muffins. 105
Gingered Peach Nuggets. 137
GLAZE (See Frostings)
Glaze, Brown Sugar. 164
Glynden's Best Ever Cookies. 252
Golden Cauliflower Casserole. 183
Golden Wassail. 45
Gourmet Chicken with Mushrooms. 134
Grammy Lucy's Million Dollar Fudge. 271
Grandma Bules' Pear Butter. 321
Grandma's Cherry Pudding. 231
Grandma Rikli's Strawberry Preserves. 320
Grandma's Sweet & Sauerkraut. 182
Grandmother's Angel Biscuits. 102
Grandmother's Brown Sugar Syrup. 109
Grandmother's Cheesecake. 213
Grandmother Thole's Green Bean Soup. 58
Grandmother's White Bread. 114
Granite of Cabernet. 244
GRANOLA
All Protein Crunch Granola. 349
Granola. 348
Granola Bars. 348
Great Mid-West Especiale. 158

GREEN BEANS
Bacon Flavored Green Beans. 76
Country Style Fresh Green Beans. 282
Crowd Pleasin' Green Beans. 295
Easy Green Bean Casserole. 360
Grandmother Thole's Green Bean Soup. . . . 58
Marinated Green Beans. 75
Sauteed Green Beans. 186
Scalloped Green Beans. 186
Sweet 'n' Sour Green Beans. 187
GREEK
Cabbage Rolls. .141
Chicken Kapama. 130
Green Onion Sandwiches. 25
Grilled Lemon Chicken. 369
Grits. 187,188
Gumbo, Creole. .293

H

HAM
Cider Jelly Glazed Ham. 162
Ham & Broccoli Roll-ups. 158
Ham & Cheese Souffle. 161
Ham Empanadas. 275
Ham Mustard Sauce. 165
Ham 'n' Potato Salad. 87
Ham & Potato Scallop. 160
Ham Salad Mold. 88
Our Easter Parade Ham Loaf. 161
Party Ham. 160
Smoked Ham Balls. 40
Sweet-Sour Mustard Sauce. 165
Topping for Ham Loaf or Ham. 162
HAMBURGER (See BEEF, GROUND)
Hamburger Crunch. 366
Hannah's Rolls. .119
Harvest Potatoes. 193
Haystacks. 353
Hearts of Palm Salad. 294
Heath Ice Cream Pie. 362
Heavenly Cheesecake. 212
Herb Parmesan Bread. 120
Herb Roasted Chicken Breasts. 309
Hershey Bar Cake. 215
Hite's Delight (Cheese Potato Sticks). 191
Hobo Bread. 111
Holiday Peas. 195
HONEY
Honey Dip. 37
Honeyed Whole Wheat Bread. 112
Orange Honey Butter. 109
Sesame Chicken w/Honey Dip. 37
HORS D'OEUVRES (See APPETIZERS)
Horseradish Sauce. 163
Hot Bacon Dressing. 93
Hot Broccoli Dip. 93
Hot Buttered Rum. 46
Hot Buttered Rum 'n' Cream. 46
Hot Cinnamon Cider. 46
Hot Clam Cheese Dip. 28
Hot Crab Cocktail. 28
Hot Crab Dip. 27
Hot Fruit Compote. 275
Hot Walnut 'n' Beef Dip. 26
Hummas Bi Tahini. 27

I

ICE CREAM (See ICES AND SHERBETS,
FROZEN DESSERTS)
Blythe Spirit. 241
Butterfinger Ice Cream. 242
Cherry Ice Cream. 370
Chocolate Mint Ice Cream. 242
Ice Cream. 283

Oklahoma Ice Cream. 245
  Strawberry Ice Cream. 309
Ice Cream Muffins. 333
ICES AND SHERBETS
  Buttermilk Sherbet. 310
  Cranberry Ice. 242
  Granite of Cabernet. 244
  Lemon Sherbet. 243
  Raspberry Freeze. 248
  Strawberry Ice. 315
ICINGS (See Frostings)
Imperial Chicken. 134
In A Hurry Cheese Bread. 359
Indian Pudding. 304
Indian Tea. 47
Individual Egglets. 176
Inland Paella. 287
Italian Dinner. 305-306
ITALIAN
  Alfredo Sauce. 167
  Brown Derby Spaghetti Sauce. 305
  Cenci. 251
  Chicken Alberghetti. 127
  Italian Cheese-It Casserole. 142
  Italian Chops Casserole. 165
  Italian Cream Cake. 220
  Italian Sauced Fish. 310
  Italian Spaghetti Sauce. 143
  Italian Style Peas. 195
  Italian Zucchini. 196
  Jerry's Veal Parmesan. 147
  Kathryn Masteryanni's Spaghetti Sauce. . . 145
  Lasagna. 146, 315, 365
  No Noodle Lasagna. 315
  Pop Over Pizza. 144
  White Clam Sauce. 306

J

J-Bar Bean Bake. 181
JAMS, JELLIES, PRESERVES (Pages 318-321)
  Apple Butter. 318
  Grandma Bules' Pear Butter. 321
  Grandma Rikli's Strawberry Preserves. . . . 320
  Oklahoma Sand Plum Jelly. 321
  Peach Jam. 319
  Pickled Peaches. 320
  Pine-Cot Marmalade. 319
  Watermelon Preserves. 320
Jane Lee's Vegetable Marinade. 80
Janie's Buttermilk Pancakes. 107
Jeannette's Creamy Cottage Potatoes. 190
Jeannine Bower's Hot Artichoke Spread. 29
JERKY
  Beef Jerky. 346
  Sweet & Simple Jerky. 382
Jerry's Veal Parmesan. 147
Jinx's Peanut Butter Fudge. 269
John's Onion Soup. 59
Judge's Favorite Coffee Cake. 118
Jumpin' Jimminey Jello Cookies. 331
Just Everybody's Favorite Chocolate
  Sheet Cake. 216

K

Kahlua. 47
Kahlua Mousse. 239
Kathryn Masteryanni's Spaghetti Sauce. 145
Kathy's Carrot Cake. 211
Keeler's Favorite Beer Batter for Fish
  or Chicken. 132
KIDS' STUFF (Pages 325-349)
  All Protein Crunch Granola. 349
  Beef Jerky. 346
  Buttery Caramel Corn. 345
  Cat-wich. 339
  Celery Canoes. 344
  Children's House Playdough. 327
  Crazy Corn. 347
  Curious George Sandwich. 339
  Easy Pigs in Blankets. 340
  Eggy Pancakes. 347
  Energy Candy. 328
  Firesticks. 331
  Flying Saucer Sicle Saver. 326
  Fractional Fudge Cookies. 330
  Frilly Milly Salad. 338
  Fruity Banana Drink. 335
  Funny Bunny Salad. 337
  Funny Face Franks. 345
  Ghosty Toasty. 340
  Granola. 348
  Granola Bars. 348
  Ice Cream Muffins. 333
  Jumpin' Jimminey Jello Cookies. 331
  Kool-Ade Punch. 335
  Love in the Lunch Box. 327
  Monster Cookies. 330
  Muscle-Man Munchies. 331
  Orange Julius. 335
  Peanut Butter Bars. 332
  Peanut Butter Cookies. 332
  Pocketwich. 341
  Pronto Pizza Man. 341
  Puzzle Cookies For Children. 333
  Rainbow Ade. 334
  Rainbow Ice. 334
  Roly Poly Roundups. 342
  Rudolph Sandwiches. 342
  Santa Apples. 329
  Superman Steak. 343
  Surprise Cupcakes. 336
  Sweetheart Sandwiches. 334
  Ticklish Tea. 336
  Trail Mix. 346
  Yummy Popcorn. 349
Kir. 296
Kitty's Mayonnaise. 93
Kona Inn Banana Bread. 97
Kool-Ade Punch. 335

L

La Puerta Taco Dip. 29
LAMB
  Italian Chops Casserole. 165
  Rice Dressing (Hashwah). 145
Lasagna. 146, 315, 365
Layered Potato Salad. 80
Layered Spinach Salad. 83
LEFT-OVERS
  Chicken Tetrazzini. 131
  Fried Potato Patties. 360
  Turkey Treasure. 369
Legacy Wine Punch. 48
LEMON
  Frozen Lemon Pudding. 245
  Lemon Chess Pie. 225
  Lemon Clouds. 258
  Lemon Glaze. 222
  Lemon-Marinated Vegetables. 78
  Lemon Nut Bread. 99
  Lemon Roll. 239
  Lemon Sherbet. 243
  Lemon Squares. 262
  Sweet Lemon Yogurt Cake. 290
Lime Pickles. 324
Linda Wilson's Banana Dressing. 92
Linda Wilson's Chocolate Roll &
  Chocolate Sauce. 238
LOW CALORIE
  Almond Milk. 308

Apricot Fizzie. 308
Baked Green Tomatoes. 309
Beef & Snow Peas. 144
Buttermilk Sherbet. 310
Carroonies. 311
Charcoaled Fish. .311
Cucumber Dressing. 312
Diabetic Applesauce Cookies. 313
Herb Roasted Chicken Breasts. 309
Italian Sauced Fish. 310
No-Bake Cherry Cheesecake. 312
No Gain Apple Spice Cake. 313
No-Noodle Lasagna. 315
Prairie Pep Up. 314
Sociologist's Sugarless Soda Bread. 316
Strawberry Ice. . . . . 309 & 315
Sweet & Simple Jerky. 382
Tuna Broccoli Casserole. 314
Love in the Lunch Box. 327

M

Macaroni-Salmon Salad. 89
Mallard, Roasted. .380
MAIN DISH (See CHICKEN, BEEF, PORK,
CASSEROLES, MAIN DISH SALADS, SOUPS
& STEWS. Pages 125-176)
Make Ahead Cole Slaw. 73
Mama Sessions Vegetable Stew. 73
Manna Bread. 122
Many Vegetable Casserole. 201
MARINADES
Charcoaled Fish. 311
Marinated Brisket. 140
Marinated Broccoli. 73
Marinated Garden Salad. 77
Marinated Green Beans. 75
Marinated Mushrooms. 188
Marinated Salad. 77
Marinated Vegetable Salad. 84
Shish-Ka-Bob Marinade. 152
Marty's Special Dressing. 93
Mashed Potatoes Parmesan. 192
MEATS (See Specific Category)
Meat Loaf Supreme. 148
MEATBALLS
Cocktail Meatballs. 19
Meatball Rosé. 147
Meatballs, Swedish. 153
Mellow Cranberry Salad. 70
MENUS, GOURMET
Creole Dinner. .292
Fiesta Dinner. .284
New England Dinner. 301
Night in Milan. 305
Pioneer Oklahoma Dinner. 281
Spring Luncheon. 274
Mexicali Corn Bread. 98
MEXICAN
Fiesta Dinner. 284-288
Great Mid-West Especiale. 158
Ham Empanadas. 275
Inland Paella. .287
La Puerta Taco Dip. 29
Mexicali Corn Bread. 98
Mexican Casserole. 154
Mexican Cheese Casserole. 175
Mucho Grande Layers. 31
Party Enchiladas. 149
Quick Chili Rellenos. 358
Ranch House "Chickenchilada". 136
Rancho de Chimayo. 34
Rice w/Sour Cream & Chilies. 206
Ruth Bondurant's Salsa. 33
Sombrero Spread. 284
Taco Casserole. 154

Too Easy Tamale Dip. 38
Zucchini Mexican Style. 288
Microwave Peanut Brittle. 270
Millionaire Pie. 225
Mint Julep. 48
Minted Pears. 357
Miss Bonnie's Fried Chicken w/Her
Original Chicken Fried Biscuits. 133
Molasses Cookies. 254
Monster Cookies. .330
Mother's Bean Soup. 60
Mother Templeman's Butter Horn Rolls. 119
Mother Wiles Rolls. 114
Mount of Olives Surprise. 289
MOUSSE
Kahlua Mousse. 239
M-M-M-Mousse Au Easy. 356
Orange Chocolate Mousse. 233
Shrimp Mousse. 91
Mucho Grande Layers. 31
MUFFINS (See also BREAD)
Banana Oatmeal Muffins. 106
Berry Best Muffins. 103
Chocolate Chip Orange Muffins. 104
Chocolate Muffins. 103
Ice Cream Muffins. 333
Muffins by the Pail Full. 104
Pure Bran Muffins. 105
Refrigerator Ginger Bread Muffins. 105
Muscle-Man Munchies. 331
MUSHROOMS
Chicken-Mushroom Soup. 57
Creamy Mushroom Salad. 76
Gourmet Chicken in Mushrooms. 134
Marinated Mushrooms. 188
Mushroom & Asparagus Soup. 363
Mushrooms 'n' Cream. 189
Mushrooms and Quail. 379
Mushrooms Supreme. 31
Pickled Mushrooms. 30
Sausage Stuffed Mushrooms. 33
Scalloped Mushrooms. 190
Stuffed Mushrooms in Bacon. 36
Swiss Mushrooms. 76
Quiche Aux Champignons. 174
Mustard Sauce for Ham. 163
Mustard Sauce, Sweet-Sour. 163

N

Never Fail Pie Crust. 229
New England Dinner. 301-304
No-Bake Cherry Cheesecake. 312
No-Fail French Bread. 116
No Gain Apple Spice Cake. 318
No-Knead Oatmeal Bread. 117
No-Noodle Lasagna. 315
NUTS (See also PECAN, WALNUT, PEANUTS)
Lemon Nut Bread. 99
Nutty Pie. 371
Seasoned Pecans. 36
Swedish Nuts. 37

O

OATMEAL
Banana Oatmeal Muffins. 106
Chocolate Oatmeal Pie. 224
No-Knead Oatmeal Bread. 117
Oatmeal Cake. 218
Oatmeal Carmeletas. 262
Okie Bollen. 253
Okie Okra. 189
OKLAHOMA
Oklahoma Baked Green Beans. 179
Oklahoma Bread Pudding w/Whiskey
Sauce. 232

Oklahoma Brown Candy (Aunt Bill's)........268
"Oklahoma Crude" Cake.................216
Oklahoma Ice Cream..................245
Oklahoma Joy Juice...................47
Oklahoma Sand Plum Jelly............321
OKRA
  Okie Okra...........................189
  Okra Gumbo.........................190
  Pickled Okra.........................322
  Ruby's Dilled Okra...................322
OMELET
  Baked Salmon Omelet................170
ONIONS
  Cheese Onion Rounds................18
  French Onion Soup...................59
  Green Onion Sandwiches.............25
  John's Onion Soup...................59
Open Faced Crab Meat Sandwich..........278
Open House Punch....................48
Opera Roll...........................269
ORANGE
  Caramel Oranges....................240
  French Orange Sauce.................109
  Orange Chocolate Mousse............233
  Orange Cranberry Relish..............303
  Orange Glazed Sweet Potatoes........193
  Orange Honey Butter.................109
  Orange Julius.......................335
  Orange & Vegetable Salad............286
ORIENTAL
  Chinese Chicken....................129
  Chinese Stew.......................56
  Roney Egg Rolls....................34
  Sukiyaki............................157
  Soy Chestnuts......................37
  Sweet & Sour Pork..................164
Our Easter Parade Ham Loaf.............161
Outdoor Smoked Brisket................139
Oven Stew..........................62
OYSTER
  Smoked Oyster Dip..................41

P

PANCAKES (See BREADS)
Paradise Chicken Salad.................88
Parisian Chicken Dinner.................135
Parmesan Bread......................120
Parmesan Chicken....................130
Parmesan Chicken w/Pasta.............137
Party Casserole.......................365
Party Enchiladas......................149
Party Ham...........................160
Party Pizzas.........................30
Pastas..............................306
Paupiettes de Porc à la Tourangelle........298
PEACHES
  "Come On Over" Cake................354
  Crunchy Peach Cobbler..............355
  Gingered Peach Nuggets.............137
  Peach Cobbler......................241
  Peach Jam..........................319
  Peaches 'n' Cream Salad.............68
  Pickled Peaches.....................318
  Simple Peach Cobbler...............353
PEANUT
  Caramel Corn.......................265
  Energy Candy.......................328
  Fractional Fudge Cookies.............330
  Frozen Peanut Butter Pie.............247
  Jinx's Peanut Butter Fudge............269
  Microwave Peanut Brittle.............270
  Peanut Brittle.......................270
  Peanut Butter Bars..................332
  Peanut Butter Brownies..............260
  Peanut Butter Cookies.............253,332

Peanut Butter Cookies w/
  Chocolate Kisses...................253
Peanut Butter Pie......................362
Peanut Clusters.......................354
Peanutty Break-ups....................261
Reese Cup Candy.....................272
PEARS
  Grandma Bules' Pear Butter..........321
  Minted Pears........................357
  Pear Tart...........................300
PEAS
  Fancy Foreign Peas..................194
  French Style Green Peas.............295
  Holiday Peas........................195
  Italian Style Peas...................195
  Prairie Pea Salad....................78
  24 Hour Layered Salad..............84
PECANS
  Calico Pecan Ball...................16
  Chocolate Covered Fondant..........264
  Chocolate Pecan Pie................223
  Fancy Pecan Pie....................226
  Nutty Pie...........................371
  Opera Roll..........................269
  Pecan Butter........................109
  Pecan Chews.......................272
  Pecan Clusters......................258
  Pecan Cream Cheese Icing...........222
  Pecan Cups.........................272
  Pecan Patties.......................357
  Oklahoma Brown Candy (Aunt Bill's)......268
  Seasoned Pecans...................36
  Shirley Bellmon's Pecan Pie..........226
  Simple Cinnamon Pecan Bread.......122
  Suzybelle's Pralines.................271
PEPPERONI
  Bite-Size Pepperoni Pizzas...........14
Petite Cheese Cakes...................259
PHEASANT
  Broiled Pheasant....................378
  Pheasant w/Madeira.................377
  Pheasant Pie.......................374
  Pheasant w/Wild Rice...............378
  Roast Pheasant w/Brandy & Cream.......377
Picalilli.............................323
Pickled Mushrooms...................30
PICKLES & PRESERVING
  Aunt Eunice's Pickled Beets..........322
  Bread & Butter Pickles..............324
  Cold Pickles........................324
  Lime Pickles........................324
  Picalilli............................323
  Pickled Beets.......................322
  Pickled Mushrooms.................30
  Pickled Okra........................322
  Ruby's Dilled Okra..................322
Picnic Cake.........................219
Pico de Gallo........................286
PIES
  Buttermilk Pie......................223
  Caramel Ice Cream Pie..............248
  Cherry Pie Filling...................362
  Chocolate Oatmeal Pie..............224
  Chocolate Pecan Pie................223
  Coffee Sundae Pie..................246
  Cranberry Pie.......................224
  Creamy Strawberry Pie in Coconut Crust....228
  Crunch Topping for Pies.............228
  Easy Chocolate Pie.................370
  Easy Pineapple Cream Pie...........356
  Fancy Pecan Pie....................226
  Frozen Peanut Butter Pie.............247
  Frozen Strawberry Pie...............371
  Heath Ice Cream Pie................362
  Lemon Chess Pie...................225

Millionaire Pie.........................225
Nutty Pie.............................371
Oklahoma Apple Crisp.................283
Peach Cobbler........................241
Peanut Butter Pie....................362
Pheasant Pie.........................374
Pineapple Pie........................226
Pumpkin Ice Cream Pie...............370
Shirley Bellmon's Pecan Pie..........226
Simple Peach Cobbler.................353
Sour Cream Apple Pie.................227
Sour Cream Raisin Pie................227
Strawberry Pie.............227,228,357
Summer Chocolate Pie................223
Tumbleweed Pie......................246
PIE CRUSTS
    Brandied Chocolate Crust...........229
    Creative Coconut Crust.............228
    Crumb Lining.......................357
    Never Fail Pie Crust...............229
    Rich & Buttery Pie Crust...........230
    Tart Crust.........................300
    Very Flaky Pastry..................230
Pine Cot Marmalade....................319
PINEAPPLE
    Easy Pineapple Cream Pie...........356
    Pine-Cot Marmalade.................319
    Pineapple a la Chantilly........... 69
    Pineapple Pie......................226
    Pineapple Yum Yum.................. 70
Pioneer Oklahoma Dinner...........281-283
Pita Bread............................115
PIZZA
    Bite-Size Pepperoni Pizzas......... 14
    Party Pizzas....................... 30
    Pizza P.D.Q........................364
    Pop Over Pizza.....................144
    Pronto Pizza Man...................341
Playdough, Children's House...........327
PLUM
    Oklahoma Sandplum Jelly............321
    Plum Pleasures..................... 32
    Plum Pudding (Modern Style)........234
Pocketwich............................341
Pop Corn..........................347,349
Pop Over Pizza........................144
Popovers..........................98,304
Poppyseed Cake........................218
Poppyseed Dressing.................... 92
PORK (See also HAM, SAUSAGE)
    Cheese Sausage Souffle Roll........159
    Cider Jelly Glazed Ham.............162
    Ham & Broccoli Roll-ups............158
    Ham & Cheese Souffle...............161
    Ham 'n Potato Salad................ 87
    Ham & Potato Scallop...............160
    Italian Chops Casserole............165
    Meat Loaf Supreme..................148
    Our Easter Parade Ham Loaf.........161
    Party Ham..........................160
    Paupiettes de Porc à la Tourangelle.......298
    Pork Tenderloin....................165
    Sausage & Rice Casserole...........167
    Stuffed Pork Chops.................166
    Sweet & Sour Pork..................164
Pots De Creme.........................234
POTATO
    Bacon Cheese Potatoes..............194
    Better Cheddar Potatoes............361
    Dilly Potato Sauce.................192
    Favorite Fried Potato Patties......360
    German Potato Salad................ 79
    Ham 'n Potato Salad................ 87
    Ham & Potato Scallop...............160
    Harvest Potatoes...................193

Hite's Delight (Cheese Potato Sticks)......191
Jeannette's Creamy Cottage Potatoes......190
Layered Potato Salad................ 80
Mashed Potatoes Parmesan...........192
Orange Glazed Sweet Potatoes.......193
Potachos........................... 32
Potato Bacon Chowder............... 61
Potato Soup........................ 61
Shrimp Potato Salad................ 89
Sliced Potato Salad................ 79
Swedish Potatoes...................191
Potachos........................... 32
POULTRY (See Specific Variety)
Prairie Firewater.................... 49
Prairie Pea Salad................... 78
Prairie Pep Up......................314
Pralines............................271
PRESERVES (See also JELLIES & JAMS)
    Grandma Rikli's Strawberry Preserves.....320
    Pine Cot Marmalade.................319
    Peach Jam..........................319
    Watermelon Preserves...............320
Pronto Pizza Man......................341
PUDDINGS
    Date Pudding.......................231
    Frozen Lemon Pudding...............245
    Grandma's Cherry Pudding...........231
    Indian Pudding.....................304
    Oklahoma Bread Pudding w/Whiskey
        Sauce..........................232
    Plum Pudding.......................234
    Sinful Pudding.....................233
PUMPKIN
    Pumpkin Bread...................... 99
    Pumpkin Cake Roll..................219
    Pumpkin Date Bread.................100
    Pumpkin Ice Cream Pie..............370
    Pumpkin Squares....................240
PUNCH (See BEVERAGES)
Punchy Sangria....................... 49
Pure Bran Muffins....................105
Puzzle Cookies for Children..........333

Q
QUAIL
    Filet of Quail Breast Fried........281
    Quail & Dried Beef.................378
    Quail & Mushrooms..................379
    Roast Quail........................379
    Stuffed Quail......................379
QUICHE
    Bacon and Sausage Quichelets....... 15
    Crab Quiche........................ 22
    Quiche Aux Champignons.............174
    "Square Dancers"................... 39
    Vegetable Quiche...................173
Quick Blender Crepes..................366
Quick Breads......................96-109
Quick Chili Rellenos..................358
Quick Chocolate Cake for Chocoholics.......353
Quick Crabmeat Soup..................363
Quick Ice Cream Muffins..............333

R
Rah Rah Roast........................153
Rainbow Ade..........................334
Rainbow Ice..........................334
RAISINS
    Raisin-Apple Stuffing for Wild Goose.....380
    Sour Cream Raisin Pie..............227
Ranch House "Chickenchilada".........136
Rancho de Chimayo.................... 34
Randall's Roll-ups...................123

RASPBERRY
Raspberry Freeze...................248
Raspberry Soup.................... 33
Raspberries 'n Cream...............237
Ratatouille........................199
Rattlesnake Appetizer..............381
Raw Apple Cake....................209
Reese Cup Candy...................272
Refrigerator Gingerbread Muffins....105
Refrigerator Rolls..................113
RELISH
Corn Relish.......................323
Cranberry Orange Relish............303
Picalilli..........................323
RICE
Curried Beef & Rice Dinner..........151
Curried Chicken w/Saffron Rice......131
Everyone's Favorite Broccoli & Rice....181
Rice Dressing (Hashwah)............145
Rice w/Sour Cream & Chilies.........206
Sausage & Rice Casserole...........167
Wild Rice Baron...................150
Rich & Buttery Pie Crust............230
Roast Mallard.....................380
Roast Pheasant w/Brandy & Cream....377
Roast Quail.......................379
Rode Kool (Red Cabbage)...........182
Roly Poly Round-Ups...............342
ROLLS (See BREADS)
Roman Artichoke Hearts............289
Roney Egg Rolls................... 34
Royal French Dressing.............. 94
Ruby's Dilled Okra.................322
Rudolph Sandwiches...............342
RUM
Hot Buttered Rum................. 46
Hot Buttered Rum 'N Cream......... 46
Rum Cake........................222
Ruth Bondurant's Salsa............. 33
Ruth's Brisket.....................140
Ruth's Raised Cinnamon Rolls.......121

S
Salad Delight...................... 71
SALAD DRESSINGS
Creamy Chili Salad Dressing.........286
Cucumber Dressing.................312
Curry Connection.................. 92
Hot Bacon Dressing................ 93
Kitty's Mayonnaise................. 93
Linda Wilson's Banana Dressing...... 92
Marty's Special Dressing............ 93
Poppy Seed Dressing............... 92
Royal French Dressing.............. 94
Vinaigrette Dressing...........299, 303
SALADS, FRUIT
Blueberry Salad................... 66
Blueberry Banana Bonanza.......... 66
Cherry Pie Filling Salad.............362
Christmas Salad................... 67
Cranberry Freeze.................. 67
Cranberry Salad................... 68
Easy Fruit Salad................... 70
Frilly Milly Salad..................338
Frozen Fruit Salad................. 70
Fruit Salad....................... 69
Funny Bunny Salad................337
Hot Fruit Compote.................275
Mellow Cranberry Salad............. 70
Orange & Vegetable Salad...........286
Peaches 'n' Cream Salad............ 68
Pineapple a la Chantilly............. 69
Pineapple Yum Yum................ 70
Salad Delight..................... 71
Seven-Up Salad................... 71

SALAD, MAIN DISH
Chicken Salad.................... 85
Chicken Salad Mold............... 85
Crab Louie....................... 86
Crabacado....................... 86
Different Tuna Salad...............364
Ham 'n' Potato Salad.............. 87
Ham Salad Mold.................. 88
Macaroni-Salmon Salad............ 89
Paradise Chicken Salad............ 88
Sherrel's Favorite Tuna Salad........ 90
Shrimp Mousse................... 91
Shrimp Potato Salad............... 89
Shrimp Rémoulade..............91, 292
Shrimp with Avocados............. 90
SALAD, VEGETABLE
Avocado Jello Salad............... 72
Avocado & Shrimp Fiesta...........285
Avocado-Spinach Salad............ 72
Bacon Flavored Green Beans........ 76
Calico Salad..................... 74
Cauliflower-Bacon Salad........... 74
Cherokee Strip Cole Slaw...........282
City Slicker Carrots................ 81
Creamy Mushroom Salad........... 76
Cucumbers in Sour Cream.......... 75
Easy Fresh Vegetable Salad.........363
Famous Fast Salad................364
German Potato Salad............... 79
Hearts of Palm Salad..............294
Jane Lee's Vegetable Marinade...... 80
Layered Potato Salad.............. 80
Layered Spinach Salad............. 83
Lemon-Marinated Vegetables....... 78
Make Ahead Cole Slaw............. 73
Marinated Broccoli................ 73
Marinated Garden Salad........... 77
Marinated Green Beans............ 75
Marinated Salad.................. 77
Marinated Vegetable Salad......... 84
Orange & Vegetable Salad..........286
Pico de Gallo....................286
Prairie Pea Salad................. 78
Rancho de Chimayo............... 34
Roman Artichoke Hearts............289
Serendipity Salad................. 83
Sliced Potato Salad............... 79
Spaghetti Salad.................. 82
Spinach Gelatin.................. 82
Swiss Mushrooms................. 76
24 Hour Layered Salad............. 84
Wheatheart Tabouli Salad.......... 81
SALMON
Baked Salmon Croquettes..........168
Baked Salmon Omelets.............170
Macaroni-Salmon Salad............ 89
Salmon Souffle Pie................170
Supreme Salmon Spread........... 40
Whole Salmon Baked in Foil.........302
SALSA
Ruth Bondurant's Salsa............. 33
Sandtarts.......................257
Sandwich Luncheon............278-280
SANDWICHES
Cat-wich........................339
Cucumber Tea Sandwiches......... 20
Curious George Sandwich..........339
Funny Face Franks................345
Green Onion Sandwiches.......... 25
Open-Faced Crabmeat Sandwich....278
Pocket-wich.....................341
Roly Poly Round-Ups..............342
Rudolph Sandwiches..............342
Show-Stopper Sandwiches......... 35
Sweetheart Sandwiches............344

Santa Apples............................329
SAUCES, DESSERTS
  Brandy Sauce........................288
  Chocolate Fondue....................232
  Chocolate Sauce.....................238
  Chocolate Sauce for Ice Cream.......243
  French Orange Sauce.................109
  Orange Honey Butter.................109
  Pecan Butter........................109
  Rum-Butterscotch Sauce..............248
  Whiskey Sauce w/Oklahoma Bread
    Pudding...........................232
SAUCES, OTHER
  Alfredo Sauce.......................167
  Barbeque Sauce......................155
  Bearnaise Sauce.....................295
  Bechamel Sauce......................367
  Brown Derby Sauce...................305
  Brown Sugar Glaze...................164
  Cheese Sauce........................306
  Chili Sauce, Homegrown..............320
  Cider Cinnamon Sauce................162
  Cream Sauce....................202, 299
  Croquette Sauce.....................168
  Dilly Potato Sauce..................192
  Easy Meat Loaf Topper...............149
  Ham Mustard Sauce...................165
  Hollandaise Sauce...................295
  Homegrown Chili Sauce...............320
  Horseradish Sauce...................163
  Remoulade Sauce.....................292
  Rochambeau, Brown Sauce.............295
  Sour Cream Gravy....................166
  Spaghetti Sauce.....................396
  Suellen's Wonderful Cheese Sauce....306
  Susie's Bar-B-Que Sauce.............165
  Sweet-Sour Mustard Sauce............165
  The Curry Connection................ 92
  Topping for Ham Loaf or Ham.........162
  Vegie Cheese Sauce..................205
  Vermouth Dip........................291
  Vinaigrette Sauce......279, 285, 294, 299
  White Clam Sauce....................306
  White Wine Sauce....................302
  Wild West Hot Dip................... 41
SAUERKRAUT
  Company Sauerkraut..................206
  Grandma's Sweet and Sauerkraut......182
SAUSAGE
  Bacon & Sausage Quichelets.......... 15
  Cheese Sausage Souffle Roll.........159
  Easy Pigs in Blankets...............340
  Panhandle Eggs......................175
  Party Pizzas........................ 30
  Pizza P.D.Q.........................364
  Sausage & Rice Casserole............167
  Sausage Stuffed Mushrooms........... 33
  Sausage Swirls...................... 36
  Sweet-Sour Smokies.................. 35
  Wild West Hot Dip................... 41
Sauteed Green Beans w/Butter & Cheese.....186
Scalloped Green Beans...................186
Scalloped Mushrooms.....................190
SCALLOPS
  Coquille St. Jacques................169
SEAFOOD (See Specific Variety)
Seasoned Pecans......................... 36
Serendipity Salad....................... 83
SHERBETS (See ICES & SHERBETS)
Sherrel's Favorite Tuna Salad.......... 90
Sherried Beef..........................150
Shirley Bellmon's Pecan Pie............226
Shish-Ka-Bob Marinade..................152
SHRIMP
  Avocado & Shrimp Fiesta.............285

Charcoaled Shrimp......................168
Coquille St. Jacques...................169
Shrimp & Asparagus Round-Up............171
Shrimp Florentine......................171
Shrimp Mousse.......................... 91
Shrimp Potato Salad.................... 89
Shrimp Remoulade.......................292
Shrimp Remoulade (New Orleans Style)... 91
Shrimp Spread.......................... 37
Shrimp with Avocados................... 90
Shrimp Victoria........................172
Shrimply "Devine"...................... 38
Show Stopper Sandwiches................ 35
Simple Cinnamon Pecan Bread............122
Simple Peach Cobbler...................353
Sinful Pudding.........................233
"Slice a Sugar" Cookie.................256
Sliced Potato Salad.................... 79
Smoked Ham Balls....................... 40
Smoked Oyster Dip...................... 41
Smothered Steak........................156
SNACKS (See also APPETIZERS)
  All Protein Crunch Granola..........349
  Beef Jerky (Kids)...................346
  Buttery Caramel Corn................345
  Carroonies..........................311
  Celery Canoes.......................344
  Crazy Corn..........................347
  Energy Candy........................328
  Firesticks..........................331
  Ghosty Toasty.......................340
  Granola.............................348
  Granola Bars........................348
  Pronto Pizza Man....................341
  Sweet & Simple Jerky................382
  Trail Mix...........................346
  Yummy Popcorn.......................349
Sociologist's Sugarless Soda Bread.....316
Soft Nestle Cookies....................263
Sombrero Spread........................284
Sorbet, Strawberry.....................277
SOUFFLES
  Ambidextrous Souffle................195
  Cheese Sausage Souffle Roll.........195
  Ham & Cheese Souffle................161
  Salmon Souffle Pie..................170
  Western Souffle.....................176
SOUPS
  Asparagus Soup......................297
  Avocado Cream Soup.................. 53
  Beer Cheese Soup.................... 54
  Black Bean Soup..................... 53
  Cabbage Soup........................ 58
  Cheese Soup......................... 55
  Chicken Mushroom Soup............... 57
  Chili con Carne..................... 56
  Chili Queen's Chili................. 54
  Chinese Stew........................ 56
  Corn & Cheese Chowder............... 55
  Cream of Asparagus Soup............. 52
  Cream of Zucchini Soup..............301
  Creole Gumbo........................292
  Curried Broccoli Soup............... 57
  Fiesta Soup.........................285
  French Onion Soup................... 59
  Gazpacho............................ 25
  Grandmother Thole's Green Bean Soup.... 58
  John's Onion Soup................... 59
  Mama Sessions Vegetable Stew........ 60
  Mother's Bean Soup.................. 60
  Mushroom and Asparagus Soup.........363
  Plum Pleasures...................... 32
  Potato Bacon Chowder................ 61
  Potato Soup......................... 61
  Puree of Asparagus w/Tarragon.......297

Quick Crabmeat Soup................363
Raspberry Soup.....................33
Spinach Cheese Soup...............62
Steak Soup........................63
Tiffany's Bean Pot Soup............63
Sour Cream Apple Pie..............227
Sour Cream Biscuits................102
Sour Cream Gravy..................166
Sour Cream Raisin Pie..............227
Soy Chestnuts......................37
SPAGHETTI
Brown Derby Spaghetti Sauce...........305
Italian Spaghetti Sauce...................143
Kathryn Masteryanni's Spaghetti Sauce.....145
Spaghetti Salad........................82
Spice Cake.....................221, 313
Spiced Apple Cider.....................49
SPINACH
Ambidextrous Souffle...................195
Avocado Spinach Salad..................72
Baked Spinach Casserole................196
Layered Spinach Salad..................83
Shrimp Florentine......................171
Spinach Casserole......................196
Spinach Cheese Soup...................62
Spinach Gelatin........................82
Super Spinach Dip.....................39
Tomatoes Rockefeller..................202
SPREADS (See APPETIZERS)
Spring Luncheon.....................274-277
Square Dancers.......................39
SQUASH
Baked Squash Supreme.................198
Cheese Please Squash..................197
Italian Zucchini........................196
Ratatouille...........................199
Stuffed Squash (Kousa)...........146, 197
Zippy Zucchini........................198
Zucchini Mexican Style.................288
Zucchini Parmesan.....................199
Zucchini Surprise......................200
Steak Soup........................63
STEW (See SOUPS)
STRAWBERRIES
Blythe Spirit..........................241
Creamy Strawberry Pie in Coconut Crust....228
Deep Fried Strawberries w/Vanilla Sauce...280
Frozen Strawberry Pie..................371
Frozen Strawberry Squares..............247
Grandma Rikli's Strawberry Preserves......320
Strawberry Bread......................100
Strawberry Ice........................315
Strawberry Ice Cream..................309
Strawberry Pie..............227, 228, 357
Strawberry Shortcake...................221
Strawberry Sorbet......................277
Stuffed Eggs Mornay...................276
Stuffed Mushrooms with Bacon...........36
Stuffed Pork Chops....................166
Stuffed Quail.........................379
Stuffed Round Steak...................156
Stuffed Squash (Kousa)................146
Stuffed Summer Squash................197
Sugar Cookies........................256
Sukiyaki.............................157
Summer Chocolate Pie.................223
Summertime Beets.....................180
Sunny's Fabulous Cheese Dip...........35
Super Spinach Dip....................39
Superman Steak......................345
Supreme Salmon Spread...............40
Surprise Cupcakes....................336
Susie's Bar-B-Que Sauce...............155
Suzybelle's Pralines...................271
Swedish Meat Balls...................153

Swedish Nuts.........................38
Swedish Potatoes....................191
Sweet Lemon Yogurt Cake.............290
Sweet Potatoes......................193
Sweet & Simple Jerky.................382
Sweet 'n' Sour Baked Chicken..........136
Sweet 'n' Sour Beets.................180
Sweet-Sour Green Beans..............187
Sweet-Sour Mustard Sauce............165
Sweet & Sour Pork...................164
Sweet-Sour Smokies..................35
Sweetheart Sandwiches...............344
Swiss Mushrooms.....................76
SYRUP (See also SAUCES)
Grandmother's Brown Sugar Syrup........109

T
Tabouli..............................81
Taco Casserole......................154
Tart Crust...........................300
TEA (See BEVERAGES)
Texas Gold Bars.....................355
Three Vegetable Casserole............205
Ticklish Tea.........................336
Tiffany's Bean Pot Soup..............63
Toffee..............................271
TOMATO
Baked Green Tomatoes................309
Escalloped Tomatoes..................201
Fried Green Tomatoes.................203
Gazpacho...........................25
Picalilli............................323
Tomatoes Rockefeller................202
Too Easy Tamale Dip..................38
Topping for Ham Loaf or Ham..........162
Topping for Pies......................228
Trail Mix............................346
True Grits...........................187
Tumbleweed Pie......................246
TUNA
Different Tuna Salad...................364
Sherrel's Favorite Tuna Salad...........90
Tuna Broccoli Casserole...............314
TURKEY
Stuffing for.........................138
Turkey Treasure......................369
TURNIP
Creamy Turnips w/Dill Weed...........202
Tuxedo Cheese Cake..................214
24 Hour Layered Salad................84

U
Uno Nolt'e en Milano................305-306

V
Vanilla Bars.........................355
VEAL
Jerry's Veal Parmesan................147
VEGETABLES
Ambidextrous Souffle.................195
Asparagus Casserole.................178
Asparagus Parmesan.................358
Avocado Jello Salad..................72
Avocado-Spinach Salad...............72
Bacon Cheese Potatoes..............194
Bacon Flavored Green Beans..........76
Baked Artichoke Hearts..............179
Baked Green Tomatoes...............309
Baked Spinach Casserole............196
Baked Squash Supreme..............198
Better Cheddar Potatoes.............361
Brussels Sprouts & Cashews..........182
Calico Salad........................74
Carrots Au Gratin...................183
Cauliflower-Bacon...................74

Celery w/Buttered Bread Crumbs.........184
Cheese Please Squash..................197
Christmas Casserole...................204
"City Slicker" Carrots.................81
Company Sauerkraut....................206
Corn Casserole........................184
Country Style Fresh Green Beans........282
Creamy Mushroom Salad.................76
Creamy Turnips w/Dill Weed............202
Crowd Pleasin' Green Beans............185
Cucumbers in Sour Cream...............75
Dilly Potato Sauce....................192
Easy Cheesey Potatoes.................361
Easy Fresh Vegetable Salad............363
Easy Green Bean Casserole.............360
Eggplant Parmesan.....................200
Escalloped Tomatoes...................201
Everyone's Favorite Broccoli & Rice......181
Fancy Foreign Peas....................194
Fancy Grits...........................188
Favorite Fried Potato Patties..........360
French-Style Green Peas...............295
Fried Green Tomatoes..................203
Garden of Gethsemane Vegetables
    w/Vermouth Dip....................291
Garden Vegetable Bake.................204
German Potato Salad....................79
Golden Cauliflower Casserole...........183
Grandma's Sweet & Sauerkraut..........182
Harvest Potatoes......................193
Hite's Delight (Cheese Potato Sticks)......191
Holiday Peas..........................195
Italian Style Peas....................195
Italian Zucchini......................196
J-Bar Bean Bake.......................181
Jane Lee's Vegetable Marinade..........80
Jeannette's Creamy Cottage Potatoes......190
Layered Potato Salad...................80
Layered Spinach Salad..................83
Lemon-Marinated Vegetables.............78
Make Ahead Cole Slaw...................73
Mama Sessions Vegetable Stew..........60
Many Vegetable Casserole..............201
Marinated Broccoli.....................73
Marinated Garden Salad.................77
Marinated Green Beans..................75
Marinated Mushrooms...................188
Marinated Salad........................77
Marinated Vegetable Salad..............84
Mashed Potatoes Parmesan..............192
Mushrooms 'n' Cream...................189
Okie Okra.............................189
Oklahoma Baked Beans..................179
Okra Gumbo............................190
Orange Glazed Sweet Potatoes..........193
Oven Stew.............................62
Prairie Pea Salad......................78
Quick Chili Rellenos..................348
Ratatouille...........................199
Red Cabbage...........................182
Rice w/Sour Cream & Chilies...........206
Rode Kool (Red Cabbage)...............182
Roman Artichoke Hearts................289
Sauteed Green Beans w/Butter & Cheese...186
Scalloped Green Beans.................186
Scalloped Mushrooms...................190
Serendipity Salad......................83
Sliced Potato Salad....................79
Spaghetti Salad........................82
Spinach Casserole.....................196
Spinach Gelatin........................82
Stuffed Summer Squash.................197
Summertime Beets......................180
Swedish Potatoes......................191

Sweet 'n' Sour Beets..................180
Sweet-Sour Green Beans................187
Swiss Mushrooms........................76
Three Vegetable Casserole.............205
Tomatoes Rockefeller..................202
True Grits............................187
24 Hour Layered Salad..................84
Vegetable Quiche......................173
Vegetable & Water Chestnut Casserole.....203
Vegie Cheese Sauce....................205
Wheatheart Tabouli Salad...............81
Wild West Corn........................185
Zippy Zucchini........................198
Zucchini Mexican Style................288
Zucchini Parmesan.....................199
Zucchini Surprise.....................200
Venison or Elk........................381
Venison Mincemeat.....................382
Very Flaky Pastry.....................230
Vinaigrette Dressing..................303
Vinaigrette Sauce...........285, 279, 294, 299

W

WAFFLES (See BREADS)
WALNUTS
    Hot Walnut 'N Beef Dip.............26
    Walnut Cheese Spread..............41
Watermelon Preserves..................324
Weddin' Party Punch w/Sherbet..........50
Wedding Punch.........................50
Western Souffle.......................176
Wheatheart Tabouli Salad...............81
White Clam Sauce......................306
White Wine Sauce......................302
Whole Salmon Baked....................302
Whole Wheat Bread.................101, 112
Whole Wheat Egg Bread.................124
Wild Rice Baron.......................150
Wild West Corn........................185
Wild West Hot Dip......................41
Wine Sauce............................302

Y

Yogurt-Lemon Cake.....................290
Yummy Popcorn.........................349

Z

ZUCCHINI
    Cream of Zucchini Soup............301
    Zippy Zucchini....................198
    Zucchini Appetizers...............42
    Zucchini Bread....................101
    Zucchini, Italian.................196
    Zucchini Mexican Style............288
    Zucchini Parmesan.................199
    Zucchini Surprise.................200

ORDER ADDITIONAL COPIES OF STIR-UPS

P.O. Box 5877
Enid, Oklahoma
73702

Please send _____ copies of STIR-UPS at mail order price of $17.00 per book.
(This amount includes $14.95 retail price and $2.05 additional charges for postage, handling, and applicable Oklahoma sales tax.)

☐ Check enclosed (payable to STIR-UPS)
We honor MasterCard and VISA (over)

Proceeds from the sale of STIR-UPS will be used for community projects and programs. Please include the names of any gift shops or stores in your area which might like to carry STIR-UPS.

☐ Check here for free gift wrap.

Your name:_____

Street:_____

City_____ State_____Zip_____

ORDER ADDITIONAL COPIES OF STIR-UPS

P.O. Box 5877
Enid, Oklahoma
73702

Please send _____ copies of STIR-UPS at mail order price of $17.00 per book.
(This amount includes $14.95 retail price and $2.05 additional charges for postage, handling, and applicable Oklahoma sales tax.)

☐ Check enclosed (payable to STIR-UPS)
We honor MasterCard and VISA (over)

Proceeds from the sale of STIR-UPS will be used for community projects and programs. Please include the names of any gift shops or stores in your area which might like to carry STIR-UPS.

☐ Check here for free gift wrap.

Your name:_____

Street:_____

City_____ State_____Zip_____

ORDER ADDITIONAL COPIES OF STIR-UPS

P.O. Box 5877
Enid, Oklahoma
73702

Please send _____ copies of STIR-UPS at mail order price of $17.00 per book.
(This amount includes $14.95 retail price and $2.05 additional charges for postage, handling, and applicable Oklahoma sales tax.)

☐ Check enclosed (payable to STIR-UPS)
We honor MasterCard and VISA (over)

Proceeds from the sale of STIR-UPS will be used for community projects and programs. Please include the names of any gift shops or stores in your area which might like to carry STIR-UPS.

☐ Check here for free gift wrap.

Your name:_____

Street:_____

City_____ State_____Zip_____

If using Charge Card, please fill in the following:

Name_____

Address_____

City_____ State_____ Zip_____

Charge to my: ☐ VISA ☐ MasterCard

Account Number:

MASTER CARD INTERBANK NO
(No. above name on card)

| | | | | | | | | | | | | | | | | | | |

| | | | |

Expiration Date:_____
Month   Year

Customer's Signature:_____

If using Charge Card, please fill in the following:

Name_____

Address_____

City_____ State_____ Zip_____

Charge to my: ☐ VISA ☐ MasterCard

Account Number:

MASTER CARD INTERBANK NO
(No. above name on card)

| | | | | | | | | | | | | | | | | | | |

| | | | |

Expiration Date:_____
Month   Year

Customer's Signature:_____

If using Charge Card, please fill in the following:

Name_____

Address_____

City_____ State_____ Zip_____

Charge to my: ☐ VISA ☐ MasterCard

Account Number:

MASTER CARD INTERBANK NO
(No. above name on card)

| | | | | | | | | | | | | | | | | | | |

| | | | |

Expiration Date:_____
Month   Year

Customer's Signature:_____